The economic nature c

Third edition

This book brings together classic writings on the economic nature and organization of firms, including works by Ronald Coase, Oliver Williamson, and Michael Jensen and William Meckling, as well as more recent contributions by Paul Milgrom, Bengt Holmstrom, John Roberts, Oliver Hart, Luigi Zingales, and others. Part I explores the general theme of the firm's nature and place in the market economy; Part II addresses the question of which transactions are integrated under a firm's roof and what limits the growth of firms; Part III examines employer–employee relations and the motivation of labor; and Part IV studies the firm's organization from the standpoint of financing and the relationship between owners and managers.

The volume also includes a consolidated bibliography of sources cited by these authors and an introductory essay by the editors that surveys the new institutional economics of the firm and issues raised in the anthology. The collection introduces the core literature to advanced undergraduates; business and economics graduate students; and scholars in allied disciplines including law, sociology, and organization and management.

Randall S. Kroszner is the Norman R. Bobins Professor of Economics at the University of Chicago's Booth School of Business, which he joined in 1990. He was a member of the President's Council of Economic Advisers in Washington, DC, from 2001 to 2003. From March 2006 to January 2009, Professor Kroszner served as a Governor on the Board of Governors of the Federal Reserve Board. He is a specialist in the regulation of banking and financial institutions, corporate governance, international financial crises, debt restructuring, and monetary economics, and he served as director of the George J. Stigler Center for the Study of the Economy and editor of the *Journal of Law and Economics*. Professor Kroszner received his Ph.D. from Harvard University in 1990.

Louis Putterman is Professor of Economics at Brown University, where he has taught since 1980. He is coauthor of *Economics of Cooperation and the Labor-Managed Economy* (1987, with John Bonin); author of *Division of Labor and Welfare* (1990); coeditor of *Economics, Values, and Organization* (1998, with Avner Ben-Ner); and author of *Dollars and Change: Economics in Context* (2001). Professor Putterman's current research interests focus on experimental economics and development and international economics, particularly the economics of China. He edited the first edition of *The Economic Nature of the Firm* and coedited the second edition with Professor Kroszner. Professor Putterman received his Ph.D. from Yale University in 1980.

The economic nature of the firm

A reader
Third edition

Edited by

Randall S. Kroszner

UNIVERSITY OF CHICAGO

Louis Putterman

BROWN UNIVERSITY

CAMBRIDGE UNIVERSITY PRESS
Cambridge, New York, Melbourne, Madrid, Cape Town,
Singapore, São Paulo, Delhi, Mexico City

Cambridge University Press
32 Avenue of the Americas, New York, NY 10013-2473, USA

www.cambridge.org
Information on this title: www.cambridge.org/9780521141772

First published 1986
Second edition published 1996
Third edition published 2009
Reprinted 2013

A catalog record for this publication is available from the British Library.

Library of Congress Cataloging in Publication Data
The economic nature of the firm : a reader / edited by Randall S. Kroszner, Louis
Putterman. – 3rd ed.
   p. cm.
Includes bibliographical references and index.
ISBN 978-0-521-19394-8 (hardback) – ISBN 978-0-521-14177-2 (pbk.)
1. Managerial economics. 2. Business enterprises. 3. Industrial organization.
4. Microeconomics. I. Kroszner, Randy. II. Putterman, Louis G. III. Title.
HD30.22.E25 2009
338.5–dc22   2009022099

ISBN 978-0-521-19394-8 Hardback
ISBN 978-0-521-14177-2 Paperback

Contents

Part III. The employment relation, the human factor, and internal organization

Part IV. Finance and the control of the firm

Contents

Editors' preface

With the exception of this Preface and the Introduction, the present volume consists of selections from material previously published in books or professional journals. With each piece is included a source note that gives the full bibliographic reference of the original work and acknowledges those who granted permission to use the material. In the case of articles, the degree of completeness versus abridgement is indicated by the phrases "reprinted from," "reprinted with minor abridgements," "reprinted with abridgements," and "excerpted from," in increasing order of abridgement. Book excerpts are understood to constitute only small selections from the originals. The chapter or section from which each portion is taken has been indicated in section headings within such selections. Ellipses within both book and journal selections are used to indicate omitted portions. However, where footnotes have been deleted, no notation has been made, and the remaining notes have been renumbered consecutively.

Minor alterations in style have been made for purposes of consistency. The references have been gathered into a single listing at the end of the book, and bibliographic particulars have been added, when necessary and feasible, to make the references as complete as possible and to have them accord with the standard format of major professional journals. Reference data, except for citations of authors' names and the dates of publication, have been moved to this list from the text and notes. Authors' notes of acknowledgment, which often appear at the beginning of the original journal papers, have been removed on grounds that they are frequently dated or unimportant to the purposes of this volume, and in order to conserve space. In their place, a very brief biographical note on the authors has been added to each selection.

We have found inspiration and help from many sources. Putterman's introduction to the literature collected here came from both the graduate microeconomics course and further reading and discussion with Sidney Winter, then at Yale University. Kroszner encountered many of the included items as an undergraduate working with Putterman at Brown University on the first edition of this book. Kroszner went on to receive his Ph.D. in economics from Harvard University in 1990 and is currently the Norman R. Bobins Professor of Economics in the Booth School of Business of the University of Chicago.

The idea for the initial volume was encouraged by Lee Alston, Wesley Cohen, Gregory Dow, Michael McPherson, Oliver Williamson, Gordon Winston, and especially Victor Goldberg, who helped shape its contents. For our subsequent reading of the literature, we are especially indebted to Tyler Cowen, Gregory Dow, Thomas Hubbard, Joseph Kalt, Richard Langlois, Bentley MacLeod, Gil Skillman, and Luigi Zingales. We thank the authors who have given permission to reprint their work, and especially Bengt Holmstrom, Paul Milgrom, and Oliver Williamson, who also contributed suggestions and encouragement. Finally, our thanks to Robert Corey-Boulet, Debra Kao, and Vero Testa for help in assembling biographical information, copyrights, and bibliography, and to Scott Parris and others at Cambridge University Press for their support and assistance with this project.

Reintroducing *The Economic Nature*
of the Firm

RANDALL S. KROSZNER AND LOUIS PUTTERMAN

Two decades ago, noticing the increasing attention being given to questions of economic organization and the nature of firms, we compiled the initial version of this Reader. At that time, we noted the growing frequency of references to writings such as Ronald Coase's 1937 classic as well as work published in the 1970s by Armen Alchian and Harold Demsetz, Michael Jensen and William Meckling, and Oliver Williamson. The years that followed have seen those and related works serve as the core of a literature that has deepened in institutional detail, branched out into empirical studies, and inspired progress in formal analysis. Coase's pioneering role was recognized with the awarding of a Nobel Memorial Prize in Economic Science in 1991.[1] Williamson's ideas, which build on those of Coase and incorporate a number of new elements, have occupied a prominent place in the study of organizations by economists and students of related disciplines. What can be called the "new institutional economics" has had increasing influence, as shown by its treatment in a growing formal analytical literature by such writers as Oliver Hart, Bengt Holmstrom, and Paul Milgrom,[2] a marked departure from a time when the "mathematical-formalist" and nonmathematical literatures included few citations by the one of the other.[3] With unfolding research still suggesting that our original selection of "classic writings" indeed brought together core sources, with interest in the materials remaining strong, and with the fruits of more recent research providing the basis for further steps forward, we are pleased to offer our second revision of *The Economic Nature of the Firm: A Reader*.

How production and related activities are organized – and the relations among actors involved in these activities – is a subject of interest that crosses several disciplinary boundaries. As before, students of law, organizational behavior, management, finance, and related fields should find this compilation of economics sources on the organization problem useful to their own endeavors.

---

[1] On the centrality of *The Nature of the Firm* to his overall contribution, see Coase's Nobel Lecture (1992). Also see Williamson & Winter (eds.) (1991), a volume honoring the fiftieth anniversary of that paper's publication; and Williamson (1994).

[2] Some examples are Grossman & Hart (1986), Hart & Moore (1990), and Holmstrom & Milgrom (1991 [and this Reader]). Hart & Holmstrom (1987) and Holmstrom & Tirole (1989) provided surveys of the technical literature developing "new institutional economics" themes. See also the text by Milgrom & Roberts (1992).

[3] See Jensen (1983).

1

Indeed, some of these fields were concerned with issues raised in our literature at a time when economists seemed resistant to such a discussion. The debates of the 1950s and 1960s, when some neoclassical economists defended "black box" theories of the firm against "behavioralist" and "managerialist" challenges,[4] seem happily behind us, as the study of the contractual and organizational structure of business enterprises matures and incorporates new analytical tools and concepts. As economists make further contributions to the understanding of these matters, controversy about the appropriate scope for inquiry has given way to a more sustained and illuminating discussion about why there are firms, what determines firm–market boundaries, and why firms are organized as they are. The papers collected in this volume include many of the most influential contributions to this evolving body of work.

Although we see the gap between formal theory and discursive approaches as having narrowed in recent years, this volume continues to emphasize the latter. The main reason is that verbal presentations are accessible to a wider audience, including both scholars in some of the disciplines mentioned previously, law and business students, and advanced undergraduate and graduate students of economics and other disciplines. Just as the better ideas in the discursive literature tend eventually to be taken up in formal models, so the better ideas in the formal literature are soon – if not simultaneously – given nonmathematical exposition. We excerpt mostly verbal portions of some technical papers representing such ideas, and we favor discursive treatments where possible. The equations and graphs included are either unusually accessible and illuminating or are retained for a hint of the flavor of the original.[5]

We also concentrate on the theoretical literature rather than empirical work. This is the realm in which new interpretive ideas are born, although the ideas developed herein should ultimately prove their power in analyzing cases and data. Empirical literature related to the ideas represented in this volume has expanded rapidly in recent years, but doing justice to that literature would require another volume, not simply a few additions to the present one.[6]

The papers and edited texts collected herein fall into four overlapping groups. The first concerns the "division of labor" among markets, hierarchies, and other coordination devices. It consists of selections from some of the older, classic writings on our topic, plus some more recent pieces, all helping to introduce the general theme of the economic nature of the firm and its place in the market

---

[4] See Machlup (1967). Coase (1991b, p. 52) draws attention to related issues.

[5] We select, for example, Hart (1989) rather than Grossman & Hart (1986) or Hart & Moore (1990); we include Bowles & Gintis (1990a) rather than Bowles (1985) or Shapiro & Stiglitz (1984); and we excerpt from Zingales (1998) rather than Rajan & Zingales (2001).

[6] Examples of this burgeoning empirical literature include Baker & Hubbard (2003); Crocker & Masten (1991); Goldberg & Erickson (1987); Hubbard & Weiner (1991); Joskow (1985, 1987, 1988a, 1988b); Kenney & Klein (1983); Klein (1988); Leffler & Rucker (1991); Masten & Crocker (1988); and Mulherin (1986). Klein & Shelanski (1994) provided a survey.

system. The volume begins with Adam Smith's classic discussion of the division of labor in the manufacturing establishment and in society as a whole, and its relationship to the development of markets. Smith tells us how efficiency is served by bringing together many hands and assigning each to specific tasks, but his treatment of the firm remains more technological than institutional or contract-theoretic. Next is Karl Marx's discussion of the productivity effects of "cooperation" in the workshop and of the capitalist character of the factory system. In this reading, differences in character are highlighted between firm and market, production and exchange. Following then are excerpts from Knight, whose ideas on the role of risk bearing remain important to discussions of both employment and financial relationships; from Berle and Means, who set off the modern discussion of financier–manager agency problems;[7] and from Hayek, who provided the classic discussion about the relationship among information, the level of economic decision making, and the price system. Finally, having begun the part with Adam Smith's "invisible hand" view of the market, we conclude it with a selection from a recent discussion of the "visible hand" of corporate governance by Zingales.[8]

Part II of this Reader includes papers dealing with the scope of the firm. Coase's famous paper, which simultaneously presents a theory of the differences between internal and market resource allocation, initiates this literature with the argument that a firm will expand until the cost of undertaking additional transactions through market exchange falls below the cost of undertaking those transactions within a common hierarchical structure. In the pieces by Klein, Crawford, and Alchian and by Williamson, Coase's focus on costs of using the price mechanism and on limited entrepreneurial attention gives way to a theory of integrated ownership in the presence of idiosyncratic investment. Although using much the same explanatory framework as Klein et al. to account for full vertical integration,[9] Williamson's piece adds the dimension of transaction frequency and attempts to account for intermediate modes, which he labels relational (or "bilateral") and neoclassical (or "trilateral") contracting.

Whereas the Klein et al. chapter and the first Williamson chapter offer explanations for vertical integration, they have less to say about what limits the growth of firms. The fourth chapter in this part, from Williamson's 1985 book, attempts to address that issue and go beyond the managerial-attention approach of Coase and the control-loss counterpart to that approach that was used earlier

---

[7] The enormous impact of Berle & Means' *The Modern Corporation and Private Property* was demonstrated in the special issue of the *Journal of Law and Economics* (June 1983) on the fiftieth anniversary of its publication. See especially the article by Stigler & Friedland (1983). We note later how several papers in Part IV of this Reader can be viewed as responses to Berle & Means.

[8] Chandler (1977) used the phrase "visible hand" to refer to the controlling hand of corporate management.

[9] Earlier thinking along similar lines to that of Klein, Crawford, and Alchian is found in Williamson (1971, 1975).

by Williamson himself. Williamson asks why the head office of a decentralized conglomerate could not give its divisions effective autonomy, thus replicating the "high-powered incentives" of the market, while outdoing the market by the selective imposition of rationalizing and coordinating measures. His answer is that selective intervention is impossible, and that it therefore follows that the incentives facing agents in firms are typically "lower-powered" than those of independent entrepreneurs or self-employed people. Milgrom and Roberts' paper (1990a) offers another reason why hierarchy becomes costly: subordinates can pursue private ends by distorting the information they supply to their superiors, and decision makers are forced to discount the information provided them – and may even find it optimal to restrict information flows. Rather than present a unified alternative theory of firm boundaries, Holmstrom and Roberts' final chapter of the part reviews earlier theories and uses intriguing real-world examples to show how well-crafted contractual arrangements can substitute for both internal organization (i.e., the firm) and reliance on arm's-length transactions (i.e., the market).

Part III addresses internal organization and the human factor, which in most instances contracts with the firm under what some of our authors term "the employment relation." Several of the chapters give centrality to the question of how effort is elicited when the contribution of the individual is costly to observe and, hence, to appropriately reward in a team setting. Alchian and Demsetz's provocative and influential discussion, which explains the hiring of employees by a residual-claiming employer through its analysis of this problem, is the first chapter in Part III. Karl Marx had anticipated the modern agency approach to the employment relationship with his discussion of the "extraction" of "labor" from "labor power" (see Part I), and radical economists have made contributions to the internal-organization literature by expanding on Marx's insights.[10] In their now-classic "efficiency-wage" model, Shapiro and Stiglitz (1984) rediscovered the role of Marx's "reserve army of the unemployed" in parallel with radical writers such as Samuel Bowles (1985). Whereas this approach has a more macroeconomic aim in the hands of Shapiro and Stiglitz, the focus of Bowles and co-author Herbert Gintis's chapter is on other issues, including doubts about whether the capitalist employment relation is, in fact, the most efficient solution to the team-effort problem.[11]

In Chapter 15 by Williamson, Wachter, and Harris, the monitoring problem takes second place to the previously noted problem of idiosyncratic investment.

---

[10] Their emphasis on the "effort-extraction" problem contrasts with an increasing tendency to ignore Marx's labor-based value (i.e., price) theory or to treat the latter as having only normative or sociological importance. In addition to the works cited herein, see Goldberg (1980b), Stephen Marglin (1974), and Richard Edwards (1979).

[11] For a parallel exposition and interesting comments by Stiglitz & Williamson, see the exchange in the Winter 1993 issue of the *Journal of Economic Perspectives*, pp. 83–114.

These authors argue that firms attempt to prevent haggling over and possible extraction by workers of the rents from firm-specific human capital. They do this by designing internal job ladders that orient employees toward the long run, while permitting some relaxation of current period monitoring, with resulting benefits for "atmosphere" and, hence, employee effort. Competition for promotion nevertheless can be keen, as in the "tournament" models formalized by other authors.[12] We present an excerpt from Holmstrom and Milgrom's recent article, which provides new formal results on the design of incentives by principals, as Chapter 16. The authors corroborate an old intuition that offers an explanation for the "lower-powered incentives" referred to by Williamson. They also provide important insights into specialization, the way tasks are assigned and combined into jobs, and other issues.

With the partial exception of Williamson et al., the chapters considered thus far in Part III adopt a standard motivational model in which agents are strictly rational and concerned only with their private incomes and leisure. Bewley's chapter is inspired by interviews with managers whose way of explaining why wages are not reduced during recessions emphasizes behavioral considerations such as worker loyalty and reciprocity. In the full article from which the chapter is excerpted, Bewley showed how ideas reminiscent of those in George Akerlof's "gift-exchange" model and in a growing body of behavioral and experimental research (Camerer & Fehr, 2004; Fehr & Schmidt, 2003) can be formalized.

Whereas wage flexibility is rare in the firms studied by Bewley, it is found in some jobs in which profit shares account for a non-negligible part of compensation. Pencavel studies the limiting case in which workers are full residual claimants – worker-owned firms in the U.S. plywood industry.[13] His finding that worker–owners achieve higher productivity than workers in conventional companies seems at odds with Alchian and Demsetz's claim that a central agent must receive the residual so as to be motivated to monitor the production workers. Yet, his observations about why worker-ownership is relatively rare are in the tradition of Knight's views on worker risk-aversion.[14]

The final section, Part IV, concerns questions of firm organization and behavior related to financing and ownership. The first three chapters present different responses to the problem of "separation of ownership and control" in the modern corporation – the problem raised by Berle and Means in Part I. These chapters begin with Manne's frequently cited argument regarding the monitoring function of the market for corporate takeovers. Next is Fama's contribution,

---

[12] See Lazear and Rosen (1981) and Malcomson (1984).

[13] Less extreme forms of profit-sharing are studied, *inter alia*, in Blinder (ed.) (1990) and Kruse (1993).

[14] For an alternative view of the relative rarity of worker-ownership, see Hansmann (1988); for a survey of such views, see Dow & Putterman (2000).

which develops a second view of markets as monitors of internal discretionary behavior, this one focusing on managerial compensation as an ultimate source of managerial accountability. Chapter 21 is a major portion of the article by Jensen and Meckling that helped spawn a large literature in the field of corporate finance and that – similar to Manne but both more broadly and more subtly – answers questions about the financier–manager relationship with reference to the monitoring properties of capital markets.

The fourth piece of this section, Chapter 22, teams Fama and Jensen. Taking the idea that corporations incur greater agency costs than closely held firms as a given, they ask why the corporate form is ever chosen, and answer with a formal argument about capital requirements. They also provide less formalized discussions about comparative advantage in managing versus financing and about the risk-reducing benefits of limited liability and diversification.

Chapters 23 and 24 reflect the continued vibrancy of debate and contrasting viewpoints on the ability of existing capital-market arrangements to control managerial malfeasance. Holderness, Kroszner, and Sheehan's chapter argues that contrary to the predictions of Berle, Means, and many of their successors, corporate ownership by managers has become less, not more, diffuse over time. Bebchuk and Fried view corporations as rife with malfeasance and offer an agency-theoretic outlook on how managers extract value from shareholders.

The final two chapters reach beyond questions of financing to treat the institution of firm ownership more broadly. In a discursive treatment of ideas developed in more formal, co-authored papers, Hart argues that the essence of ownership is not the right to residual income or the responsibility for monitoring but rather the right to make decisions that otherwise have not been determined in prior negotiations between parties to an enterprise. In arguments reminiscent of but somewhat distinct from the ideas of Klein et al. and Williamson, Hart argues that the efficient assignment of this residual control right is to the owner of critical, often idiosyncratic, inputs and that if there are several such inputs, they should be commonly owned. In Chapter 26, Putterman integrates financial agency and control-right concerns, suggesting that the supply of risk-bearing and financing services, substantially determined by the distribution of wealth, has implications not only for the financial but also for the internal incentive structure of firms. He argues that the factors that lead to the nonidentity of owners and labor suppliers also can be viewed as being responsible for the characteristic incentive problems of the workplace. He notes that the unbundling of the control, revenue, and alienation aspects of ownership – although problematic – shows signs of alleviating the trade-offs between efficient risk bearing and provision of incentives.

We organize our discussion of the literature from which our readings are drawn around a set of themes that feature prominently in it. Viewing firms as distinctive modes of organizing economic activity, the literature attempts to explain two related questions: Why do they exist? What determines their sizes and scopes? However, two more fundamental questions that are bound up with and, in some respects, prior to the first two are: Just what is the thing we call a firm? How distinctive are firms as organizing modes? Or, relatedly: How sharp are the boundaries between them and the environments in which they operate? Because the answers to all of these questions are closely intertwined, the order in which we address them is, to some degree, arbitrary. As a matter of convenience, we choose to begin with a provisional discussion of what firms are, then move to the explanation of their existence and the determinants of their sizes and scopes, and finally address the extensive literature on the sharpness of firm–market distinctions. We inevitability begin to touch on that literature under the earlier topics, which also brings us back full circle to the question of the firm's nature.

After considering the questions just raised, the remainder of this introduction (paralleling the structure of the book) moves into a more detailed discussion of how firms are organized, focusing on two types of relationships: those involving ownership of assets and those involving contracting with labor providers. We note how contributors to the literature can be partially classified into those who view the employment contract as the essence of the firm and those who view asset ownership as its essence, with a third group seeing both sets of relations as equally important or as manifestations of a common principle. We then survey the parallel literatures on agency and incentive issues in the relations between managers and workers, on the one hand, and between owners and managers, on the other. Finally, we discuss the question of why firms might be organized as they are (e.g., with respect to the distributions of control rights and risk bearing and the concentration of ownership) and how this might matter to our view of their economic nature or essence.

What is a firm?

In standard microeconomics, as mentioned previously, firms are the economy's basic units of production, just as households are its units of consumption. Firms purchase inputs such as labor services and materials from households and from other firms, transform these inputs into goods and services, and sell the latter to households and firms with the objective of maximizing the difference between their revenue and their outlay. As between the two entities, firms differ from households in that they maximize profit rather than utility and in the different activities (i.e., consumption versus production) in which each engages.

In the literature exemplified by this Reader, however, most authors have something more in mind when referring to a firm than simply a profit-seeking transformer of inputs into outputs. A set of factor owners could hypothetically agree today to contribute their inputs at the going rate so as to produce something for which an unmet demand is perceived, divide any surplus earnings, and go their separate ways tomorrow according to newly observed opportunities. Producers' coalitions of this type would differ, however, from the literature's *firms* because the latter usually entail (1) long-term contracts between at least some input providers; and (2) an assignment of control rights in which some agents hire others and direct them in the activities of production. Rather than being momentary assemblages of cooperating factor suppliers, then, firms are ongoing organizations that manage and coordinate the activities of participating actors.

Asking where the boundaries of the firm lie raises some difficult theoretical issues. Most authors, however, have relatively simple notions of control and ownership in mind when deciding where one firm ends and another begins. Few if any question that a company having multiple plants producing the same or even different products should be treated as a single firm as long as the rights to the residual earnings and to hire and fire the managers of subunits are ultimately in the hands of the same owner or owners. We return to the centrality of ownership to both the nature and the definition of the firm later in this introduction.

Why are there firms?

That the previous discussion is but a first pass at the question of what firms are becomes clearer when we encounter the literature on *why* there are firms. If by *firm* one meant simply an entity that engages in the transformation of inputs into outputs, then the "Why are there firms?" question could be answered trivially by noting that there is a demand for the products in question at prices at least equal to the combined cost of the required inputs. However, although product demand may explain production, it hardly explains the need for an organization of production with such features as long-term contracts, risk bearing by owners, and hierarchical or centralized coordination of those engaged in the production process. "Why are there firms?" is a question to Coase, Williamson, and others because with traditional microeconomic theory assuming that the *price system* coordinates the allocation of resources to their most valued uses, such organizations might appear to have no economic *raison d'etre*.

If standard theory offered any explanation for the existence of firms, it would seem to have been a technological one. Factors of production are needed in certain combinations, and some scales of production are more efficient than others. Once a certain scale is reached, the need for coordination seems obvious. The assembly of automobiles in large factory buildings in which hundreds of workers are arrayed along assembly lines must be coordinated by some type of organizing entity. Having independently contracting workers each owning subsets of the tools and machines comprising the factory and contracting with

8

one another without the coordination of an employer is out of the question, right? However, on further inspection, this obviousness gives way to a mystery. For, as Williamson in particular has forcefully argued, there is no *technological* reason why the participants in this production process could not each operate their own firms, buying and selling their semi-assembled components as they move along the production line. Even an accepted "technological" requirement of coordination or management fails to explain the firm as organization because the contributors of varying specialized inputs could simply contract for managerial services from other specialized agents, as the musicians in an orchestra might hire a conductor or as farmers contract for storage and other services from a cooperative or other company. It is the puzzle of which *organizational* factors give rise to the existence of an overarching framework of ownership, management, and coordination that motivates the prominent hypotheses of Coase, Williamson, Alchian and Demsetz, and others.

Coase initiated the contemporary literature by pointing out that when economic agents interact with each other, they incur "transaction costs" that vary with the mode of interaction. In the market, he argued, agents interact by negotiating exchanges, with existing prices serving as signals of the opportunities facing each supplier of a service or demander of a product. In a firm, conversely, a central coordinator or entrepreneur manages the allocation of resources such as the machinery owned by him and the manpower that he employs. Were the production process to be undertaken through market interactions alone, Coase wrote, the interacting parties would have to negotiate new actions and new terms of exchange each time a change in market or technological conditions made profitable a change in the activity being undertaken. Owners of the substations of the hypothetical production line would have to determine the prices at which to exchange their semifinished products – a difficult task in the absence of external markets for such goods – and these prices would be subject to change in response to changes in factor supply, technical conditions, and so forth. Such trivial matters as a breakdown in a piece of equipment, a stoppage of electricity, or a small change in the most profitable product mix would give rise to costly renegotiation of the full set of bilateral exchanges. The costs of such renegotiation, and of what Coase referred to as the "price discovery process," could be economized by agreement to a framework of ongoing relations under which a central coordinator would be granted the authority to reassign tasks and to offer altered payments as new contingencies arose.

Whereas Coase's ideas attracted enough attention to be cited and even reprinted occasionally in the early postwar decades following their initial publication, the "transaction cost" approach was largely ignored by the modernizers of economic theory who gained increasing dominance in those years. Parsimony and mathematical rigor were the order of the day, and theories that appeared capable of predicting economic phenomena using simple axioms held sway. In such an environment, the concept of "transaction costs" tended to be viewed as a vague and plastic one, inviting suspicions that it might be casually molded to explain whatever anomalies the analyst felt unable to explain by more "rigorous" methods.

By the 1970s, however, an increasing number of economists had come to view existing theory as failing to explain the organizational dimensions of the economy at the micro level.[15] At about the time that economic theorists were beginning to attack this and related flaws by treating problems of information and agency with formal tools, Williamson developed a variant of transaction-cost economics that would dominate the organizational literature, quite broadly, and inspire significant subsequent formal analysis as well. In Williamson's approach, as in Coase's, the market and firms were treated as discrete modes of organizing economic activity, and the choice among these modes was hypothesized to be dictated by economizing with respect to the cost of transactions among the different parties involved. Whereas Coase emphasized the costs of price discovery and negotiation, however, Williamson put his emphasis on the problem of investment in assets specific to a given venture. In an argument paralleling that of by Klein, Crawford, and Alchian, he suggested that when agents contemplated investing in assets that would have far lower returns outside of the activities to which they were initially dedicated, they would become subject to the possibility that owners of complementary assets would attempt to opportunistically extract their *quasi-rents* (i.e., the difference in returns between the dedicated and next-best uses) by threatening to withdraw their inputs. The threat of quasi-rent appropriation (or, in Williamson's terminology, *hold up*) would prevent such investments from being made without organizational safeguards, of which common ownership or vertical integration was the simplest example. Thus, the stations on the hypothetical assembly line would be owned and managed by an integrated entity rather than by a multitude of separate firms transacting across market interfaces, for the organizational rather than technological reason that separate firms would risk hold up, whence any who dared own one would face unacceptable danger.

It is worth noting the link between the Williamson and Klein–Crawford–Alchian idea of asset specificity and the idea of relational exchange or contracting introduced in the law and economics literature by MacNeil (1978) and in economics literature by Goldberg (1980a). As Goldberg stated, firms or individuals having assets uniquely suited to each other's needs can engage in a "relational exchange" that differs from the "arm's-length" trade in markets for generic goods and services in that the identity of the trading partners, and their ongoing cooperation, are matters of interest to each. This may not have been the

---

[15] One economist, Harvey Leibenstein, even argued that "a branch of economics is missing – micro micro theory." See Leibenstein (1979); see also Leibenstein (1966, 1982).

case when the parties met but becomes so after they have invested in physical capital, knowledge, or other ways of serving each other's needs, occasioning the shift from large to "small numbers bargaining" that Williamson (1985) called "the great transformation." "Relational contracting" appeared in the title of Williamson's book as a reference to forms intermediate between spot-market trading and internal organization. More recently, Baker, Gibbons, and Murphy (2002) argued that relational contracting is sometimes better addressed by integration of the parties into a firm, sometimes by contractual relations among firms. Although the relational interdependence among resource owners thus resurfaces in the discussion of firm–market boundaries in the next two sections, Baker et al. nonetheless are among those agreeing that the existence of relational interactions and the governance requirements they give rise to is a major reason for the existence of firms.

Rather than transaction costs, Alchian and Demsetz's theory of the firm focused on costs of monitoring. They assumed a technological condition for the existence of firms – it is economical for many hands to produce jointly – and then joined to this a behavioral or motivational problem. When production is joint and there are no individual products from which to infer input contributions, they argued, workers have incentives to withhold promised effort unless monitored so that acts of shirking can be punished by payment adjustments or by firing. However, the classical free-rider problem afflicting effort discretion will equally afflict the provision of monitoring unless the monitor is herself monitored or is motivated by some other means. Because one cannot posit a monitor of each monitor *ad infinitum*, Alchian and Demsetz posited a final (and central) monitor who is motivated by claim to the activity's residual income and who can maximize the value of that claim (and of the right to sell the firm) by exercising discretion over the team's composition and matching resources to uses in production. Thus, firms come into being when technological conditions (e.g., increasing returns and costly measurement of input contributions) make centralized ownership and monitoring a superior alternative to either unmonitored revenue-sharing or lower-productivity small-scale production.[16]

Although Williamson rejected what he called the "technical nonseparabilities" element of Alchian and Demsetz's theory as being insufficiently general, he did not reject the idea that monitoring costs may be a determinant of organizational form. In *The Economic Institutions of Capitalism*, he labeled the

---

[16] Although Alchian & Demsetz do not rule out the possibility that revenue-sharing teams will generate some mutual monitoring, they argue that the level of such monitoring would be suboptimal because the incentive to monitor would itself be subject to a free-rider problem. By contrast, the literature on profit-sharing surveyed by Weitzman & Kruse and other papers in Blinder (ed.) (1990) often argues that mutual monitoring and the reduction of specialized monitoring costs is a key to the positive productivity effects of that practice. See also the theoretical and empirical analysis of Dong & Dow (1993) and the discussion of technological and other dimensions of the issue by Putterman (1984).

monitoring approach a "branch" of transaction-cost economics, with Yoram Barzel (1982) as its key developer (see also Kenney & Klein [1983]). Economizing on the costs of measuring intermediate outputs at each stage of the production process is at the core of Barzel's theory of the firm. Assume that it is difficult to assess the value of the output at each stage so that monitoring the inputs may provide useful information about the value of the intermediate good. Workers along a production line could be organized as separate one-worker firms or integrated into a single firm. If the workers are separate firms, then each worker–firm will have to monitor the inputs of the worker–firm directly "upstream," as well as those of all of the worker–firms in the prior stages of the production process whose products are intermediate inputs. The firm, then, emerges as a means of centralizing monitoring, thereby avoiding costly redundancy in that function.

The emphasis of transaction-cost economics on hold-up costs has inspired an immense amount of theoretical and empirical literature but also has been questioned. In the article excerpted in Part II, Milgrom and Roberts (1990a) argued that the danger of hold up could be treated as a normal business risk if it only affected the division as opposed to the size of the "pie" generated by the interacting parties. In their view, only concrete bargaining costs, such as the costs of hiring lawyers, writing more complex contracts, and unrecoverable down time due to work stoppages, should make idiosyncratic investment a factor in business integration because it makes the contractual structure of production a determinant of the pie's size. Milgrom and Roberts accordingly declared themselves to be more Coasian than Williamsonian. Nevertheless, along with Hart, Holmstrom, Zingales, and others, they join Williamson in the tradition (which goes back at least to Herbert Simon) of seeing firms as ways of getting around the need to either negotiate on the spot or to write complex contingent contracts that would be impossible or at least impossibly costly to spell out in full detail. A set of long-term, incomplete contracts between input providers and a central agent or entity (i.e., the firm) coupled with an agreed procedure for filling in details as events unfold – usually the ceding of authority to management – is the agreed essence of firms in this broadly shared tradition.

Before leaving this discussion, it is interesting to ask whether an approach that predates Coase's – namely, Knight's theory of entrepreneurship (see Part I) – in its own right constitutes a reasonable theory of why firms exist. Knight emphasized the riskiness of the production enterprise: inputs will be exhausted before the quality and quantity of output, the price at which the product can be sold, or whether it can be sold at all are known with certainty.[17] Someone will have to bear risk if production is to be undertaken, but differences in

---

[17] Israel Kirzner (1973, 1979) instead emphasized the discovery of potentially profitable opportunities as the key element of entrepreneurship. Firms may arise to aid entrepreneurs in exploiting those discoveries.

willingness to do this – partly conditioned on wealth and partly on confidence in one's ability to make appropriate judgments – suggest that this function might not be shared equally by participants in the production process. Conversely, once some agents accept these risks and guarantee the payments of others, the problem of moral hazard dictates that the risk bearers also must be given the right to supervise their insurees lest the latter take their economic security as an invitation to shirk responsibility. Thus, the firm is born as an organization of individuals engaging in a common production process with an internal division of labor where some insure and supervise and others are insured and accept supervision.

One could ask, of course, why the workers involved do not form separate firms, each with its own insurer–supervisor. If economies of supervision suffice to address that problem, then Knight's approach indeed does seem to offer a theory of the firm on a par with those discussed previously. Why it has been more influential in the fields of labor and macroeconomics than in the literature presently under discussion is something of a mystery but one to which Coase's directed criticism might offer a clue. When he wrote his own seminal paper, Coase considered Knight's approach to be "the most interesting . . . and probably the most widely accepted" explanation for the existence of firms. In arguing against it, he said that "the fact that certain people have better judgment or better knowledge does not mean that they can only get an income from it by themselves actively taking part in production." He contended that the guarantee of income to a worker does not necessitate the assuming of supervisory powers because "[a] large proportion of jobs are done to contract" where "the contractor is guaranteed a certain sum providing [only that] he performs certain acts." Coase's main reason for rejecting Knight, however, seems to be found in his statement that "nowhere does Professor Knight give a reason why the price mechanism should be superseded." This suggests that Knight's lack of commonality with the "discrete contracting modes"–"market and hierarchy" orientation of both Coase and Williamson, along with a certain antipathy to risk-centered approaches by those and related writers, caused the Knightian approach to be discounted in the post-1970 flowering of both transaction-cost and, more generally, "new institutional" economics.[18] However, the absence of a trenchant analysis of monitoring problems and the informality of Knight's treatment of what have since come to be known as agency problems have

---

[18] To be sure, Williamson suggested (1985, p. 3, footnote 3) that Coase's criticism was misplaced; lauded Knight as a precursor in the analysis of opportunism (op. cit., p. 6) and bounded rationality (p. 133) problems; and lamented that "Knight's keen behavioral insights never gained prominence" (p. 3). He continued, "[a]ttention has focused instead on the technical distinction between risk and uncertainty that he had introduced" and that "[h]ad Knight used a nontechnical term, such as 'opportunism' . . . that result might have been avoided" (op. cit., p. 3). This seems significant in view of the fact that Williamson (pp. 388–390) lists risk-neutrality as a maintained assumption of transaction-cost economics.

reduced his influence on both the "monitoring branch" of the new institutional economics and more mathematical theorizing. The influence of Knightian reasoning on the financial contracting area of firm theory will nonetheless be shown to have been strong, if not always explicitly recognized.[19]

What determines a firm's size and scope?

A prominent aspect of the Coasian approach to the firm is its argument that firms are spheres of planning and that by virtue of the importance of intrafirm planning to the overall coordination of economic activity, so-called market economies (as contrasted with "planned" economies of the now-defunct Soviet type) are, in fact, composites of planning and market coordination, with the scope of each coordinating mechanism determined by competition. As discussed, transactions come to be organized within firms rather than "in the market," according to Coase, when the supersession of the price mechanism by the authority of the entrepreneur–coordinator is more economical than a series of exchanges negotiated between the relevant parties. With regard to the question of why this does not continue to be the case as firms grow ever larger, Coase suggested that there must be diminishing returns to the coordinator's attention, including an increasing possibility of mistakes that would be more cataclysmic in nature for an extremely large firm.

Without a theory of multitier hierarchy, however, Coase's argument is incomplete. A given manager's attention indeed may be limited, but a manager might employ other managers to look after aspects or divisions of his firm; therefore, one must posit costs of agency, or some type of control loss, to complete this line of reasoning. An Alchian–Demsetz-like argument about the incentive effect of concentrated residual claims, plus some agency costs of the type implicit in their theory and expounded more explicitly by Jensen and Meckling (1976a) might do the job. Williamson (1967a), Beckmann (1983), Calvo and Wellisz (1978), and McAfee and McMillan (1991) likewise modeled tendencies for management cost per unit of output to rise as the number of managers (or of personnel managed) increases. An argument by Milgrom and Roberts reviewed herein supplies another way of supporting Coase's presumption.

Questioning the adequacy of his earlier argument, Williamson (1985 and Chapter 10 of this Reader) asked why a "super-firm," wherein what were previously independent firms are run as "autonomous" subdivisions, cannot do everything that the once-independent firms could do but at least sometimes improve

---

[19] A formalization of Knight's ideas on entrepreneurship and the assumption of risk was provided by Kihlstrom & Laffont (1979). Similar reasoning was used by Montias (1970), Meade (1972), Neuberger & James (1973), and Putterman (1993a and Part IV), and formalized by Bowles & Gintis (1995), to explain why most firms are controlled by capital suppliers. See also Dow (2003) and Pencavel (2001 and this Reader).

on their performance by imposing coordination or rationalizing moves from the corporate center. His basic answer was that one cannot simultaneously posit real divisional autonomy *and* central powers of intervention. Furthermore, if the center has the right to intervene when it sees (or claims) rationalizing opportunities, then the division heads cannot be put on "high-powered incentive" contracts mimicking those they would enjoy as independent entrepreneurs – i.e., earning precisely the net profit of the division. With such contracts, the center's right to intervene would cause managers to bear all the risks of residual claimants without the corresponding control over outcomes.[20] Neither would it be wise for the firm to make the division head a full residual claimant because he would then be tempted to exploit assets belonging to the firm for short-term gain (in Williamson's expression, to "run [the assets] into the ground"). For both of these reasons, the granting of intervention rights would tend to be accompanied by a degree of income insurance that would dilute or "lower the power" of division managers' incentives and, thus, the level of their managerial attentiveness and energies. In other words, the firm's Williamsonian advantages – providing safeguards to investors in complementary specific assets – are at some point offset by its inability to replicate the "high-powered incentives" of agents directly exposed to market forces by way of a residual claim.

In contrast to Williamson, Milgrom and Roberts explain the cost of expanded bureaucratic or hierarchical control with an argument that is applicable even when there is only one layer of management. The key to their argument is that information pertinent to optimal managerial decision making is dispersed among agents employed by the enterprise. To make fully informed decisions, a manager must elicit such information from subordinates; however, attempting to do so makes him subject to their self-interested provision of selective or distorted information. Drawing on the rent-seeking literature, Milgrom and Roberts pointed out that subordinates stand to gain personally by providing managers with suggestions and information that may advance their own careers. Because it is costly for managers to filter out good from bad information, it becomes optimal simply to restrict the information flow – although managers then act on less than full information. Moreover, the larger the organization, the larger the information-filtering costs and the larger the losses in efficiency because of decisions made with less complete information by higher-level managers. In supplying a countervailing cost likely to eventually offset any initial benefits from administering resource allocation within an organization, Milgrom and Roberts' version of the rent-seeking story thus bolsters the logic of Hayek's seminal argument that beyond some point, at least, bureaucratic

---

[20] Note here the commonality with the Knightian idea that he who bears the risk must hold the control.

centralization cannot dominate the price system as a method for using dispersed information to allocate a society's resources.[21]

Of course, whatever factors make coordination within a firm desirable in the first place also must be considered in determining its optimal scale. That scale is reached, presumably, when the marginal gains of internalization – whether due to lessened negotiation and price discovery costs, to the amelioration of asset specificity problems, or to other factors – equal the marginal costs of integrated management, such as those discussed previously. Both Coase's and Williamson's explanations of the existence of firms, for example, suggested that firms will be larger in those industries in which products pass through more stages as intermediate goods that lack their own markets and reference prices, or where the ability to flexibly redeploy resources is of greater importance. The asset-specificity approach of Williamson and of Klein, Crawford, and Alchian, as well as Hart's critical asset complementarity variant, suggests that firms will be larger, as measured by capital stocks, when production processes call for using larger sets of interspecialized assets or for more expensive individual assets within those sets. Ordinary economies of scale may be relevant here insofar as they dictate the optimal size of capital goods or the fineness (and specificity) of the internal division of labor.

In their paper (1998 and this Reader), Holmstrom and Roberts argued that single-cause theories of firms' boundaries, such as those focusing on avoidance of hold-up or agency problems, are unlikely to provide satisfactory explanations of important facts. Other problems, such as the effect of control and incentive structures on the transfer of knowledge and the potential monitoring advantages of markets, also come into play in their eclectic treatment, "offered in the hope of inspiring new theoretical research."[22]

How sharp the firm/market distinction?

We previously noted that one reason for the initially limited impact of Coase's explanation for the existence of firms is that his appeal to the phenomenon of transaction costs was viewed by some economists as vague and open to arbitrary application. Another cause of reservations regarding the Coasian theory of the firm has been its depiction of intrafirm organization as a discretely different mode of economic coordination in which managerial control supersedes (his term) the price mechanism.[23] Although perhaps not intended to do so by Coase

[21] Attempting to resolve an apparent contradiction on this point between Williamson and Hart, Putterman (1995) suggested that intrafirm coordination may put more refined information than markets can in a decision maker's hands up to a certain scale but not beyond.

[22] For still other treatments, see Nelson & Winter (1982); Teece (1980, 1982); and Langlois (2003).

[23] For example, "'vertical' integration, involving as it does the *supersession* of the price mechanism" (Coase, 1937, pp. 388–389); "It was not until machinery drew workers into one locality that

himself,[24] this approach linked itself to the debate about the virtues of planning versus the market, with Coase's argument that planning is one of the normal modes of coordination in a *market* economy being potentially provocative to the antisocialist camp.[25] Moreover, Coase's view of the firm seemed to challenge the belief that economic life could be explained in terms of rational, individual responses to market constraints and opportunities. Whether firm and market are distinct modes of organization, whether one form shades into the other, or whether the firm is nothing other than a congeries of market interactions has been a topic of debate in the literature with which we are concerned.

Coase identified the planned coordination within firms with the intended planning under socialism, suggesting that the main difference between the two was that the scope of the one was determined by competition and that of the other by political authority.[26] In viewing planning and the authority of the employment relationship as the essence of the firm and the absence of authority and governance by independent contracting as the essence of the market, Coase revisited a distinction made much earlier by an author of whose work on the topic he appeared unaware. "Division of labor within the workshop," according to Karl Marx, "implies the undisputed authority of the capitalist over men," whereas "division of labor within the society" [read: "the market"] brings into contact independent commodity-producers, who acknowledge no other authority but that of competition." Although sharing none of Marx's antipathy for the market, Coase also emphasized authority in the employment relation as a hallmark of the firm. "We can best approach the question of what constitutes a firm by considering the legal relationship normally called that of 'master and servant' or 'employer and employee'," wrote Coase, who then proceeded to quote from Batt's *Law of Master and Servant*: "It is [the] right of control or interference . . . which is the dominant characteristic in this relation and marks off the servant from an independent contractor."[27]

Much of the ensuing discussion is concerned with Coase's proposal that the line between firm and market could be drawn where the employment

---

it paid to *supersede* the price mechanism and the firm emerged" (op cit., p. 397, note 4); "nowhere does Professor Knight give a reason why the price mechanism should be *superseded*" (op cit., p. 401) (emphasis added).

[24] See Coase (1991a, 1991b).

[25] During the 1920s and 1930s, Ludwig von Mises and Hayek engaged in a lively debate with Oskar Lange, Fred Taylor, and Maurice Dobb about the possibility of rational economic calculation in a centrally planned economy – that is, one in which market forces do not determine prices. However, philosophically inspired resistance to Coase's firm–market distinction surfaced mainly in the 1970s and 1980s, without much reference to this debate. On the Socialist Calculation Debate, see Bardhan & Roemer (eds.) (1993) and Hayek (1972).

[26] Coase, 1937, p. 389, note 3, which appears in Chapter 7, Footnote 14, in this Reader.

[27] Coase, 1937, pp. 403–404. For an extended discussion of the plan–market distinction in Marx and in modern economic theory, see Pagano (1985). On the firms–markets distinction, also see Khalil (1994) and Hayek (1972).

relationship is distinguished from the hiring of an independent contractor. Masten (1988) followed Coase in citing Batt and other legal sources, suggesting that the obligation of the employee toward the employer is central to what we call a firm. By contrast, Alchian and Demsetz rejected the concept of an authority relation, arguing that because both worker and employer can terminate their relationship when they find it in their interest to do so, an employee's response to managerial directions reflects only a mutually beneficial exchange of the most conventional type. Cheung (1983) argued that it is unimportant to determine exactly what constitutes a firm and when a transaction takes place between independent agents as opposed to within firms.

Ultimately, whether the firm constitutes a domain of bureaucratic direction that is shielded from market forces or simply "a nexus for a set of contracting relationships among individuals" (see Jensen & Meckling, Chapter 21) is a function of the completeness of markets and the ability of market forces to penetrate intrafirm relationships. For example, authority as such is not modeled in the principal–agent literature, except perhaps insofar as the principal designs the contract; in these models, the principal takes the worker's market-given reservation utility as a datum, and there is no exercise of managerial control once the contract is in place. If market forces determine rewards and each agent selects the application of his endowments that brings the highest return (or utility), then there is no scope for the operation of firms as a separate allocation mechanism, over and above the market. On the other hand, factors that render markets incomplete may open up just such a possibility.

Alchian and Demsetz, for example, concede that competition for either working or monitoring positions by external market agents is insufficient to deter internal shirking. In their view, a central agent must have the power to reward effort and to penalize shirking, including possibly by firing. Although such powers do not distinguish the central agent from any other competitive actor, for Alchian and Demsetz, they indeed may do so in a nonmarket clearing environment of the type that arises in efficiency-wage models, as argued by Bowles and Gintis. Moreover, Alchian and Demsetz's view of the firm as "an alternative kind of market," although rhetorically suggestive of a more market-oriented view, is in fact not very different from that of Coase or Williamson because what is distinctive about the firm, by their account, is that the manager's superior knowledge of internal resources permits more efficient resource allocation than can be accomplished by less informed external agents. The firm does appear to be an alternative or supplementary allocative mechanism to the market, in their view.

Standing shoulder-to-shoulder with the "nexus of contracts" school, Benjamin Klein (1983, p. 373) asserted that "Coase mistakenly made a sharp distinction between intrafirm and interfirm transactions, claiming that while the latter represented market contracts, the former represented planned direction.

Economists now recognize that such a sharp distinction does not exist and that it is useful to consider also transactions occurring within the firm as representing market (contractual) relationships." Our discussion in this section suggests, however, that such a consensus has yet to be reached.[28]

On another level, however, there has been much less disagreement between the contending approaches. Insofar as the debate about the firm–market distinction concerns whether firms and markets are *discrete* alternatives or whether there are intermediate forms, with the one effectively shading into the other, most authors evince openness to the second approach. In his classic work on cooperation among firms, Richardson (1972)[29] emphasized the ubiquity of intermediate forms of organization and coordination. He argued that it is inappropriate conceptually and empirically to think of firms as "islands of planned coordination in a sea of market relations. . . . Firms are not islands but are linked together in patterns of cooperation and affiliation." He concluded that the "dichotomy between firms and market, between directed and spontaneous coordination . . . ignores the institutional fact of inter-firm cooperation and assumes away the distinct method of cooperation that this can provide."[30] Williamson's use of "relational contracting" to refer to the governance of the types of relationships that Richardson addressed was discussed previously. Interfirm relations bearing such firm-like qualities as a long-term character, incompleteness of terms, and explicit governance remedies were likewise emphasized by Goldberg (1980a), Klein, Crawford, and Alchian (1978 and this Reader), and Holmstrom and Roberts (1998 and this Reader).

Ownership relations and employment relations

As a "nexus of contracts," firms entail relations between suppliers of specific and generic inputs; sellers of managerial, technical, and other labor services; providers of equity and debt finance; and customers. However, the literature on firms as governance or control structures singles out two types of relationships for special attention. The centrality of employment relationships in approaches such as that of Coase was discussed previously. Centrality of an alternative relationship – that is, the ownership of physical assets – has been the focus of other writers, epitomized by Grossman and Hart.

[28] For another position similar to Klein's, see Cheung (1983). On the opposite end of the spectrum, see Williamson's methodological discussion on "comparative institutional assessment of discrete institutional alternatives" (1985, p. 42) and Simon (1991). In most of their work on these topics, Hart, Holmstrom, Milgrom, Roberts, Rajan, & Zingales appear to be closer in spirit to the dichotomous "market versus hierarchy" views of Coase and Williamson than to the "nexus of contracts" view of Alchian & Demsetz, Jensen & Meckling, Klein, and Cheung.

[29] See also Richardson (1990) and the foreword by David Teece.

[30] For a discussion of Richardson's work, see Loasby (1986).

Grossman and Hart (see also Hart [1989] and Chapter 25) take issue with the notion that employers exert any special degree of control over employees by virtue of the employment relation.[31] However, they suggest that the ability to determine how physical assets will be used and, therefore, which human agents will have access to them, is the essence of control of the firm. As Hart stated, the asymmetry between employer and employee glossed over by Alchian and Demsetz is that whereas the employee can sever his relationship with the employer, thus depriving the firm of his particular talents, when the employer separates the employee from the firm, he also deprives him of his tools, which stay with the employer. Even the right to residual income is secondary, in Hart's view, to the ability to make such decisions over the disposition of assets that have not been settled by prior agreement. (Rajan and Zingales' related concept of "power" is discussed subsequently.)

Most of the writers surveyed herein appear to place themselves somewhere between Coase's transaction-cost and Hart's "property-rights" approaches. Williamson and Klein, Crawford, and Alchian emphasized specificity of physical assets as a cause of internal control, but Williamson's belief in the presumptive superiority of internal audits[32] puts him closer to Coase and Alchian's (1984) view of the firm as a coalition, with some emphasis on human assets.[33] Alchian and Demsetz, in an approach more recently also favored by Holmstrom and Milgrom (see the following discussion), place the monitor–worker relationship at the center of their explanation of the firm; however, those writers also make ownership of physical assets part of the bundle of core rights held by the central agent (for reasons that again pertain to monitoring). Even Masten, whose position appears closest to Coase, stated that "the distinction between ownership and governance roles of the firm is a spurious one" (1988, p. 195).

Ownership and employment relations are distinguished by the fact that the employer, at most, can control the current services of the employee, not the stock of labor capacity itself. This distinction is important, for example, to the implications of the asset specificity paradigm. When two physical assets are highly specialized to one another, advocates of this paradigm argue, it is efficient that they be under common ownership and control. Although the same might otherwise have been said where human capital is concerned, prohibition of owning persons means that full integration of human capital (except, perhaps, that of a proprietor) into the firm is not an option. Williamson treats this

---

[31] Grossman & Hart (1986, p. 165) questioned Arrow's assumption (1975) that integration improves communication among units. Williamson (1985, p. 155), by contrast, asserts that managers have better access to company information than external auditors because of employee allegiance. Williamson, Wachter, & Harris also refer to superior intrafirm communication of employee ratings. See also the discussions in Masten (1988), Riordan (1990), and Putterman (1995).

[32] See the previous note.

[33] Another coalitional view of the firm is provided by Masahiko Aoki. See, for example, Aoki (1984).

problem by arguing that human assets are usually not as specific to the firm as physical ones and by suggesting that the risk of investing in specialized assets can be mitigated, in labor's case, by safeguards embedded in the employment contract.[34] However, collective ownership by workers or joint participation of both workers and investors in management might logically follow from the analysis in which specific human inputs are more important than nonhuman inputs (Blair, 1995).

The relationships among firm, capital goods, and employees also demand further attention when defining the firm. As Putterman (1988) argued, viewing the firm as a coalition of agents that includes its employees is inconsistent with the legal notion of the firm as economic agent (and, hence, the "legal fiction" with which Jensen and Meckling associate the firm as a nexus of contracts). That is, the firm enters employment contracts on one side of the contracting process, the employees on the other. Although not an actual person, the legal agent called "the firm" is ultimately controlled by another group of agents – its owners, who may delegate managerial tasks to a subset of employees. The firm may own certain capital goods and intangible capital, such as reputation, may also adhere to it; however, the prohibition on owning the human capital of others means that its employees are not *within* the firm, seen this way, even if their independence is attenuated while the employment relation is in effect. The distinction between the firm as a legal entity and the firm as a coalition, organization, or association of agents becomes clear when the ownership of the firm changes hands: the firm in the first sense is a tradable commodity, which the firm as an organization cannot possibly be.[35]

Workers and incentives

By concentrating on the discussion regarding the element of authority in the management of the firm's personnel, thus far, we have left aside the larger issue of incentives. Even if the manager could rely on the complete obedience of the worker to his commands – as might be suggested by a simple reading of Coase or, for example, Simon's similar treatment (1951) – motivating employees would remain a problem insofar as there are situations that must

---

[34] See Williamson, Wachter, & Harris (1975 and Chapter 15 in this Reader) and Williamson (1985, Chapter 12).

[35] Hart made a similar point: "[I]dentify the firm with all the nonhuman assets that belong to it. . . . Human assets, however, are not included. Since human assets cannot be bought or sold, management and workers presumably own their human capital both before and after any merger" (Hart, 1989, p. 1766 [and this Reader, p. 347]). Rajan & Zingales (1988, p. 388) suggested that "the property rights view" may make too much of the fact that "employees cannot be owned": "There is a sense in which employees "belong" to an organization even in a world without permanent indenture. This sense of belonging arises from the expectation "good citizens" of an organization have that they will receive a share of future organizational rents."

21

be responded to in which the employee has better information than the manager.[36] In simpler settings in which the only difficulty lies in the elicitation of effort, imperfect or costly observability and worker self-interest may render the problem equally severe.

Assuming that the firm's profits are increasing in the worker's effort and decreasing in his pay, while the worker's utility bears the opposite relationship to these variables, employer and employee interests are diametrically opposed. The resulting conflict can be resolved by contractual stipulation, but only if enforcement costs are trivial. When effort is not observable without cost, and when the cost of monitoring makes it optimal that it be imperfectly observed on the margin, workers may have incentives to shirk. Alchian and Demsetz suggest solving the problem through profit-motivated monitoring, but their solution is one in which rewards are still imperfectly correlated with effort, so a degree of shirking remains. Holmstrom (1982a) provided an alternative theoretical solution, in which the central agent observes output and does not need to monitor labor inputs. If aggregate output falls below that associated with each worker providing the socially optimal effort level, all workers are punished, although only one may have shirked. Whereas sufficient in principle to deter shirking without monitoring, the approach would appear to be impractical, whether due to incentive incompatibility, uncertain production functions, or considerations of fairness and enforceability.[37] A substantial formal literature, including Calvo and Wellisz (1978), Shapiro and Stiglitz (1984), and Bowles (1985), still attaches importance to monitoring.

Simple efficiency wage models like that of Shapiro and Stiglitz differ from the intuition of Alchian and Demsetz in that the former monitoring leads to a zero-shirking outcome. The employer pays an above-market-clearing wage to give the employee reason to prefer keeping the job then determines the probability of detecting shirking by hiring or undertaking a particular amount of monitoring. As emphasized by Bowles, monitoring and wage rents are substitutes in the elicitation of effort in such a model, and the employer's problem is to select a profit-maximizing combination of the two – which, when workers are homogeneous and there is a credible threat of firing, is one that fully deters shirking.

Williamson's approach to the incentive problem, in his joint paper with Wachter and Harris (1975 and Chapter 15 in this Reader), is one that is simultaneously a treatment of the problem of firm-specific human capital, which these authors view as being equally salient in its own right. Workers can "hold

---

[36] See the discussion of the distinction between consummate and perfunctory cooperation in Williamson, Wachter, & Harris (op. cit.). A similar idea was developed by Clague (1993) under the term "EIR behavior" (i.e., effort, initiative, and responsibility).

[37] On the relevant incentive compatability problem, see Eswaran & Kotwal (1989) and MacLeod (1987).

up" their employers for higher remuneration not only by threatening to quit – a threat that is the less credible as the specific component of skill becomes larger – but also by working in a merely "perfunctory" manner. To tie workers' interests to the firm and to reduce opportunistic haggling, workers are exposed to the possibility of advancing up a firm's internal job ladders if they exhibit "consummate" performance over time. The approach is also said to cut down on the frequency of monitoring, which carries not only direct but also indirect costs in the form of harm to worker morale or goodwill. Rather than providing an alternative explanation of the phenomenon modeled by authors such as Shapiro and Stiglitz, of course, Williamson et al. may be seen as analyzing a different type of employment situation – perhaps one involving skilled, white-collar workers as opposed to participants in the "primary labor market."

A different reason for not monitoring more intensively and, indeed, for not offering "high powered" rewards in organizations is provided by Holmstrom and Milgrom (1991a and Chapter 16 in this Reader). A worker's job may have both relatively measurable and relatively unmeasurable dimensions. If pay is made contingent on the measurable part of effort or productivity, the unmeasured aspect may be neglected. Holmstrom and Milgrom's formalization of a point frequently made in discussions of the quantity–quality trade-off inherent in piece rate systems[38] is one of a number of contributions of an analysis that considers the implications of potentially multitask jobs for reward schemes, job design, and choice between self-employment and employment by a firm (see the following discussion).

Truman Bewley's recent contribution on effort and worker morale treats the worker's choice of effort as being heavily influenced by perceived moral considerations. When choosing between reducing the wages of those already employed and laying off workers in a recession, the firm's decision is dictated, Bewley argues, largely by its understanding of worker psychology (capable of formal incorporation in worker-utility functions). Although the market may have ceased to value the product as highly as it once did, workers are assumed to view it as unfair that they be paid less for the same work. Accordingly, a wage cut would lead to lower morale and lowered productivity. It is better to send away a few workers whose unhappiness will not be on view every day to the remaining employees, themselves grateful to keep their jobs and willing to work hard to keep the employer viable. Neither monitoring nor the threat of termination for low effort plays a major role in Bewley's discussion. In essence, the employee will do a good day's work for a good day's pay out of loyalty and reciprocity.

---

[38] See Lawler (1971), Stiglitz (1975), and Nalbantian (ed.) (1987). Holmstom & Milgrom's idea also closely parallels the classical literature on the "problem of success indicators" in Soviet-type economies; see Nove (1958).

Although morale and organizational psychology may be equally important to both, the case of worker-owned firms discussed by Pencavel is, in one respect, the polar opposite of Bewley's because a distinguishing feature of these firms is that in recessions, they *do* reduce pay and *do not* lay off workers who are partners in the firm. If Bewley's characterization of worker psychology is correct, why do not the cooperative members become disgruntled and slack off when their earnings fall? Evidently, it is not just pay but also the structural relationship of the worker to the firm that determines the worker's response: the cooperative firm belongs to the workers whereas the conventional firm hires labor in someone else's interest. Moreover, unless there is a clear rule (e.g., seniority) for determining who would be laid off, the median worker would tend to resist any layoffs because he could be among those dismissed if the layoffs were truly random (Steinherr & Thisse, 1979). In other words, when the workers (and managers who can be removed by them) run the firm rather than outside owners or managers, the pain of layoffs may not so easily be limited by rendering its effects external to the decision makers.

Returning to the previous theme of monitoring and incentives, Pencavel's and much other analysis of worker-owned and more conventional firms with profit-sharing provides interesting evidence on the empirics of what economic theory predicts should be a straightforward free-rider problem. Baker, Jensen, and Murphy (1988), for example, argued that economic theory implies that the direct effect of a profit share on effort will be negligible if the firm is large enough that the effort of an individual worker makes little difference to per-worker output. However, the evidence of the plywood cooperatives discussed by Pencavel and of the more diverse group of firms discussed by Weitzman and Kruse (1990) suggests that profit-sharing is often quite effective at inducing high levels of effort, typically with less need for monitoring. Weitzman and Kruse explained the efficacy of profit-sharing using a repeated game approach. They noted that the problem of effort choice under a sharing scheme has the characteristic of an n-person prisoners' dilemma, that the problem is typically played out repeatedly over time, and that the literature on such games shows that both efficient and inefficient equilibria are possible.[39] They also noted that profit-sharing may induce mutual monitoring and moral pressure on fellow workers and that even if the incentives to engage in such monitoring or pressuring are small, the effects could be substantial under appropriate configurations of workplace technology and preferences.[40] The recent experimental literature on

---

[39] MacLeod (1987) models this explicitly for a workers' cooperative.

[40] A discussion of the relative importance of incentives to monitor versus technology of monitoring was provided by Putterman (1984) in a critical appraisal of Alchian & Demsetz's approach. Mutual monitoring and peer pressure were discussed by Bradley & Gelb (1981) and Kandel & Lazear (1992), among others.

the role of anger or negative reciprocity in causing group members to take on themselves the disciplining of free riders is also pertinent here.[41]

Agency and finance

Many of the theories discussed so far (e.g., those of Coase and of Alchian and Demestz) assume that the manager of the firm is himself the owner and residual claimant. Such an assumption may be an appropriate simplification for some purposes, and it more or less may reflect the realities of many smaller firms. Because managers and owners are different individuals in many larger firms, it leaves a considerable area in need of further theoretical analysis. To be sure, the owner–manager relationship is amenable to some of the same agency-theoretic treatment as that between managers and workers; therefore, one might expect to find here mostly variations on themes already explored. In fact, however, the problem involves some rather different considerations, partly because it is bound up with questions of financial contracting in which institutions having no exact parallels in the sphere of labor play an important role.

As noted previously, the literature on financial agency owes much to Berle and Means's (1932) view that because dispersed shareholders have little incentive to closely monitor the managers of a corporation, nonowner managers are able to direct firms toward ends other than profit-seeking. Authors such as Manne, Fama, and Jensen and Meckling respond to Berle and Means by identifying ways in which financial institutions might make managers responsive to the interests of outside owners despite diffuse ownership and small managerial ownership stakes. Although disagreeing about the degree to which such institutions align managers' and shareholders' interests, all find reason for skepticism of Berle and Means's view.

Manne's article (1965 and Chapter 19 in this Reader) is a seminal contribution to the literature on the market for corporate control. He argued that the potential of a corporate takeover (i.e., a controlling equity interest being bought by outside investors who believe that the firm can be more profitable under alternative management) keeps the incumbent managers vigilant, even if the frequency of actual takeovers is relatively low. The effectiveness of takeovers as a disciplinary device has been the subject of much debate and research.[42] Authors such as Grossman and Hart (1980) argued that in theory, free-rider problems may reduce the effectiveness of the takeover market. Various defense strategies employed by incumbent management also may reduce the discipline that takeovers provide. The evidence on takeovers, however, indicates that on average, actual takeovers are effective means for improving

---

[41] See, e.g., Fehr & Gächter (2000).
[42] See, e.g., the Symposium in the *Journal of Economic Perspectives*, Winter 1988.

corporate performance, in terms of both returns to stockholders and operating efficiency.[43]

Fama's basic argument (in his 1980 paper and in Chapter 20 of this Reader) was that in the long run, managers can expect to be rewarded in direct proportion to their contributions to shareholder wealth, and that they accordingly have essentially perfect incentives to maximize firm value (or, equivalently, the present discounted value of the firm's future profit stream). He presented a formal model in which managers earn current wages equal to weighted averages of estimated past marginal productivity (i.e., contribution to firm value). Although current pay fails to reflect current performance, the assumption that estimates of past performance are unbiased means that lifetime compensation is expected to change in exact proportion to changes in current effectiveness. In arguing that compensation accurately tracks past performance, Fama relied heavily on the assumptions that (1) competition among managers causes the information needed for such tracking to reach those who set or approve compensation; and (2) no alternative considerations influence those decision makers – assumptions with which Bebchuk and Fried take issue.

Jensen and Meckling model an owner–manager who, for portfolio diversification or other reasons, seeks to reduce his ownership stake.[44] In this model, the manager's choice between maximizing the value of his firm and enjoying consumption on the job is determined by preferences and relative prices, with the price to the manager of consumption on the job being an increasing function of his ownership stake. Because a reduction in the size of the manager's stake leads to a lower price and therefore a larger amount of consumption, it also produces a decline in the firm's value. Potential outside owners rationally anticipate this effect; therefore, a manager cannot sell shares at the value they would have had were he full owner but rather must accept an appropriately reduced price. The upshot is that the manager personally bears the cost of his value-reducing actions, which gives him an incentive to bond himself or to invite monitoring so as to be able to enjoy a reduced ownership stake with less personal wealth reduction. Whereas Jensen and Meckling differ from Fama because "managerial shirking" or nonwealth maximizing behavior is not fully eliminated, in their model, their argument has the similar implication that rational capital markets make managers pay for their personal consumption, creating a pressure toward verifiable wealth-maximizing by managers with even small ownership stakes.[45]

---

[43] Jarrell, Brickley, & Netter (1988); Kaplan (1989); and Healy, Palepu, & Ruback (1992) documented the consequences of takeovers and buyouts.

[44] A formalization of Jensen and Meckling in which the demand for a limited stake is endogenous was provided by Kihlstrom & Matthews (1990).

[45] Indeed, the argument may hold even for managers with no stakes, provided that they at least occasionally have reason to raise outside equity because it implies that the cost of such equity – or the value at which shares can be sold – is proportional to the level of anticipated malfeasance.

Because the costliness of determining when behavior is wealth-maximizing means that managers are never perfect agents of owners, in their model, Jensen and Meckling's analysis suggests that resources invested in a firm will always have their highest return when the manager is full owner. Why then do we, in practice, observe many firms whose managers hold small or zero shares? Just as Alchian and Demsetz argue that production takes place in teams despite the fact that it is not economically rational to eliminate all shirking under team production – in that case, due to the countervailing benefits of economies of scale – so it can be argued that delegating management is sometimes efficient, despite persistent agency costs that, in principle, could be eliminated by full owner-management. The countervailing benefits in the case of management and ownership, according to Fama and Jensen (1985 and Chapter 22 in this Reader), come from a few main sources.

First, those authors argue, there is not always a perfect coincidence between the possession of managerial talent and the possession of the resources with which to finance a firm. Because an owner-run firm will return less value in the hands of an owner who is an incompetent manager, there may be gains from trade between wealthy financiers and nonwealthy talented managers, despite agency costs. Second, even if all wealthy people were talented managers, there might not be enough people sufficiently wealthy to individually own all of the potentially profitable firms, especially firms able to use profitably extremely large amounts of capital. Third, risk-averse individuals have a preference for holding diversified portfolios of assets and are willing to sacrifice some wealth in order to do so. Finally, the costs of attracting large numbers of individuals to share the burden of financing a large firm are lowered by letting new financiers join and old ones leave freely, without the permission of the incumbents and by the rules of limited liability. Although a given project in theory could be better managed by a solo owner–manager, Fama and Jensen suggest in their diagrammatic argument that it may be better to have it slightly inefficiently managed by professional managers at an optimal level of capitalization than to have it efficiently managed by an owner–manager at a suboptimal level of capitalization. Thus, larger or riskier projects tend to have outside financing, whereas smaller or less risky projects tend to be owned and financed by the people who manage them.

The notions that corporations are likely to suffer from agency problems or that the long-term trend in large corporations has been toward more diffuse ownership have not gone uncontested. Demsetz (1983), for example, resisted the idea that managers who are partial or nonowners will enjoy more consumption on the job than full owner–managers. The crux of Demsetz's argument is that consumption on the job is not necessarily bad for the full owner manager because there is nothing irrational about a manager engaging in some of his consumption at work if he values it at least as much as the cost in reduced profits. Because an outside owner places no direct value on a hired manager's consumption on the job, however, and because in addition he has difficulty in monitoring it, he may forbid some forms of consumption that he would engage in if he were managing the firm himself. Demsetz also departs from some of the literature by resisting the characterization of corporations as "diffusely held," providing evidence of significant ownership concentration in many large firms, of substantial shareholding by upper-level managers, and of a large share of the compensation of upper-level managers that derives from shareholding.[46]

The concentration of ownership, its impact on performance, and its changes over time have been the subject of a number of detailed empirical investigations. Demsetz and Lehn (1985) empirically studied the determinants of ownership structure in 511 U.S. corporations and found no significant relationship between ownership concentration and accounting profit rates.[47] Holderness, Kroszner, and Sheehan (1999, 2000, and Chapter 23 in this Reader) compared a cross-section of approximately 1,500 publicly traded U.S. firms in 1935 with a modern sample of more than 4,200 traded firms in 1995 and found that contrary to received wisdom, the mean percentage of common stock held by a firm's officers and directors rose from 13 percent in 1935 to 21 percent in 1995. They found no evidence that insider ownership was substituting for mechanisms such as incentive-based pay, board monitoring, the market for corporate control, or product-market competition, each of which operate at least as intensively now as compared with the earlier period. Instead, they argued that the overall average lower level of volatility and the greater hedging and diversification opportunities open to both managers and firms today had lowered the costs to managers of holding large equity stakes in their firms. The top management of publicly traded corporations thus faces more intensive pressure from a variety of incentive-alignment devices today than in the pre-WWII period.

Both popular and academic concerns about managerial malfeasance nevertheless have grown, fueled in part by the large and well-publicized scandals of the past few years. In the academic literature, Bebchuk has been a persistent and articulate exponent of the view that corporation CEOs have had considerable freedom to pursue their own interests at the expense of shareholders. In

---

[46] Because the emphasis in this Reader is on the theoretical rather than empirical literature, and because the material presented in Demsetz (1983) is no more than an "opening shot" in a widening and still contentious literature, we have not reprinted most of the portion of the paper dealing with this part of Demestz's argument. The interested reader may wish to see pp. 387–390 in Demsetz (1983), along with Demsetz & Lehn (1985). Holderness, Kroszner, & Sheehan (1999, 2000) examined how ownership structure has evolved since the 1930s. Jensen & Warner (1988) presented a thorough survey of the empirical literature on ownership and corporate governance.

[47] Jensen & Warner (1988) presented a thorough survey of the empirical literature on ownership and corporate governance. See also Morck, Shleifer, & Vishny (1988); Kole & Lehn (1999); La Porta, Lopez-de-Silanes, & Shleifer (1999); and McConnell & Servaes (1990).

Chapter 24 in this Reader, Bebchuk and Fried argue that board members have insufficient incentive to treat managerial proposals with the critical independence that their role as agents of shareholders demands of them. Contrary to Fama, they identify a number of ways in which CEO self-interest, agency and collective-action problems, and the structure of U.S. corporations may leave shareholders poorly served.

Why should ownership confer control?

Beyond questions of agency such as those addressed by the authors discussed thus far, one can ask broader questions about the nature of the ownership both of firms' assets and of firms as such. Alchian and Demsetz argue that firms will own many of the capital goods with which they work because the cost of having their rate of usage and resulting deterioration monitored by outside owners can thus be avoided. Holmstrom and Milgrom point out that when the direct user of the machine is an employee and when the rate of utilization and maintenance is difficult for even the employer to observe, it may be better for the worker to own the machine (and perhaps to be self-employed). This is particularly the case because the existence of this problem may make it optimal for the employer to desist from offering high-powered incentives for the measurable tasks that the employee performs with the machine (for reasons discussed previously). Whether the worker will become self-employed, in their model, depends on his degree of risk aversion. However, Williamson's point about trade between owners of interspecialized assets, Barzel's point about the cost of monitoring stages of a sequential production process, or the general point of the asset-specificity approach (shared by Klein, Crawford, and Alchian and by Grossman and Hart) that assets specialized to each other may best be owned in common may also rule out the hiving off of the worker and machine as a separate firm.

Milgrom and Roberts criticize the asset-specificity arguments of Williamson and of Klein, Crawford, and Alchian. The appropriation of rents from one party to a specialized exchange by another party to that same exchange, they point out, is a redistribution of the returns from the joint project but need not affect the aggregate level of those returns. Because the appropriation hazard does not affect efficiency, risk-neutral parties should simply proceed to contract for the exchange, deducting any estimated anticipation of appropriation from their reservation prices. Their argument is said to hold even for some specifications of risk aversion. A possible answer, however, is that efficiency would be affected if the parties invested real resources in efforts at appropriation (e.g., temporarily shutting down a railroad to add credibility to a threat to do so permanently unless better compensated). Such a response, indeed, is very much in the rent-seeking tradition from which Milgrom and Roberts' own theory of bureaucracy derives.[48] The presence of asymmetric information – which might, for example, lead to the adoption of such bargaining strategies – is also precluded in Milgrom and Roberts' critique.

As discussed previously, Hart argues that Williamson is unclear about what disciplinary advantages a manager has relative to an independent contractor and, therefore, why production should take place in a firm rather than through market contracts. Hart's approach instead emphasizes the importance of residual control rights over assets which are complementary to the labor input, so that discipline over labor is exercised only indirectly. The theory implies that interspecialized assets should be owned in common and that the owner of a resource that is critical to a project should hold the residual rights of control.

Hart's property-rights approach thus might be thought to constitute a theory of why the capital owner must run the firm, but this is not really the case – or at least not without additional assumptions or restrictions. This is because if all of the interspecialized or critical resources are capital goods, then transfer of ownership to a different party has no consequence for efficiency.[49] It is only when the owner of a specialized or critical capital good also has specialized human capital (e.g., unique knowledge of how to employ that good) that the theory dictates the identity of the owner. Specialized human capital dictates ownership, whereas specialized physical capital does not because only the former, in principle, is not transferable.

Rajan and Zingales (1998) went so far as to argue that "[t]he ownership of physical assets is not the only source of power within a firm, nor necessarily the most effective in promoting relationship-specific investments." They define a "power"-allocating mechanism that they call "access," defining the latter as "the ability to use, or work with, a critical resource." The critical resource need not be a physical asset (e.g., it could be an idea) and it need not be the case that the person with "access" has formal property rights in it (i.e., it could be a relationship with a person or persons).

Williamson (1985, Chapter 12) and Putterman (1993a) inquired into why it is the providers of capital who own and control most firms.[50] Williamson argues that while credit can be provided to firms where redeployable assets are available as collateral, specialized and intangible assets must be financed by equity holders, who provide funds without guaranteed return of even the invested principal. He compares equity holders to managers and other investors in firm-specific assets, arguing that only the former lack contractual safeguards of the type that managers can obtain through their terms of employment. The

---

[48] This seems to be the idea behind Milgrom & Roberts' informal treatment of the issue in their textbook; see Milgrom & Roberts (1992), pp. 307–308.

[49] That is, while the theory implies that *some* capital owner should own the firm, it does not imply that *any particular* capital owner must do so.

[50] See also Hansmann (1996).

unprotected status of equity holders thus calls for the grant of control over the firm.

Putterman (1993a) suggested that this argument by Williamson, although couched in terms of asset specificity, is essentially a variant of the Knightian argument about moral hazard and risk-bearing. According to that argument (as discussed previously), the bearer of risk, who guarantees a return to other agents in the firm, demands control rights as a way of ensuring that the insured agents do not abuse their security. Putterman further pointed out that despite the alleged separation of ownership and control in corporations, ultimate control rights remain in the hands of the shareholders and indeed *must* remain there if the mechanisms discussed by Manne, Fama, and others are to be of any effect.[51] Thus, Knight's intuition about moral hazard appears to have enormous explanatory power even in the world of the large corporation. Putterman also argued that the primary determinant of who holds that bundle of control, residual, and alienation rights that we call ownership, is probably the ability and willingness to provide financial resources and bear risk, a Knightian approach shorn of the emphasis on nonfinancial aspects of entrepreneurship.[52] He pointed out that identification of the boundaries of the firm with the boundaries of common ownership is perhaps underappreciated (e.g., in Williamson's transaction-cost economics) and suggested that the disassociation of ownership from labor should be seen as the fundamental source of the incentive problems that preoccupy so much of the internal organization literature. Whereas worker ownership in some cases can address those problems and also may give workers direct utility, workers' limited wealth and consequent high risk aversion and demand for portfolio diversification make that option quite costly to them and correspondingly rare.

Conclusion

In this introduction, we considered some of the major issues addressed by the literature sampled in our Reader: What is a firm? Why are there firms? What determines firms' sizes and scopes? How sharp is the distinction between intrafirm transactions and transactions in the market? We found most authors treating firms as somewhat distinctive devices for coordinating production activities, marked by long-term contracts and by an assignment of residual control rights to a subset of agents who supply equity finance. However, we found

[51] That the market for corporate control could not exist without the attachment of control rights to shareholding is obvious. Fama's argument that managerial compensation will track how well managers perform from the shareholders' standpoint also makes no sense without "the market for outside takeovers providing discipline of last resort." Fama & Jensen (1983a) assigned a similar role to shareholders' control rights.

[52] For an alternative viewpoint emphasizing the importance of existing wealth as a means of attracting finance, rather than the ability to bear risk, see Newman (1995).

considerable controversy regarding the strength of the firm–market distinction, paralleling controversy over the meaning of authority within the organization.

We found a variety of explanations for organization of activity in firms, ranging from Coase's economizing on the costs of pricing transactions to Williamson's safeguards against appropriation of quasi-rents to Barzel's economizing on and Alchian and Demsetz's motivation of monitoring effort and to Knight's provision of insurance in exchange for control. Determinants of firm size similarly varied, including the domain of interspecialized-assets consideration implicit in the asset-specificity approach and corresponding technological considerations in the monitoring approaches, with arguments about high- and low-powered incentives, costs of bureaucracy, and limited managerial attention called on to provide upper limits.

Finally, we discussed two key relations observed in firms – those of ownership and those of employment – by pointing to a difference among authors regarding the relative importance of each to the nature of the firm. The remainder of our discussion reviewed the models of the employment relationship and incentives that constitute Part III and the analyses of financial agency and ownership issues that constitute Part IV of this Reader.

The literature on the economic nature – in particular, the internal and contractual structure of firms – has progressed considerably from the days when neoclassical economists ignored institutions and institutionalists were ill-prepared to discourse with formal theorists. Where once an interest in what was going on inside "the black box" of the firm had a faint scent of disloyalty to the enterprise of economics, such an interest is now part of the frontier of economic research. Not all "neo-institutional" insights have been absorbed by formal theory, so theorists seeking better answers to the still-perplexing questions of the field would do well to explore the literature sampled here. The fact that firm theorists disagree among themselves about firm–market boundaries, the nature of the employment relation, and other issues may be a reflection of a field that is still relatively youthful, but it also holds out the promise of more lively discussion yet to come. We are pleased to present this sourcebook for that discussion to the latest generation of participants.

PART I

Within and among firms: the division of labor

CHAPTER 1

From *The Wealth of Nations*

ADAM SMITH

Adam Smith (1723–1790) was born in Kirkcaldy, Scotland. He received a Master of Arts degree from the University of Glasgow in 1740 and subsequently was Professor of Moral Philosophy at that university from 1752 to 1763 and Commissioner of Customs for Scotland from 1778 to 1790. *The Wealth of Nations* established Smith as the founding figure in classical political economy.

Of the division of labour

(From book I, chapter 1)

The greatest improvement in the productive powers of labour, and the greater part of the skill, dexterity, and judgment with which it is any where directed, or applied, seem to have been the effects of the division of labour.

The effects of the division of labour, in the general business of society, will be more easily understood by considering in what manner it operates in some particular manufactures. It is commonly supposed to be carried furthest in some very trifling ones; not perhaps that it really is carried further in them than in others of more importance: but in those trifling manufactures which are destined to supply the small wants of but a small number of people, the whole number of workmen must necessarily be small; and those employed in every different branch of the work can often be collected into the same workhouse and placed at once under the view of the spectator. In those great manufactures, on the contrary, which are destined to supply the great wants of the great body of the people, every different branch of the work employs so great a number of workmen that it is impossible to collect them all into the same workhouse. We can seldom see more, at one time, than those employed in one single branch. Though in such manufactures, therefore, the work may really be divided into a much greater number of parts, than in those of a more trifling nature, the division is not near so obvious and has accordingly been much less observed.

From Adam Smith, *An Inquiry into the Nature and Causes of The Wealth of Nations*, originally published 1776. Excerpted from the Modern Library Edition, edited by Edwin Cannan. New York, 1937.

To take an example, therefore,[1] from a very trifling manufacture, but one in which the division of labour has been very often taken notice of, the trade of the pin maker; a workman not educated to this business (which the division of labour has rendered a distinct trade) nor acquainted with the use of the machinery employed in it (to the invention of which the same division of labour has probably given occasion) could scarce, perhaps, with his utmost industry, make one pin in a day and certainly could not make twenty. But in the way in which this business is now carried on, not only the whole work is a peculiar trade, but it is divided into a number of branches, of which the greater part are likewise peculiar trades. One man draws out the wire, another straights it, a third cuts it, a fourth points it, a fifth grinds it at the top for receiving the head; to make the head requires two or three distinct operations; to put it on, is a peculiar business, to whiten the pins is another; it is even a trade by itself to put them into the paper; and the important business of making a pin is, in this manner, divided into about eighteen distinct operations, which, in some manufactories, are all performed by distinct hands, though in others the same man will sometimes perform two or three of them. I have seen a small manufactory of this kind where ten men only were employed, and where some of them consequently performed two or three distinct operations. But though they were very poor, and therefore but indifferently accommodated with the necessary machinery, they could, when they exerted themselves, make among them about twelve pounds of pins in a day. There are in a pound upwards of four thousand pins of a middling size. Those ten persons, therefore, could make among them upwards of forty-eight thousand pins in a day. Each person, therefore, making a tenth part of forty-eight thousand pins, might be considered as making four thousand eight hundred pins in a day. But if they had all wrought separately and independently, and without any of them having been educated to this particular business, they certainly could not each of them have made twenty, perhaps not one pin in a day; that is, certainly, not the two hundred and fortieth, perhaps not the four thousand eight hundredth part of what they are at present capable of performing, in consequence of a proper division and combination of their different operations.

In every other art and manufacture, the effects of the division of labour are similar to what they are in this very trifling one; though, in many of them, the labour can neither be so much subdivided nor reduced to so great a simplicity of operation. The division of labour, however, so far as it can be introduced, occasions, in every art, a proportionable increase of the productive powers of labour. The separation of different trades and employments from one another seems to have taken place, in consequence of this advantage. This separation

---

[1] Another and perhaps more important reason for taking an example like that which follows is the possibility of exhibiting the advantages of division of labour in statistical form.

too is generally carried furthest in those countries which enjoy the highest degree of industry and improvement; what is the work of one man in a rude state of society, being generally that of several in an improved one.

. . .

This great increase of the quantity of work, which, in consequence of the division of labour, the same number of people are capable of performing, is owing to three different circumstances; first, to the increase of dexterity in every particular workman; secondly, to the saving of the time which is commonly lost in passing from one species of work to another; and lastly, to the invention of a great number of machines which facilitate and abridge labour and enable one man to do the work of many.

First, the improvement of the dexterity of the workman necessarily increases the quantity of the work he can perform; and the division of labour, by reducing every man's business to some one simple operation, and by making this operation the sole employment of his life, necessarily increases very much the dexterity of the workman. A common smith, who, though accustomed to handle the hammer, has never been used to make nails, if upon some particular occasion he is obliged to attempt it, will scarce, I am assured, be able to make above two or three hundred nails in a day, and those too very bad ones. A smith who has been accustomed to make nails, but whose sole or principal business has not been that of a nailer, can seldom with his utmost diligence make more than eight hundred or a thousand nails in a day. I have seen several boys under twenty years of age who had never exercised any other trade but that of making nails, and who, when they exerted themselves, could make, each of them, upwards of two thousand three hundred nails in a day. The making of a nail, however, is by no means one of the simplest operations. The same person blows the bellows, stirs or mends the fire as there is occasion, heats the iron, and forges every part of the nail: In forging the head too he is obliged to change his tools. The different operations into which the making of a pin, or of a metal button, is subdivided, are all of them much more simple, and the dexterity of the person, of whose life it has been the sole business to perform them, is usually much greater. The rapidity with which some of the operations of those manufacturers are performed, exceeds what the human hand could, by those who had never seen them, be supposed capable of acquiring.

Secondly, the advantage which is gained by saving the time commonly lost in passing from one sort of work to another is much greater than we should at first view be apt to imagine it. It is impossible to pass very quickly from one kind of work to another that is carried on in a different place and with quite different tools. A country weaver, who cultivates a small farm, must lose a good deal of time in passing from his loom to the field and from the field to his loom. When the two trades can be carried on in the same workhouse, the loss of time is no doubt much less. It is even in this case, however, very considerable. A man commonly saunters a little in turning his hand from one sort of employment to another. When he first begins the new work he is seldom very keen and hearty; his mind, as they say, does not go to it, and for some time he rather trifles than applies to good purpose. The habit of sauntering and of indolent careless application, which is naturally, or rather necessarily, acquired by every country workman who is obliged to change his work and his tools every half hour, and to apply his hand in twenty different ways almost every day of his life, renders him almost always slothful and lazy and incapable of any vigorous application even on the most pressing occasions. Independent, therefore, of his deficiency in point of dexterity, this cause alone must always reduce considerable the quantity of work which he is capable of performing.

Thirdly, and lastly, every body must be sensible how much labour is facilitated and abridged by the application of proper machinery. It is unnecessary to give any example. I shall only observe, therefore, that the invention of all those machines by which labour is so much facilitated and abridged seems to have been originally owing to the division of labour. Men are much more likely to discover easier and readier methods of attaining any object, when the whole attention of their minds is directed towards that single object, than when it is dissipated among a great variety of things. But in consequence of the division of labour, the whole of every man's attention comes naturally to be directed towards some one very simple object. It is naturally to be expected, therefore, that some one or other of those who are employed in each particular branch of labour should soon find out easier and readier methods of performing their own particular work, wherever the nature of it admits of such improvement. A great part of the machines made use of in those manufactures in which labour is most subdivided were originally the inventions of common workmen, who, being each of them employed in some very simple operation, naturally turned their thoughts towards finding out easier and readier methods of performing it. Whoever has been much accustomed to visit such manufactures must frequently have been shewn very pretty machines, which were the inventions of such workmen, in order to facilitate and quicken their own particular part of the work. In the first fire engines, a boy was constantly employed to open and shut alternately the communication between the boiler and the cylinder, according as the piston either ascended or descended. One of those boys, who loved to play with his companions, observed that, by tying a string from the handle of the valve which opened this communication to another part of the machine, the valve would open and shut without his assistance and leave him at liberty to divert himself with his play fellows. One of the greatest improvements that has been made upon this machine, since it was first invented, was in this manner the discovery of a boy who wanted to save his own labour.

All the improvements in machinery, however, have by no means been the inventions of those who had occasion to use the machines. Many improvements have been made by the ingenuity of the makers of the machines, when to make them became the business of a peculiar trade; and some by that of those who are called philosophers or men of speculation, whose trade it is not to do any thing but to observe every thing and who, upon that account, are often capable of combining together the powers of the most distant and dissimilar objects. In the progress of society, philosophy or speculation becomes, like every other employment, the principal or sole trade and occupation of a particular class of citizens. Like every other employment too, it is subdivided into a great number of different branches, each of which affords occupation to a peculiar tribe or class of philosophers; and this subdivision of employment in philosophy, as well as in every other business, improves dexterity and saves time. Each individual becomes more expert in his own peculiar branch, more work is done upon the whole, and the quantity of science is considerably increased by it.

It is the great multiplication of the productions of all the different arts, in consequence of the division of labour, which occasions, in a well-governed society, that universal opulence which extends itself to the lowest ranks of the people. Every workman has a great quantity of his own work to dispose of beyond what he himself has occasion for; and every other workman being exactly in the same situation, he is enabled to exchange a great quantity of his own goods for a great quantity, or, what comes to the same thing, for the price of a great quantity of theirs. He supplies them abundantly with what they have occasion for, and they accommodate him as amply with what he has occasion for, and a general plenty diffuses itself through all the different ranks of the society.

Observe the accommodation of the most common artificer or day labourer in a civilized and thriving country, and you will perceive that the number of people of whose industry a part, though but a small part, has been employed in procuring him this accommodation, exceeds all computation. The woollen coat, for example, which covers the day labourer, as coarse and rough as it may appear, is the produce of the joint labour of a great multitude of workmen. The shepherd, the sorter of wool, the wool comber or carder, the dyer, the scribbler, the spinner, the weaver, the fuller, the dresser, with many others, must all join their different arts in order to complete even this homely production. How many merchants and carriers, besides, must have been employed in transporting the materials from some of those workmen to others who often live in a very distant part of the country! How much commerce and navigation in particular, how many shipbuilders, sailors, sail makers, rope makers must have been employed in order to bring together the different drugs made use of by the dyer, which often come from the remotest corners of the world! What a variety of labour too is necessary in order to produce the tools of the meanest of those workmen! To say nothing of such complicated machines as the ship of the sailor, the mill of the fuller, or even the loom of the weaver, let us consider only what a variety of labour is requisite in order to form that very simple machine, the shears with which the shepherd clips the wool. The miner, the builder of the furnace for smelting the ore, the feller of the timber, the burner of the charcoal to be made use of in the smelting house, the brick maker, the bricklayer, the workmen who attend the furnace, the millwright, the forger, the smith must all of them join their different arts in order to produce them. Were we to examine, in the same manner, all the different parts of his dress and household furniture; the coarse linen shirt which he wears next his skin; the shoes which cover his feet; the bed which he lies on and all the different parts which compose it; the kitchengrate at which he prepares his victuals; the coals which he makes use of for that purpose, dug from the bowels of the earth and brought to him perhaps by a long sea and a long land carriage; all the other utensils of his kitchen; all the furniture of his table; the knives and forks; the earthen or pewter plates upon which he serves up and divides his victuals; the different hands employed in preparing his bread and his beer; the glass window which lets in the heat and the light and keeps out the wind and the rain, with all the knowledge and art requisite for preparing that beautiful and happy invention, without which these northern parts of the world could scarce have afforded a very comfortable habitation; together with the tools of all the different workmen employed in producing those different conveniences; if we examine, I say, all these things, and consider what a variety of labour is employed about each of them, we shall be sensible that without the assistance and cooperation of many thousands, the very meanest person in a civilized country could not be provided, even according to, what we very falsely imagine, the easy and simple manner in which he is commonly accommodated. Compared, indeed, with the more extravagant luxury of the great, his accommodation must no doubt appear extremely simple and easy; and yet it may be true, perhaps that the accommodation of an European prince does not always so much exceed that of an industrious and frugal peasant, as the accommodation of the latter exceeds that of many an African king, the absolute master of the lives and liberties of ten thousand naked savages.

. . .

That the division of labour is limited by the extent of the market

(From book 1, chapter 3)

As it is the power of exchanging that gives occasion to the division of labour, so the extent of this division must always be limited by the extent of that power, or in other words, by the extent of the market. When the market is very small, no person can have any encouragement to dedicate himself entirely to one employment, for want of the power to exchange all that surplus part of the produce of his own labour, which is over and above his own consumption, for such parts of the produce of other men's labour as he has occasion for.

There are some sorts of industry, even of the lowest kind, which can be carried on no where but in a great town. A porter, for example, can find employment and subsistence in no other place. A village is by much too narrow a sphere for him; even an ordinary market town is scarce large enough to afford him constant occupation. In the lone houses and very small villages which are scattered about in so desert a country as the Highlands of Scotland, every farmer must be butcher, baker, and brewer for his own family. In such situations we can scarce expect to find even a smith, a carpenter, or a mason within less than twenty miles of another of the same trade. The scattered families that live at eight or ten miles distance from the nearest of them must learn to perform themselves a great number of little pieces of work, for which, in more populous countries, they would call in the assistance of those workmen. Country workmen are almost every where obliged to apply themselves to all the different branches of industry that have so much affinity to one another as to be employed about the same sort of materials. A country carpenter deals in every sort of work that is made of wood; a country smith in every sort of work that is made of iron. The former is not only a carpenter, but a joiner, a cabinet maker, and even a carver in wood, as well as a wheelwright, a ploughwright, a cart and wagon maker. The employments of the latter are still more various. It is impossible there should be such a trade as even that of the nailer in the remote and inland parts of the Highlands of Scotland. Such a workman at the rate of a thousand nails a day, and three hundred working days in the year, will make three hundred thousand nails in the year. But in such a situation it would be impossible to dispose of one thousand, that is, of one day's work in the year.

As by means of water carriage a more extensive market is opened to every sort of industry than what land carriage alone can afford it, so it is upon the seacoast, and along the banks of navigable rivers, that industry of every kind naturally begins to subdivide and improve itself, and it is frequently not till a long time after that those improvements extend themselves to the inland parts of the country.

. . .

On joint stock companies

(From book V, chapter 1)

Joint stock companies, established either by royal charter or by act of parliament differ in several respects, not only from regulated companies but from private copartneries.

First, in a private copartnery, no partner, without the consent of the company, can transfer his share to another person or introduce a new member into the company. Each member, however, may, upon proper warning, withdraw from the copartnery and demand payment from them of his share of the common stock. In a joint stock company, on the contrary, no member can demand payment of his share from the company; but each member can, without their consent, transfer his share to another person and thereby introduce a new member. The value of a share in a joint stock is always the price which it will bring in the market; and this may be either greater or less, in any proportion, than the sum which its owner stands credited for in the stock of the company.

Secondly, in a private copartnery, each partner is bound for the debts contracted by the company to the whole extent of his fortune. In a joint stock company, on the contrary, each partner is bound only to the extent of his share.

The trade of a joint stock company is always managed by a court of directors. This court, indeed, is frequently subject, in many respects, to the controul of a general court of proprietors. But the greater part of those proprietors seldom pretend to understand any thing of the business of the company, and when the spirit of faction happens not to prevail among them, give themselves no trouble about it, but receive contentedly such half yearly or yearly dividend as the directors think proper to make to them. This total exemption from trouble and from risk, beyond a limited sum, encouraged many people to become adventurers in joint stock companies, who would, upon no account, hazard their fortunes in any private copartnery. Such companies, therefore, commonly draw to themselves much greater stocks than any private copartnery can boast of. The trading stock of the South Sea Company, at one time, amounted to upwards of thirty-three millions eight hundred thousand pounds. The dividend capital of the Bank of England amounts, at present, to ten millions seven hundred and eighty thousand pounds. The directors of such companies, however, being the managers rather of other people's money than of their own, it cannot well be expected, that they should watch over it with the same anxious vigilance with which the partners in a private copartnery frequently watch over their own. Like the stewards of a rich man, they are apt to consider attention to small matters as not for their master's honour and very easily give themselves a dispensation from having it. Negligence and profusion, therefore, must always prevail, more or less, in the management of the affairs of such a company. It is upon this account that joint stock companies for foreign trade have seldom been able to maintain the competition against private adventurers. They have, accordingly, very seldom succeeded without an exclusive privilege, and frequently have not succeeded with one. Without an exclusive privilege they have commonly mismanaged the trade. With an exclusive privilege they have both mismanaged and confined it.

. . .

But a joint stock company, consisting of a small number of proprietors, with a moderate capital, approaches very nearly to the nature of the private copartnery and may be capable of nearly the same degree of vigilance and attention.

. . .

On education

(From book V, chapter 1)

In the progress of the division of labour, the employment of the far greater part of those who live by labour, that is, of the great body of the people, comes to be confined to a few very simple operations, frequently to one or two. But the understandings of the greater part of men are necessarily formed by their ordinary employments. The man whose whole life is spent in performing a few simple operations, of which the effects too are, perhaps, always the same, or very nearly the same, has no occasion to exert his understanding or to exercise his invention in finding out expedients for removing difficulties which never occur. He naturally loses, therefore, the habit of such exertion and generally becomes as stupid and ignorant as it is possible for a human creature to become. The torpor of his mind renders him, not only incapable of relishing or bearing a part in any rational conversation, but of conceiving any generous, noble, or tender sentiment, and consequently of forming any just judgment concerning many even of the ordinary duties of private life. Of the great and extensive interests of his country he is altogether incapable of judging; and unless very particular pains have been taken to render him otherwise, he is equally incapable of defending his country in war. The uniformity of his stationary life naturally corrupts the courage of his mind and makes him regard with abhorrence the irregular, uncertain, and adventurous life of a soldier. It corrupts even the activity of his body, and renders him incapable of exerting his strength with vigour and perseverance, in any other employment than that to which he has been bred. His dexterity at his own particular trade seems, in this manner, to be acquired at the expense of his intellectual, social, and marital virtues. But in every improved and civilized society this is the state into which the labouring poor, that is, the great body of the people, must necessarily fall, unless government takes some pains to prevent it.

It is otherwise in the barbarous societies, as they are commonly called, of hunters, of shepherds, and even of husbandmen in that rude state of husbandry which precedes the improvement of manufactures and the extension of foreign commerce. In such societies the varied occupations of every man oblige every man to exert his capacity and to invent expedients for removing difficulties which are continually occurring. Invention is kept alive, and the mind is not suffered to fall into that drowsy stupidity, which, in a civilized society, seems to benumb the understanding of almost all the inferior ranks of people. In those barbarous societies, as they are called, every man, it has already been observed, is a warrior. Every man too is in some measure a statesman and can form a tolerable judgment concerning the interest of the society and the conduct of those who govern it. How far their chiefs are good judges in peace, or good leaders in war, is obvious to the observation of almost every single man among them. In such a society indeed, no man can well acquire that improved and refined understanding, which a few men sometimes possess in a more civilized state. Though in a rude society there is a good deal of variety in the occupations of every individual, there is not a good deal in those of the whole society. Every man does, or is capable of doing, almost every thing which any other man does, or is capable of doing. Every man has a considerable degree of knowledge, ingenuity, and invention; but scarce any man has a great degree. The degree, however, which is commonly possessed, is generally sufficient for conducting the whole simple business of the society. In a civilized state, on the contrary, though there is little variety in the occupations of the greater part of individuals, there is an almost infinite variety in those of the whole society. These varied occupations present an almost infinite variety of objects to the contemplation of those few, who, being attached to no particular occupation themselves, have leisure and inclination to examine the occupations of other people. The contemplation of so great a variety of objects necessarily exercises their minds in endless comparisons and combinations, and renders their understandings, in an extraordinary degree, both acute and comprehensive. Unless those few, however, happen to be placed in some very particular situations, their great abilities, though honourable to themselves, may contribute very little to the good government or happiness of their society. Notwithstanding the great abilities of those few, all the nobler parts of the human character may be, in a great measure, obliterated and extinguished in the great body of the people.

The education of the common people requires, perhaps, in a civilized and commercial society, the attention of the public more than that of people of some rank and fortune. People of some rank and fortune are generally eighteen or nineteen years of age before they enter upon that particular business, profession, or trade by which they propose to distinguish themselves in the world. They have before that full time to acquire, or at least to fit themselves for afterwards acquiring, every accomplishment which can recommend them to the public esteem, or render them worthy of it.

. . .

It is otherwise with the common people. They have little time to spare for education. Their parents can scarce afford to maintain them even in infancy. As soon as they are able to work, they must apply to some trade by which they can earn their subsistence. That trade too is generally so simple and uniform as to give little exercise to the understanding; while, at the same time, their labour is both so constant and so severe that it leaves them little leisure and less inclination to apply to, or even to think of, any thing else.

But though the common people cannot, in any civilized society, be so well instructed as people of some rank and fortune, the most essential parts of education, however, to read, write, and account, can be acquired at so early a period of life that the greater part even of those who are to be bred to the lowest occupations have time to acquire them before they can be employed in those occupations. For a very small expense the public can facilitate, can encourage, and can even impose upon almost the whole body of the people, the necessity of acquiring those most essential parts of education.

. . .

CHAPTER 2

From *Capital*

KARL MARX

Karl Marx (1818–1883) was born in Trier, Germany. He earned a Ph.D. degree at the University of Jena in 1841. Beginning in 1849, he resided in London where he took up economic studies in the British Museum. His three-volume work, *Capital*, is the cornerstone of what has come to be known as Marxian political economy.

The buying and selling of labour-power

(From chapters 5 and 6)

. . .

We have shown that surplus-value cannot be created by circulation, and, therefore, that in its formation, something must take place in the background, which is not apparent in the circulation itself.

. . .

The consumption of labour-power is completed, as in the case of every other commodity, outside the limits of the market or of the sphere of circulation. Accompanied by Mr. Moneybags and by the possessor of labour-power, we therefore take leave for a time of this noisy sphere, where everything takes place on the surface and in view of all men, and follow them both into the hidden abode of production, on whose threshold there stares us in the face "No admittance except on business." Here we shall see, not only how capital produces, but how capital is produced. We shall at last force the secret of profit making.

This sphere that we are deserting, within whose boundaries the sale and purchase of labour-power goes on, is in fact a very Eden of the innate rights of man.

From Karl Marx, *Capital: A Critique of Political Economy, Volume 1: The Process of Capitalist Production*, edited by Frederick Engels, originally published 1867. Excerpted from the translation of the Third German Edition by Samuel Moore and Edward Aveling. New York: International Publishers, 1967.

There alone rule Freedom, Equality, Property, and Bentham. Freedom, because both buyer and seller of a commodity, say of labour-power, are constrained only by their own free will. They contract as free agents, and the agreement they come to is but the form in which they give legal expression to their common will. Equality, because each enters into relation with the other, as with a simple owner of commodities, and they exchange equivalent for equivalent. Property, because each disposes only of what is his own. And Bentham, because each looks only to himself. The only force that brings them together and puts them in relation with each other is the selfishness, the gain and the private interests of each. Each looks to himself only, and no one troubles himself about the rest, and just because they do so, do they all, in accordance with the preestablished harmony of things, or under the auspices of an all-shrewd providence, work together to their mutual advantage, for the common weal and in the interest of all.

On leaving this sphere of simple circulation or of exchange of commodities, which furnishes the "Free-trade Vulgaris" with his views and ideas, and with the standard by which he judges a society based on capital and wages, we think we can perceive a change in the physiognomy of our dramatis personae. He, who before was the money owner, now strides in front as capitalist; the possessor of labour-power follows as his labourer. The one with an air of importance, smirking, intent on business; the other, timid and holding back, like one who is bringing his own hide to market and has nothing to expect but – a hiding.

. . .

Division of labour and manufacture

(From chapter 14)

. . .

Section 4. – division of labour in manufacture, and division of labour in society

We first considered the origin of Manufacture, then its simple elements, then the detail labourer and his implements, and finally, the totality of the mechanism. We shall now lightly touch upon the relation between the division of labour in manufacture and the social division of labour, which forms the foundation of all production of commodities.

. . .

Since the production and the circulation of commodities are the general prerequisites of the capitalist mode of production, division of labour in manufacture demands that division of labour in society at large should previously have attained a certain degree of development. Inversely, the former division reacts upon and develops and multiplies the latter.

. . .

But, in spite of the numerous analogies and links connecting them, division of labour in the interior of a society, and that in the interior of a workshop, differ not only in degree but also in kind. The analogy appears most indisputable where there is an invisible bond uniting the various branches of trade. For instance the cattle breeder produces hides, the tanner makes the hides into leather, and the shoemaker, the leather into boots. Here the thing produced by each of them is but a step towards the final form, which is the product of all their labours combined. There are, besides, all the various industries that supply the cattle breeder, the tanner, and the shoemaker with the means of production. Now it is quite possible to imagine, with Adam Smith, that the difference between the above social division of labour and the division in manufacture is merely subjective, exists merely for the observer, who, in a manufacture, can see with one glance all the numerous operations being performed on one spot, while in the instance given above, the spreading out of the work over great areas, and the great number of people employed in each branch of labour, obscure the connexion. But what is it that forms the bond between the independent labours of the cattle breeder, the tanner, and the shoemaker? It is the fact that their respective products are commodities. What, on the other hand, characterises division of labour in manufactures? The fact that the detail labourer produces no commodities.[1] It is only the common product of all the detail labourers that becomes a commodity. Division of labour in society is brought about by the purchase and sale of the products of different branches of industry, while the connexion between the detail operations in a workshop is due to the sale of the labour-power of several workmen to one capitalist, who applies it as combined labour-power. The division of labour in the workshop implies concentration of the means of production in the hands of one capitalist; the division of labour in society implies their dispersion among many independent producers of commodities. While within the workshop, the iron law of proportionality subjects definite numbers of workmen to definite

---

[1] "There is no longer anything which we can call the natural reward of individual labour. Each labourer produces only some part of a whole, and each part, having no value or utility in itself, there is nothing on which the labourer can seize, and say: It is my product; this I will keep to myself." (Th. Hodgeskin, 1825, p. 25.)

functions, in the society outside the workshop, chance and caprice have full play in distributing the producers and their means of production among the various branches of industry. The different spheres of production, it is true, constantly tend to an equilibrium: for, on the one hand, while each producer of a commodity is bound to produce a use value, to satisfy a particular social want, and while the extent of these wants differs quantitatively, still there exists an inner relation which settles their proportions into a regular system, and that system one of spontaneous growth; and, on the other hand, the law of the value of commodities ultimately determines how much of its disposable working time society can expend on each particular class of commodities. But this constant tendency to equilibrium, of the various spheres of production, is exercised only in the shape of a reaction against the constant upsetting of this equilibrium. The a priori system on which the division of labour, within the workshop, is regularly carried out becomes in the division of labour within the society an a posteriori, nature-imposed necessity, controlling the lawless caprice of the producers, and perceptible in the barometrical fluctuations of the market prices. Division of labour within the workshop implies the undisputed authority of the capitalist over men, that are but parts of a mechanism that belongs to him. The division of labour within the society brings into contact independent commodity producers, who acknowledge no other authority but that of competition, of the coercion exerted by the pressure of their mutual interests; just as in the animal kingdom, the *bellum omnium contra omnes* more or less preserves the conditions of existence of every species. The same bourgeois mind which praises division of labour in the workshop, life-long annexation of the labourer to a partial operation, and his complete subjection to capital as being an organisation of labour that increases its productiveness – that same bourgeois mind denounces with equal vigour every conscious attempt to socially control and regulate the process of production as an inroad upon such sacred things as the rights of property, freedom, and unrestricted play for the bent of the individual capitalist. It is very characteristic that the enthusiastic apologists of the factory system have nothing more damning to urge against a general organisation of the labour of society than that it would turn all society into one immense factory.

In a society with capitalist production, anarchy in the social division of labour and despotism in that of the workshop are mutual conditions the one of the other . . . .

. . .

While division of labour in society at large, whether such division be brought about or not by exchange of commodities, is common to economic formations of society the most diverse, division of labour in the workshop, as practised by manufacture, is a special creation of the capitalist mode of production alone.

. . .

The knowledge, the judgment, and the will, which, though in ever so small a degree, are practised by the independent peasant or handicraftsman, in the same way as the savage makes the whole art of war consist in the exercise of his personal cunning – these faculties are now required only for the workshop as a whole. Intelligence in production expands in one direction, because it vanishes in many others. What is lost by the detail labourers is concentrated in the capital that employs them. It is a result of the division of labour in manufactures that the labourer is brought face to face with the intellectual potencies of the material process of production, as the property of another and as a ruling power. This separation begins in simple cooperation, where the capitalist represents the single workman, the oneness and the will of the associated labour. It is developed in manufacture which cuts down the labourer into a detail labourer. It is completed in modern industry, which makes science a productive force distinct from labour and presses it into the service of capital.

. . .

"The understandings of the greater part of men," says Adam Smith, "are necessarily formed by their ordinary employments. The man whose whole life is spent in performing a few simple operations . . . has no occasion to exert his understanding . . . . He generally becomes as stupid and ignorant as it is possible for a human creature to become." After describing the stupidity of the detail labourer he goes on: "The uniformity of his stationary life naturally corrupts the courage of his mind . . . . It corrupts even the activity of his body and renders him incapable of exerting his strength with vigour and perseverance in any other employments than that to which he has been bred. His dexterity at his own particular trade seems in this manner to be acquired at the expense of his intellectual, social, and martial virtues. But in every improved and civilised society, this is the state into which the labouring poor, that is, the great body of the people, must necessarily fall."[2] For preventing the complete deterioration of the great mass of the people by division of labour, A. Smith recommends education of the people by the State, but prudently, and in homoeopathic doses. G. Garnier, his French translator and commentator, who, under the first French Empire, quite naturally developed into a senator, quite as naturally opposes him on this point. Education of the masses, he urges, violates the first law of the

[2] A. Smith (1937 [1776]), Bk. v., ch. i, art. ii.

division of labour, and with it "our whole social system would be proscribed." "Like all other divisions of labour," he says, "that between hand labour and head labour is more pronounced and decided in proportion as society (he rightly uses this word, for capital, landed property, and their State) becomes richer. This division of labour, like every other, is an effect of past, and a cause of future progress... ought the government then to work in opposition to this division of labour, and to hinder its natural course? Ought it to expend a part of the public money in the attempt to confound and blend together two classes of labour, which are striving after division and separation?"[3]

Some crippling of body and mind is inseparable even from division of labour in society as a whole. Since, however, manufacture carries this social separation of branches of labour much further, and also, by its peculiar division, attacks the individual at the very roots of his life, it is the first to afford the materials for, and to give a start to, industrial pathology.

"To subdivide a man is to execute him, if he deserves the sentence, to assassinate him if he does not.... The subdivision of labour is the assassination of a people."[4]

. . .

The factory

(From chapter 15, section 4)

... Every kind of capitalist production, in so far as it is not only a labour process but also a process of creating surplus value, has this in common, that it is not the workman that employs the instruments of labour, but the instruments of labour that employ the workman. But it is only in the factory system that this inversion for the first time acquires technical and palpable reality. By means of its conversion into an automaton, the instrument of labour confronts the labourer, during the labour process, in the shape of capital, of dead labour, that dominates, and pumps dry, living labour-power. The separation of the intellectual powers of production from the manual labour, and the conversion of those powers into the might of capital over labour, is, as we have already shown, finally completed by modern industry erected on the foundation of machinery. The special skill of each individual insignificant factory operative vanishes as an infinitesimal quantity before the science, the gigantic physical forces, and the mass of labour that are embodied in the factory mechanism and, together with that mechanism, constitute the power of the "master."

. . .

[3] G. Garnier (1796), vol. V. of his translation of A. Smith, pp. 4–5.
[4] D. Urquhart (1856), p. 119.

CHAPTER 3

From *Risk, Uncertainty, and Profit*

FRANK KNIGHT

Frank Knight (1885–1972) was born in McLean County, Illinois. He received a Ph.D. degree from Cornell University in 1916. When his book *Risk, Uncertainty and Profit* was published in 1921, he was Associate Professor of Economics at the State University of Iowa. He later became Morton D. Hall Distinguished Service Professor of Social Science and Philosophy at the University of Chicago.

Structures and methods for meeting uncertainty

(From chapter 8)

. . .

It is therefore seen that the insurance principle can be applied even in the almost complete absence of scientific data for the computation of rates. . . .

. . . The fact which limits the application of the insurance principle to business risks generally is not therefore their inherent uniqueness alone, and the subject calls for further examination. This task will be undertaken in detail in the next chapter, which deals with entrepreneurship. At this point we may anticipate to the extent of making two observations: first, the typical uninsurable (because unmeasurable and this because unclassifiable) business risk relates to the exercise of judgment in the making of decisions by the business man; second, although such estimates do tend to fall into groups within which fluctuations cancel out and hence to approach constancy and measurability, this happens only *after the fact* and, especially in view of the brevity of a man's active life, can only to a limited extent be made the basis of prediction.

Excerpted from Frank Knight, *Risk, Uncertainty and Profit*. New York: Houghton Mifflin Co., 1921; eighth impression published by Kelley and Millman, New York, 1957.

Furthermore, the classification or grouping can only to a limited extent be carried out by any agency outside the person himself who makes the decisions because of the peculiarly obstinate connection of a *moral hazard* with this sort of risks. The decisive factors in the case are so largely on the inside of the person making the decisions that the "instances" are not amenable to objective description and external control.

Manifestly these difficulties, insuperable when the "consolidation" is to be carried out by an external agency such as an insurance company or association, fall away in so far as consolidation can be effected within the scale of operations of a single individual; and the same will be true of an organization if responsibility can be adequately centralized and unity of interest secured. The possibility of thus reducing uncertainty by transforming it into a measurable risk through grouping constitutes a strong incentive to extend the scale of operations of a business establishment. This fact must constitute one of the important causes of the phenomenal growth in the average size of industrial establishments which is a familiar characteristic of modern economic life. In so far as a single business man, by borrowing capital or otherwise, can extend the scope of his exercise of judgment over a greater number of decisions or estimates, there is a greater probability that bad guesses will be offset by good ones and that a degree of constancy and dependability in the total results will be achieved. In so far uncertainty is eliminated and the desideratum of rational activity realized.

Not less important is the incentive to substitute more effective and intimate forms of association for insurance, so as to eliminate or reduce the moral hazard and make possible the application of the insurance principle of consolidation to groups of ventures too broad in scope to be "swung" by a single enterpriser. Since it is capital which is especially at risk in operations based on opinions and estimates, the form of organization centers around the provisions relating to capital. It is undoubtedly true that the reduction of risk to borrowed capital is the principal desideratum leading to the displacement of individual enterprise by the partnership and the same fact with reference to both owned and borrowed capital explains the substitution of corporate organization for the partnership. The superiority of the higher form of organization over the lower from this point of view consists both in the extension of the scope of operations to include a larger number of individual decisions, ventures, or "instances," and in the more effective unification of interest which reduces the moral hazard connected with the assumption by one person of the consequences of another person's decisions.

The close connection between these two considerations is manifest. It is the special "risk" to which large amounts of capital loaned to a single enterpriser are subject which limits the scope of operations of this form of business unit by making it impossible to secure the necessary property resources. On the other hand, it is the inefficiency of organization, the failure to secure effective unity of interest, and the consequent large risk due to moral hazard when a partnership grows to considerable size, which in turn limit its extension to still larger magnitudes and bring about the substitution of the corporate form of organization. With the growth of large fortunes it becomes possible for a limited number of persons to carry on enterprises of greater and greater magnitude, and today we find many very large businesses organized as partnerships. Modifications of partnership law giving this form more of the flexibility of the corporation with reference to the distribution of rights of control, of participation in income, and of title to assets in case of dissolution have also contributed to this change.

With reference to the first of our two points above mentioned, the extension of the scope of operations, the corporation may be said to have solved the organization problem. There appears to be hardly any limit to the magnitude of enterprise which it is possible to organize in this form, so far as mere ability to get the public to buy the securities is concerned. On the second score, however, the effective unification of interests, though the corporation has accomplished much in comparison with other forms of organization, there is still much to be desired. Doubtless the task is impossible, in any absolute sense; nothing but a revolutionary transformation in human nature itself can apparently solve this problem finally, and such a change would, of course, obliterate all moral hazards at once, without organization. In the meanwhile the internal problems of the corporation, the protection of its various types of members and adherents against each other's predatory propensities, are quite as vital as the external problem of safeguarding the public interests against exploitation by the corporation as a unit.

Another important aspect of the relations of corporate organization to risk involves what we have called "diffusion" as well as consolidation. The minute divisibility of ownership and ease of transfer of shares enables an investor to distribute his holdings over a large number of enterprises in addition to increasing the size of a single enterprise. The effect of this distribution on risk is evidently twofold. In the first place, there is to the investor a further offsetting through consolidation; the losses and gains in different corporations in which he owns stock must tend to cancel out in large measure and provide a higher degree of regularity and predictability in his total returns. And again, the chance of loss of a small fraction of his total resources is of less moment even proportionally than a chance of losing a larger part.

. . .

Enterprise and profit

(From chapter 9)

. . .

When uncertainty is present and the task of deciding what to do and how to do it takes the ascendancy over that of execution, the internal organization of the productive groups is no longer a matter of indifference or a mechanical detail.[1] Centralization of this deciding and controlling function is imperative; a process of "cephalization," such as has taken place in the evolution of organic life, is inevitable, and for the same reasons as in the case of biological evolution. Let us consider this process and the circumstances which condition it. The order of attack on the problem is suggested by the classification worked out in Chapter VII of the elements in uncertainty in regard to which men may in large measure differ independently.

In the first place, occupations differ in respect to the kind and amount of knowledge and judgment required for their successful direction as well as in the kind of abilities and tastes adapted to the routine operation. Productive groups or establishments now compete for managerial capacity as well as skill, and a considerable rearrangement of personnel is the natural result. The final adjustment will place each producer in the place where his particular combination of the two kinds of attributes seems to be most effective.

But a more important change is the tendency of the groups themselves to specialize, finding the individuals with the greatest managerial capacity of the requisite kinds and placing them in charge of the work of the group, submitting the activities of the other members to their direction and control. It need hardly be mentioned explicitly that the organization of industry depends on the fundamental fact that the intelligence of one person can be made to direct in a general way the routine manual and mental operations of others. It will also be taken into account that men differ in their powers of effective control over other men as well as in intellectual capacity to decide what should be done. In addition, there must come into play the diversity among men in degree of confidence in their judgment and powers and in disposition to act on their opinions, to "venture." This fact is responsible for the most fundamental change of all in the form of organization, the system under which the confident and venturesome "assume the risk" or "insure" the doubtful and timid by guaranteeing to the latter a specified income in return for an assignment of the actual results.

---

[1] See above, Chapter IV, p. 106, note. [ed: in the book from which this excerpt is taken]

Uncertainty thus exerts a fourfold tendency to select men and specialize functions: (1) an adaptation of men to occupations on the basis of kind of knowledge and judgment; (2) a similar selection on the basis of degree of foresight, for some lines of activity call for this endowment in a very different degree from others; (3) a specialization within productive groups, the individuals with superior managerial ability (foresight and capacity of ruling others) being placed in control of the group and the others working under their direction; and (4) those with confidence in their judgment and disposition to "back it up" in action specialize in risk taking. The close relations obtaining among these tendencies will be manifest. We have not separated confidence and venturesomeness at all, since they act along parallel lines and are little more than phases of the same faculty – just as courage and the tendency to minimize danger are proverbially commingled in all fields, though they are separable in thought. In addition the tendencies number (3) and (4) operate together. With human nature as we know it, it would be impracticable or very unusual for one man to guarantee to another a definite result of the latter's actions without being given power to direct his work. And on the other hand the second party would not place himself under the direction of the first without such a guaranty. The result is a "double contract" of the type famous in the history of the evasion of usury laws. It seems evident also that the system would not work at all if good judgment were not in fact generally associated with confidence in one's judgment on the part both of himself and others. That is, men's judgment of their own judgment and of others' judgment as to both kind and grade must in the large be much more right than wrong.[2]

The result of this manifold specialization of function is *enterprise and the wage system of industry*. Its existence in the world is a direct result of the fact of uncertainty; our task in the remainder of this study is to examine this phenomenon in detail in its various phases and divers relations with the economic activities of man and the structure of society. It is not necessary or inevitable, not the only conceivable form or organization, but under certain conditions has certain advantages, and is capable of development in different degrees. The essence of enterprise is the specialization of the function of *responsible direction* of economic life, the neglected feature of which is the inseparability of these *two* elements, *responsibility* and *control*. Under the enterprise system, a special social class, the business men, direct economic activity; they are in the strict sense the producers, while the great mass of the population merely furnish them with productive services, placing their persons and their property at the disposal of this class; the entrepreneurs *also* guarantee to those who furnish productive services a fixed remuneration. Accurately to

---

[2] The statement implies that a man's judgment has in an effective sense a true or objective value. This assumption will be justified by the further course of the argument.

define these functions and trace them through the social structure will be a long task, for the specialization is never complete; but at the end of it we shall find that in a free society the two are essentially inseparable. Any degree of effective exercise of judgment, or making decisions, is in a free society coupled with a corresponding degree of uncertainty bearing, of taking the responsibility for those decisions.

. . .

CHAPTER 4

From *The Modern Corporation and Private Property*

ADOLF A. BERLE, JR., AND GARDINER C. MEANS

Adolf A. Berle, Jr. (1895–1971) was born in Boston, Massachusetts. He received his Masters of Arts degree from Harvard University and graduated from Harvard Law School in 1916. He became a Professor of Corporate Law at Columbia Law School in 1927 and remained on that school's faculty until his retirement in 1964. As a member of Franklin D. Roosevelt's "brain trust," he held several government posts, including Assistant Secretary of State between 1938 and 1944.

Gardiner C. Means (1896–1988) was born in Windham, Connecticut. He received his Ph.D. in economics from Harvard University in 1933. He held a series of positions in the federal government and in later years was an independent consultant and author.

Property in transition

(Book I, chapter 1)

. . .

... The typical business unit of the 19th century was owned by individuals or small groups; was managed by them or their appointees; and was, in the main, limited in size by the personal wealth of the individuals in control. These units have been supplanted in ever greater measure by great aggregations in which tens and even hundreds of thousands of workers and property worth hundreds of millions of dollars, belonging to tens or even hundreds of thousands of individuals, are combined through the corporate mechanism into a single producing organization under unified control and management. ...

Such an organization of economic activity rests upon two developments, each of which has made possible an extension of the area under unified control. The factory system, the basis of the industrial revolution, brought an increasingly large number of workers directly under a single management. Then,

Excerpted from Adolf A. Berle, Jr., and Gardiner C. Means, *The Modern Corporation and Private Property.* New York: Commerce Clearing House, Inc., 1932.

the modern corporation, equally revolutionary in its effect, placed the wealth of innumerable individuals under the same central control. By each of these changes the power of those in control was immensely enlarged and the status of those involved, worker or property owner, was radically changed. The independent worker who entered the factory became a wage laborer surrendering the direction of his labor to his industrial master. The property owner who invests in a modern corporation so far surrenders his wealth to those in control of the corporation that he has exchanged the position of independent owner for one in which he may become merely recipient of the wages of capital.

. . .

Growing out of this separation are two characteristics, almost as typical of the quasi-public corporation as the separation itself – mere size and the public market for its securities. It is precisely this separation of control from ownership which makes possible tremendous aggregations of property. The Fords and the Mellons, whose personal wealth is sufficient to finance great enterprises, are so few, that they only emphasize the dependence of the large enterprise on the wealth of more than the individual or group of individuals who may be in control. The quasi-public corporation commands its supply of capital from a group of investors frequently described as the "investing public." It draws these savings to itself either directly, as individuals purchase stocks or bonds, or indirectly, as insurance companies, banks, and investment trusts receive these savings and invest them in corporate securities. To secure these funds it must commonly avail itself of an open market in its securities – usually by listing shares on a stock exchange, or, less importantly, by maintaining a private or "unlisted" market. So essential, in fact, is the open market to the quasi-public corporation that it may be considered almost as characteristic of that type of corporation as the separation of ownership from control and the great aggregation of wealth.

. . .

. . . The separation of ownership from control produces a condition where the interests of owner and of ultimate manager may, and often do, diverge, and where many of the checks which formerly operated to limit the use of power disappear. Size alone tends to give these giant corporations a social significance not attached to the smaller units of private enterprise. By the use of the open market for securities, each of these corporations assumes obligations towards the investing public which transforms it from a legal method clothing the rule of a few individuals into an institution at least nominally serving investors who have embarked their funds in its enterprise. New responsibilities towards the owners, the workers, the consumers, and the State thus rest upon the shoulders of those in control. In creating these new relationships, the quasi-public corporation may fairly be said to work a revolution. It has destroyed the unity that we commonly call property – has divided ownership into nominal ownership and the power formerly joined to it. Thereby the corporation has changed the nature of profit-seeking enterprise. This revolution forms the subject of the present study.

Examination of the changes produced can properly commence with the new relationships between the owners on the one hand and control on the other, and it is these relationships with which this book will deal. This involves the area roughly termed "corporation finance" – the relations between the corporation as managed by the group in control, and those who hold participations in it – its stockholders, bondholders, and, to some extent, its other creditors. The change in internal organization – the relation of the corporation to its workers, its plant organization and its technical problem of production – we cannot consider at this time. Nor can we here deal with its external relationships, on the one hand with its customers – the terms on which it furnishes to them its products or its services – and on the other hand, with the political state – the government by which it may be in some degree controlled, or over which it may have a measure of dominance. Here we are concerned only with a fundamental change in the form of property, and in the economic relationships which rest upon it.

Outwardly the change is simple enough. Men are less likely to own the physical instruments of production. They are more likely to own pieces of paper, loosely known as stocks, bonds, and other securities, which have become mobile through the machinery of the public markets. Beneath this, however, lies a more fundamental shift. Physical control over the instruments of production has been surrendered in ever growing degree to centralized groups who manage property in bulk, supposedly, but by no means necessarily, for the benefit of the security holders. Power over industrial property has been cut off from the beneficial ownership of this property – or, in less technical language, from the legal right to enjoy its fruits. Control of physical assets has passed from the individual owner to those who direct the quasi-public institutions, while the owner retains an interest in their product and increase. We see, in fact, the surrender and regrouping of the incidence of ownership, which formerly bracketed full power of manual disposition with complete right to enjoy the use, the fruits, and the proceeds of physical assets. There has resulted the dissolution of the old atom of ownership into its component parts, control and beneficial ownership.

This dissolution of the atom of property destroys the very foundation on which the economic order of the past three centuries has rested. Private enterprise, which has molded economic life since the close of the middle ages, has been rooted in the institution of private property. Under the feudal system, its predecessor, economic organization grew out of mutual obligations and privileges derived by various individuals from their relation to property which no one of them owned. Private enterprise, on the other hand, has assumed an owner of the instruments of production with complete property rights over those instruments. Whereas the organization of feudal economic life rested upon an elaborate system of binding customs, the organization under the system of private enterprise has rested upon the self-interest of the property owner – a self-interest held in check only by competition and the conditions of supply and demand. Such self-interest has long been regarded as the best guarantee of economic efficiency. It has been assumed that, if the individual is protected in the right both to use his own property as he sees fit and to receive the full fruits of its use, his desire for personal gain, for profits, can be relied upon as an effective incentive to his efficient use of any industrial property he may possess.

In the quasi-public corporation, such an assumption no longer holds. As we have seen, it is no longer the individual himself who uses his wealth. Those in control of that wealth, and therefore in a position to secure industrial efficiency and produce profits, are no longer, as owners, entitled to the bulk of such profits. Those who control the destinies of the typical modern corporation own so insignificant a fraction of the company's stock that the returns from running the corporation profitably accrue to them in only a very minor degree. The stockholders, on the other hand, to whom the profits of the corporation go, cannot be motivated by those profits to a more efficient use of the property, since they have surrendered all disposition of it to those in control of the enterprise. The explosion of the atom of property destroys the basis of the old assumption that the quest for profits will spur the owner of industrial property to its effective use. It consequently challenges the fundamental economic principle of individual initiative in industrial enterprise. It raises for reexamination the question of the motive force back of industry, and the ends for which the modern corporation can be or will be run.

. . .

The new concept of the corporation

(From Book IV, chapter 4)

. . .

. . . Neither the claims of ownership nor those of control can stand against the paramount interests of the community. The present claims of both contending parties now in the field have been weakened by the developments described in this book. It remains only for the claims of the community to be put forward with clarity and force. Rigid enforcement of property rights as a temporary protection against plundering by control would not stand in the way of the modification of these rights in the interest of other groups. When a convincing system of community obligations is worked out and is generally accepted, in that moment the passive property right of today must yield before the larger interests of society. Should the corporate leaders, for example, set forth a program comprising fair wages, security to employees, reasonable service to their public, and stabilization of business, all of which would divert a portion of the profits from the owners of passive property, and should the community generally accept such a scheme as a logical and human solution of industrial difficulties, the interests of passive property owners would have to give way. Courts would almost of necessity be forced to recognize the result, justifying it by whatever of the many legal theories they might choose. It is conceivable – indeed it seems almost essential if the corporate system is to survive – that the "control" of the great corporations should develop into a purely neutral technocracy, balancing a variety of claims by various groups in the community and assigning to each a portion of the income stream on the basis of public policy rather than private cupidity.

. . .

CHAPTER 5

The use of knowledge in society

FRIEDRICH HAYEK

Friedrich Hayek (1899–1992) was born in Vienna, Austria. He earned degrees in law and politics at the University of Vienna in 1921 and 1923, and in 1940, he received a Doctor of Science degree in economics from the University of London. At the time this paper was published, he was Tooke Professor of Political Economy and Statistics at the London School of Economics. He later served as professor at the University of Chicago and the University of Freiburg. In 1974, he was awarded the Nobel Memorial Prize in Economic Science.

I

What is the problem we wish to solve when we try to construct a rational economic order?

On certain familiar assumptions the answer is simple enough. *If* we possess all the relevant information, *if* we can start out from a given system of preferences, and *if* we command complete knowledge of available means, the problem which remains is purely one of logic. That is, the answer to the question of what is the best use of the available means is implicit in our assumptions. The conditions which the solution of this optimum problem must satisfy have been fully worked out and can be stated best in mathematical form: put at their briefest, they are that the marginal rates of substitution between any two commodities or factors must be the same in all their different uses.

This, however, is emphatically *not* the economic problem which society faces. And the economic calculus which we have developed to solve this logical problem, though an important step toward the solution of the economic problem of society, does not yet provide an answer to it. The reason for this is that the "data" from which the economic calculus starts are never for the whole society "given" to a single mind which could work out the implications, and can never be so given.

The peculiar character of the problem of a rational economic order is determined precisely by the fact that the knowledge of the circumstances of which

Reprinted in abridged form from Friedrich Hayek, "The Use of Knowledge in Society," *The American Economic Review*, 35 (1945): 519–30, by permission of the editors.

we must make use never exists in concentrated or integrated form but solely as the dispersed bits of incomplete and frequently contradictory knowledge which all the separate individuals possess. The economic problem of society is thus not merely a problem of how to allocate "given" resources – if "given" is taken to mean given to a single mind which deliberately solves the problem set by these "data." It is rather a problem of how to secure the best use of resources known to any of the members of society for ends whose relative importance only these individuals know. Or, to put it briefly, it is a problem of the utilization of knowledge not given to anyone in its totality.

This character of the fundamental problem has, I am afraid, been rather obscured than illuminated by many of the recent refinements of economic theory, particularly by many of the uses made of mathematics. Though the problem with which I want primarily to deal in this paper is the problem of a rational economic organization, I shall in its course be led again and again to point to its close connections with certain methodological questions. Many of the points I wish to make are indeed conclusions toward which diverse paths of reasoning have unexpectedly converged. But as I now see these problems, this is no accident. It seems to me that many of the current disputes with regard to both economic theory and economic policy have their common origin in a misconception about the nature of the economic problem of society. This misconception in turn is due to an erroneous transfer to social phenomena of the habits of thought we have developed in dealing with the phenomena of nature.

II

In ordinary language we describe by the word "planning" the complex of inter-related decisions about the allocation of our available resources. All economic activity is in this sense planning; and in any society in which many people collaborate, this planning, whoever does it, will in some measure have to be based on knowledge which, in the first instance, is not given to the planner but to somebody else, which somehow will have to be conveyed to the planner. The various ways in which the knowledge on which people base their plans is communicated to them is the crucial problem for any theory explaining the economic process. And the problem of what is the best way of utilizing knowledge initially dispersed among all the people is at least one of the main problems of economic policy – or of designing an efficient economic system.

The answer to this question is closely connected with that other question which arises here, that of *who* is to do the planning. It is about this question that all the dispute about "economic planning" centers. This is not a dispute about whether planning is to be done or not. It is a dispute as to whether planning is to be done centrally, by one authority for the whole economic system, or is to be divided among many individuals. Planning in the specific sense in which the term is used in contemporary controversy necessarily means central planning – direction of the whole economic system according to one unified plan. Competition, on the other hand, means decentralized planning by many separate persons. The halfway house between the two, about which many people talk but which few like when they see it, is the delegation of planning to organized industries, or, in other words, monopoly.

Which of these systems is likely to be more efficient depends mainly on the question, under which of them we can expect that fuller use will be made of the existing knowledge. And this, in turn, depends on whether we are more likely to succeed in putting at the disposal of a single central authority all the knowledge which ought to be used but which is initially dispersed among many different individuals, or in conveying to the individuals such additional knowledge as they need in order to enable them to fit their plans in with those of others.

. . .

IV

If it is fashionable today to minimize the importance of the knowledge of the particular circumstances of time and place, this is closely connected with the smaller importance which is now attached to change as such. Indeed, there are few points on which the assumptions made (usually only implicitly) by the "planners" differ from those of their opponents as much as with regard to the significance and frequency of changes which will make substantial alterations of production plans necessary. Of course, if detailed economic plans could be laid down for fairly long periods in advance and then closely adhered to, so that no further economic decisions of importance would be required, the task of drawing up a comprehensive plan governing all economic activity would appear much less formidable.

It is, perhaps, worth stressing that economic problems arise always and only in consequence of change. So long as things continue as before, or at least as they were expected to, there arise no new problems requiring a decision, no need to form a new plan. The belief that changes, or at least day-to-day adjustments, have become less important in modern times implies the con-tention that economic problems also have become less important. This belief in the decreasing importance of change is, for that reason, usually held by the same people who argue that the importance of economic considerations has been driven into the background by the growing importance of technological knowledge.

Is it true that, with the elaborate apparatus of modern production, economic decisions are required only at long intervals, as when a new factory is to be erected or a new process to be introduced? Is it true that, once a plant has been built, the rest is all more or less mechanical, determined by the character of the plant, and leaving little to be changed in adapting to the ever-changing circumstances of the moment?

The fairly widespread belief in the affirmative is not, so far as I can ascertain, borne out by the practical experience of the business man. In a competitive industry at any rate – and such an industry alone can serve as a test – the task of keeping cost from rising requires constant struggle, absorbing a great part of the energy of the manager. How easy it is for an inefficient manager to dissipate the differentials on which profitability rests, and that it is possible, with the same technical facilities to produce with a great variety of costs, are among the commonplaces of business experience which do not seem to be equally familiar in the study of the economist. The very strength of the desire, constantly voiced by producers and engineers, to be able to proceed untrammeled by considerations of money costs, is eloquent testimony to the extent to which these factors enter into their daily work.

. . .

V

If we can agree that the economic problem of society is mainly one of rapid adaptation to changes in the particular circumstances of time and place, it would seem to follow that the ultimate decisions must be left to the people who are familiar with these circumstances, who know directly of the relevant changes and of the resources immediately available to meet them. We cannot expect that this problem will be solved by first communicating all this knowledge to a central board which, after integrating *all* knowledge, issues its orders. We must solve it by some form of decentralization. But this answers only part of our problem. We need decentralization because only thus can we ensure that the knowledge of the particular circumstances of time and place will be promptly used. But the "man on the spot" cannot decide solely on the basis of his limited but intimate knowledge of the facts of his immediate surroundings. There still remains the problem of communicating to him such further information as he needs to fit his decisions into the whole pattern of changes of the larger economic system.

How much knowledge does he need to do so successfully? Which of the events which happen beyond the horizon of his immediate knowledge are of relevance to his immediate decision, and how much of them need he know?

There is hardly anything that happens anywhere in the world that *might* not have an effect on the decision he ought to make. But he need not know of these events as such, nor of *all* their effects. It does not matter for him *why* at the particular moment more screws of one size than of another are wanted, *why* paper bags are more readily available than canvas bags, or *why* skilled labor, or particular machine tools, have for the moment become more difficult to acquire. All that is significant for him is *how much more or less* difficult to procure they have become compared with other things with which he is also concerned, or how much more or less urgently wanted are the alternative things he produces or uses. It is always a question of the relative importance of the particular things with which he is concerned, and the causes which alter their relative importance are of no interest to him beyond the effect on those concrete things of his own environment.

It is in this connection that what I have called the economic calculus proper helps us, at least by analogy, to see how this problem can be solved, and in fact is being solved, by the price system. Even the single controlling mind, in possession of all the data for some small, self-contained economic system, would not – every time some small adjustment in the allocation of resources had to be made – go explicitly through all the relations between ends and means which might possibly be affected. It is indeed the great contribution of the pure logic of choice that it has demonstrated conclusively that even such a single mind could solve this kind of problem only by constructing and constantly using rates of equivalence (or "values," or "marginal rates of substitution"), i.e., by attaching to each kind of scarce resource a numerical index which cannot be derived from any property possessed by that particular thing, but which reflects, or in which is condensed, its significance in view of the whole means–end structure. In any small change he will have to consider only these quantitative indices (or "values") in which all the relevant information is concentrated; and by adjusting the quantities one by one, he can appropriately rearrange his dispositions without having to solve the whole puzzle *ab initio*, or without needing at any stage to survey it at once in all its ramifications.

Fundamentally, in a system where the knowledge of the relevant facts is dispersed among many people, prices can act to coordinate the separate actions of different people in the same way as subjective values help the individual to coordinate the parts of his plan. It is worth contemplating for a moment a very simple and commonplace instance of the action of the price system to see what precisely it accomplishes. Assume that somewhere in the world a new opportunity for the use of some raw material, say tin, has arisen or that one of the sources of supply of tin has been eliminated. It does not matter for our purpose – and it is very significant that it does not matter – which of these two causes has made tin more scarce. All that the users of tin need to know is that some of the tin they used to consume is now more profitably employed elsewhere, and that in consequence they must economize tin. There is no need for the great majority of them even to know where the more urgent need has arisen or in favor of what other needs they ought to husband the supply. If only some of them know directly of the new demand, and switch resources over to it, and if the people who are aware of the new gap thus created in turn fill it from still other sources, the effect will rapidly spread throughout the whole economic system and influence not only all the uses of tin but also those of its substitutes and the substitutes of these substitutes, the supply of all the things made of tin, and their substitutes, and so on; and all this without the great majority of those instrumental in bringing about these substitutions knowing anything at all about the original cause of these changes. The whole acts as one market, not because any of its members survey the whole field, but because their limited individual fields of vision sufficiently overlap so that through many intermediaries the relevant information is communicated to all. The mere fact that there is one price for any commodity – or rather that local prices are connected in a manner determined by the cost of transport, etc. – brings about the solution which (it is just conceptually possible) might have been arrived at by one single mind possessing all the information which is in fact dispersed among all the people involved in the process.

. . .

CHAPTER 6

Corporate governance

LUIGI ZINGALES

Luigi Zingales was born in 1963 in Padova, Italy. He earned his Ph.D. in economics from the Massachusetts Institute of Technology in 1992. That year, he joined the faculty at the Graduate School of Business at the University of Chicago, where he currently serves as the Robert C. McCormack Professor of Entrepreneurship and Finance.

While some of the questions have been around since Berle and Means (1932), the term 'corporate governance' did not exist in the English language until twenty years ago. In the last two decades, however, corporate governance issues have become important not only in the academic literature, but also in public policy debates. During this period, corporate governance has been identified with takeovers, financial restructuring, and institutional investors' activism. But what exactly is corporate governance? Why is there a corporate governance 'problem'? Why does Adam Smith's invisible hand not automatically provide a solution? What role do takeovers, financial restructuring, and institutional investors play in a corporate governance system?

. . .

1. When do we need a governance system?

The word 'governance' is synonymous with the exercise of authority, direction, and control. These words, however, seem strange when used in the context of a free-market economy. Why do we need any form of authority? Isn't the market responsible for allocating all resources efficiently without the intervention of authority? The basic (neoclassical) undergraduate microeconomics courses rarely mention the words 'authority' and 'control'.

In fact, neoclassical microeconomics describes well only one set of transactions, which Williamson (1985) calls 'standardized'. Consider, for instance, the purchase of a commodity, like wheat. There are many producers of the same quality of wheat and many potential customers. In this context, Adam Smith's

Reprinted in abridged form from Luigi Zingales, "Corporate Governance," *The New Palgrave Dictionary of Economics and the Law* (2008): 497–502. Reprinted with the permission of Palgrave Macmillan.

invisible hand ensures that the good is provided efficiently without the need of any form of authority.

Many daily transactions, however, do not fit this simple example. Consider for instance the purchase of a customized machine. The buyer must contact a manufacturer and agree upon the specifications and the final price. Unlike the case of wheat, the signing of the agreement does not represent the end of the relationship between the buyer and the seller. Producing the machine requires some time. During this time many events can occur, which alter the cost of producing the machine as well as the buyer's willingness to pay for it. More importantly, before the agreement was signed, the market for manufacturers was competitive. Once production has begun, though, the buyer and the seller are trapped in a situation of bilateral monopoly. The customized machine probably has a higher value to the buyer than to the market. On the other hand, the contracted manufacturer has probably the lowest cost to finish the machine. The difference between what the two parties generate together and what they can obtain in the marketplace represents a quasi-rent, which needs to be divided *ex post*. In dividing this surplus Adam Smith's invisible hand is of no help, while authority does play a role.

In the spirit of Williamson (1985), I define a *governance system* as the complex set of constraints that shape the *ex post* bargaining over the quasi-rents generated in the course of a relationship. A main role in this system is certainly played by the initial contract. But the contract, most likely, will be incomplete, in the sense that it will not fully specify the division of surplus in every possible contingency (this might be too costly to do or outright impossible because the contingency was unanticipated). This creates an interesting distinction between decisions made *ex ante* (when the two parties entered a relationship and irreversible investments were sunk) and *ex post* (when the quasi-rents are divided). This contract incompleteness also creates room for bargaining.

The outcome of the bargaining will be affected by several factors besides the initial contract. First, which party has ownership of the machine while it is in the production process. Second, the availability of alternatives: how costly is it for the buyer to delay receiving the new machine; how costly is it for the manufacturer to delay the receipt of the final payment; how much more costly is it to have the job finished by another manufacturer, etc. Finally, a major role in shaping the bargaining outcome is played by the institutional environment. For example: how effective and rapid is law enforcement; what are the professional norms; how quickly and reliably does information about the manufacturer's performance travel across potential clients, etc. All these conditions constitute a governance system.

As illustrated by the machine example, there are two necessary conditions for a governance system to be needed. First, the relationship must generate some quasi-rents. In the absence of quasi-rents, the competitive nature of the market will eliminate any scope for bargaining. Second, the quasi-rents are not perfectly allocated *ex ante*. If they were, then there would be no scope for bargaining either.

2. Corporate governance

. . .

There are two main definitions of the firm available in the literature. The first, introduced by Alchian and Demsetz (1972), is that the firm is a nexus of contracts. According to this definition, there is nothing unique to corporate governance, which is simply a more complex version of standard contractual governance.

The second definition, due to Grossman and Hart (1986) and Hart and Moore (1990) (GMH henceforth), is that the firm is a collection of physical assets that are jointly owned. Ownership matters because it confers the right to make decisions in all the contingencies unspecified by the initial contract. On the one hand, this definition has the merit of differentiating between a simple contractual relationship and a firm. Since the firm is defined by the non-contractual element (i.e., the allocation of ownership), corporate governance (as opposed to contractual governance) is defined by the effect of this non-contractual element. Not surprisingly, the focus of the corporate governance literature in the last decade has been the allocation of ownership (hence this literature is called the property rights view of the firm). On the other hand, this definition has the drawback of excluding any stakeholder other than the owner of physical assets from being important to our understanding of the firm.

More recently, Rajan and Zingales (1997 and 1998) have proposed a broader definition. They define the firm as a nexus of specific investments: a combination of mutually specialized assets and people. Unlike the nexus of contracts approach, this definition explicitly recognizes that a firm is a complex structure that cannot be instantaneously replicated. Unlike the property rights view, this definition recognizes that all the parties who are mutually specialized belong to the firm, be they workers, suppliers, or customers. While this definition does not necessarily coincide with the legal definition, it does coincide with the economic essence of a firm: a network of specific investments that cannot be replicated by the market.

3. Incomplete contracts and governance

In an Arrow–Debreu economy it is assumed that agents can costlessly write all state-contingent contracts. As a result, all decisions are made *ex ante* and all quasi-rents are allocated *ex ante*. Thus, there is no room for governance.

More surprisingly, even if we relax the assumption that every state-contingent contract can be written and admit that certain future contingencies are not observable (and thus not contractible), we still find no room for governance as long as one can costlessly write contracts on all future observable variables.

Recall the example of the customized machine, and assume that the manufacturer's effort is unobservable to others and is, therefore, not contractible. The neoclassical approach to this problem is to design a mechanism (hence the name 'mechanism design'), contingent on all publicly observable variables, which provides the manufacturer with the best possible incentives to exert effort. Myerson (1979) shows that all optimal mechanisms are equivalent to a revelation (direct) mechanism in which the agent (manufacturer) publicly announces his information and receives compensation contingent on his announcement. An important consequence of this result is that, in the mechanism design approach, delegation (giving an agent discretion over certain decisions) is always weakly dominated by a fully centralized mechanism, where all decisions are made *ex ante* by the designer. The mechanism design approach reproduces several distinguishing features of an Arrow–Debreu economy: all decisions are made *ex ante* and only executed *ex post*; as a result, all conflicts are resolved and all rents are allocated *ex ante*. This leaves no room for *ex post* bargaining. All these features are incompatible with not only my definition of governance, but also with any meaningful (i.e., related to the sense in which this term has been used) definition of governance. This is best illustrated with two examples.

One of the crucial questions in corporate governance is in whose interest should corporate directors act? In the mechanism design approach this question cannot even be raised. All possible future conflicts are resolved *ex ante* and the initial contract specifies how directors will behave in any observable state of the world. However, since this question is raised all the time, it must be that all possible conflicts are not resolved *ex ante*.

Second, the mechanism design approach avoids renegotiation: the initial contract is designed such that the agents do not want to renegotiate. As a result, the designer wants to make renegotiation as inefficient as possible: this reduces the cost of providing incentives to the agents with no efficiency costs, since renegotiation never occurs in equilibrium (Aghion et al. 1997). If this result were to be taken seriously, the optimal public policy approach would be to preserve any inefficiency in the system in order to avoid destroying its beneficial incentives *ex ante*. In reality, though, the jurisprudential approach is completely different. For example, courts do not support punitive damages that are considered excessive with respect to the issue at stake.

Only in a world where some contracts contingent on future observable variables are costly (or impossible) to write *ex ante*, is there room for governance *ex post*. Only in such a world are there quasi-rents that must be divided *ex post* and real decisions that must be made. Finally, only in a world of incomplete contracts can we define what a firm is and discuss corporate governance as being different from contractual governance. Not surprisingly, the theory of governance is intimately related to the emergence and evolution of the incomplete contracts paradigm.

A fundamental milestone in this evolution is the residual rights of control concept introduced by Grossman and Hart (1986). In a world of incomplete contracts, it is necessary to allocate the right to make *ex post* decisions in unspecified contingencies. This residual right is both meaningful and valuable. It is meaningful because it confers the discretion to make decisions *ex post*. It is valuable because this discretion can be used strategically in bargaining over the surplus.

. . .

5. Who should control the firm?

To show the utility of the framework developed thus far, I will use it to address one of the most controversial issues in corporate governance: Who should control the firm? In particular, I will analyse it with regard to the first objective of a corporate governance system. For an analysis focused on the second objective the reader is referred to Hansmann (1996) and for an analysis focused on the third to Fama and Jensen (1983a and 1983b).

As far as the first objective is concerned, the allocation of control is important because it affects the division of surplus. By controlling a firm's decisions, a party can ensure itself of more and more valuable options without the collaboration of the other parties. This guarantees the controlling party a larger share of the surplus within the relationship. Thus, in the framework outlined above, the question of who should control the firm can be rephrased as: Whose investments need more protection in the *ex post* bargaining? Again, the answer to this question is indissolubly linked to the underlying theory of the firm.

In the nexus of contracts view, the firm 'is just a legal fiction which serves as a focus for the complex process in which the conflicting objectives of individuals . . . are brought in equilibrium within a framework of contractual relationship' (Jensen and Meckling 1976a: 312). Thus, according to this view each party is fully protected by its contract with the exception of the shareholders, who accept a residual payoff because they possess a comparative advantage in diversifying risk. As a result, shareholders need the protection insured by control.

While widely popular, this explanation is unsatisfactory. The contractual protection provided to the parties involved in the nexus of contracts is only complete if contracts are complete. But if contracts are complete, then the statement that shareholders are in control is meaningless. In fact, in a world of complete contracts all the decisions are made *ex ante*, and thus shareholders are no more in control than are the workers: everything is contained in the initial grand contract. Furthermore, as I have already argued in section 3, this conclusion is inconsistent with the existence of a debate on what a company should do.

Alternatively, if contracts are incomplete, then the argument that all other parties are fully protected by their contractual relationships does not automatically follow. In fact, in this context one should ask why shareholders need more protection than other parties to the nexus of contracts. I will return to this issue momentarily.

In the property rights view of the firm, the reason why shareholders should be in control is straightforward. Control is allocated so as to maximize the incentives to make human-capital specific investments. The owner of the firm will generally be the worker with the most expropriable investment. In other words, the property rights approach does not deal with outside shareholders, and, thus, it applies only to entrepreneurial firms.

Outside of the GHM framework, the typical justification for why shareholders (or more generally the providers of finance) are in control is based on a combination of three arguments. Shareholders need more protection because: (1) their investment is more valuable; (2) other stakeholders can protect their investments better through contracts; (3) other stakeholders have other sources of power *ex post* that protect their investments.

Of the three arguments, the first is clearly unfounded. Reviewing the empirical evidence on the return on specialized human capital, Blair (1995) estimates that the quasi-rents generated by specialized human capital are as big as accounting profits, which are likely to overestimate the quasi-rent generated by physical capital. Hence, there is no ground to dismiss human capital investments as second order to physical capital investments.

The second argument is harder to dismiss. Since we lack a fully satisfactory theory of why contracts are incomplete, we cannot easily argue which contracts are more incomplete. Nevertheless, it is hard to argue that human capital investments are easier to contract than physical capital investments. If there is one contingency that is easily verifiable, it is the provision of funds. Thus, it is not obvious why providers of funds are at a comparative disadvantage.

The most convincing argument is probably the third. As Williamson (1985) puts it,

the suppliers of finance bear a unique relation to the firm: The whole of their investment in the firm is potentially placed at hazard. By contrast, the productive assets (plant and equipment; human capital) of suppliers of raw material, labor, intermediate product, electric power, and the like normally remains in the suppliers' possession.

Thus, the other stakeholders have a better outside option in the *ex post* bargaining and they do not need the protection ensured via the residual rights of control.

74

Even this argument, however, is not fully satisfactory. In fact, it only suggests that the suppliers of finance should have some form of contractual protection – it does not necessarily imply that they should be protected via the residual rights of control.

A satisfactory explanation of why the residual right belongs to the shareholders can only be obtained in a theory of the firm that explicitly accounts for the existence of different stakeholders and models the interaction between contractual (e.g., ownership) and noncontractual sources of power (e.g., unique human capital investments). An attempt in this direction is made by Rajan and Zingales (1998).

To understand the argument note that the residual right of control over an asset always increases the share of surplus captured by its owner (who has the opportunity to walk away with the asset), but it does not necessarily increase her marginal incentive to specialize. If, as is likely, a more specialized asset has less value outside the relationship for which it has been specialized, then specialization decreases the owner's outside opportunity and, thus, her share of the quasi-rents. Owning a physical asset, then, makes an agent more reluctant to specialize it. As a result, the residual right of control is best allocated to a group of agents who need to protect their investment against *ex post* expropriation, but who have little control on how much the asset is specialized.

Consider now the different members of the specific investments nexus that makes up the firm. Most of the specific investments which form this nexus are in human capital and, therefore, can neither be contracted nor delegated *ex ante*. Granting the residual right to any of these members will have a negative effect on their incentive to specialize.

By contrast, since the provision of funds is easily contractible, funds will be provided in the optimal amount as long as their providers receive sufficient surplus *ex post*. Thus, allocating the residual rights of control to the providers of funds has the positive effect of granting them enough surplus *ex post*, while avoiding the negative effect of reducing their marginal incentives.

Once they have provided funds, however, financial investors might be reluctant to use these funds for very specialized projects, for fear of seeing their share of the return go down. Thus, it is optimal that, while retaining a residual right of control over the assets, the providers of funds delegate the right to specialize the assets to a third party, who does not internalize the opportunity loss generated by this specialization. This third party, thus, should not be in the position of a mere agent, who owes a duty of obedience to the principal, but should be granted the independence to act in the interest of the firm (i.e., the whole body of members of the nexus of specific investments), and not only of the shareholders. Blair and Stout (1997) claim that this is the role American corporate law attributes to the board of directors.

In sum, a broader definition of the firm allows us to understand why the residual right of control is allocated to the providers of capital and why its use is mostly delegated to a board of directors.

. . .

8. Summary and conclusions

In this essay I have tried to summarize the results obtained by applying the incomplete contracts approach to corporate governance. In a world where all future observable contingencies can be costlessly contracted upon *ex ante*, there is no room for governance. By contrast, in an incomplete contracts world, corporate governance can be defined as the set of conditions that shapes the *ex post* bargaining over the quasi-rents generated by a firm. A governance system has efficiency effects both *ex ante*, through its impact on the incentives to make relationship-specific investments, and *ex post*, by altering the conditions under which bargaining takes place. A governance system also affects the level and the distribution of risk.

The incomplete contracts approach has been very successful in explaining the corporate governance of entrepreneurial firms. It can explain how ownership is allocated and how capital structure is chosen. By contrast, it is difficult for this approach to cope with the complexity of large publicly traded companies. Nevertheless, recent contributions in the area are able to account for some important features of large corporations: the allocation of ownership to the providers of capital who are dispersed and the importance of internal organization.

Many aspects, however, remain to be investigated. First, and foremost, the role of the board of directors. Second, the interaction between the different mechanisms of corporate governance. While we have many models that describe how each mechanism works in isolation, we know very little about how they interact. The effects are not obvious. For example, debt and takeovers are generally thought, in isolation, to be two instruments that reduce the amount of quasi-rents appropriated by management. But the use of debt may crowd out the effectiveness of takeovers, increasing rather than decreasing managerial rents (Novaes and Zingales 1995). Third, the normative implications of this approach deserve more attention. In a world of incomplete contracts, privately optimal governance can be inefficient *ex ante* and *ex post*. Of course, this is only a theoretical possibility, whose relevance needs to be assessed in the data. The most important contribution, however, will arise from a development of the underlying theory. Without a better understanding of why contracts are incomplete, all the results are merely provisional.

PART II

The scope of the firm

CHAPTER 7

The nature of the firm

RONALD COASE

Ronald Coase was born in Middlesex, England, in 1910. He received a Bachelor's (B. Com.) degree from the University of London in 1932 and a Doctor of Science degree in economics from the same school in 1951. When this article was published, he was Assistant Lecturer at the London School of Economics. He is currently Professor Emeritus of Economics and Senior Fellow in Law and Economics at the University of Chicago Law School. In 1991, he was awarded the Nobel Memorial Prize in Economic Science.

Economic theory has suffered in the past from a failure to state clearly its assumptions. Economists in building up a theory have often omitted to examine the foundations on which it was erected. This examination is, however, essential not only to prevent the misunderstanding and needless controversy which arise from a lack of knowledge of the assumptions on which a theory is based, but also because of the extreme importance for economics of good judgment in choosing between rival sets of assumptions. For instance, it is suggested that the use of the word "firm" in economics may be different from the use of the term by the "plain man."[1] Since there is apparently a trend in economic theory towards starting analysis with the individual firm and not with the industry,[2] it is all the more necessary not only that a clear definition of the word "firm" should be given but that its difference from a firm in the "real world," if it exists, should be made clear. Mrs. Robinson has said that "the two questions to be asked of a set of assumptions in economics are: Are they tractable? and: Do they correspond with the real world?"[3] Though, as Mrs. Robinson points out, "more often one set will be manageable and the other realistic," yet there may well be branches of theory where assumptions may be both manageable and realistic. It is hoped to show in the following paper that a definition of a firm may be obtained which is not only realistic in that it corresponds to what is meant by a firm in the real world, but is tractable by two of the most powerful instruments of economic analysis developed by Marshall, the idea of the margin and that of substitution, together giving the idea of substitution at

Reprinted from Ronald Coase, "The Nature of the Firm," *Economica*, 4 (1937): 386–405, by permission of the publisher.
[1] Joan Robinson (1932), p. 12.   [2] See N. Kaldor (1934b).   [3] Kaldor (op. cit.), p. 6.

the margin.[4] Our definition must, of course, "relate to formal relations which are capable of being *conceived* exactly."[5]

I

It is convenient if, in searching for a definition of a firm, we first consider the economic system as it is normally treated by the economist. Let us consider the description of the economic system given by Sir Arthur Salter.[6] "The normal economic system works itself. For its current operation it is under no central control; it needs no central survey. Over the whole range of human activity and human need, supply is adjusted to demand, and production to consumption, by a process that is automatic, elastic and responsive." An economist thinks of the economic system as being coordinated by the price mechanism and society becomes not an organization but an organism.[7] The economic system "works itself." This does not mean that there is no planning by individuals. These exercise foresight and choose between alternatives. This is necessarily so if there is to be order in the system. But this theory assumes that the direction of resources is dependent directly on the price mechanism. Indeed, it is often considered to be an objection to economic planning that it merely tries to do what is already done by the price mechanism.[8] Sir Arthur Salter's description, however, gives a very incomplete picture of our economic system. Within a firm, the description does not fit at all. For instance, in economic theory we find that the allocation of factors of production between different uses is determined by the price mechanism. The price of factor A becomes higher in X than in Y. As a result, A moves from Y to X until the difference between the prices in X and Y, except in so far as it compensates for other differential advantages, disappears. Yet in the real world, we find that there are many areas where this does not apply. If a workman moves from department Y to department X, he does not go because of a change in relative prices, but because he is ordered to do so. Those who object to economic planning on the grounds that the problem is solved by price movements can be answered by pointing out that there is planning within our economic system which is quite different from the individual planning mentioned above and which is akin to what is normally called economic planning. The example given above is typical of a large sphere in our modern economic system. Of course, this fact has not been ignored by economists. Marshall introduces organization as a fourth factor of production; J. B. Clark gives the coordinating function to the entrepreneur;

[4] J. M. Keynes (1933), pp. 223–4.   [5] L. Robbins (1932), p. 63.

[6] This description is quoted with approval by D. H. Robertson (1930), p. 85, and by Arnold Plant (1932). It appears in *Allied Shipping Control*, pp. 16–17.

[7] See F. A. Hayek (1933).   [8] See F. A. Hayek (1933).

Professor Knight introduces managers who coordinate. As D. H. Robertson points out, we find "islands of conscious power in this ocean of unconscious cooperation like lumps of butter coagulating in a pail of buttermilk."[9] But in view of the fact that it is usually argued that coordination will be done by the price mechanism, why is such organization necessary? Why are there these "islands of conscious power"? Outside the firm, price movements direct production, which is coordinated through a series of exchange transactions on the market. Within a firm, these market transactions are eliminated and in place of the complicated market structure with exchange transactions is substituted the entrepreneur-coordinator, who directs production.[10] It is clear that these are alternative methods of coordinating production. Yet having regard to the fact that if production is regulated by price movements, production could be carried on without any organization at all, well might we ask, why is there any organization?

Of course, the degree to which the price mechanism is superseded varies greatly. In a department store, the allocation of the different sections to the various locations in the building may be done by the controlling authority or it may be the result of competitive price bidding for space. In the Lancashire cotton industry, a weaver can rent power and shop room and can obtain looms and yarn on credit.[11] This coordination of the various factors of production is, however, normally carried out without the intervention of the price mechanism. As is evident, the amount of "vertical" integration, involving as it does the supersession of the price mechanism, varies greatly from industry to industry and from firm to firm.

It can, I think, be assumed that the distinguishing mark of the firm is the supersession of the price mechanism. It is, of course, as Professor Robbins points out, "related to an outside network of relative prices and costs,"[12] but it is important to discover the exact nature of this relationship. This distinction between the allocation of resources in a firm and the allocation in the economic system has been very vividly described by Mr. Maurice Dobb when discussing Adam Smith's conception of the capitalist:

... It began to be seen that there was something more important than the relations inside each factory or unit captained by an undertaker; there were the relations of the undertaker with the rest of the economic world outside his immediate sphere ... the undertaker busies himself with the division of labour inside each firm and he plans and organises consciously,

[9] D. H. Robertson (1930), p. 85.

[10] In the rest of this paper I shall use the term entrepreneur to refer to the person or persons who, in a competitive system, take the place of the price mechanism in the direction of resources.

[11] *Survey of Textile Industries*, p. 26.   [12] L. Robbins (1932), p. 71.

but

. . . he is related to the much larger economic specialisation of which he himself is merely one specialised unit. Here, he plays his part as a single cell in a larger organism, mainly unconscious of the wider role he fills.[13]

In view of the fact that while economists treat the price mechanism as a coordinating instrument, they also admit the coordinating function of the "entrepreneur," it is surely important to inquire why coordination is the work of the price mechanism in one case and of the entrepreneur in another. The purpose of this paper is to bridge what appears to be a gap in economic theory between the assumption (made for some purposes) that resources are allocated by means of the price mechanism and the assumption (made for other purposes) that this allocation is dependent on the entrepreneur-coordinator. We have to explain the basis on which, in practice, this choice between alternatives is effected.[14]

II

Our task is to attempt to discover why a firm emerges at all in a specialized exchange economy. The price mechanism (considered purely from the side of the direction of resources) might be superseded if the relationship which replaced it was desired for its own sake. This would be the case, for example, if some people preferred to work under the direction of some other person. Such individuals would accept less in order to work under someone, and firms would arise naturally from this. But it would appear that this cannot be a very important reason, for it would rather seem that the opposite tendency is operating if one judges from the stress normally laid on the advantage of "being one's own master."[15] Of course, if the desire was not to be controlled but to control, to exercise power over others, then people might be willing to give up something in order to direct others; that is, they would be willing to pay others more than they could get under the price mechanism in order to be able to direct them. But this implies that those who direct pay in order to be able to do this and are

[13] Maurice Dobb (1925), p. 20 Cf.; also, Henderson, (1922), pp. 3–5.

[14] It is easy to see when the State takes over the direction of an industry that, in planning it, it is doing something which was previously done by the price mechanism. What is usually not realized is that any business man in organizing the relations between his departments is also doing something which could be organized through the price mechanism. There is therefore a point in Mr. Durbin's answer to those who emphasize the problems involved in economic planning that the same problems have to be solved by business men in the competitive system. (See Durbin, 1936.) The important difference between these two cases is that economic planning is imposed on industry while firms arise voluntarily because they represent a more efficient method of organizing production. In a competitive system, there is an "optimum" amount of planning!

[15] See Harry Dawes (1934), who instances "the trek to retail shopkeeping and insurance work by the better paid of skilled men due to the desire (often the main aim in life of a worker) to be independent" (p. 86).

not paid to direct, which is clearly not true in the majority of cases.[16] Firms might also exist if purchasers preferred commodities which are produced by firms to those not so produced; but even in spheres where one would expect such preferences (if they exist) to be of negligible importance, firms are to be found in the real world.[17] Therefore there must be other elements involved.

The main reason why it is profitable to establish a firm would seem to be that there is a cost of using the price mechanism. The most obvious cost of "organizing" production through the price mechanism is that of discovering what the relevant prices are.[18] This cost may be reduced, but it will not be eliminated, by the emergence of specialists who will sell this information. The costs of negotiating and concluding a separate contract for each exchange transaction which takes place on a market must also be taken into account.[19] Again, in certain markets, e.g., produce exchanges, a technique is devised for minimizing these contract costs; but they are not eliminated. It is true that contracts are not eliminated when there is a firm but they are greatly reduced. A factor of production (or the owner thereof) does not have to make a series of contracts with the factors with whom he is cooperating within the firm, as would be necessary, of course, if this cooperation were as a direct result of the working of the price mechanism. For this series of contracts is substituted one. At this stage, it is important to note the character of the contract into which a factor enters that is employed within a firm. The contract is one whereby the factor, for a certain remuneration (which may be fixed or fluctuating), agrees to obey the directions of an entrepreneur *within certain limits*.[20] The essence of the contract is that it should only state the limits to the powers of the entrepreneur. Within these limits, he can therefore direct the other factors of production.

There are, however, other disadvantages – or costs – of using the price mechanism. It may be desired to make a long-term contract for the supply of some article or service. This may be due to the fact that if one contract is made for a longer period, instead of several shorter ones, then certain costs of making each contract will be avoided. Or, owing to the risk attitude of the people concerned, they may prefer to make a long rather than a short-term

[16] Nonetheless, this is not altogether fanciful. Some small shopkeepers are said to earn less than their assistants.

[17] G. F. Shove (1933), p. 116, note I, points out that such preferences may exist, although the example he gives is almost the reverse of the instance given in the text.

[18] According to N. Kaldor (1934a), it is one of the assumptions of static theory that: "All the relevant prices are known to all individuals." But this is clearly not true of the real world.

[19] This influence was noted by Professor Usher when discussing the development of capitalism. He says: "The successive buying and selling of partly finished products were sheer waste of energy" (1921, p. 13). But he does not develop the idea nor consider why it is that buying and selling operations still exist.

[20] It would be possible for no limits to the powers of the entrepreneur to be fixed. This would be voluntary slavery. According to Professor Batt (1929), p. 18, such a contract would be void and unenforceable.

contract. Now, owing to the difficulty of forecasting, the longer the period of the contract is for the supply of the commodity or service, the less possible, and indeed, the less desirable it is for the person purchasing to specify what the other contracting party is expected to do. It may well be a matter of indifference to the person supplying the service or commodity which of several courses of action is taken, but not to the purchaser of that service or commodity. But the purchaser will not know which of these several courses he will want the supplier to take. Therefore, the service which is being provided is expressed in general terms, the exact details being left until a later date. All that is stated in the contract is the limits to what the persons supplying the commodity or service are expected to do. The details of what the supplier is expected to do are not stated in the contract but are decided later by the purchaser. When the direction of resources (within the limits of the contract) becomes dependent on the buyer in this way, that relationship which I term a "firm" may be obtained.[21] A firm is likely therefore to emerge in those cases where a very short-term contract would be unsatisfactory. It is obviously of more importance in the case of services – labor – than it is in the case of the buying of commodities. In the case of commodities, the main items can be stated in advance and the details which will be decided later will be of minor significance.

We may sum up this section of the argument by saying that the operation of a market costs something and by forming an organization and allowing some authority (an "entrepreneur") to direct the resources, certain marketing costs are saved. The entrepreneur has to carry out his function at less cost, taking into account the fact that he may get factors of production at a lower price than the market transactions which he supersedes, because it is always possible to revert to the open market if he fails to do this.

The question of uncertainty is one which is often considered to be very relevant to the study of the equilibrium of the firm. It seems improbable that a firm would emerge without the existence of uncertainty. But those, for instance, Professor Knight, who make the *mode of payment* the distinguishing mark of the firm – fixed incomes being guaranteed to some of those engaged in production by a person who takes the residual, and fluctuating, income – would appear to be introducing a point which is irrelevant to the problem we are considering. One entrepreneur may sell his services to another for a certain sum of money, while the payment to his employees may be mainly or wholly a share in profits.[22] The significant question would appear to be why the allocation of resources is not done directly by the price mechanism.

---

[21] Of course, it is not possible to draw a hard and fast line which determines whether there is a firm or not. There may be more or less direction. It is similar to the legal question of whether there is the relationship of master and servant or principal and agent. See the discussion of this problem presented later.

[22] The views of Professor Knight are examined later in more detail.

Another factor that should be noted is that exchange transactions on a market and the same transactions organized within a firm are often treated differently by governments or other bodies with regulatory powers. If we consider the operation of a sales tax, it is clear that it is a tax on market transactions and not on the same transactions organized within the firm. Now since these are alternative methods of "organization" – by the price mechanism or by the entrepreneur – such a regulation would bring into existence firms which otherwise would have no raison d'être. It would furnish a reason for the emergence of a firm in a specialized exchange economy. Of course, to the extent that firms already exist, such a measure as a sales tax would merely tend to make them larger than they would otherwise be. Similarly, quota schemes, and methods of price control which imply that there is rationing, and which do not apply to firms producing such products for themselves, by allowing advantages to those who organize within the firm and not through the market, necessarily encourage the growth of firms. But it is difficult to believe that it is measures such as have been mentioned in this paragraph which have brought firms into existence. Such measures would, however, tend to have this result if they did not exist for other reasons.

These, then, are the reasons why organizations such as firms exist in a specialized exchange economy in which it is generally assumed that the distribution of resources is "organized" by the price mechanism. A firm, therefore, consists of the system of relationships which comes into existence when the direction of resources is dependent on an entrepreneur.

The approach which has just been sketched would appear to offer an advantage in that it is possible to give a scientific meaning to what is meant by saying that a firm gets larger or smaller. A firm becomes larger as additional transactions (which could be exchange transactions coordinated through the price mechanism) are organized by the entrepreneur and becomes smaller as he abandons the organization of such transactions. The question which arises is whether it is possible to study the forces which determine the size of the firm. Why does the entrepreneur not organize one less transaction or one more? It is interesting to note that Professor Knight considers that:

... the relation between efficiency and size is one of the most serious problems of theory, being, in contrast with the relation for a plant, largely a matter of personality and historical accident rather than of intelligible general principles. But the question is peculiarly vital because the possibility of monopoly gain offers a powerful incentive to *continuous and unlimited* expansion of the firm, which force must be offset by some equally powerful one making for decreased efficiency (in the production of money income) with growth in size, if even boundary competition is to exist.[23]

[23] Frank Knight (1933).

Professor Knight would appear to consider that it is impossible to treat scientifically the determinants of the size of the firm. On the basis of the concept of the firm developed above, this task will now be attempted.

It was suggested that the introduction of the firm was due primarily to the existence of marketing costs. A pertinent question to ask would appear to be (quite apart from the monopoly considerations raised by Professor Knight), why, if by organizing one can eliminate certain costs and in fact reduce the cost of production, are there any market transactions at all?[24] Why is not all production carried on by one big firm? There would appear to be certain possible explanations.

First, as a firm gets larger, there may be decreasing returns to the entrepreneur function, that is, the costs of organizing additional transactions within the firm may rise.[25] Naturally a point must be reached where the costs of organizing an extra transaction within the firm are equal to the costs involved in carrying out the transaction in the open market, or to the costs of organizing by another entrepreneur. Secondly, it may be that as the transactions which are organized increase, the entrepreneur fails to place the factors of production in the uses where their value is greatest, that is, fails to make the best use of the factors of production. Again, a point must be reached where the loss through the waste of resources is equal to the marketing costs of the exchange transaction in the open market or to the loss if the transaction was organized by another entrepreneur. Finally, the supply price of one or more of the factors of production may rise, because the "other advantages" of a small firm are greater than those of a large firm.[26] Of course, the actual point where the expansion of the firm ceases might be determined by a combination of the factors mentioned above. The first two reasons given most probably correspond to the economists' phrase of "diminishing returns to management."[27]

The point has been made in the previous paragraph that a firm will tend to expand until the costs of organizing an extra transaction within the firm

[24] There are certain marketing costs which could only be eliminated by the abolition of "consumers' choice" and these are the costs of retailing. It is conceivable that these costs might be so high that people would be willing to accept rations because the extra product obtained was worth the loss of their choice.

[25] This argument assumes that exchange transactions on a market can be considered as homogeneous; which is clearly untrue in fact. This complication is taken into account later.

[26] For a discussion of the variation of the supply price of factors of production to firms of varying size, see E. A. G. Robinson (1931). It is sometimes said that the supply price of organizing ability increases as the size of the firm increases because men prefer to be the heads of small independent businesses rather than the heads of departments in a large business. See Jones (1927), p. 531, and Macgregor (1906), p. 63. This is a common argument of those who advocate rationalization. It is said that larger units would be more efficient, but owing to the individualistic spirit of the smaller entrepreneurs, they prefer to remain independent, apparently in spite of the higher income which their increased efficiency under rationalization makes possible.

[27] This discussion is, of course, brief and incomplete. For a more thorough discussion of this particular problem, see N. Kaldor (1934b) and E. A. G. Robinson (1934).

become equal to the costs of carrying out the same transaction by means of an exchange on the open market or the costs of organizing in another firm. But if the firm stops its expansion at a point below the costs of marketing in the open market and at a point equal to the costs of organizing in another firm, in most cases (excluding the case of "combination"[28]), this will imply that there is a market transaction between these two producers, each of whom could organize it at less than the actual marketing costs. How is the paradox to be resolved? If we consider an example the reason for this will become clear. Suppose *A* is buying a product from *B* and that both *A* and *B* could organize this marketing transaction at less than its present cost. *B*, we can assume, is not organizing one process or stage of production, but several. If *A* therefore wishes to avoid a market transaction, he will have to take over all the processes of production controlled by *B*. Unless *A* takes over all the processes of production, a market transaction will still remain, although it is a different product that is bought. But we have previously assumed that as each producer expands he becomes less efficient; the additional costs of organizing extra transactions increase. It is probable that *A*'s cost of organizing the transactions previously organized by *B* will be greater than *B*'s cost of doing the same thing. *A* therefore will take over the whole of *B*'s organization only if his cost of organizing *B*'s work is not greater than *B*'s cost by an amount equal to the costs of carrying out an exchange transaction on the open market. But once it becomes economical to have a market transaction, it also pays to divide production in such a way that the cost of organizing an extra transaction in each firm is the same.

Up to now it has been assumed that the exchange transactions which take place through the price mechanism are homogeneous. In fact, nothing could be more diverse than the actual transactions which take place in our modern world. This would seem to imply that the costs of carrying out exchange transactions through the price mechanism will vary considerably as will also the costs of organizing these transactions within the firm. It seems therefore possible that, quite apart from the question of diminishing returns, the costs of organizing these transactions within the firm may be greater than the costs of carrying out the exchange transactions in the open market. This would necessarily imply that there were exchange transactions carried out through the price mechanism, but would it mean that there would have to be more than one firm? Clearly not, for all those areas in the economic system where the direction of resources was not dependent directly on the price mechanism could be organized within one firm. The factors which were discussed earlier would seem to be the important ones, though it is difficult to say whether "diminishing returns to management" or the rising supply price of factors is likely to be the more important.

[28] A definition of this term is given later.

Other things being equal, therefore, a firm will tend to be larger:

(a) the less the costs of organizing and the slower these costs rise with an increase in the transactions organized;
(b) the less likely the entrepreneur is to make mistakes and the smaller the increase in mistakes with an increase in the transactions organized;
(c) the greater the lowering (or the less the rise) in the supply price of factors of production to firms of larger size.

Apart from variations in the supply price of factors of production to firms of different sizes, it would appear that the costs of organizing and the losses through mistakes will increase with an increase in the spatial distribution of the transactions organized, in the dissimilarity of the transactions, and in the probability of changes in the relevant prices.[29] As more transactions are organized by an entrepreneur, it would appear that the transactions would tend to be either different in kind or in different places. This furnishes an additional reason why efficiency will tend to decrease as the firm gets larger. Inventions which tend to bring factors of production nearer together, by lessening spatial distribution, tend to increase the size of the firm.[30] Changes like the telephone and the telegraph which tend to reduce the cost of organizing spatially will tend to increase the size of the firm. All changes which improve managerial technique will tend to increase the size of the firm.[31,32]

It should be noted that the definition of a firm which was given above can be used to give more precise meanings to the terms "combination" and

[29] This aspect of the problem is emphasized by N. Kaldor (1934b). Its importance in this connection had been previously noted by E. A. G. Robinson (1931), pp. 83–106. This assumes that an increase in the probability of price movements increases the costs of organizing within a firm more than it increases the cost of carrying out an exchange transaction on the market – which is probable.

[30] This would appear to be the importance of the treatment of the technical unit by E. A. G. Robinson (1931), pp. 27–33. The larger the technical unit, the greater the concentration of factors and therefore the firm is likely to be larger.

[31] It should be noted that most inventions will change both the costs of organizing and the costs of using the price mechanism. In such cases, whether the invention tends to make firms larger or smaller will depend on the relative effect on these two sets of costs. For instance, if the telephone reduces the costs of using the price mechanism more than it reduces the costs of organizing, then it will have the effect of reducing the size of the firm.

[32] An illustration of these dynamic forces is furnished by Maurice Dobb (1928), p. 68. "With the passing of bonded labour the factory, as an establishment where work was organised under the whip of the overseer, lost its raison d'être until this was restored to it with the introduction of power machinery after 1846." It seems important to realize that the passage from the domestic system to the factory system is not a mere historical accident but is conditioned by economic forces. This is shown by the fact that it is possible to move from the factory system to the domestic system, as in the Russian example, as well as vice versa. It is the essence of serfdom that the price mechanism is not allowed to operate. Therefore, there has to be direction from some organizer. When, however, serfdom passed, the price mechanism was allowed to operate. It was not until machinery drew workers into one locality that it paid to supersede the price mechanism and the firm again emerged.

"integration."[33] There is a combination when transactions which were previously organized by two or more entrepreneurs become organized by one. This becomes integration when it involves the organization of transactions which were previously carried out between the entrepreneurs on a market. A firm can expand in either or both of these two ways. The whole of the "structure of competitive industry" becomes tractable by the ordinary technique of economic analysis.

III

The problem which has been investigated in the previous section has not been entirely neglected by economists, and it is now necessary to consider why the reasons given above for the emergence of a firm in a specialized exchange economy are to be preferred to the other explanations which have been offered.

It is sometimes said that the reason for the existence of a firm is to be found in the division of labor. This is the view of Professor Usher, a view which has been adopted and expanded by Mr. Maurice Dobb. The firm becomes

... the result of an increasing complexity of the division of labour.... The growth of this economic differentiation creates the need for some integrating force without which differentiation would collapse into chaos; and it is as the integrating force in a differentiated economy that industrial forms are chiefly significant.[34]

The answer to this argument is an obvious one. The "integrating force in a differentiated economy" already exists in the form of the price mechanism. It is perhaps the main achievement of economic science that it has shown that there is no reason to suppose that specialization must lead to chaos.[35] The reason given by Mr. Maurice Dobb is therefore inadmissible. What has to be explained is why one integrating force (the entrepreneur) should be substituted for another integrating force (the price mechanism).

The most interesting reasons (and probably the most widely accepted) which have been given to explain this fact are those to be found in Professor Knight's *Risk, Uncertainty and Profit.* His views will be examined in some detail.

Professor Knight starts with a system in which there is no uncertainty:

... acting as individuals under absolute freedom but without collusion men are supposed to have organised economic life with the primary and secondary division of labour, the use of capital, etc., developed to the point familiar in present-day America. The principal fact which calls for the exercise of the imagination is the internal organisation of

---

[33] This is often called "vertical integration," combination being termed "lateral integration."

[34] Maurice Dobb (1928), p. 10. Professor Usher's views are to be found in Usher (1921), pp. 1–18.

[35] Cf. J. B. Clark (1900), p. 19, who speaks of the theory of exchange as being the "theory of the organisation of industrial society."

the productive groups or establishments. With uncertainty entirely absent, every individual being in possession of perfect knowledge of the situation, there would be no occasion for anything of the nature of responsible management or control of productive activity. Even marketing transactions in any realistic sense would not be found. The flow of raw materials and productive services to the consumer would be entirely automatic.[36]

Professor Knight says that we can imagine this adjustment as being "the result of a long process of experimentation worked out by trial-and-error methods alone," while it is not necessary "to imagine every worker doing exactly the right thing at the right time in a sort of 'pre-established harmony' with the work of others. There might be managers, superintendents, etc., for the purpose of coordinating the activities of individuals," though these managers would be performing a purely routine function, "without responsibility of any sort."[37]

Professor Knight then continues:

With the introduction of uncertainty – the fact of ignorance and the necessity of acting upon opinion rather than knowledge – into this Eden-like situation, its character is entirely changed. . . . With uncertainty present, doing things, the actual execution of activity, becomes in a real sense a secondary part of life; the primary problem or function is deciding what to do and how to do it.[38]

This fact of uncertainty brings about the two most important characteristics of social organization.

In the first place, goods are produced for a market on the basis of entirely impersonal prediction of wants, not for the satisfaction of the wants of the producers themselves. The producer takes the responsibility of forecasting the consumers' wants. In the second place, the work of forecasting and at the same time a large part of the technological direction and control of production are still further concentrated upon a very narrow class of producers, and we meet with a new economic functionary, the entrepreneur. . . . When uncertainty is present and the task of deciding what to do and how to do it takes the ascendancy over that of execution the internal organisation of the productive groups is no longer a matter of indifference or a mechanical detail. Centralisation of this deciding and controlling function is imperative, a process of "cephalisation" is inevitable.[39]

The most fundamental change is:

. . . the system under which the confident and venturesome assume the risk or insure the doubtful and timid by guaranteeing to the latter a specified income in return for an assignment of the actual results. . . . With human nature as we know it, it would be impracticable or very unusual for one man to guarantee to another a definite result of the latter's actions without being given power to direct his work. And on the other hand the second party would not place himself under the direction of the first without such

---

[36] Frank Knight (1921), p. 267.   [37] Knight (1921), pp. 267–8.
[38] Knight (1921), p. 268.   [39] Knight (1921), pp. 268–95.

a guarantee.... The result of this manifold specialisation of function is the enterprise and wage system of industry. Its existence in the world is the direct result of the fact of uncertainty.[40]

These quotations give the essence of Professor Knight's theory. The fact of uncertainty means that people have to forecast future wants. Therefore, you get a special class springing up who direct the activities of others to whom they give guaranteed wages. It acts because good judgment is generally associated with confidence in one's judgment.[41]

Professor Knight would appear to leave himself open to criticism on several grounds. First of all, as he himself points out, the fact that certain people have better judgment or better knowledge does not mean that they can only get an income from it by themselves actively taking part in production. They can sell advice or knowledge. Every business buys the services of a host of advisers. We can imagine a system where all advice or knowledge was bought as required. Again, it is possible to get a reward from better knowledge or judgment not by actively taking part in production but by making contracts with people who are producing. A merchant buying for future delivery represents an example of this. But this merely illustrates the point that it is quite possible to give a guaranteed reward providing that certain acts are performed without directing the performance of those acts. Professor Knight says that "with human nature as we know it it would be impracticable or very unusual for one man to guarantee to another a definite result of the latter's actions without being given power to direct his work." This is surely incorrect. A large proportion of jobs are done to contract, that is, the contractor is guaranteed a certain sum providing he performs certain acts. But this does not involve any direction. It does mean, however, that the system of relative prices has been changed and that there will be a new arrangement of the factors of production.[42] The fact that Professor Knight mentions that the "second party would not place himself under the direction of the first without such a guarantee" is irrelevant to the problem we are considering. Finally, it seems important to notice that even in the case of an economic system where there is no uncertainty Professor Knight considers that there would be coordinators, though they would perform only a routine function. He immediately adds that they would be "without responsibility of any sort," which raises the question by whom are they paid and why? It seems

---

[40] Knight (1921), pp. 269–70.   [41] Knight (1921), p. 270.

[42] This shows that it is possible to have a private enterprise system without the existence of firms. Though, in practice, the two functions of enterprise, which actually influences the system of relative prices by forecasting wants and acting in accordance with such forecasts, and management, which accepts the system of relative prices as being given, are normally carried out by the same persons, yet it seems important to keep them separate in theory. This point is further discussed later.

that nowhere does Professor Knight give a reason why the price mechanism should be superseded.

IV

It would seem important to examine one further point and that is to consider the relevance of this discussion to the general question of the "cost curve of the firm."

It has sometimes been assumed that a firm is limited in size under perfect competition if its cost curve slopes upward,[43] while under imperfect competition, it is limited in size because it will not pay to produce more than the output at which marginal cost is equal to marginal revenue.[44] But it is clear that a firm may produce more than one product and, therefore, there appears to be no prima facie reason why this upward slope of the cost curve in the case of perfect competition or the fact that marginal cost will not always be below marginal revenue in the case of imperfect competition should limit the size of the firm.[45] Mrs. Robinson[46] makes the simplifying assumption that only one product is being produced. But it is clearly important to investigate how the number of products produced by a firm is determined, while no theory which assumes that only one product is in fact produced can have very great practical significance.

It might be replied that under perfect competition, since everything that is produced can be sold at the prevailing price, then there is no need for any other product to be produced. But this argument ignores the fact that there may be a point where it is less costly to organize the exchange transactions of a new product than to organize further exchange transactions of the old product. This point can be illustrated in the following way. Imagine, following von Thunen, that there is a town, the consuming centre, and that industries are located around this central point in rings. These conditions are illustrated in the following diagram in which A, B, and C represent different industries.

Imagine an entrepreneur who starts controlling exchange transactions from x. Now as he extends his activities in the same product (B), the cost of organising increases until at some point it becomes equal to that of a dissimilar product which is nearer. As the firm expands, it will therefore from this point include more than one product (A and C). This treatment of the problem is obviously incomplete,[47] but it is necessary to show that merely proving that the cost

[43] See Kaldor (1934b) and Robinson (1934).

[44] Mr. Robinson calls this the imperfect competition solution for the survival of the small firm.

[45] Mr. Robinson's conclusion, (op cit.) p. 249, note 1, would appear to be definitely wrong. He is followed by Horace J. White, Jr. (1936), p. 645, note 27. Mr. White states: "It is obvious that the size of the firm is limited in conditions of monopolistic competition."

[46] Robinson (1934).

[47] As has been shown above, location is only one of the factors influencing the cost of organising.

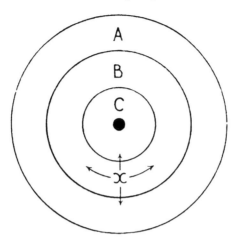

curve turns upwards does not give a limitation to the size of the firm. So far we have only considered the case of perfect competition; the case of imperfect competition would appear to be obvious.

To determine the size of the firm, we have to consider the marketing costs (that is, the costs of using the price mechanism), and the costs of organising of different entrepreneurs, and then we can determine how many products will be produced by each firm and how much of each it will produce. It would, therefore, appear that Mr. Shove[48] in his article on "imperfect competition" was asking questions which Mrs. Robinson's cost curve apparatus cannot answer. The factors mentioned above would seem to be the relevant ones.

V

Only one task now remains, and that is to see whether the concept of a firm which has been developed fits in with that existing in the real world. We can best approach the question of what constitutes a firm in practice by considering the legal relationship normally called that of "master and servant" or "employer and employee."[49] The essentials of this relationship have been given as follows:

[48] G. F. Shove, "The Imperfection of the Market," *Economic Journal*, March, 1933, p. 115. In connection with an increase in demand in the suburbs and the effect on the price charged by suppliers, Mr. Shove asks, "... why do not the old firms open branches in the suburbs?" If the argument in the text is correct, this is a question which Mrs. Robinson's apparatus cannot answer.

[49] The legal concept of "employer and employee" and the economic concept of a firm are not identical, in that the firm may imply control over another person's property as well as over their labor. But the identity of these two concepts is sufficiently close for an examination of the legal concept to be of value in appraising the worth of the economic concept.

(1) The servant must be under the duty of rendering personal services to the master or to others on behalf of the master, otherwise the contract is a contract for sale of goods or the like.

(2) The master must have the right to control the servant's work, either personally or by another servant or agent. It is this right of control or interference, of being entitled to tell the servant when to work (within the hours of service) and when not to work, and what work to do and how to do it (within the terms of such service) which is the dominant characteristic in this relation and marks off the servant from an independent contractor, or from one employed merely to give to his employer the fruits of his labour. In the latter case, the contractor or performer is not under the employer's control in doing the work or effecting the service; he has to shape and manage his work so as to give the result he has contracted to effect.[50]

We thus see that it is the fact of direction which is the essence of the legal concept of "employer and employee," just as it was in the economic concept which was developed above. It is interesting to note that Professor Batt says further:

That which distinguishes an agent from a servant is not the absence or presence of a fixed wage or the payment only of commission on business done, but rather the freedom with which an agent may carry out his employment.[51]

We can, therefore, conclude that the definition we have given is one which approximates closely to the firm as it is considered in the real world.

Our definition is, therefore, realistic. Is it manageable? This ought to be clear. When we are considering how large a firm will be the principle of marginalism works smoothly. The question always is, will it pay to bring an extra exchange transaction under the organizing authority? At the margin, the costs of organizing within the firm will be equal either to the costs of organizing in another firm or to the costs involved in leaving the transaction to be "organized" by the price mechanism. Business men will be constantly experimenting, controlling more or less, and in this way, equilibrium will be maintained. This gives the position of equilibrium for static analysis. But it is clear that the dynamic factors are also of considerable importance, and an investigation of the effect changes have on the cost of organizing within the firm and on marketing costs generally will enable one to explain why firms get larger and smaller. We thus have a theory of moving equilibrium. The above analysis would also appear to have clarified the relationship between initiative or enterprise and management. Initiative means forecasting and operates through the price mechanism by the making of new contracts. Management proper merely reacts to price changes, rearranging the factors of production under its

[50] Batt (1929), p. 6.   [51] Batt (1929), p. 7.

control. That the business man normally combines both functions is an obvious result of the marketing costs which were discussed above. Finally, this analysis enables us to state more exactly what is meant by the "marginal product" of the entrepreneur. But an elaboration of this point would take us far from our comparatively simple task of definition and clarification.

CHAPTER 8

Vertical integration, appropriable rents, and the competitive contracting process

BENJAMIN KLEIN, ROBERT CRAWFORD,
AND ARMEN ALCHIAN

Benjamin Klein was born in 1943 in New York City. He earned his Ph.D. in economics from the University of Chicago in 1970. When this article was published, he was a member of the faculty of the University of California at Los Angeles, where he is currently Professor of Economics, Emeritus.

Robert Crawford was born in 1943 in Medicine Hat, Alberta, Canada. He received a Ph.D. in economics from Carnegie-Mellon University in 1976. Since 1978, he has been Associate Professor of Managerial Economics at Brigham Young University.

Armen Alchian was born in 1914 in Fresno, California. He received a Ph.D. in economics at Stanford University in 1943. When this article was published, he was Professor of Economics at the University of California, Los Angeles, where he is currently Professor Emeritus.

More than forty years have passed since Coase's fundamental insight that transaction, coordination, and contracting costs must be considered explicitly in explaining the extent of vertical integration.[1] Starting from the truism that profit-maximizing firms will undertake those activities that they find cheaper to administer internally than to purchase in the market, Coase forced economists to begin looking for previously neglected constraints on the trading process that might efficiently lead to an intrafirm rather than an interfirm transaction. This paper attempts to add to this literature by exploring one particular cost of using the market system – the possibility of postcontractual opportunistic behavior.

Opportunistic behavior has been identified and discussed in the modern analysis of the organization of economic activity. Williamson, for example, has referred to effects on the contracting process of "*ex post* small numbers opportunism,"[2] and Teece has elaborated:

Reprinted with abridgements from Benjamin Klein, Robert Crawford, and Armen Alchian, "Vertical Integration, Appropriable Rents, and the Competitive Contracting Process," *Journal of Law and Economics*, 21 (1978): 297–326. Copyright © 1978. Reprinted with the permission of the University of Chicago Press.

[1] R. H. Coase (1937).   [2] Oliver E. Williamson (1975).

Even when all of the relevant contingencies can be specified in a contract, contracts are still open to serious risks since they are not always honored. The 1970's are replete with examples of the risks associated with relying on contracts... [O]pen displays of opportunism are not infrequent and very often litigation turns out to be costly and ineffectual.[3]

The particular circumstance we emphasize as likely to produce a serious threat of this type of reneging on contracts is the presence of appropriable specialized quasi rents. After a specific investment is made and such quasi rents are created, the possibility of opportunistic behavior is very real. Following Coase's framework, this problem can be solved in two possible ways: vertical integration or contracts. The crucial assumption underlying the analysis of this paper is that, as assets become more specific and more appropriable quasi rents are created (and therefore the possible gains from opportunistic behavior increase), the costs of contracting will generally increase more than the costs of vertical integration. Hence, *ceteris paribus*, we are more likely to observe vertical integration.

I. Appropriable quasi rents of specialized assets

Assume an asset is owned by one individual and rented to another individual. The quasi-rent value of the asset is the excess of its value over its salvage value, that is, its value in its next best *use* to another renter. The potentially appropriable specialized portion of the quasi rent is that portion, if any, in excess of its value to the second highest-valuing *user*. If this seems like a distinction without a difference, consider the following example.

Imagine a printing press owned and operated by party A. Publisher B buys printing services from party A by leasing his press at a contracted rate of $5,500 per day. The amortized fixed cost of the printing press is $4,000 per day and it has a current salvageable value if moved elsewhere of $1,000 (daily rental equivalent). Operating costs are $1,500 and are paid by the printing press owner, who prints final printed pages for the publisher. Assume also that a second publisher C is willing to offer at most $3,500 for daily service. The current quasi rent on the installed machine is $3,000 (= $5,500 − $1,500 − $1,000), the revenue minus operating costs minus salvageable value. However, the daily quasi rent from publisher B relative to use of the machine for publisher C is only $2,000 (= $5,500 − $3,500). At $5,500 revenue daily from publisher B the press owner would break even on his investment. If the publisher were then able to cut his offer for the press from $5,500 down to almost $3,500, he would still have the press service available to him. He would be appropriating $2,000 of the quasi rent from the press owner. The $2,000 difference between

---

[3] David J. Teece (1976).

his prior agreed-to daily rental of $5,500 and the next best revenue available to the press once the machine is purchased and installed is less than the quasi rent and therefore is potentially appropriable. If no second party were available at the present site, the entire quasi rent would be subject to threat of appropriation by an unscrupulous or opportunistic publisher.

Our primary interest concerns the means whereby this risk can be reduced or avoided. In particular, vertical integration is examined as a means of economizing on the costs of avoiding risks of appropriation of quasi rents in specialized assets by opportunistic individuals. This advantage of joint ownership of such specialized assets, namely, economizing on contracting costs necessary to insure nonopportunistic behavior, must of course be weighed against the costs of administering a broader range of assets within the firm.[4]

An appropriable quasi rent is not a monopoly rent in the usual sense, that is, the increased value of an asset protected from market entry over the value it would have had in an open market. An appropriable quasi rent can occur with no market closure or restrictions placed on rival assets. Once installed, an asset may be so expensive to remove or so specialized to a particular user that if the price paid to the owner were somehow reduced, the asset's services to that user would not be reduced. Thus, even if there were free and open competition for entry to the market, the specialization of the installed asset to a particular user (or more accurately the high costs of making it available to others) creates a quasi rent but no "monopoly" rent. At the other extreme, an asset may be costlessly transferable to some other user at no reduction in value, while at the same time, entry of similar assets is restricted. In this case, monopoly rent would exist, but no quasi rent.

We can use monopoly terminology to refer to the phenomenon we are discussing as long as we recognize that we are not referring to the usual monopoly created by government restrictions on entry or referring to a single supplier or even highly concentrated supply. One of the fundamental premises of this paper is that monopoly power, better labeled "market power," is pervasive. Because of transaction and mobility costs, "market power" will exist in many situations not commonly called monopolies. There may be many potential suppliers of a particular asset to a particular user but once the investment in the asset is made, the asset may be so specialized to a particular user that monopoly or monopsony market power, or both, is created.

---

[4] Vertical integration does not completely avoid contracting problems. The firm could usefully be thought of as a complex nonmarket contractual network where very similar forces are present. Frank Knight stressed the importance of this more than 50 years ago when he stated:" "[T]he internal problems of the corporation, the protection of its various types of members and adherents against each other's predatory propensities, are quite as vital as the external problem of safeguarding the public interest against exploitation by the corporation as a unit." Frank H. Knight (1965).

Vertical integration, appropriable rents, competitive contracting process

A related motive for vertical integration that should not be confused with our main interest is the optimal output and pricing between two successive monopolists or bilateral monopolists (in the sense of marginal revenue less than price). A distortion arises because each sees a distorted marginal revenue or marginal cost.[5] While it is true that this successive monopoly distortion can be avoided by vertical integration, the results of the integration could, for that purpose alone, be achieved by a long term or a more detailed contract based on the true marginal revenue and marginal costs. Integrated ownership will sometimes be utilized to economize on such precontractual bargaining costs. However, we investigate a different reason for joint ownership of vertically related assets – the avoidance of postcontractual opportunistic behavior when specialized assets and appropriable quasi rents are present. One must clearly distinguish the transaction and information costs of reaching an agreement (discovering and heeding true costs and revenues and agreeing upon the division of profits) and the enforcement costs involved in assuring compliance with an agreement, especially one in which specialized assets are involved. It is this latter situation which we here explore as a motivation for intrafirm rather than interfirm transactions.

We maintain that, if an asset has a substantial portion of quasi rent which is strongly dependent upon some other particular asset, both assets will tend to be owned by one party. For example, reconsider our printing press example. Knowing that the press would exist and be operated even if its owner got as little as $1,500, publisher B could seek excuses to renege on his initial contract to get the weekly rental down from $5,500 to close to $3,500 (the potential offer from publisher C, the next highest-valuing user at its present site). If publisher B could effectively announce he was not going to pay more than, say, $4,000 per week, the press owner would seem to be stuck. This unanticipated action would be opportunistic behavior (which by definition refers to unanticipated nonfulfillment of the contract) if the press owner had installed the press at a competitive rental price of $5,500 anticipating (possibly naively) good faith by the publisher. The publisher, for example, might plead that his newspaper business is depressed and he will be unable to continue unless rental terms are revised.

Alternatively, and maybe more realistically, because the press owner may have bargaining power due to the large losses that he can easily impose on the publisher (if he has no other source of press services quickly available), the press owner might suddenly seek to get a higher rental price than $5,500 to capture some newly perceived increase in the publisher's profits. He could do this by alleging breakdowns or unusually high maintenance costs. This type of opportunistic behavior is difficult to prove and therefore litigate.

[5] This matter of successive and bilateral monopoly has long been known and exposited in many places. See, for example, Robert Bork (1954); Fritz Machlup and Martha Taber (1960), where the problem is dated back to Cournot's statement in 1838.

As we shall see, the costs of contractually specifying all important elements of quality varies considerably by type of asset. For some assets it may be essentially impossible to effectively specify all elements of quality and therefore, vertical integration is more likely. But even for those assets used in situations where all relevant quality dimensions can be unambiguously specified in a contract, the threat of production delay during litigation may be an effective bargaining device. A contract therefore may be clearly enforceable but still subject to postcontractual opportunistic behavior. For example, the threat by the press owner to break its contract by pulling out its press is credible even though illegal and possibly subject to injunctive action. This is because such an action, even in the very short run, can impose substantial costs on the newspaper publisher.[6]

This more subtle form of opportunistic behavior is likely to result in a loss of efficiency and not just a wealth-distribution effect. For example, the publisher may decide, given this possibility, to hold or seek standby facilities otherwise not worthwhile. Even if transactors are risk neutral, the presence of possible opportunistic behavior will entail costs as real resources are devoted to the attempt to improve posttransaction bargaining positions in the event such opportunism occurs. In particular, less specific investments will be made to avoid being "locked in."[7] In addition, the increased uncertainty of quality and quantity leads to larger optimum inventories and other increased real costs of production.

This attention to appropriable specialized quasi rents is not novel. In addition to Williamson's[8] pathbreaking work in the area, Goldberg's[9] perceptive analysis of what he calls the "hold up" problem in the context of government regulation is

---

[6] While newspaper publishers generally own their own presses, book publishers generally do not. One possible reason book publishers are less integrated may be because a book is planned further ahead in time and can economically be released with less haste. Presses located in any area of the United States can be used. No press is specialized to one publisher, in part because speed in publication and distribution to readers are generally far less important for books than newspapers, and therefore appropriable quasi rents are not created. Magazines and other periodicals can be considered somewhere between books and newspapers in terms of the importance of the time factor in distribution. In addition, because magazines are distributed nationally from at most a few plants, printing presses located in many different alternative areas are possible competitors for an existing press used at a particular location. Hence, a press owner has significantly less market power over the publisher of a magazine compared to a newspaper and we find magazines generally printed in nonpublisher-owned plants. (See W. Eric Gustafson, 1959.) But while a magazine printing press may be a relatively less specific asset compared to a newspaper printing press, appropriable quasi rents may not be trivial (as possibly they are in the case of book printing). The magazine printing contract is therefore unlikely to be of a short-term one-transaction form but will be a long-term arrangement.

[7] The relevance for private investments in underdeveloped, politically unstable, that is, "opportunistic," countries is painfully obvious. The importance for economic growth of predictable government behavior regarding the definition and enforcement of property rights has frequently been noted.

[8] Oliver E. Williamson (1971) and Williamson (1975).   [9] Victor P. Goldberg (1976).

what we are discussing in a somewhat different context. Goldberg indicates how some government regulation can usefully be considered a means of avoiding or reducing the threat of loss of quasi rent. (Goldberg treats this as the problem of providing protection for the "right to be served.") He also recognizes that this force underlies a host of other contractual and institutional arrangements such as stockpiling, insurance contracts, and vertical integration. Our analysis will similarly suggest a rationale for the existence of particular institutions and the form of governmental intervention or contractual provisions as alternatives to vertical integration in a wide variety of cases.

II. Contractual solutions

The primary alternative to vertical integration as a solution to the general problem of opportunistic behavior is some form of economically enforceable long-term contract. Clearly a short-term (for example, one transaction, non-repeat sale) contract will not solve the problem. The relevant question then becomes when will vertical integration be observed as a solution and when will the use of the market-contracting process occur. Some economists and lawyers have defined this extremely difficult question away by calling a long-term contract a form of vertical integration.[10] Although there is clearly a continuum here, we will attempt not to blur the distinction between a long-term rental agreement and ownership. We assume the opportunistic behavior we are concentrating on can occur only with the former.[11]

For example, if opportunism occurs by the owner-lessor of an asset failing to maintain it properly for the user-lessee and hence unexpectedly increasing the effective rental price, legal remedies (proving contract violation) may be very costly. On the other hand, if the user owned the asset, then the employee who failed to maintain the asset properly could merely be fired.[12] If the employee

[10] See, for example, Friedrich Kessler and Richard H. Stern (1959).

[11] It is commonly held that users of assets that can be damaged by careless use and for which the damage is not easy to detect immediately are more likely to own rather than rent the assets. However, these efficient maintenance considerations apply to short-term contracts and are irrelevant if the length of the long-term rental contract coincides with the economic life of the asset. Abstracting from tax considerations, the long-term contract remains less than completely equivalent to vertical integration only because of the possibility of postcontractual opportunistic reneging. These opportunistic possibilities, however, may also exist within the firm; see note 4 *supra*.

[12] We are abstracting from any considerations of a firm's detection costs of determining proper maintenance. Ease of termination also analytically distinguishes between a franchiser–franchisee arrangement and a vertically integrated arrangement with a profit-sharing manager. If cheating occurs, it is generally cheaper to terminate an employee rather than a franchisee. (The law has been changing recently to make it more difficult to terminate either type of laborer.) But the more limited job-tenure rights of an employee compared to a franchisee reduce his incentive to invest in building up future business, and the firm must trade off the benefits and costs of the alternative arrangements. A profit-sharing manager with an explicit long-term employment contract would essentially be identical to a franchisee.

could still effectively cheat the owner-user of the asset because of his specific ability to maintain the asset, then the problem is that vertical integration of a relevant asset, the employee's human capital, has not occurred. For the moment, however, we will concentrate solely on the question of long-term rental versus ownership of durable physical assets.[13]

Long-term contracts used as alternatives to vertical integration can be assumed to take two forms: (1) an explicitly stated contractual guarantee legally enforced by the government or some other outside institution or (2) an implicit contractual guarantee enforced by the market mechanism of withdrawing future business if opportunistic behavior occurs. Explicit long-term contracts can, in principle, solve opportunistic problems, but, as suggested already, they are often very costly solutions. They entail costs of specifying possible contingencies and the policing and litigation costs of detecting violations and enforcing the contract in the courts.[14] Contractual provisions specifying compulsory arbitration or more directly imposing costs on the opportunistic party (for example, via bonding) are alternatives often employed to economize on litigation costs and to create flexibility without specifying every possible contingency and quality dimension of the transaction.

Since every contingency cannot be cheaply specified in a contract or even known and because legal redress is expensive, transactors will generally also rely on an implicit type of long-term contract that employs a market rather than legal enforcement mechanism, namely, the imposition of a capital loss by the withdrawal of expected future business. This goodwill market-enforcement mechanism undoubtedly is a major element of the contractual alternative to vertical integration. Macaulay provides evidence that relatively informal, legally unenforceable contractual practices predominate in business relations and that reliance on explicit legal sanctions is extremely rare.[15] Instead, business firms are said to generally rely on effective extralegal market sanctions, such as the depreciation of an opportunistic firm's general goodwill because of the anticipated loss of future business, as a means of preventing nonfulfillment of contracts.

One way in which this market mechanism of contract enforcement may operate is by offering to the potential cheater a future "premium," more precisely, a

---

[13] The problems involved with renting specific human capital are discussed below.

[14] The recent Westinghouse case dealing with failure to fulfill uranium-supply contracts on grounds of "commercial impossibility" vividly illustrates these enforcement costs. Nearly three years after outright cancellation by Westinghouse of their contractual commitment, the lawsuits have not been adjudicated and those firms that have settled with Westinghouse have accepted substantially less than the original contracts would have entitled them to. A recent article by Paul L. Joskow (1977) analyzes the Westinghouse decision to renege on the contract as anticipated risk sharing and therefore, using our definition, would not be opportunistic behavior. However, the publicity surrounding this case and the judicial progress to date are likely to make explicit long-term contracts a less feasible alternative to vertical integration in the situations we are analyzing.

[15] Stewart Macaulay (1963).

price sufficiently greater than average variable (that is, avoidable) cost to assure a quasi-rent stream that will exceed the potential gain from cheating.[16] The present-discounted value of this future premium stream must be greater than any increase in wealth that could be obtained by the potential cheater if he, in fact, cheated and were terminated. The offer of such a long-term relationship with the potential cheater will eliminate systematic opportunistic behavior.[17]

The larger the potential one-time "theft" by cheating (the longer and more costly to detect a violation, enforce the contract, switch suppliers, and so forth) and the shorter the expected continuing business relationship, the higher this premium will be in a nondeceiving equilibrium. This may therefore partially explain both the reliance by firms on long-term implicit contracts with particular suppliers and the existence of reciprocity agreements among firms. The premium can be paid in seemingly unrelated profitable reciprocal business. The threat of termination of this relationship mutually suppresses opportunistic behavior.[18]

---

[16] The following discussion of the market enforcement mechanism is based upon the analysis of competitive equilibrium under costly quality information developed in Benjamin Klein and Keith Leffler (1979), which formally extends and more completely applies the analysis in Benjamin Klein (1974). It is similar to the analysis presented in Gary S. Becker and George J. Stigler (1974), of insuring against malfeasance by an employer. This market-enforcement mechanism is used in Benjamin Klein and Andrew McLaughlin (1978) (unpublished manuscript), to explain franchising arrangements and particular contractual provisions such as resale price maintenance, exclusive territories, initial specific investments, and termination clauses.

[17] Formally, this arrangement to guarantee nonopportunistic behavior unravels if there is a last period in the relationship. No matter how high the premium, cheating would occur at the start of the last period. If transactors are aware of this, no transaction relying on trust (that is, the expectation of another subsequent trial) will be made in the penultimate period, because it becomes the last period, and so on. If some large lump-sum, final-period payment such as a pension as part of the market-enforcement scheme, as outlined by Gary S. Becker and George J. Stigler (1974), this last-period problem is obvious. One solution to this unrecognized last-period problem is the acceptance of some continuing third party (for example, escrow agents or government enforcers) to prevent reneging on the implicit contracts against reneging we are outlining. Alternatively, the potential loss of value of indefinitely long-lived salable brand-name assets can serve as deterrents to cheating even where the contract between two parties has a last period. If one party's reputation for nonopportunistic dealings can be sold and used in later transactions in an infinite-time-horizon economy, the firm that cheats in the "last" period to any one buyer from the firm experiences a capital loss. This may partially explain the existence of conglomerates and their use of identifying (not product-descriptive) brand names.

[18] Although it may not always be in one's narrow self-interest to punish the other party in such a reciprocal relationship since termination may impose a cost on both, it may be rational for one to adopt convincingly such a reaction function to optimally prevent cheating. R. L. Trivers (1971) discusses similar mechanisms such as "moralistic aggression" which he claims have been genetically selected to protect reciprocating altruists against cheaters. Similarly, throughout the discussion we implicitly assume that cheating individuals can only cheat once and thereafter earn the "competitive" rate of return. They may, however, be forced to earn less than the competitive wage if they are caught cheating, that is, take an extra capital loss (collusively, but rationally) imposed by other members of the group. This may explain why individuals may prefer to deal in business relations with their own group (for example, members of the same church or the same country club) where effective social sanctions can be imposed against opportunistic behavior. Reliance on such

The premium stream can be usefully thought of as insurance payments made by the firm to prevent cheating.[19] As long as both parties to the transaction make the same estimate of the potential short-run gain from cheating, the quantity of this assurance that will be demanded and supplied will be such that no opportunistic behavior will be expected to occur.[20] If postcontractual reneging is anticipated to occur, either the correct premium will be paid to optimally prevent it or, if the premium necessary to eliminate reneging is too costly, the particular transaction will not be made.

We are not implicitly assuming here that contracts are enforced costlessly and cannot be broken, but rather that given our information-cost assumptions, parties to a contract know exactly when and how much a contract will be broken. An unanticipated broken contract, that is, opportunistic behavior, is therefore not possible in this particular equilibrium. In the context of this model, expected wealth maximization will yield some opportunistic behavior only if we introduce a stochastic element. This will alter the informational equilibrium state such that the potential cheater's estimate of the short-run gain from opportunistic behavior may be at times greater than the other firm's estimate. Hence, less than an optimal premium will be paid and opportunistic behavior will occur.

The firms collecting the premium payments necessary to assure fulfillment of contractual agreements in a costly information world may appear to be earning equilibrium "profits" although they are in a competitive market. That is, there may be many, possibly identical, firms available to supply the services of nonopportunistic performance of contractual obligations yet the premium will not be competed away if transactors cannot costlessly guarantee contractual performance. The assurance services, by definition, will not be supplied unless the premium is paid and the mere payment of this premium produces the required services.

Any profits are competed away in equilibrium by competitive expenditures on fixed (sunk) assets, such as initial specific investments (for example, a sign) with low or zero salvage value if the firm cheats, necessary to enter and obtain this preferred position of collecting the premium stream.[21] These fixed (sunk)

reciprocal business relationships and group enforcement mechanisms is more likely where governmental enforcement of contracts is weaker. Nathaniel H. Leff (1978), for example, documents the importance of such groups in less-developed countries. Industries supplying illegal products and services would likely be another example.

[19] It is, of course, an insurance scheme that not only pools risks but also alters them.

[20] As opposed to the analysis of Michael R. Darby and Edi Karni (1973), the equilibrium quantity of opportunistic behavior or "fraud" will be zero under our assumptions of symmetrical information.

[21] A more complete analysis of market equilibrium by the use of specific capital in guaranteeing contract enforcement is developed in Benjamin Klein and Keith Leffler (1979).

costs of supplying credibility of future performance are repaid or covered by future sales on which a premium is earned. In equilibrium, the premium stream is then merely a normal rate of return on the "reputation," or "brand-name" capital created by the firm by these initial expenditures. This brand-name capital, the value of which is highly specific to contract fulfillment by the firm, is analytically equivalent to a forfeitable collateral bond put up by the firm which is anticipated to face an opportunity to take advantage of appropriable quasi rents in specialized assets.

While these initial specific investments or collateral bonds are sometimes made as part of the normal (minimum-cost) production process and therefore at small additional cost, transaction costs and risk considerations do make them costly. We can generally say that the larger the appropriable specialized quasi rents (and therefore the larger the potential short-run gain from opportunistic behavior) and the larger the premium payments necessary to prevent contractual reneging, the more costly this implicit contractual solution will be. We can also expect the explicit contract costs to be positively related to the level of appropriable quasi rents since it will pay to use more resources (including legal services) to specify precisely more contingencies when potential opportunities for lucrative contractual reneging exist.

Although implicit and explicit contracting and policing costs are positively related to the extent of appropriable specialized quasi rents, it is reasonable to assume, on the other hand, that any internal coordination or other ownership costs are not systematically related to the extent of the appropriable specialized quasi rent of the physical asset owned. Hence we can reasonably expect the following general empirical regularity to be true: the lower the appropriable specialized quasi rents, the more likely that transactors will rely on a contractual relationship rather than common ownership. And conversely, integration by common or joint ownership is more likely, the higher the appropriable specialized quasi rents of the assets involved.

III. Example of appropriable specialized quasi rent

This section presents examples of quasi rents where the potential for their appropriation serves as an important determinant of economic organization. A series of varied illustrations, some quite obvious and others rather subtle, will make the analysis more transparent and provide suggestive evidence for the relevance of the protection of appropriable quasi rents as an incentive to vertically integrate. It also suggests the direction of more systematic empirical work that obviously is required to assess the significance of this factor relative to other factors in particular cases. Where this force towards integration (that is, the economizing on contracting costs necessary to assure nonopportunistic behavior in the presence of appropriable quasi rents) does not appear to dominate, important insights regarding the determinants of particular contracting costs and contract provisions are thereby provided.[22]

. . .

B. Petroleum industry

Appropriable quasi rents exist in specialized assets of oil refineries, pipelines, and oil fields. This leads to common ownership to remove the incentive for individuals to attempt to capture the rents of assets owned by someone else.

Suppose several oil wells are located along a separately owned pipeline that leads to a cluster of independently owned refineries with no alternative crude supply at comparable cost. Once all the assets are in place (the wells drilled and the pipeline and refineries constructed) the oil-producing properties and the refineries are specialized to the pipeline. The portion of their value above the value to the best alternative user is an appropriable specialized quasi rent. The extent of the appropriable quasi rent is limited, in part, by the costs of entry to a potential parallel pipeline developer. Since pipelines between particular oil-producing properties and particular refineries are essentially natural monopolies, the existing pipeline owner may have a significant degree of market power.

These specialized producing and refining assets are therefore "hostage" to the pipeline owner. At the "gathering end" of the pipeline, the monopsonist pipeline could and would purchase all its oil at the same well-head price regardless of the distance of the well from the refinery. This price could be as low as the marginal cost of getting oil out of the ground (or its reservation value for future use, if higher) and might not generate a return to the oil-well owner sufficient to recoup the initial investment of exploration and drilling. At the delivery-to-refinery end of the pipeline, the pipeline owner would be able to appropriate the "specialized-to-the-pipeline quasi rents" of the refineries. The pipeline owner could simply raise the price of crude oil at least to the price of alternative sources of supply to each refinery that are specialized to the pipeline. Given the prospects of such action, if the pipeline owner were an independent monopsonist facing the oil explorers and a monopolist to the refinery owners, everyone (explorers and refiners) would know in advance their vulnerability to rent extraction. Therefore

---

[22] It is important to recognize that not only will contracting and enforcement costs of constraining opportunistic behavior determine the form of the final economic arrangement adopted by the transacting parties, but they will also influence the firm's production function. That is, the level of specific investment and therefore the size of the potentially appropriable quasi rent is not an independent "technological" datum in each of these following cases, but is economically determined in part by transaction costs.

oil-field owners and refinery owners would, through shared ownership in the pipeline, remove the possibility of subsequent rent extraction.

The problem would not be completely solved if just the oil field or the refineries (but not both) were commonly owned with the pipeline, since the local monopoly (or monopsony) would persist vis-à-vis the other. Prospectively, one would expect the common ownership to extend to all three stages. If several refineries (or oil fields) were to be served by one pipeline, all the refinery (or oil field) owners would want to jointly own the pipeline. A common practice is a jointly owned company which "owns" the pipeline with the shares by producers and refiners in the pipeline company corresponding roughly to the respective shares of oil to be transported.[23]

Consider other inputs in the production process. The oil tanker, for example, is specialized to crude oil transportation. But since it is essentially equivalued by many alternative users, the appropriable quasi rent is near zero. So we would expect oil tankers not to be extensively owned by refiners or producers. Similarly, the assets used for refinery construction are not specialized to any single refiner or refinery and they should also not be commonly owned with the refinery.

. . .

C. Specific human capital

The previous analysis has dealt with examples of physical capital. When specific human capital is involved, the opportunism problem is often more complex and, because of laws prohibiting slavery, the solution is generally some form of explicit or implicit contract rather than vertical integration.

For example, consider the following concrete illustration from the agricultural industry. Suppose someone owns a peach orchard. The ripened peaches, ready for harvest, have a market value of about $400,000. So far costs of $300,000 have been paid and the remaining harvesting and shipping costs will

---

[23] Jane Atwood and Paul Kobrin (1977) find an extremely high positive correlation between a firm's crude production and its share of ownership in the pipeline. On the other hand, natural gas pipelines, although apparently economically similar in terms of potentially appropriable quasi rents, do not appear to be vertically integrated. Rather than joint-ownership arrangements with the gas producers, these pipelines are often independently owned. The difference may be due to more effective FPC (and now the Federal Energy Regulatory Commission) regulation (of the wellhead and citygate gas prices and the implied pipeline tariff) compared to the direct Interstate Commerce Commission regulation of oil pipelines as common carriers. Regulation of oil pipeline tariffs could, for example, be easily evaded by opportunistic decreases in the wellhead prices paid for oil. More complete government regulation of gas prices may effectively prevent opportunistic behavior by the natural gas pipeline owners, and thereby serve as an alternative to vertical integration (see Victor P. Goldberg, 1976). Edmund Kitch informs us that the evidence does indicate a much greater degree of vertical integration of natural gas pipelines in the period before FPC regulation.

be $50,000 ($5,000 transport and $45,000 labor), leaving $50,000 as the competitive return on the owner's capital. Assume the laborers become a union (one party to whom the crop is now specialized) and refuse to pick unless paid $390,000. That would leave $5,000 for transport and only $5,000 for the owner of the peach orchard, instead of the $350,000 necessary to cover incurred costs and the cost of capital. If the union had power to exclude other pickers, it could extract all the appropriable quasi rent of that year's crop specialized to that particular labor union's service. The union would be extracting not just the usual monopoly rents involved in raising wages, but also the short-run appropriable quasi rents of the farmer's specific assets represented by the ripened peaches. This gain to the union is a one-period return because obviously the farmer will not make any additional specific investments in the future if he knows it will be appropriated by the union.

To reduce this risk of appropriation, the farmer may have a large clan family (or neighbors of similar farms) do his picking. Because of diseconomies of scale, however, this "cooperative" solution is not generally the lowest-cost arrangement and some reliance on market contracting will be necessary. The individual farmer, for example, may want the labor union to put up a forfeitable bond to compensate him in the event the union under threat of strike asks for more wages at harvest time. Alternatively, but equivalently, the collateral put up by the union could be the value of the brand-name capital of the union, a value which will depreciate if its leaders engage in opportunistic behavior. The farmer would then make a continuing brand-name payment to the union (similar to the premium payment noted above) for this collateral.[24]

The market value of the union's reputation for reliability of contract observance is the present-discounted value of these brand-name payments which will be greater than any short-run opportunistic gain to the union leaders that could be obtained by threats at harvest time. These payments which increase the cost to the union of opportunistic behavior would be substantial for a perishable product with a large appropriable quasi rent. It is therefore obvious why producers of highly perishable crops are so antagonistic to unionization of field labor. They would be especially hostile to unions without established reputations regarding fulfillment of contract and with politically motivated (and possibly myopic) leaders.[25]

---

[24] If the premium is a payment of the union per unit time, then the arrangement is identical to a collateral-bond arrangement where the union collects the interest on the bond as long as no opportunistic behavior occurs. Because of possible legal difficulties of enforcing such an arrangement, however, the premium may be reflected in the price (that is, a higher wage).

[25] It is interesting to note in this context that California grape farmers preferred the established Teamsters Union to the new, untried, and apparently more politically motivated field-workers union organized by Cesar Chavez.

Since unions are not "owned," union leaders will not have the proper incentive to maximize the union's value; they will tend more to maximize returns during their tenure. If, however, union

Vertical integration, appropriable rents, competitive contracting process

In addition to implicit (brand-name) contracts, opportunistic union behavior may be prevented by use of explicit contracts, often with some outside arbitration as an element of the contract-enforcement mechanism. Although it is difficult for an outsider to distinguish between opportunistic behavior and good-faith modifications of contract, impartial arbitration procedures may reduce the necessity of explicitly specifying possible contingencies and thereby reduce the rigidity of the explicit long-term contract.[26]

When the problem is reversed and quasi rents of firm-specific human capital of employees may be opportunistically appropriated by the firm, implicit and explicit long-term contracts are also used to prevent such behavior. Because of economies of scale in monitoring and enforcing such contracts, unions may arise as a contract cost-reducing institution for employees with investments in specific human capital.[27]

In addition to narrow contract-monitoring economies of scale, a union creates a continuing long-term employment relationship that eliminates the last-period (or transient employee) contract-enforcement problem and also creates bargaining power (a credible strike threat) to more cheaply punish a firm that violates the contract. Even when the specific human-capital investment is made by the firm, a union of employees may similarly reduce the contract-enforcement costs of preventing individual-worker opportunism. There are likely to be economies of scale in supply credibility of contract fulfillment, including the long-term continuing relationship aspect of a union. The existence of a union not only makes it more costly for a firm to cheat an individual worker in his last period but also makes it more costly for an individual worker in his last period to

leadership (ownership) were salable, the leaders would have the optimal incentive to invest in and conserve the union's brand-name capital. They therefore would not engage in opportunistic actions that may increase current revenue while decreasing the market value of the union. "Idealistic" union leaders that do not behave as if they own the union may, in fact, produce less wealth-maximizing action than would "corrupt" leaders, who act as if they personally own the union. Alternatively, the current members of the union may have control, not in the sense of having directly salable shares, but in the sense that the valuable union asset can be transferred to their children or relatives. If government regulations force union members to give away these rights to future rents (for example, by forcing them to admit minorities and eliminate nepotism), we can expect them to intentionally depreciate or not create the reputation capital of the union by opportunistic strikes. See Benjamin Klein (1974) where similar problems with regard to the supply of money by nonprivately owned, nonwealth-maximizing firms are discussed.

[26] An interesting legal case in this area is *Publishers' Ass'n v. Newspaper & Mail Del. Union*, 114 N.Y.S. 2d, 401 (1952). The union authorized and sanctioned a strike against the *New York Daily News* although the collective bargaining agreement had "no-strike" and arbitration clauses. *The Daily News* took the union to arbitration, and the arbitrator found actual damages of $2,000 and punitive damages of $5,000 if the union again violated the contract. (The court, however, overturned the punitive damages for technical reasons.) See David E. Feller (1973) for a discussion of the flexibility obtained with arbitration provisions in labor contracts.

[27] We should explicitly note that we are not considering unions as cartelizing devices, the usually analyzed motivation for their existence. This force is obviously present in many cases (for example, interstate trucking) but is distinct from our analysis.

cheat the firm, because the union has the incentive (for example, withholding pension rights) to prevent such an externality on the continuing workers. Therefore unions are more likely to exist when the opportunistic cheating problem is greater, namely, when there is more specific human capital present.[28]

. . .

D. Leasing inputs and ownership of the firm

Examination of leasing companies should reveal that leases are less common (or too expensive) for assets with specialized quasi rents that could be appropriated by the lessee or lessor. Leasing does not occur in the obvious cases of elevators or the glass of windows in an office building where postinvestment bilaterally appropriable quasi rents are enormous, while the furniture in the building is often rented. In banks, the safe is owned by the bank, but computers (though not the memory discs) are sometimes rented.[29] Though this may seem like resorting to trivialities, the fact that such leasing arrangements are taken for granted merely corroborates the prior analysis.

The standard example of leasing arrangements occurs with transportation capital, such as the planes, trucks, or cars used by a firm. This capital is generally easily movable and not very specific. But leasing arrangements are far from universal because some of this capital can be quite specific and quasi rents appropriated. For example, early American steam locomotives were specialized to operating conditions such as high speed, hill climbing, short hauls, heavy loads, sharp corners, as well as types of coal for fuel. Slight differences in engines created significant differences in operating costs. High specialization made it desirable for the rail companies to own locomotives (as well as the land on which water was available for steam). The advent of the more versatile, less specialized, diesel locomotive enabled more leasing and equipment trust financing. Similarly, Swift, the meat packer and innovator of the refrigerator car for transporting slaughtered beef, owned the specialized refrigerator cars it used.[30]

[28] When allowing for this "reverse" effect of employee-specific capital, and therefore higher wages, on the formation of unions, the usual positive effect of unions on wages appears to vanish. See, for example, O. Ashenfelter and G. Johnson (1972) and Peter Schmidt and Robert P. Strauss (1976).

[29] In addition to computers being less specific and hence possessing smaller appropriable quasi rents than elevators, firms (for example, IBM) that supply computers generally possess extremely valuable brand names per unit of current sales due to a large anticipated growth in demand. Since there are some quasi rents associated with the use of a computer by a bank that could possibly be appropriated by threat of immediate removal, we would expect that if rental contracts existed, they would be more likely be with highly credible firms with high anticipated demand growth.

[30] The great bulk of all refrigerator cars are not owned by the railroads, but rather by shipper-users such as packers and dairy companies. See Robert S. Henry (1942).

Vertical integration, appropriable rents, competitive contracting process

On the other hand, some capital may be quite specific to other assets in a firm's productive process and yet leased rather than owned. These cases provide useful insights into the nature of the contracting costs underlying our analysis. For example, consider the fact that agricultural land, a highly specific asset, is not always owned but often is rented. Land rented for farming purposes is typically for annual crops, like vegetables, sugar beets, cotton, or wheat, while land used for tree crops, like nuts, dates, oranges, peaches, apricots, or grape vines – assets that are highly specialized to the land – is usually owned by the party who plants the trees or vines.[31] However, long-term rental arrangements even for these "specialized asset" crops are not entirely unknown.

It is instructive to recognize why land-rental contracts, rather than vertical integration, can often be used without leading to opportunistic behavior. The primary reason is because it is rather cheap to specify and monitor the relevant contract terms (the quality of the good being purchased) and to enforce this particular rental contract. In addition, the landowner generally cannot impose a cost on the farmer by pulling the asset out or reducing the quality of the asset during the litigation process. Note the contrast with labor rental where it is essentially impossible to effectively specify and enforce quality elements (for example, all working conditions and the effort expended by workers) and where the possibility of withdrawal by strike or lockout is real and costly. Therefore, we do observe firms making highly specific investments in, for example, trees or buildings on land they do not own but only rent long term.[32] This is because credible postcontractual opportunistic threats by the landowner are not possible. However, if the landowner can vary the quality of the land, for example, by controlling the irrigation system to the crops or the electricity supply to a building, then a significant possibility of postinvestment opportunistic behavior exists, and we would therefore expect vertical integration.[33]

[31] While 25% of vegetable and melon farms in California in 1974 were fully owned by the farm operator, 82% of fruit and nut tree farms were fully owned, a significantly different ownership proportion at the 99% confidence interval. Similarly, the ownership proportions of cash grain and cotton farms were 40% and 39%, respectively, both also significantly different at the 99% confidence interval from the proportions of fruit and nut tree farm ownership. See 1 U.S. Dep't of Commerce, Bureau of the Census, 1974 Census of Agriculture, State and County Data, pt. 5, at tab. 28. Summary by Tenure of Farm Operator and Type of Organization, *id.*, 1974, California, pp. 1–29 to 1–30.

[32] Rental terms may be related to sales of the firm using the land in order to share the risk of real-value changes and to reduce the risk of nominal land-value changes involved with a long-term contract.

[33] Coase's example of a monopolist selling more of a durable good, say land, after initially selling a monopoly quantity at the monopoly price is analytically identical to the problem of postcontractual opportunistic behavior. Existing contractual relationships indicate, however, that the land case may be relatively easy to solve because it may not be expensive to make a credible contract regarding the remaining land. But, one of Coase's indicated solutions, the short-term rental rather than sale of the land is unlikely because it would discourage specific (to land) investments by the renter (such as building a house, developing a farm, and so forth) for fear of appropriation. See R. H. Coase (1972).

One specific asset that is almost always owned by the firm is its trade-name or brand-name capital and, in particular, the logo it uses to communicate to consumers. If this asset were rented from a leasing company, the problems would be obvious. The firm would be extremely hesitant to make any investments to build up its goodwill, for example, by advertising or by successful performance, because such investments are highly specific to that "name." The quasi rents could be appropriated by the leasing company through increases in the rental fee for the trade name. Not only would the firm not invest in this specific asset, but there would be an incentive for the firm to depreciate a valuable rented brand name. Although these problems seem insurmountable, rental of the capital input of a firm's brand name is not entirely unknown. In fact, franchisors can be thought of as brand-name leasing companies. A franchisee is fundamentally a renter of the brand-name capital (and logo) owned by the franchisor. Because of the specific capital problems noted above, direct controls are placed on franchisee behavior. The rental payment is usually some form of profit-sharing arrangement, and, although the franchisee is legally considered to be an independent firm, the situation is in reality much closer to vertical integration than to the standard contractual relationship of the independent market.

Finally, the analysis throws light on the important question of why the owners of a firm (the residual claimants) are generally also the major capitalists of the firm.[34] As we have seen, owners may rent the more generalized capital but will own the firm's specific capital. This observation has implications for recent discussions of "industrial democracy," which fail to recognize that although employees may own and manage a firm (say, through their union), they will also have to be capitalists and own the specific capital. It will generally be too costly, for example, for the worker-owners to rent a plant because such a specific investment could be rather easily appropriated from its owners after it is constructed. Therefore it is unlikely to be built. A highly detailed contractual arrangement together with very large brand-name premium payments by the laborers would be necessary to assure nonopportunistic behavior. This is generally too expensive an alternative and explains why capitalists are usually the owners of a firm.[35]

[34] We are grateful to Earl Thompson for discerning this implication.

[35] Armen A. Alchian and Harold Demsetz, "Production, Information Costs, and Economic Organization," 62 *Am. Econ. Rev.* 777 (1972), claim that if the owner of the firm also owns the firm's capital, it supplies evidence that he can pay for rented inputs, including labor. This appears to be incorrect since the owner could supply credibility by using some of his assets completely unrelated to the production process, such as treasury bonds, for collateral. Michael C. Jensen and William H. Meckling (unpublished manuscript, Feb. 1977) emphasize the costs of monitoring managerial performance and the maintenance of rented capital, and the problems of efficiently allocating risks in a pure-rental firm. They also note that it is "impossible" for a firm to rent all the productive capital assets because many of them are intangible and therefore "it is impossible to repossess the asset if the firm refused to pay the rental fee" (1977, p. 20). This argument is

E. Social institutions

Much of the previous analysis has dealt with tangible capital. Contractual arrangements involving such assets are often cheaper than complete vertical integration, even when the assets are highly specific (for example, the land-rental case). As the discussion on human capital suggests, however, when the specific assets involved are intangible personal assets, the problems of contract enforcement become severe. In addition, when the number of individuals involved (or the extent of the specific capital) becomes very large, ownership arrangements often become extremely complex.

For example, consider country clubs. Golf country clubs are social, in addition to being golfing, organizations. Sociability of a country club involves substantial activities away from the golf course: dinners, dances, parties, cards, games, and general social activities with friends who are members of the club. However, some golf courses are operated with very few social activities for the set of members and their families. The social clubs (usually called "country clubs") are mutually owned by the members, whereas golf courses with virtually no off-course social activity often are privately owned with members paying daily golf fees without owning the golf course.

Mutual ownership is characteristic of the social country club because the specialized quasi rent of friendship is collected by each member whose friendship is specialized to the other members. The members' behavior toward one another constitutes an investment in forming valuable friendships, a congenial milieu, and rapport among the members. Each member has invested in creating that congenial milieu and atmosphere specialized to the other members. And its value could be stolen or destroyed by opportunistic behavior of a party authorized to admit new members.

To see how, suppose the club were owned by someone other than the members. Once the membership value is created by the interpersonal activities of the members, the owner of the club could then start to raise the fees for continuing members. Assuming some costs of the members moving away en masse and forming a new club, the owner could expropriate by higher fees some of the specialized quasi-rent value of the sociability created by the members' specialization to each other in their own group. Alternatively, the owner could threaten to break the implicit contract and destroy some of the sociability capital by selling admission to "undesirable" people who want to consort with the existing members.

similar to our analysis of opportunistic behavior. However, rather than asserting that such rentals are impossible, we would merely recognize the extremely high contracting costs generally present in such situations. More importantly, we claim that such an argument also extends to the rental of tangible specific capital.

Similarly, if the social country club were owned by the members as a corporation with each member owning a share of stock salable without prior approval of existing members (as is the case for the business corporation), a single member could, by threatening to sell to an "undesirable" potential member, extract some value of congeniality from the current members, as a payment for not selling.[36]

An extreme case of this general problem is a marriage. If each mate had a transferable share salable to a third party, there would be far fewer marriages with highly specific investments in affection and children. If a relationship is not one of specialized interest (specialized to a particular other party) or if it required no investment by any member, then the marriage relationship would be more like a corporation. As it is one of highly specific investments, marriages have historically been mutually owned entities, with permission of both parties generally required for alteration of membership. Government arbitration of this relationship to prevent postinvestment opportunistic behavior by either party can contribute toward lower bargaining costs and investments of resources (recoverable dowries) by both parties to improve their respective postinvestment bargaining positions, and, most importantly, create confidence that opportunistic behavior will not be successful. The legislative movement to "no-fault" divorce suggests that modern marriages may have less specific assets than formerly.[37]

. . .

IV. Concluding comment

We should emphasize in conclusion that most business relationships are neither likely to be as simple as the standard textbook polar cases of vertical integration or market contract nor as easily explained as some of the above examples. When particular examples are examined in detail, business relationships are

---

[36] The "free-rider" problems of bribing an opportunistic member to prevent sale to an "undesirable" member are obvious. This analysis could be applied to social clubs such as Elks, Masonic Order, and so forth.

[37] Similarly, people whose work is highly specialized to each other will be partners (common ownership). For example, attorneys that have become highly specialized to their coattorneys will become partners, whereas new associates will at first be employees. A small team of performers (Laurel and Hardy, Sonny and Cher) who were highly specialized to each other would be "partners" (co-owners) rather than employee and employer. While it is still difficult to enforce such contracts and prevent postcontractual opportunistic behavior by either party, joint ownership creates an incentive for performance and specific investment not present in an easily terminable employer–employee contract that must rely solely on the personal brand-name reputation of contracting parties. Trust, including the reputation of certifying institutions such as theatrical agents, law schools, and so on, and the presence of social sanctions against opportunistic partners remain important.

often structured in highly complex ways not represented by either a simple rental contract or by simple vertical integration. . . .

. . .

. . . Once we attempt to add empirical detail to Coase's fundamental insight that a systematic study of transaction costs is necessary to explain particular forms of economic organization, we find that his primary distinction between transactions made within a firm and transactions made in the marketplace may often be too simplistic. Many long-term contractual relationships (such as franchising) blur the line between the market and the firm. It may be more useful to merely examine the economic rationale for different types of particular contractual relationships in particular situations and consider the firm as a particular kind or set of interrelated contracts.[38] Firms are therefore, by definition, formed and revised in markets and the conventional sharp distinction between markets and firms may have little general analytical importance. The pertinent economic question we are faced with is, "what kinds of contracts are used for what kinds of activities, and why?"

[38] If we think of firms as collections of interrelated contracts rather than the collection of goods operative in the contracts, the question of who "owns" the firm (the set of contacts) appears somewhat nonsensical. It may be useful to think solely of a set of claimants to various portions of the value consequences of the contractual coalition, with no "owner" of the firm.

CHAPTER 9

The governance of contractual relations

OLIVER WILLIAMSON

Oliver Williamson was born in Superior, Wisconsin, in 1932. He received a Ph.D. in economics at Carnegie-Mellon University in 1963. When this chapter was published, he was Gordon B. Tweedy Professor of Economics of Law and Organization at Yale University. Since 1988, he has taught at the University of California, Berkeley, where he is currently Edgar F. Kaiser Professor, Emeritus, of Business Administration, Economics, and Law.

. . .

Contractual variety is the source of numerous puzzles with which the study of the economic institutions of capitalism is appropriately concerned. Transaction cost economics maintains that such variety is mainly explained by underlying differences in the attributes of transactions. Efficiency purposes are served by matching governance structures to the attributes of transactions in a discriminating way.

. . .

1. Contracting traditions

There is widespread agreement that the discrete transaction paradigm – "sharp in by clear agreement; sharp out by clear performance" (Macneil, 1974, p. 738) – has served both law and economics well. But there is also increasing awareness that many contractual relations are not of this well-defined kind. A deeper understanding of the nature of contract has emerged as the legal-rule emphasis associated with the study of discrete contracting has given way to a more general concern with the contractual purposes to be served. Macneil's distinctions among classical, neoclassical, and relational law are instructive.

1.1 Classical contract law

As Macneil observes, any system of contract law has the purpose of facilitating exchange. What is distinctive about classical contract law is that it attempts to do so by enhancing discreteness and intensifying "presentiation" (1978, p. 862), where presentiation has reference to efforts to "make or render present in place or time; to cause to be perceived or realized at present" (1978, p. 863, n. 25). The economic counterpart to complete presentiation is contingent claims contracting, which entails comprehensive contracting whereby all relevant future contingencies pertaining to the supply of a good or service are described and discounted with respect to both likelihood and futurity.

Classical contract law endeavors to implement discreteness and presentiation in several ways. For one thing, the identity of the parties to a transaction is treated as irrelevant. In that respect it corresponds exactly with the "ideal" market transaction in economics. Second, the nature of the agreement is carefully delimited, and the more formal features govern when formal (for example, written) and informal (for example, oral) terms are contested. Third, remedies are narrowly prescribed so that, "should the initial presentiation fail to materialize because of nonperformance, the consequences are relatively predictable from the beginning and are not open-ended" (Macneil, 1978, p. 864). Additionally, third-party participation is discouraged (p. 864). The emphasis is thus on legal rules, formal documents, and self-liquidating transactions.

1.2 Neoclassical contract law

Not every transaction fits comfortably into the classical contracting scheme. In particular, for long-term contracts executed under conditions of uncertainty complete presentiation is apt to be prohibitively costly if not impossible. Problems of several kinds arise. First, not all future contingencies for which adaptations are required can be anticipated at the outset. Second, the appropriate adaptations will not be evident for many contingencies until the circumstances materialize. Third, except as changes in states of the world are unambiguous, hard contracting between autonomous parties may well give rise to veridical disputes when state-contingent claims are made. In a world where (at least some) parties are inclined to be opportunistic, whose representations are to be believed?

Faced with the prospective breakdown of classical contracting in such circumstances, three alternatives are available. One would be to forgo such transactions altogether. A second would be to remove those transactions from the market and organize them internally instead. Adaptive, sequential decision making would then be implemented under unified ownership and with the assistance of hierarchical incentive and control systems. Third, a different

117

contracting relation that preserves trading but provides for additional governance structure might be devised. This last brings us to what Macneil refers to as neoclassical contracting.

As Macneil observes, "Two common characteristics of long-term contracts are the existence of gaps in their planning and the presence of a range of processes and techniques used by contract planners to create flexibility in lieu of either leaving gaps or trying to plan rigidly" (1978, p. 865). Third-party assistance in resolving disputes and evaluating performance often has advantages over litigation in serving these functions of flexibility and gap filling. . . .

A recognition that the world is complex, that agreements are incomplete, and that some contracts will never be reached unless both parties have confidence in the settlement machinery thus characterizes neoclassical contract law. . . .

. . .

1.3 Relational contracting

The pressures to sustain ongoing relations "have led to the spinoff of many subject areas from the classical, and later the neoclassical, contract law system, e.g., much of corporate law and collective bargaining" (Macneil, 1978, p. 885). Progressively increasing the "duration and complexity" of contracts has thus resulted in the displacement of even neoclassical adjustment processes by adjustment processes of a more thoroughly transaction-specific, ongoing-administrative kind. The fiction of discreteness is fully displaced as the relation takes on the properties of a "minisociety with a vast array of norms beyond those centered on the exchange and its immediate processes" (Macneil, 1978, p. 901). By contrast with the neoclassical system, where the reference point for effecting adaptations remains the original agreement, the reference point under a truly relational approach is the "entire relation as it has developed [through] time. This may or may not include an 'original agreement'; and if it does, may or may not result in great deference being given it" (Macneil, 1978, p. 890).

The spinoff to which Macneil refers notwithstanding, commercial law, labor law, and corporate law all possess striking commonalities.

2. Efficient governance

As discussed above, the principal dimensions for describing transactions are asset specificity, uncertainty, and frequency. It will facilitate the argument in this section to assume that uncertainty is present in sufficient degree to pose an adaptive, sequential decision requirement, and to focus on asset specificity and frequency. Three frequency classes – one-time, occasional, and recurrent – and three asset specificity classes – nonspecific, mixed, and highly specific – will be considered. To simplify the argument further, the following assumptions are made: (1) Suppliers and buyers intend to be in business on a continuing basis; thus the special hazards posed by fly-by-night firms can be disregarded. (2) Potential suppliers for any given requirement are numerous – which is to say that *ex ante* monopoly in ownership of specialized resources is assumed away. (3) The frequency dimension refers strictly to buyer activity in the market. (4) The investment dimension refers to the characteristics of investments made by suppliers.

Although discrete transactions are intriguing – for example, purchasing local spirits from a shopkeeper in a remote area of a foreign country one expects never again to visit or refer his friends – few transactions have such a totally isolated character. For those that do not, the difference between one-time and occasional transactions is not apparent. Accordingly, only occasional and recurrent frequency distinctions will be maintained. The two-by-three matrix shown in Figure 9.1 thus describes the six types of transactions to which governance structures must be matched. Illustrative transactions appear in the cells.

The question now is how Macneil's contracting classifications correspond to the description of transactions in Figure 9.1. Several propositions are suggested immediately: (1) Highly standardized transactions are not apt to require specialized governance structure. (2) Only recurrent transactions will support a highly specialized governance structure. (3) Although occasional transactions of a nonstandardized kind will not support a transaction-specific governance structure, they require special attention nonetheless. In terms of

		Investment Characteristics		
		Nonspecific	Mixed	Idiosyncratic
Frequency	Occasional	Purchasing standard equipment	Purchasing customized equipment	Constructing a plant
	Recurrent	Purchasing standard material	Purchasing customized material	Site-specific transfer of intermediate product across successive stages

Figure 9.1. Illustrative Transactions

119

Macneil's three-way classification of contract, classical contracting presumably applies to all standardized transactions (whatever the frequency), relational contracting develops for transactions of a recurring and nonstandardized kind, and neoclassical contracting is needed for occasional nonstandardized transactions.

Specifically, classical contracting is approximated by what is described below as market governance, neoclassical contracting involves trilateral governance, and the relational contracts that Macneil describes are organized in bilateral or unified governance structures. Consider these seriatim.

2.1 Market governance

Market governance is the main governance structure for nonspecific transactions of both occasional and recurrent contracting. Markets are especially efficacious when recurrent transactions are contemplated, since both parties need only consult their own experience in deciding to continue a trading relationship or, at little transitional expense, turn elsewhere. Being standardized, alternative purchase and supply arrangements are presumably easy to work out.

Nonspecific but occasional transactions are ones for which buyers (and sellers) are less able to rely on direct experience to safeguard transactions against opportunism. Often, however, rating services or the experience of other buyers of the same good can be consulted. Given that the good or service is of a standardized kind, such experience rating, by formal and informal means, will provide incentives for parties to behave responsibly.

To be sure, such transactions take place within and benefit from a legal framework. But such dependence is not great. As S. Todd Lowry puts it, "the traditional economic analysis of exchange in a market setting properly corresponds to the legal concept of *sale* (rather than contract), since sale presumes arrangements in a market context and requires legal support primarily in enforcing transfers of title" (1976, p. 12). He would thus reserve the concept of contract for exchanges where, in the absence of standardized market alternatives, the parties have designed "patterns of future relations on which they could rely" (1976, p. 13).

The assumptions of the discrete contracting paradigm are rather well satisfied for transactions where markets serve as a main governance mode. Thus the specific identity of the parties is of negligible importance; substantive content is determined by reference to formal terms of the contract; and legal rules apply. Market alternatives are mainly what protect each party against opportunism by his opposite. Litigation is strictly for settling claims; concentrated efforts to sustain the relation are not made, because the relation is not independently valued.

2.2 Trilateral governance

The two types of transactions for which trilateral governance is needed are occasional transactions of the mixed and highly specific kinds. Once the principals to such transactions have entered into a contract, there are strong incentives to see the contract through to completion. Not only have specialized investments been put in place, the opportunity cost of which is much lower in alternative uses, but the transfer of those assets to a successor supplier would pose inordinate difficulties in asset valuation. The interests of the principals in sustaining the relation are especially great for highly idiosyncratic transactions.

Market relief is thus unsatisfactory. Often the setup costs of a transaction-specific governance structure cannot be recovered for occasional transactions. Given the limits of classical contract law for sustaining such transactions, on the one hand, and the prohibitive cost of transaction-specific (bilateral) governance, on the other, an intermediate institutional form is evidently needed.

Neoclassical contract law has many of the sought-after qualities. Thus rather than resorting immediately to court-ordered litigation – with its transaction-rupturing features – third-party *assistance* (arbitration) in resolving disputes and evaluating performance is employed instead. (The use of the architect as a relatively independent expert to determine the content of form construction contracts is an example [Macneil, 1978, p. 566].) Also, the expansion of the specific performance remedy in past decades is consistent with continuity purposes – though Macneil declines to characterize specific performance as the "primary neoclassical contract remedy" (1978, p. 879). The section of the Uniform Commercial Code that permits the "seller aggrieved by a buyer's breach . . . unilaterally to maintain the relation" is yet another example.

2.3 Bilateral governance

The two types of transactions for which specialized governance structure are commonly devised are recurring transactions supported by investments of the mixed and highly specific kinds. The fundamental transformation applies because of the nonstandardized nature of the transactions. Continuity of the trading relation is thus valued. The transactions' recurrent nature potentially permits the cost of specialized governance structures to be recovered.

Two types of transaction-specific governance structures for intermediate product market transactions can be distinguished: bilateral structures, where the autonomy of the parties is maintained, and unified structures, where the transaction is removed from the market and organized within the firm subject to an authority relation (vertical integration). Bilateral structures have only recently received the attention they deserve, and their operation is least well understood. . . .

Highly idiosyncratic transactions are ones where the human and physical assets required for production are extensively specialized, so there are no obvious scale economies to be realized through interfirm trading that the buyer (or seller) is unable to realize himself (through vertical integration). In the case, however, of mixed transactions, the degree of asset specialization is less complete. Accordingly, outside procurement for those components may be favored by scale economy considerations.

As compared with vertical integration, outside procurement also maintains high-powered incentives and limits bureaucratic distortions.... Problems with market procurement arise, however, when adaptability and contractual expense are considered. Whereas internal adaptations can be effected by fiat, outside procurement involves effecting adaptations across a market interface. Unless the need for adaptations has been contemplated from the outset and expressly provided for by the contract, which often is impossible or prohibitively expensive, adaptations across a market interface can be accomplished only by mutual, follow-on agreements. Inasmuch as the interests of the parties will commonly be at variance when adaptation proposals (originated by either party) are made, a dilemma is evidently posed.

On the one hand, both parties have an incentive to sustain the relationship rather than to permit it to unravel, the object being to avoid the sacrifice of valued transaction-specific economies. On the other hand, each party appropriates a separate profit stream and cannot be expected to accede readily to any proposal to adapt the contract. What is needed, evidently, is some way for declaring admissible dimensions for adjustment such that flexibility is provided under terms in which both parties have confidence. This can be accomplished partly by (1) recognizing that the hazards of opportunism vary with the type of adaptation proposed and (2) restricting adjustments to those where the hazards are least. But the spirit within which adaptations are effected is equally important (Macaulay, 1963, p. 61).

. . .

2.4 Unified governance

Incentives for trading weaken as transactions become progressively more idiosyncratic. The reason is that as human and physical assets become more specialized to a single use, and hence less transferable to other uses, economies of scale can be as fully realized by the buyer as by an outside supplier. The choice of organizing mode then turns entirely on which mode has superior adaptive properties. As discussed in Chapter 4 of Williamson (1985), vertical integration will ordinarily appear in such circumstances.

The advantage of vertical integration is that adaptations can be made in a sequential way without the need to consult, complete, or revise interfirm agreements. Where a single ownership entity spans both sides of the transaction, a presumption of joint profit maximization is warranted. Thus price adjustments in vertically integrated enterprises will be more complete than in interfirm trading. And, assuming that internal incentives are not misaligned, quantity adjustments will be implemented at whatever frequency serves to maximize the joint gain to the transaction.

Unchanging identity at the interface coupled with extensive adaptability in both price and quantity is thus characteristic of highly idiosyncratic transactions. Market contracting gives way to bilateral contracting, which in turn is supplanted by unified contracting (internal organization) as asset specificity progressively deepens.[1]

The efficient match of governance structures with transactions that results from the foregoing is shown in Figure 9.2.

3. Uncertainty

The proposed match of governance structures with transactions considers only two of the three dimensions for describing transactions: asset specificity and frequency. The third dimension, uncertainty, is assumed to be present in sufficient degree to pose an adaptive, sequential decision problem. The occasion to make successive adaptations arises because of the impossibility (or costliness) of enumerating all possible contingencies and/or stipulating appropriate adaptations to them in advance. The effects on economic organization of increases in uncertainty above that threshold level have not, however, been considered.

As indicated earlier, nonspecific transactions are ones for which continuity has little value, since new trading relations can be easily arranged by both parties. Increasing the degree of uncertainty does not alter this. Market governance

---

[1] Note that this transaction cost rationale for internal organization is very different from that originally advanced by Coase. He argued that there are two factors that favor organizing production in the firm as compared with the market: the cost of "discovering what the relevant prices are" is purportedly lower, and the "costs of negotiating and concluding a separate contract for each exchange transaction which takes place on a market" are reduced (Coase, 1952, p. 336). His 1972 treatment of the main differences between firms and markets invokes precisely these same two factors (Coase, 1972, p. 63). Expressed in terms of the behavioral assumptions on which I rely, Coase (implicitly) acknowledges bounded rationality but makes no reference to opportunism. Indeed, to contend, as he does, that Knight offers no reason for superseding the price system, since "[w]e can imagine a system where all advice or knowledge was bought as required" (Coase, 1952, p. 346), is essentially to deny that markets for information are beset by opportunism. Coase is not only silent on the contracting hazards and maladaptations on which I rely to explain nonstandard contracting, but he makes no mention of the need to dimensionalize transactions, which is the key to the discriminating approach. Those differences notwithstanding, the debts of transaction cost economics to Coase's early work are beyond adequate acknowledgment.

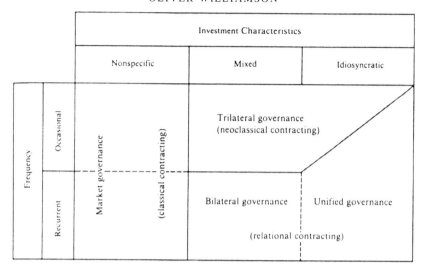

Figure 9.2. Efficient Governance

(classical contracting) thus holds across standardized transactions of all kinds, whatever the degree of uncertainty.

Matters change when asset specificity is introduced. Since continuity now matters, increasing the degree of parametric uncertainty makes it more imperative to organize transactions within governance structures that have the capacity to "work things out." Failure to support transaction-specific assets with protective governance structures predictably results in costly haggling and maladaptiveness. Efforts to restore a position on the shifting contract curve may be forgone for this reason. The intrusion of behavioral uncertainty, which is associated with unique events, compounds the difficulties.

. . .

Transactions with mixed investment attributes pose especially interesting organizational problems. Unless an appropriate market-assisted governance structure can be devised, such transactions may "flee" to one of the polar extremes as the degree of uncertainty increases. One possibility would be to sacrifice valued design features in favor of a more standardized good or service. Market governance would then apply. Alternatively, the valued design features could be preserved (perhaps even enhanced) and the transaction assigned to internal organization instead. Sometimes, however, it will be feasible to devise nonstandard contracts. . . . Where that is done (and is not prohibited by public

124

policy), bilateral contracting relations between nominally autonomous contracting agents can often survive the stresses of greater uncertainty.

Reductions in uncertainty, of course, warrant shifting transactions in the opposite direction – although such shifts may be delayed if the assets in question are long-lived. To the extent that uncertainty decreases as an industry matures, which is the usual case, the benefits that accrue to internal organization (vertical integration) presumably decline. Accordingly, greater reliance on market procurement is commonly feasible for transactions of recurrent trading in mature industries.

. . .

5. The distribution of transactions

The study of contractual relations plainly involves more than an examination of discrete markets on the one hand and hierarchical organization on the other. As Llewellyn observed in 1931, the exchange spectrum runs the full gamut from pure market to hierarchy and includes complex "future deals" located between market and hierarchy extremes (1931, p. 727). Similarly, George Richardson remarks that "what confronts us is a continuum passing from transactions, such as those on organized commodity markets, where the cooperation element is minimal, through intermediate areas in which there are linkages of traditional connection and good will, and finally to those complex and interlocking clusters, groups and alliances which represent cooperation fully and formally developed" (1972, p. 887). Both Richardson's examples and those more recently developed and discussed by Arthur Stinchcombe (1983) demonstrate that activity in the middle range is extensive. Stewart Macaulay's empirical examination of commercial contracting practices (1963) confirms this.

Suppose that transactions were to be arrayed in terms of the degree to which parties to the trade maintained autonomy. Discrete transactions would thus be located at the one extreme; highly centralized, hierarchical transactions would be at the other; and hybrid transactions (franchising, joint ventures, other forms of nonstandard contracting) would be located in between. What would the resulting distribution of transactions look like?

The three leading candidates are (1) the bimodal distribution, where most transactions cluster at one or the other extreme, (2) the normal distribution, whence the extremes are rare and most transactions display an intermediate degree of interdependence, and (3) the uniform transaction. Whereas I was earlier of the view that transactions of the middle kind were very difficult to organize and hence were unstable, on which account the bimodal distribution was more accurately descriptive (Williamson, 1975), I am now persuaded that transactions in the middle range are much more common. (Such transactions have, moreover, been the object of increasing attention in the economic,[2] legal,[3] and organizations[4] literatures.) But inasmuch as standardized commodity transactions are numerous and as administrative organization is similarly widespread, the tails of the distribution are thick. By a process of elimination, the uniform distribution appears most nearly to correspond with the world of contract as it is. Whatever the empirical realities, greater attention to transactions of the middle range will help to illuminate an understanding of complex economic organization. If such transactions flee to the extremes, what are the reasons? If such transactions can be stabilized, what are the governance processes?

[2] See especially Chapters 7, 8, 10, and 13 [of Williamson (1985)] and the numerous references to the recent economic literature therein.

[3] Macaulay (1963); Macneil (1974); Clarkson, Miller and Muris (1978); Atiyah (1979); Goetz and Scott (1983); Palay (1984); Masten (1984); and Kronman (1985) are examples.

[4] Stinchcombe (1983), Harrison White (1981), Robert Eccles (1981), and Granovetter (1983) are examples.

CHAPTER 10

The limits of firms: incentive and bureaucratic features

OLIVER WILLIAMSON

Oliver Williamson is the Edgar F. Kaiser Professor, Emeritus, of Business Administration, Economics, and Law at the University of California, Berkeley. See also the previous chapter by Williamson.

Why can't a large firm do everything that a collection of small firms can do and more? That is a variant of a question asked many times before for which an adequate answer has never been devised – to wit, what is responsible for limitations in firm size? Yet another way of putting the same issue is this: Why not organize everything in one large firm?

The trade-off model in Chapter 4 [of Williamson (1985)] offers two reasons why a firm would eschew integration: economies of scale and scope may be sacrificed if the firm attempts to make for itself what it can procure in the market, and the governance costs of internal organization exceed those of market organization where asset specificity is slight.... The first is not a thoroughly comparative explanation. If economies of scale are realized by the outside supplier, then the same economies can be preserved upon merger by instructing the supplier to service the market in the future just as it has in the past. The fundamental limitation to firm size thus must turn on the governance cost disabilities of internal organization where asset specificity is insubstantial. But wherein do the firm's comparative disabilities in those governance cost... respects reside?...

. . .

1. A chronic puzzle

Frank Knight made early reference to the limitations to firm size puzzle when, in 1921, he observed that the "diminishing returns to management is a subject often referred to in economic literature, but in regard to which there is a dearth of scientific discussion" (1965, p. 286, n. 1). And in 1933 he elaborated as follows:

The relation between efficiency and size of firm is one of the most serious problems of theory, being, in contrast with the relation for a plant, largely a matter of personality and historical accident rather than of intelligible general principles. But the question is peculiarly vital, because the possibility of monopoly gain offers a powerful incentive to *continuous and unlimited* expansion of the firm, which force must be offset by some equally powerful one making for decreased efficiency [1965, p. xxiii; emphasis in original].

. . .

A different way of posing the issue is in terms not of horizontal but of vertical integration. Thus Ronald Coase inquired, "Why does the entrepreneur not organize one less transaction or one more?" (1952, p. 339). More generally the issue is, "Why is not all production carried on in one big firm?" (p. 340).

Various answers have been advanced. They all suffer, however, from a failure to adopt and maintain the relevant comparative institutional standard. Thus consider Knight's response: "The question of diminishing returns from entrepreneurship is really a matter of the amount of uncertainty present. To imagine that a man could adequately manage a business enterprise of indefinite size and complexity is to imagine a situation in which effective uncertainty is entirely absent" (1965, pp. 286–87). In effect, Knight attributes limitations upon entrepreneurship to a condition of bounded rationality. As uncertainty increases, problems of organization become increasingly complex, and bounds on cognitive competence are reached. But he does not address the issues in a genuinely comparative manner.

Thus suppose that two firms are competing. In principle, net gains ought always to be available by merging the two. Economies of scale can be more fully exploited. Certain overhead and rivalry expenses can be curtailed. And product prices may improve – at least temporarily. Joining the two does not increase the aggregate uncertainty. Since the gaming moves and replies of rivalry have been removed, uncertainty has arguably been reduced. Moreover – and this is the really critical point – decisions need not be forced to the top but can always be assigned to the level at which the issues are most appropriately resolved. Specifically, by conferring semiautonomous status on what had previously been fully autonomous firms in the premerger period, the best of both worlds can presumably be realized. If, for example, demand or cost interaction effects are such that net gains can be had by moving decisions to the top, it will be done. Those decisions, however, that are most efficiently made at operating levels will remain there. Intervention at the top thus always occurs *selectively*, which is to say only upon a showing of expected net gains. The resulting combined firm can therefore do everything that the two autonomous firms could do previously *and more*. The same argument applies, moreover, not

128

merely to horizontal mergers but also to vertical and conglomerate mergers. The upshot is that, possible public policy restraints (against monopoly, vertical integration, or aggregate size) aside, a compelling reason to explain why all production is not concentrated in one large firm is not reached by Knight's argument.

Although other efforts to explain limitations on firm size have since been made, none addresses the issues in the way I have just posed it. And none really disposes of the puzzle. Thus consider my treatment of limits on firm size in terms of the "control loss" phenomenon (Williamson, 1967b). It involved the application to hierarchical organization of what F. C. Bartlett referred to as the serial reproduction effect in transmitting messages or images between individuals. . . . Bartlett illustrated this graphically with a line drawing of an owl which, when redrawn successively by eighteen individuals, each sketch based on its immediate predecessor, ended up as a recognizable cat; and the farther from the initial drawing one moved, the greater the distortion experienced (1932, pp. 180–81).

I applied the same argument to the firm size dilemma by invoking bounded rationality and noting that limited spans of control are thereby implied. If any one manager can deal directly with only a limited number of subordinates, then increasing firm size necessarily entails adding hierarchical levels. Transmitting information across these levels experiences the losses to which Bartlett referred, which are cumulative and arguably exponential in form. As firm size increases and successive levels of organization are added, therefore, the effects of control loss eventually exceed the gains. A limit upon radial expansion is thus reached in this way.

Plausible though the argument seemed at the time, it does not permit selective intervention of the kind described above. Rather, the entire firm is managed from the top. All information that has a bearing on decisions is transmitted across successive levels from bottom to top; all directives follow the reverse flow down.

The scenario thus contemplates comprehensive (unselective) linkages between stages. Internal organization need not, however, adopt this structure. Suppose instead that the parent firm deals with each of its parts by exercising forbearance with respect to those activities where no net gains are in prospect (in which event the parent directs the operating part to replicate small firm behavior) and intervenes wherever coordination yields net gains. The puzzle to which I referred at the outset is evidently restored – or at least the serial reproduction loss "solution" does not apply – if such selective intervention is admitted.

. . .

2. Integration of an owner-managed supply stage

The obvious answer to the puzzle of why firms do not comprehensively integrate is that selective intervention is not feasible. But why should that be? If the reasons were obvious, the puzzle of what is responsible for limitations on firm size would not persist.

I attempt here to identify some of the main reasons why selective intervention breaks down. So as to facilitate the argument, assume that an owner-managed supplier is acquired by the buyer.[1] Assume that this ownership change is accomplished as follows:

1. A price at which the assets are transferred is agreed to.
2. The formula for determining the price at which product is to be transferred from the supply division to the buying division is stipulated.
3. So as to encourage cost economizing, the high-powered incentives that characterize markets are carried over into the firm. Accordingly, the supply division is advised that it will appropriate its net revenues – which are defined as gross revenues less the sum of operating costs, user charges (for asset maintenance and depreciation), and other relevant expenses (e.g., for R & D).
4. Selective intervention will obtain. Accordingly, the supply division is advised to conduct business as usual with the following exception: The supplier will accede to decisions by the buyer to adapt to new circumstances, thereby to realize collective gains, without resistance. Failure to accede is cause for and gives rise to termination.

Unified ownership of the assets of the two stages thus (1) preserves high-powered incentives (rule 3), (2) provides for selective intervention (rule 4), and (3) precludes costly haggling (rule 4). The last two features permit adaptive sequential decision-making economies to be realized by merging what had previously been nonintegrated stages of organization.

[1] Readers familiar with the recent examination of the costs of vertical integration by Sanford Grossman and Oliver Hart (1984) will recognize that they, like I, trace these costs to incentive impairments that attend unified ownership of successive stages. Their work on these matters and mine were contemporaneous, but I have nevertheless benefited from their treatment and specifically recommend it to those who wish to see these issues developed in a more formal way. Despite similarities, their work and mine differ in the following significant respects: (1) they ignore the very factors – asset malutilization, accounting contrivances – that I regard as central to incentive distortions in firms; (2) they deny that internal and market organization differ in auditing respects; (3) their "even-handed" insistence that high-powered (transfer pricing) incentives apply in all ownership regimes asymmetrically denies adaptability advantages to integration that weaker (e.g., cost plus) incentives coupled with unified ownership would support; and (4) they disregard the bureaucratic consequences of internal organization. My discussion in this section features asset utilization and accounting effects. Auditing differences are treated in section 4, salaried management in the preacquisition supply stage is the subject of section 3, and bureaucratic features are addressed in section 5.

The limits of firms

Implicit in the argument is the assumption that the two stages are operating in a bilateral exchange relation with each other by reason of investments in transaction-specific assets. Such specificity can take at least four forms: site specificity, physical asset specificity, human asset specificity, and dedicated assets. It will be convenient here to consider only physical asset specificity.

Indeed, given rule 4 above, human asset specificity is effectively ruled out. As developed more fully in Chapter 10 [of Williamson (1985)], it is in the mutual interests of firm and worker to safeguard the employment relation against abrupt termination (by either party) wherever labor develops firm-specific skills and knowledge during the course of its employment. Accordingly, the rule do this/do that or terminate is maladapted to the needs of the parties where firm-specific human assets are considerable. The argument here therefore assumes that the bilateral exchange relation is due entirely to a condition of physical asset specificity. Rule 4 thus applies, whereunder failure to accede to any order to adapt will be cause for termination. Upon realization that successor managements can always be brought in to implement change orders as requested, the incumbent management always acquiesces.

Were this the end of the story, selective intervention with net gains would presumably obtain. In fact, however, numerous measurement difficulties stand in the way of implementing a merger agreement that is attended by high-powered incentives. Some of them operate to the disadvantage of the buyer, some work to the disadvantage of the supplier, and others impose losses on both.

2.1 Asset utilization losses

The former owner-manager of the supply stage becomes the manager of the supply division upon sale of the supply stage assets to the buyer. The change of status has immediate and serious incentive effects if the high-powered incentive rules described above are employed. For one thing, the manager who appropriates the net receipts associated with the supply division no longer has the same incentives to utilize equipment with equivalent care and to incur identical preventive maintenance. Since, by assumption, the manager has no firm-specific human assets at stake, the manager behaves myopically with respect to the enterprise. The object being to maximize immediate net receipts, labor costs will be saved by utilizing equipment intensively, and maintenance expense will be deferred to a successor management. Having been paid for his assets upon giving up ownership status, the manager of the supply division proceeds to run them into the ground and leaves the firm to invest his augmented net receipts elsewhere.

To be sure, there are checks against asset abuses of both kinds. The new asset owner may insist that certain utilization and maintenance procedures be observed and furthermore monitor the supply division for compliance. Note, however, that added monitoring costs – unneeded in the nonintegrated state – have now been introduced. Additionally, reputation effects can deter managers from behaving irresponsibly. These, however, are imperfect. Some managers may shrug them off if the immediate gains are large enough and if they cannot be required to disgorge their ill-gotten gains. (Swiss bank accounts have attractive features in that respect.)

The upshot is that efficient asset utilization and the use of high-powered incentives experience tensions in an integrated firm – tensions that do not arise when the two production stages are independent. Contrary to the type of selective intervention that I postulated in section 1, the integrated firm *cannot* wholly replicate outside procurement in "business as usual" respects. Instead there are *unavoidable side effects.*

2.2 Accounting contrivances

The price at which a supplier agrees to sell his assets to the buyer will vary with the stream of net receipts that he projects in the postmerger period. Given the high-powered incentives described above, that stream will vary with (1) revenues, (2) costs, and (3) continued employment.

One hazard is that the supplier will be "promised" a favorable net receipt stream, hence accept a low price for transferring asset ownership, only to learn to his dismay that his employment has been terminated. Suppose, out of awareness of such a hazard, the supplier demands and receives a guarantee of continued employment. Such guarantees accomplish little, however, if the net receipts of the supply division can be altered substantially through the exercise of accounting discretion. Expropriation can then be accomplished by indirection.

Net receipts can be squeezed in either or both of two ways. For one, revenues can be reduced by cutting transfer prices. For another, cost imputations can be raised. The supply division is vulnerable in both respects.

Given the impossibility of comprehensive contracting, the transfer pricing rule that is stipulated at the outset will necessarily be incomplete. So as to correct against misalignments, prices will need to be reset periodically to reflect changing circumstances. This can be done by consulting the market if asset specificity is zero. Complications intrude, however, when even a slight degree of asset specificity appears. Thus although the terms under which product is traded between autonomous parties are disciplined by the credible threat that the supplier will retire his specialized assets, rather than use them to support the supplier's specialized procurement needs, if mutually acceptable terms are not reached, the manager of the supply division in the integrated firm does not have the same option. If push comes to shove, the physical assets are no longer his to retire (or, more generally, redeploy). Employment guarantees notwithstanding, the manager of the supply division can, if he refuses to accept the proposed terms, be brushed aside. (He is simply "reassigned.") Upon merger, therefore, the determination of transfer prices has, in effect, become a decision for the purchasing division (which now owns the assets of both parts) to reach unilaterally. The hazard is obvious: Despite assurances to the contrary, prices will be set so as to squeeze the net receipts of the supply stage.

Cost determination is problematic, moreover, whatever the degree of asset specificity. Whereas each stage determines its own accounting practices in the premerger regime, that is no longer permitted – indeed, is wholly implausible – upon merger. Instead, responsibility for the accounting rules will be concentrated on the asset owner. Explicit agreements that limit accounting discretion notwithstanding, the supply stage runs the risk that costs will be reset to its disadvantage.

The upshot is that the supply stage is better advised to discount very heavily any promise that favorable net receipt streams are in prospect and to realize its full bargaining advantage by extracting maximum asset valuation terms at the outset – because a squeeze is in prospect thereafter. But there is more to it. If the use of high-powered incentives in firms is inherently subject to corruption, then the notion that the integrated firm can do everything that the nonintegrated parts could accomplish is a fiction. Instead, the integrated firm does better in some respects and worse in others.

2.3 Incentive ramifications

High-powered incentives in firms give rise to difficulties of two kinds: The assets of the supply stage are not utilized with due care, and the net revenue stream of the supply stage is subject to manipulation. Upon realization that high-powered incentives in firms experience such disabilities, lower-powered incentives are apt to be introduced instead. Were the supply stage management to be compensated mainly by salary and become subject to periodic monitoring (decision review, auditing, and the like), the supply stage would have less need to be concerned with accounting chicanery, and the asset owner's concern with asset dissipation would be lessened.

Low-powered incentives have well-known adaptability advantages. That, after all, is what commends cost plus contracting. But such advantages are not had without cost – which explains why cost plus contracting is embraced reluctantly (Williamson, 1967b). Our first explanation for why firms do not everywhere supplant markets thus is that (1) firms cannot mimic the high-powered incentives of markets without experiencing added costs; (2) although recourse by firms to lower-powered incentives is thereby indicated, that too comes at a cost; and (3) those added costs of internal organization are not offset by comparative adaptability gains under circumstances where [assets are nonspecific], since those are precisely the conditions under which the identity of the parties does not matter, whence classical market contracting works well. The net governance costs of acquiring an owner-operated supply stage are thus positive where asset specificity is slight. . . .

More generally, the argument is this: Incentives and controls are adapted to the attributes of each organizational alternative. To attempt to "hold the rules as nearly constant as possible," on the theory that what works well in one regime ought to apply equally to another, is thus mistaken. The powers and limits of each form of organization must be discovered and respected.

. . .

3. Acquisition of a supply stage in which ownership and management are separated

Suppose, *arguendo*, that vertical integration *of the kind described above* experiences the incentive disabilities that are ascribed to it. It is nevertheless noteworthy that the conditions described above are very special. In particular I have assumed that ownership and management are joined in the preacquisition supply stage. What if that condition does not obtain?

Suppose that an independent supplier undergoes an ownership change before an acquisition of the supplier is even contemplated. Suppose, in particular, that what had been a closely held, owner-managed firm becomes a diffusely held firm in which none of the management has a significant equity interest.

The hazards of using high-powered (net receipt) incentives to compensate the management of this firm will be evident to owners and managers alike. Owners will recognize the asset dissipation hazards, and managers will be concerned that owners will retain influence over accounting, thus posing a risk that net receipt realizations will be manipulated. When those consequences are foreseen, high-powered incentives in this now diffusely owned firm will give way to incentives of a lower-powered kind. Salaried compensation will therefore obtain.

The critical question is whether, in view of the above-described changes that attend the change in ownership of the premerger supply stage, merger incurs any added costs. If it does not, then the acquisition by a purchasing stage of a supply stage in which the ownership has already been sold off would offer the prospect of gain without cost. The gains would presumably take the same form as those ascribed to merger previously: Subgoal pursuit by the supply stage management would be attenuated, so that coordination between the two stages would be accomplished more easily and effectively in the postmerger period when common ownership obtains.

The firm size dilemma to which I referred at the outset would then be restored with only a minor change. The puzzle would now read as follows: Why are not all *diffusely owned* production stages placed under unified ownership, thereby to be organized and operated as one large firm? Unless undisclosed costs of merger are discovered, we are mainly back where we started. Put differently, section 2 is an explication of the Berle and Means problem and does not provide an explanation for limits on vertical integration outside of that special context.

Unremarked merger consequences of three kinds warrant consideration. For one thing, to observe that ownership and management are separated does not establish that ownership is thereafter wholly lacking in control. Differential control effects within merged and nonmerged entities is thus one possibility. Second, the fact that managements in both pre- and postmerger regimes are salaried does not necessarily imply that compensation is disconnected from net receipts. Finally, the possibility that integration affects the internal politics of the corporation with systematic performance consequences warrants scrutiny. The first two consequences are considered here. The third is addressed in section 4.

. . .

4. The costs of bureaucracy

The costs of acquisition discussed in section 2 are mainly ones that will accrue to any separation of ownership from control, merger-related or otherwise. Although the costs of acquisition discussed in section 3 are not confounded in ownership and control respects, they are also more speculative in nature and are probably weaker in effect. The question thus arises as to whether there are other costs of merger that have yet to be identified. In particular, are there undisclosed "costs of bureaucracy" that obtain when successive production stages are joined?

Philip Selznick contends that "the most important thing about [nonmarket] organizations is that, though they are tools, each nevertheless has a life of its own" (1949, p. 10). Instrumental intentions notwithstanding, formal structures can "never succeed in conquering the nonrational dimensions of organizational behavior" (Selznick, 1948, p. 25). Richard Scott summarizes the argument as follows:

[O]rganizational rationality is constrained by "the recalcitrance of the tools of action": persons bring certain characteristics to the organization and develop other commitments as members that restrict their capacity for rational action; organizational procedures become valued ends in themselves; the organization strikes bargains with its environment that compromise present objectives and limit future possibilities [1981, p. 91].

What are the ramifications of such views for economic approaches to the study of organization? One possible economic response is to regard the conditions to which Selznick, Scott, and others refer as noise. Aberrations from rationality are thus treated as error terms. A stronger response is to deny that such behavior even exists. Neither is proposed here. Instead, an informed economic approach to the study of organization will display an interest in and *thereafter make provision for* all regularities of whatever kind. If the behavior in question is systematic, allowance can be made for it in making comparative institutional choices and in organizational design respects. Thus, if some forms of organization are less subject to bureaucratic distortions than others, this will be taken into account in assessing alternative modes. Within modes where distortions are especially severe, moreover, it may be possible to mitigate such conditions by devising checks or organizational reforms.

By comparison with the market failure literature, the literature on bureaucratic failure is relatively underdeveloped. The discussion here merely attempts to identify some of the main life-cycle features that beset internal organization. As compared with market organization, internal organization displays a differential propensity to manage complexity, to forgive error, and to engage in logrolling.

4.1 The propensity to manage

A propensity to manage seems to characterize all forms of bureaucratic organization. To be sure, the public sector is widely thought to be especially culpable in this respect – and probably is. Charles Morris captures the spirit in his reference to "the cost of good intentions." What he characterizes as "the new rationalist style in government" was based on "a confident optimism that the most intractable problems would give way before the resolute assault of intelligent, committed people" (1980, p. 3). But the same attitude also characterizes the private sector (Feldman and March, 1981).

Actually, the propensity to manage has two parts rather than just one. The part to which Morris refers is the *instrumental* propensity: Decision makers project a capacity to manage complexity that is repeatedly refuted by events. Although such a propensity is well-intentioned, problems regularly turn out to be more difficult and/or managerial competence more limited than managers of complexity originally project (Perrow, 1983). Counterexamples to the contrary notwithstanding, this is the main opinion.

The second type of propensity is more reprehensible. It is the *strategic* propensity to use the resources of the organization to pursue subgoals. If, for the reasons given in section 2, pecuniary incentives in firms are weaker than those in markets, then political games and preferences have greater sway. Efforts to tilt the organization, often through greater hands-on management, commonly result.

Odysseus-type solutions are often attractive where *ex ante* resolve is known regularly to break down in the face of recurrent exigencies/temptations. Out of awareness that the call of the Sirens would be well-nigh irresistible, Odysseus instructed that he should be bound to the mast. As Jon Elster points out, "binding oneself is a privileged way of resolving the problem of weakness of will" (1979, p. 37). Such self-denial benefits can be realized within the firm if mergers for which the advocates can identify only limited prospective benefits are refused. The uncounted, but nevertheless predictable, costs attributable to the future propensity to manage will thereby assuredly be avoided.

4.2 Forgiveness

Systems of justice vary systematically with organization. Families are ordinarily presumed to have deep knowledge of the transactions that occur between or impinge on the membership, to employ long time horizons, and to be relatively forgiving.[2] Markets, in contrast, are presumed to have less knowledge of idiosyncratic circumstances, employ shorter time horizons, and are relatively severe (unforgiving).

For the reasons given in section 5, internal organization enjoys comparative auditing advantages. Accordingly, the integrated firm has greater capacity to reach informed decisions on the merits than do nonintegrated trading entities. The confounding of risks and decisions, which complicates market assessments, can thus be unpacked with greater precision and confidence internally. In principal, therefore, internal asset managers can better ascertain whether to continue funding a project than could the capital market.

But there are at least two further consequences. First, the prospect of penalty can and often does elicit inordinate energies. The market is a severe taskmaster. Unless escalator clauses have been expressly agreed to from the outset, unexpected cost increases are absorbed rather than passed through when transactions are mediated by the market. By contrast, unexpected cost increases that occur in trades within the firm are apt to be negotiable. The justification for such increases can be examined more fully within the firm, and the hazards of misrepresentation are less severe than in the market. But internal organization is thereby denied access to the supranormal energies that the market is able to mobilize. It is unrealistic to expect that such efforts will be expended if reasoned or plausible explanations can be advanced to support the cost increases in question: Reasoning systems are expected to behave in reasoning ways. (Academics, being the ultimate reasoners, are often unsuited for administrative positions on that account.)

Second, the net benefit calculus employed by firm and market differ. Indeed, a useful definition of forgiveness, at least for purposes of evaluating commercial

---

[2] Of these three aspects, which are all related, forgiveness is the most important and distinctive.

transactions, is whether "excuses" are evaluated strictly with reference to a pecuniary net benefit calculus or not. As between the two, the market is expected to employ a stricter pecuniary net benefit calculus than is the firm. In this sense, it is less forgiving. A leading reason for this is that the firm maintains greater separability among transactions with the market than it can for transactions that are organized internally.

It is thus easy for a firm to terminate a supplier of a good or service that is supported by nonspecific assets ($k = 0$) at the first indication of failure. Were this same transaction to be organized internally, however, the firm would conduct an inquiry and consider second chances. Partly this is a manifestation of the aforementioned auditing advantage of internal organization. But it is also the case that the firm is unable to treat each internal transaction in a fully separable way. In effect, internal transactions of the $k = 0$ [ed.: nonspecific asset] kind benefit from an association with other internal transactions for which $k > 0$ [ed.: assets are specific].

Thus whereas continuity of transactions of the latter kind is valued from a pecuniary net benefit standpoint, the same is not true for the former. Firms that internalize transactions of both kinds are unable, however, to treat each in a fully discriminating way. A rational decision to "work things out" when things go wrong for $k > 0$ transactions spills over and infects transactions of the $k = 0$ kind. It is unacceptable, both to insiders and to interested observers, for the firm to behave differently. Simple regard for human dignity demands that due process be respected. Barnard's remarks about informal organization are apposite: One of the purposes served by informal organization is that of "maintaining the personality of the individual against certain effects of formal organizations which tend to disintegrate the personality" (Barnard, 1938, p. 122).

Thus whereas extreme market outcomes can be accepted as the luck of the draw, administrative actions are interpreted by all of the affected parties, including interested outsiders (associates, family, friends, and so forth), as merit choices. That places a severe burden of due process on internal organization. A plausible case will not do; a preponderance of evidence is needed if severe penalties are to be meted out. Out of awareness that they operate under the protection of a norm of internal due process, individuals are able to exploit the internal organization in minimum performance respects, and some do.

To be sure, the above described weakening of incentives applies strictly to $k = 0$ activities. The possibility that a merit choice environment intensifies incentives within the firm, as compared with the market, for $k > 0$ activities is not denied. It suffices, however, for the purposes of the argument, that due process spillovers are responsible for incentive attenuation for the $k = 0$ condition.

4.3 Logrolling

Again the issue is not whether internal organization experiences costs but whether differential costs are incurred in moving from nonintegrated to integrated status. I submit that internal operating and investment decisions are more subject to politicization.

a. Operating decisions

Alvin Gouldner contends that the norm of reciprocity is as important and universal as the incest taboo (1961). It finds expression throughout human society – across cultures and degrees of development and over time. Opportunities to give effect to reciprocity, however, vary with the circumstances. In general those opportunities are greater within more highly integrated organization than in less. Moreover, those opportunities are apt to be given expression – which is a manifestation of the earlier described tendency for internal traders to be more accommodating than autonomous traders. This is not necessarily a bad thing; the prospect of such accommodation is a factor that weighs favorably in evaluating trades that are supported by specific assets. The possibility that it will go beyond the objective merits to include reciprocal managerial back-scratching is, however, a matter for concern and is appropriately taken into account in the decision to internalize incremental transactions.

b. Investment renewal biases

An internal procurement bias is supported by a number of factors. For one thing, the internal supplier that produces mainly for internal uses may be judged to be at a relative disadvantage in the marketplace. The internal supplier may lack both the large and experienced marketing organization and the established customer connections to which nonintegrated external suppliers have access. In consideration of such conditions, and if fixed costs are nonredeployed, a "preference" for internal procurement might seem appropriate – at least so long as the external price exceeds the variable cost of internal supply.

This may be a specious argument, however, since the nonredeployability of assets may easily be overstated (there may be a secondhand market for the machinery in question) and individual equipment renewal decisions ought eventually to be made with reference to the long-run viability of the internal facility. Managers are notably reluctant, however, to abolish their own jobs, even in the face of employment guarantees. The problems with such guarantees are that while continued employment may be secure, assurances that status will be maintained when a position is eliminated, and that promotion prospects will not be upset upon removal from a known promotion ladder, are unenforceable. A preference for internal supply is thus to be expected and may manifest itself by urging that each equipment replacement decision be made serially, in semi-independent fashion. A fundamentally nonviable internal capability may be uncritically preserved in this way.

4.4 Further remarks

The main benefits of vertical integration, according to the transaction cost economics point of view adopted here, take the form of governance rather than production cost savings. They are discerned by examining the problems that attend autonomous contracting when the parties to a trade are operating in a bilateral exchange relation. The main costs of vertical integration are more difficult to discover, however. They are plainly not of a neoclassical production function kind. Neither are differential governance cost features transparent. Analysis at a more microanalytic level is evidently needed.

. . .

Just as transaction cost reasoning and the examination of microanalytic phenomena has helped to illuminate the factors responsible for market failure, however, I conjecture that similar headway can be made against the subject of bureaucracy if a concerted effort is made here as well.

. . .

5. Low-powered incentives in markets

A symmetrical treatment of economic organization will examine not merely the strains that result when the high-powered incentives associated with markets are introduced into firms, but will also consider whether the low-powered incentives employed by firms can be introduced without strain into markets. The latter question is the matter of concern here.

Assume, for the purposes of this section, that the innovative tensions discussed in 2.4 [in Williamson (1985)] are slight. Assume further that the amount of physical asset specificity at the supply stage is great. Integration is thus the indicated form of organization.

Suppose, as a consequence of the factors discussed in subsections 2.1 and 2.2, that the integrated firm decides to transfer product between divisions on the cost plus terms. The supply division thus accedes to requests from the procurement division that it adapt the quantity or quality of the product without resistance. Lest costs be permitted to escalate or economizing opportunities go unnoticed or be forgone, however, the supply division is periodically reviewed in cost and decision respects. Suppose, *arguendo*, that the resulting performance is judged to be satisfactory.

The limits of firms

If such low-powered incentives coupled with periodic auditing have advantages in firms, why not replicate the same with markets? That is a different way of putting the question that I posed at the outset – only here the question is, why can't the market replicate the firm? It will be useful to address the question by examining the following more operational statement of the problem: What are the consequences of cost plus contracting between autonomous firms?

Interfirm and intrafirm cost plus contracting differ in at least two significant respects. Both are related to the fact that an autonomous firm has an added degree of freedom that an integrated division does not: It can take its assets and flee. The first difference is that an independent supplier has an incentive to incur costs for strategic purposes that the internal supply division did not. The second is that interfirm auditing cannot be presumed to be as effective as intrafirm auditing.

The strategic difference is this: The independent firm has a stronger incentive to make investments for which reimbursements can plausibly be claimed – in plant and equipment and in human capital – if they give it an added capability to compete for other business. To be sure, both external supplier and the internal supply division can be advised (and may agree) that they are to supply exclusively to the needs of the procurement division. But enforcing such a provision against an independent supplier is apt to be much more difficult. Court ordering is much less effective than administrative fiat in effecting preferences on these matters.

It is sometimes argued that interfirm and intrafirm audits are indistinguishable. Thus Sanford Grossman and Oliver Hart "assume that integration in itself does not make any new variable observable to both parties. Any audits which an employer can have done of her subsidiary are also feasible when the subsidiary is a separate company" (1984, p. 5). I submit that there are reasons to believe otherwise. Specifically, market and internal organization differ in "informal organization" respects. . . . Although Armen Alchian does not make reference to informal organization, he nevertheless acknowledges that "anyone vulnerable to [a] threat of loss (if the coalition is impaired) will seek to preserve not only the coalition but also to reduce the possibility of that threat from the other members of the coalition" (1984, p. 9). If a stronger mutual interest in organizational integrity can be presumed among members of an integrated organization than would exist between independent trading units – because their destinies are more closely tied in the former than in the latter case – then internal auditors can expect to receive greater cooperation, including even hints as to where the "dead bodies lie," than can be presumed when auditing across an autonomous ownership boundary is attempted.

Indeed, the external auditor can ordinarily anticipate only perfunctory cooperation. Since if "our" costs are disallowed then "our" profits will decline and

141

"our" viability may be jeopardized, the employees of the independent supply stage will engage in cost justification and cover-up.

To be sure, divisions also engage in obfuscation and cover-up against internal auditors. Division managements cannot, however, take the physical assets they have accumulated through cost overruns and flee. Termination with and without assets makes a difference. If, therefore, heads must roll in an integrated division where cost excesses have become great, and if guilty and innocent in these circumstances go down together, then it is easy to understand how those who are not implicated in malfeasance will collaborate early and actively with internal auditors.

The upshot is that cost plus contracting in markets cannot be presumed to be identical to cost plus contracting in firms. Transferring a transaction out of the firm and into the market therefore will rarely occur on unchanged cost plus terms but will instead be attended by incentive and governance realignments.

This repeats the argument advanced earlier: Incentives and governance structures that are observed to work well in one organizational milieu do not transfer uncritically to others. To the contrary, organization form, incentive instruments, and governance safeguards must be derived simultaneously.

. . .

CHAPTER 11

Bargaining costs, influence costs, and the organization of economic activity

PAUL MILGROM AND JOHN ROBERTS

Paul Milgrom was born in Detroit, Michigan, in 1948. He received a Ph.D. in business from Stanford University in 1979. When this paper was published, he was Professor of Economics at Stanford University. Since 1993, he has been the Shirley R. and Leonard W. Ely, Jr., Professor of Humanities and Science and Professor of Economics at Stanford University.

John Roberts was born in Winnipeg, Manitoba, in 1945. He received a Ph.D. in economics from the University of Minnesota in 1972. When this article was published, he was the Jonathan B. Lovelace Professor of Economics in the Graduate School of Business, Stanford University. He is presently the John H. and Irene S. Scully Professor in Economics, Strategic Management, and International Business in the same School.

This chapter is concerned with the economics of organization and management, a relatively new area of study that seeks to analyze the internal structure and workings of economic organizations, the division of activity among these organizations, and the management of relations between them through markets or other higher-level, encompassing organizations.

The dominant approach to this subject is transaction cost economics, as introduced by Coase (1937, 1960) and developed by several others since, most notably Williamson (1975, 1985). The main tenet of Coase's theory is that economic activities tend to be organized efficiently – that is, so as to maximize the expected total wealth of the parties affected.[1] In this context, two sorts of costs

Reprinted with abridgments from Paul Milgrom and John Roberts, "Bargaining Costs, Influence Costs, and the Organization of Economic Activity," pp. 57–89 in James Alt and Kenneth Shepsle, eds., *Perspectives on Positive Political Economy*, Cambridge: Cambridge University Press. Copyright © Cambridge University Press 1990. Reprinted with the permission of Cambridge University Press.

[1] Identifying efficiency with expected total wealth maximization requires assumptions that are maintained throughout most of this literature, including risk neutrality (preferences being linear in a freely transferable good, usually money, in terms of which values are expressed), access to a smoothly functioning capital market, and common beliefs about the likelihoods of uncertain events. All of these are clearly restrictive. An important implication of the hypothesis of wealth maximization is that the actions that should (and will) be taken and the way in which benefits of joint action will be shared are determined separately. In particular, such factors as relative bargaining power are irrelevant in determining economic organization. This prediction contrasts sharply with those of Marxian theories, in which power and class interests are prime determinants.

are customarily identified – those of physical production and distribution and those of carrying out necessary exchanges. Because these are typically treated as distinct and separable, the efficiency hypothesis becomes one of transaction cost minimization: The division of activities among firms and between a firm and the market is determined by whether a particular transaction is most efficiently conducted in a market setting or under centralized authority within a firm.

This approach has two conceptual problems. First, the total costs a firm incurs cannot generally be expressed as the sum of production costs – depending only on the technology and the inputs used – and transaction costs – depending only on the way transactions are organized. In general, these two kinds of costs must be considered together; efficient organization is not simply a matter of minimizing transaction costs. Second, the general theory is too vague to be useful. If an existing institution or arrangement appears to be inefficient, one can always claim that it is simply because the observer has not recognized all the relevant transaction costs. To give the theory more power and to generate more specific predictions, recent developments of transaction cost economics have focused on identifying the major components of transaction costs and how they affect the efficient form of organization.

Our principal purpose here is to add two elements to this theory. First, we will argue that the crucial costs associated with using markets to carry out transactions (rather than bringing them within a more complex, formal organization) are the costs of bargaining over short-term arrangements between independent economic agents. This accentuation of short-term bargaining costs contrasts with received theory (as presented by Williamson), which emphasizes asset specificity, uncertainty, and frequency of dealings as the key factors. Second, we identify certain costs attached to the centralized, discretionary decision-making power inherent in formal economic organizations such as firms. Particularly important among these are the costs of essentially political activity within the organization, which we call *influence* costs: the losses that arise from individuals within an organization seeking to influence its decisions for their private benefit (and from their perhaps succeeding in doing so) and from the organization's responding to control this behavior. These costs are an important disability of centralized control and help to explain why integrated internal organization does not always supplant market relations between independent entities.

. . .

Critique and extension of the received theory

Received transaction cost theory emphasizes the implications of the incompleteness of contracts that cover actions to be taken in the uncertain future. However, we will argue that this emphasis is somewhat misplaced. Instead, we will show that the key to evaluating the efficacy of market transactions is the costs of negotiating suitably detailed short-term contracts. If these costs were always zero, then organizing economic activity through market exchange would always be perfectly efficient. On the other hand, when the costs of negotiating periodic exchange agreements are sufficiently high, then regardless of other factors, such as the presence or absence of specialized assets, potentially important savings are to be realized by placing the activity under a central authority, which can quickly settle potentially costly disputes.

To understand these claims we must first understand what we mean by the terms "short-term" and "bargaining costs." When describing contracts "short-term" refers to a period short enough so that all the information that is relevant for current decisions is already available. Short-term contracts, by definition, do not specify how to act in the longer term as new circumstances arise. We interpret "bargaining costs" expansively, just as we did the term "transaction costs," to include all the costs associated with multilateral bargaining, competitive bidding, and other voluntary mechanisms for determining a mutually acceptable agreement. Bargaining costs include not only the wages paid to the bargainers or the opportunity costs of their time but also the costs of monitoring and enforcing the agreement and any losses from failure to reach the most efficient agreement possible in the most efficient fashion.

With these definitions, having zero short-term bargaining costs means that the bargainers require negligible physical and human resources to reach efficient short-term contracts. (A short-term contract is *efficient* if there is no other feasible *short-term* contract that both parties would prefer.) However, by definition, bargainers cannot commit themselves through a short-term contract to restrict their long-term behavior in any way, even though they may recognize the long-term impacts of their short-term decisions. For example, the parties to a short-term contract may agree on what investments in specialized assets to make this year and who will pay for these, but they cannot commit themselves to behave benignly next year toward the party who, having paid for the investment, has appropriable quasi rents.

To establish the key role of bargaining costs, suppose that the costs of negotiating short-term contracts were zero. We consider a two-party relationship (such as between a supplier and a customer) for which efficient production demands that the supplier, the customer, or both invest in specialized assets. We assume that the parties meet the standard assumptions of the transaction cost literature in that each is a risk-neutral, financially unconstrained, expected-wealth-maximizing[2] bargainer. The two also share common beliefs about the

---

[2] This assumption includes the possibilities that the bargainers maximize the expected present value of profits at some fixed discount rates or at discount rates that properly reflect the correlation of project returns with other aggregate risks. These objectives for the firm are widely used in the theory of financial economics.

relative likelihoods of various future contingencies and both are farsighted in the sense that they understand how their current actions and agreements will affect future bargaining opportunities and behavior. They are also opportunistic in the sense that their behavior at any time does not depend on past unbonded promises or on how past costs and benefits have been shared. Finally, we assume that contracts governing prices and behavior in the distant future are prohibitively costly to write because too many contingencies need to be evaluated and described (that is, there is too much uncertainty) but that contracts governing prices, bonus payments, and the actions to be taken in the near term, over which the relevant conditions are already known, are costless to write.

In general Williamsonian terms, the situation involves opportunistic behavior, imperfect long-term contracting, specialized assets, and uncertainty about the future. According to transaction-cost theorists, these conditions are sufficient to prevent a market arrangement based on a series of short-term contracts from yielding an efficient outcome. Nevertheless, we claim that if the costs of bargaining over short-term arrangements were zero – a condition that is apparently consistent with our other specifications – then the market outcome would be efficient. That is, the actions taken by the parties both in the short run *and in the long run* would in *all contingencies* be identical to those that would have been specified in the "ideal contract" – the efficient (possibly long-term and complete) contract the parties would sign if there were no restrictions at all on contracting.

Before proving this proposition and explaining the argument supporting it and the defect in received theory, we should emphasize two points. First, given our assumptions of risk neutrality and common beliefs, the actions taken under an efficient contract do not depend on the bargaining power of the parties involved: Only the distribution of the fruits of the bargain depend on bargaining power. Conversely, because the parties are risk neutral, if the actions they take coincide with those that would be specified in the ideal contract, then the arrangement is efficient, regardless of the payments made between the parties. Second, we do not claim that the inability to write complete contracts has no effect on the way the parties' share risks: By their very definition, incomplete contracts imply a limited capacity to make inter-temporal or contingent

---

Interestingly, the assumption that the parties are risk-neutral maximizers of expected wealth without financial constraints plays an important role in our analysis. The assumed absence of financial constraints severely limits the applicability of the analysis contained in this section to the problem of investments in human capital, because laws against slavery prohibit the use of human capital as loan collateral. The assumption is also likely to fail in applications to public projects involving health, safety, or environmental quality – projects for which the public's preferences are not easily expressed in terms of risk neutrality and expected pecuniary gains.

When the assumption fails, the efficiency of actions can no longer generally be considered separately from distributional considerations.

transfers. What *is* unaffected is the set of actions the parties will eventually take and hence the agreement's efficiency.

. . .

To illustrate, consider the relationship between Fisher Body (the supplier) and General Motors (the customer) analyzed by Klein, Crawford, and Alchian. Suppose the relationship lasts for two periods. In the first period, the parties reach an agreement about plant site and design . . . and about the share of the cost of constructing the plant each will bear. Such an agreement specifies only the immediate actions the parties will take and how they will be compensated for these. In the second period, the parties negotiate prices, possibly a fixed transfer payment, quality standards, and a delivery schedule . . . in full knowledge of the circumstances then prevailing (e.g., current model year body designs, demands for various models, the costs and availabilities of steel and substitute materials, and so on, . . . as well as the previously made investments). By our assumption of costless bargaining, regardless of the first-period agreement, the second-period agreement will be efficient given the conditions that prevail then.

Now consider what would happen if the parties were to agree in the initial period to make the efficient plant site and design decisions. Then, the actions taken in the second period would, in all circumstances, agree with those specified under the hypothetical ideal contract. We therefore conclude that the parties could sign a short-term contract in the first period that would lead to them making efficient decisions in both the first and second periods. Actually, by varying who pays for the initial investment in the plant, all distributions of the fruits of these efficient decisions can be attained. Any contract, therefore, that leads to inefficient decision making can be improved upon for both parties by some contract that leads to efficient decision making. Thus, if the costs of short-term bargaining were zero, the agreement reached would indeed lead to efficient actions.

What, then, was wrong with the argument advanced in the first section of this chapter? Why shouldn't the fear of opportunism by General Motors make Fisher Body unwilling to enter into the arrangement? The answer is that Fisher can be compensated for the risk by having General Motors bear part of the plant's cost. Why, then, shouldn't General Motors fear that Fisher will appropriate its quasi rents? Because the agreement can call for General Motors to pay for only as much of the plant's earnings as it expects to appropriate in future negotiations. Threats of appropriation are simply distributional threats; they are not threats to efficient action as long as bargaining costs are zero. Among risk-neutral parties with common beliefs and no private information, distributional threats can be compensated by initial cash payments. The efficiency of market arrangements is limited only by the costs of negotiating efficient short-term contracts. This conclusion points to the central importance of bargaining costs in determining the efficiency of market transactions. We shall study the origins and determinants of bargaining costs in the next section.

The preceding analysis relied on the assumptions that all parties are risk neutral and that they can contract for current actions without restriction. The first of these assumptions is not reasonable when contracting parties are individuals, and the second fails when current actions cannot be precisely monitored. Nevertheless, as Fudenberg, Holmstrom, and Milgrom (1990) have shown, the conclusion that short-term contracts are as good as long-term contracts when no bargaining costs are involved applies equally to situations involving risk-averse bargainers and imperfectly observed actions, provided contractual payments in each period can be made to depend on any information obtained during the period and provided no new information about any period's actions arrives only in later periods.

Our other criticism of early transaction cost theories concerns their relative silence regarding the source, nature, and magnitude of the costs incurred in nonmarket transactions. Indeed, despite the firm beliefs of many economists that markets often hold great advantages over nonmarket forms of organization, *received* transaction cost theory leaves unclear why market transactions are *ever* to be preferred to nonmarket ones.

Identifying the costs of general nonmarket transactions is a task to be approached with great caution. As Chandler (1962) has documented, business organizations have changed substantially and repeatedly over the past century, and the disabilities (transaction costs) suffered by an older form of organization may be overcome by its replacement. Perhaps wisely, then, transaction cost theorists for a long time were largely silent about the source and nature of the costs of centralized organization, although they were certainly aware of the problem. Quite recently, however, Williamson (1985) and Grossman and Hart (1986) have addressed explicitly the disabilities of nonmarket organization.

. . .

[W]e believe that [their] incentive arguments have substantial force. Nevertheless, these theories miss an important class of generally identifiable costs of internal organization that do not depend specifically on control of assets. In the section titled "Costs of Centralized Authority," we argue that the crucial distinguishing characteristic of a firm is not the pattern of asset ownership but the substitution of centralized authority for the relatively unfettered negotiations that characterize market transactions. And, we argue, the very existence of this centralized authority is incompatible with a thoroughgoing policy of efficient selective intervention. The authority to intervene inevitably implies the authority to intervene inefficiently. Yet such interventions, even if they are inefficient overall, can be highly beneficial for particular individuals and groups. Thus, either inefficient interventions will be made and resources will be expended to bring them about or to prevent them, or else the authority to intervene must be restricted. This implies that some efficient interventions must be foregone.

. . .

Costs of centralized authority

. . .

Why can't a centrally planned, consciously coordinated system always do at least as well as an unplanned, decentralized one? For many years scholars, failing to find an answer to this question, have boldly (and we think wrongly) concluded that there is no answer. . . .

Substantially the same puzzle arises in trying to explain why there are any limits to a firm's size and scope. Thus, economists have asked, "Why, if by organizing one can eliminate certain costs and in fact reduce the cost of production, are there any market transactions at all? Why is not all production carried out by one big firm?" And, "Why can't a large firm do everything that a collection of small firms can do, and more?"

The form of these questions assumes that benign, costless, *selective interventions* of the type Williamson considered are possible. This requires a decision maker with the authority to intervene, the interest in doing so only when appropriate, and the ability to consider and reject interventions without distorting the behavior of others in the organization. We argue that these requirements realistically cannot be met.

We take the view that what most distinguishes any centralized organization is the authority and autonomy of its top decision makers or management – that is, their broad rights to intervene in lower-level decisions and the relative immunity of their decisions from intervention by others.[3] Increases in centralized authority carry with them increases in the discretionary power to intervene. This increased power necessarily has costs that are avoided in more decentralized contexts. From this perspective, the principles that guide a firm's decision whether to manufacture an input (centralized organization) or to buy it from an independent supplier (decentralized organization) can be applied equally well to evaluate the relative productive efficiency of capitalist and socialist economic systems.

---

[3] This contrasts with Coase's view (1937, p. 389) that "the distinguishing mark of the firm is the supersession of the price mechanism" and with the view of Alchian and Demsetz (1972) that a firm is principally a "nexus of contracts."

Two kinds of costs generally accompany increases in discretionary central-ized authority. Both have the same fundamental cause: The very existence of such authority makes possible its inappropriate use. The first kind arises because those with discretionary authority may misuse it directly, on their own initiative. The second arises because others in the organization may attempt to persuade or manipulate those with authority to use it excessively or inappropriately. Inap-propriate interventions, the attempts to induce them, and the organization's efforts to control both – all generate costs of increased centralization.

The first source of the costs of centralized, discretionary authority is inap-propriate interventions that occur because individuals with increased authority are unable or unwilling to resist interfering where or in ways that they should not. This may happen simply because the individuals feel an imperative to manage – that is, after all, what managers are paid to do! Business people often cite this imperative to intervene as a characteristic and a cost of gov-ernment bureaucracies: Bureaucrats look for something to do, whether or not their intervention is likely to be helpful. Private managers are presumably not immune to this failure, let alone to believing that their interventions will be beneficial when they are actually unlikely to be. Another possible reason for inappropriate intervention is that individuals in authority may have personal interests in decisions: Will the empty lot next to the apartment building owned by the park commissioner's cousin be converted into a city park? Will the executive's protégé be appointed to replace a retiring division head? For any of these reasons, authority will be exercised more often and in other ways than efficiency alone dictates.

In a related vein are the costs of outright corruption, which is possible only with discretionary centralized authority: The central authority may seek bribes or other favors and may block efficient decisions when bribes are not paid. . . .

Note that monetary bribes themselves do not necessarily represent an eco-nomic inefficiency, because they are but transfers. Rather, the costs of corruption arise first because productive decisions are distorted, either from favoring those who pay bribes or from punishing those who refuse. Secondly, if trust between individuals and faith in the system facilitate economic activity, widespread corruption and bribery may result in further, less direct, but possibly more significant costs.

These costs of discretionary authority depend on flaws in decision makers' incentives, intelligence, or character. Presumably, then, they can be reduced or even eliminated by vesting authority in honest, wise individuals and by giving them incentives to care about organizational performance. However, discretionary authority results in a second kind of cost which is incurred even when the central authority is both incorruptible and intelligent enough not to interfere in operations without good reason. These are what we call *influence costs*.

Influence costs arise first because individuals and groups within the organization expend time, effort, and ingenuity in attempting to affect others' decisions to their benefit and secondly because inefficient decisions result either directly from these influence activities or, less directly, from attempts to prevent or control them.

At first blush, it might seem easy to avoid these costs: Simply have decision makers ignore attempts at influence. If this does not provide a sufficient incentive to deter influence activities, severely punish any such behavior. In some circumstances, this may in fact be possible, and we will assume that organizations follow this policy whenever feasible. However, an essential difficulty exists with such an approach. The policy of ignoring attempts at influence – and, indeed, the policy of selective intervention more generally – is not what macroeconomists call "dynamically consistent" or what game theorists call "subgame perfect." *Ex post,* when relevant information is available and those at lower levels have already taken actions that cannot be reversed, there will be interventions that are now organizationally desirable and that the center will thus want to take. However, recognition of the center's *ex post* incentives will alter the behavior of the organization's members in ways that are organizationally dysfunctional. Thus, the center would like to be able to commit *ex ante* to not making these interventions – that is, to restrict its own discretion. For example, decision makers might want to motivate workers by committing to promote the most productive one. However, after the fact, they would want to renege and promote the worker who, on the basis of training and other credentials, appears best qualified. As long as central decision makers reserve for themselves the right to make selective interventions, commitments are impossible, if only because of the impossibility of complete contracting. Thus, the possibility of attempts at influence will remain and will inevitably exert costs (Milgrom and Roberts, 1988a).

One reason influence is inevitable is that decision makers must rely on others for information that is not easily available to them directly. Central office executives are not islands unto themselves; they commonly rely extensively on others for information, suggestions, and analyses to reach decisions. Moreover, the employees affected by a decision are often the very ones executives must rely on. In such circumstances, employees will have strong reasons to try to influence decisions, and their attempts at influence will impose costs on the organization. For example, employees may distort the information they report or withhold information from the central office and from other employees. Candidates for possible promotions may spend valuable time polishing their credentials, thereby establishing their qualifications for the desired assignment at the expense of current performance (Milgrom and Roberts, 1988a). Managers, worried about how higher authorities will evaluate their performance, may avoid risky but profitable investments because such investments pose career risks if they turn out badly (Holmstrom, 1982b). Or, less specifically, employees may simply waste time trying to figure out what issues are on the agenda, how they might be personally affected, and how to shape decisions to their benefit. The loss of productivity from these distortions in the way employees spend their time, report their information, and make their decisions is one category of influence costs. These are costs of discretionary authority because they arise only when an authority exists whose decisions can be influenced.

A second sort of influence cost arises when central authorities make suboptimal decisions because of employees' influence activities, particularly their suppressing or distorting information. In some situations these distortions may be undone by properly accounting for individuals' incentives, and efficient decisions may still be reached (Milgrom and Roberts, 1986). However, when these incentives are unclear or when the underlying information is so complex that unscrambling is impossible, decision makers will have to rely on information that they know is incomplete or inaccurate. Consider, for example, the problems of the U.S. Congress in dealing with military appropriations. Congress must rely on the military for information, and it understands that the military may have incentives to distort the information that it provides. But it is impossible for Congress to disentangle interservice rivalries, individual career ambitions, and genuine concerns with national security, all of which motivate particular spending requests. Even if the incentives of those providing the information to distort or suppress it could be determined, the impossible problem of inferring what information they actually have would still remain. In such complex circumstances, decisions must be based on fundamentally incorrect information, and inefficient decisions must be expected.

The incentives to attempt to influence an organization's decisions are, to some extent, endogenous. The costs and benefits of influence activities depend on an organization's information-gathering and decision-making procedures and on its reward systems. Thus, careful organizational design can at least partially control the direct costs of influence activities. For example, Holstrom and Ricart (1986) have investigated how capital budgeting practices that reward investment and growth per se and establish high internal hurdle rates for investments can help alleviate managers' natural reluctance to undertake risky but profitable investments. Milgrom (1988) and Milgrom and Roberts (1988a) have examined how compensation and promotion policies can be used to make employees more nearly indifferent about company decisions, thereby reducing resistance to change and other organizationally unproductive influence activities. As an alternative to using compensation policies and promotion criteria to control incentives to attempt influence, Milgrom and Roberts also explored limiting communication between decision makers and potentially affected parties and otherwise restricting these parties' involvement in decision making.

152

Even the very boundaries of the firm can become design variables used to control influence. The widespread practice of spinning off or isolating unprofitable subsidiaries can be partly interpreted in these terms: It is done to prevent the subsidiary's employees and management from imposing large influence costs on the organization through attempts to claim corporate resources to cover their losses and thereby to avoid having to become efficient or to curtail operations. Similarly, a university's policy of requiring its schools to be "tubs on their own bottoms," each individually responsible for its revenues and expenditures (subject to formula payments to or from the central administration), limits influence activities that would amount to raids on other schools' or the university's resources. For example, when universities centrally determine and fund salaries, research support, and teaching loads, faculties have incentives to try to get more for themselves from the center by invoking comparisons with other schools and departments rather than by raising their own resources. Of course, they can (and do) still make the same complaints when financial boundaries exist between schools, but they have less to gain by doing so because resources cannot easily be shifted from the envied to the envious.

Of course, such responses as these bring costs of their own. Worthwhile investments will be foregone, and managers may seek out the wrong investment opportunities; less qualified people will be assigned to key positions; too many valued employees will quit to increase their pay; bad decisions will be made because communication has been restricted and available information is not used; and desirable resource transfers between divisions will not be effected. These costs of employing policies and organizational structures that would be inefficient if influence activities were not a problem are then in themselves a third category of influence costs.

In this context, an important element of organizational design involves trading off these various costs. For example, Japanese firms make use both of wage policies and of organizational rules to facilitate extensive involvement of their employees in decision making without encouraging excessive attempts at influence. Lifetime employment for key decision makers, relatively small wage differentials within age cohorts, relatively low wages for senior executives, and promotions based largely on seniority combine to insulate employees from the effects of the firm's investment and promotion decisions and to make promotion decisions relatively immune to influence.

. . .

Taken together, the activities just described could consume a major portion of division heads', and central office personnel's, time, diverting them from more productive activities. The boundaries between independent firms reduce the possibilities for influence. Consequently, those boundaries reduce influence costs.

. . .

The validity of these arguments depends on our characterization of the firm as a centrally controlled organization considerably free from outside intervention. In capitalist economies, several institutions support executives' having much more extensive control over their firms than do courts or government agencies acting from outside. First, property rights tend to limit government interventions more than executive interventions because property rights over the firm generally reside at the executive level or higher. Thus, a court, a governmental regulatory agency, and a firm's central office can all order a plant that is polluting the environment to cease operations until the problem is fixed, but the central office can also replace the plant manager if it finds that to be the most effective way to do the job. Second, executives generally have better and more fluid information systems than courts or government agencies do. Managers in firms hear most of the important information they need in conversations and meetings where they can query sources informally to resolve ambiguities and acquire needed detail. In contrast, agencies and courts must rely on written reports or adversary proceedings. Finally, executives can deliver incentives directly where they count most – to individual employees – and can tailor the incentives to take the form either of rewards, such as pay increases, bonuses, promotions, or desirable assignments, or of punishments, such as undesirable assignments or layoffs. The incentives courts and government agencies offer consist mostly of threats to collect penalties against the firm's treasury.

. . .

Summary and conclusions

. . .

Whenever a central authority, whether a governmental unit or an executive in a firm, has discretion to intervene, certain identifiable costs are incurred. These include (1) a tendency for the authority to intervene excessively, both because intervening is that authority's job and because the authority may have a personal interest (licit or illicit, but in either case differing from the organization's interests) in certain decisions; (2) increased time devoted to influence activities and a corresponding reduction in organizational productivity, as interested parties seek to have the authority intervene in particular ways or to adopt their favored alternatives; (3) poorer decision making resulting from the distortion of information associated with influence activities; and (4) a loss of efficiency as the organization adapts its structure and policies to control influence activities and their costs.

We believe that these ideas about influence cost are important in analyzing organizations. For example, they might be used to examine issues of corporate control, financial structure, bankruptcy, proxy fights, and takeovers. Moreover, because influence activities are essentially political and because the theory applies equally to public and private organizations, we believe that it may also prove valuable in the more general study of political economy.

CHAPTER 12

The boundaries of the firm revisited

BENGT HOLMSTROM AND JOHN ROBERTS

Bengt Holmstrom was born in 1949 in Helsinki, Finland. He earned his Ph.D. in economics from the Graduate School of Business, Stanford University, in 1978. When this article was published, he was Edwin J. Beinecke Professor of Management Studies, Yale School of Management. He is presently the Paul A. Samuelson Professor of Economics at Massachusetts Institute of Technology.

John Roberts is the John H. and Irene S. Scully Professor of Economics, Strategic Management and International Business in the Graduate School of Business, Stanford University. See also the chapter by Roberts and Milgrom.

Why do firms exist? What is their function, and what determines their scope? These remain the central questions in the economics of organization. They are also central questions for business executives and corporate strategists. The worldwide volume of corporate mergers and acquisitions exceeded $1.6 trillion in 1997. It is hard to imagine that so much time, effort and investment bankers' fees would be spent on adjusting firm boundaries unless there was some underlying economic gain. Indeed, the exceptional levels of merger and acquisition activity over the past two decades are a strong indication that economically significant forces do determine organizational boundaries.

The study of firm boundaries originated with the famous essay by Coase (1937), who raised the question of why we observe so much economic activity inside formal organizations if, as economists commonly argue, markets are such powerful and effective mechanisms for allocating scarce resources. Coase's answer was in terms of the costs of transacting in a world of imperfect information. When the transaction costs of market exchange are high, it may be less costly to coordinate production through a formal organization than through a market.

In large part thanks to the work of Williamson (1975, 1985), recent decades have seen a resurgence of interest in Coase's fundamental insight that firm

Reprinted in abridged form from Bengt Holmstrom and John Roberts, "The Boundaries of the Firm Revisited," *Journal of Economic Perspectives,* 12, 4(1998): 73–94. Reprinted with the permission of the American Economic Association.

boundaries can be explained by efficiency considerations. Our understanding of firm boundaries has been sharpened by identifying more precisely the nature and sources of transaction costs in different circumstances. In the process, the focus of attention has shifted away from the coordination problems originally emphasized by Coase and towards the role of firm boundaries in providing incentives. In particular, the most influential work during the last two decades on why firms exist, and what determines their boundaries, has been centered on what has come to be known as the "hold-up problem."

. . .

The next section of the paper will review the two strains of work that have dominated the research on the boundaries of the firm: transaction cost economics and property rights theory. Both theories, while quite different in their empirical implications, focus on the role of ownership in supporting relationship-specific investments in a world of incomplete contracting and potential hold-ups. There is much to be learned from this work.

In this essay, however, we argue for taking a much broader view of the firm and the determination of its boundaries. Firms are complex mechanisms for coordinating and motivating individuals' activities. They have to deal with a much richer variety of problems than simply the provision of investment incentives and the resolution of hold-ups. Ownership patterns are not determined solely by the need to provide investment incentives, and incentives for investment are provided by a variety of means, of which ownership is but one. Thus, approaches that focus on one incentive problem that is solved by the use of a single instrument give much too limited a view of the nature of the firm, and one that is potentially misleading.

. . .

Investment incentives are not provided by ownership alone

There is no doubt that hold-up problems are of central concern to business people. In negotiating joint venture agreements, venture capital contracts, or any of a number of other business deals, much time is spent on building in protections against hold-ups. At the same time, such contracts are *prima facie* evidence that hold-up problems do not get resolved solely by integration of buyer and seller into a single party – the firm. Indeed, there seems to be something of a trend today toward disintegration, outsourcing, contracting out, and dealing through the market rather than bringing everything under the umbrella of the organization. This trend has seen the emergence of alternative, often ingenious solutions to hold-up problems.

Japanese subcontracting

The pattern of relations between Japanese manufacturing firms and their suppliers offers a prominent instance where the make-buy dichotomy and related theorizing have been less than satisfactory. Although the basic patterns apply in a number of industries (including, for example, electronics), the practices in the automobile industry are best documented (Asanuma, 1989, 1992). These patterns have spread from Japan to the auto industry in the United States and elsewhere, and from autos to many other areas of manufacturing. These practices feature long-term, close relations with a limited number of independent suppliers that seem to mix elements of market and hierarchy. Apparently, these long-term relations substitute for ownership in protecting specific assets.

Two points of contrast in the treatment of specific investments between traditional U.S. practice and the Japanese model present particular problems for the received theory. The first concerns investments in designing specialized parts and components. Traditional U.S. practice featured either internal procurement or arm's length, short-term contracting. Design-intensive products were very often procured internally (Monteverde and Teece, 1982).[1] When products were outsourced, the design was typically done by the automaker, with the drawings being provided to the suppliers. This pattern is what hold-up stories would predict, for the investment in design is highly specific and probably cannot be protected fully by contracts; thus, external suppliers will not make such relationship-specific investments, for fear that they will be held up by buyers after their investments are in place. In stark contrast, it is normal practice for Japanese auto firms to rely on their suppliers to do the actual design of the products supplied. The design costs are then to be recovered through the sale price of the part, with the understanding that this price will be adjusted in light of realized volumes.

A second contrast: traditional U.S. practice has been that physical assets specific to an automaker's needs are owned by the automaker. This clearly applies in the case of internally procured items, but it also holds in cases where the assets are used by the external supplier in its own factory. For example, the dies used in making a particular car part will belong to the automaker, even though they are used in the supplier's plant on the supplier's presses. Again, this accords well with the transaction cost story of potential hold-up by the automaker.[2] In Japan, in contrast, these specific investments are made by the supplier, who

---

[1] However, this pattern did not become standard until decades after the founding of the industry. Earlier, something akin to the practices associated now with the Japanese was the norm. See Helper (1991).

[2] An alternative story is more in the line of Williamson's earlier discussions emphasizing inefficiencies in ex post bargaining. The useful life of a die far exceeds the one-year contracting period. If the supplier owned the die, changing suppliers would require negotiating the sale of the die to the new supplier, and this could be costly and inefficient.

retains ownership of the dies. This would seem to present the automaker with temptations to appropriate the returns on these assets, once the supplier has made the relationship-specific investment. Moreover, because the Japanese auto manufacturers typically have a very small number of suppliers of any part, component or system, the supplier would also seem to be in a position to attempt opportunistic renegotiation by threatening to withhold supply for which there are few good, timely substitutes.

The Japanese pattern is directly at odds with transaction cost theory. Meanwhile, the divergence in ownership of the dies between the two countries presents problems for attempts to explain ownership allocation solely in terms of providing incentives for investment.[3]

In Japanese practice, explicit contracting is not used to overcome the incentive problems involved in outsourced design and ownership of specific assets. In fact, the contracts between the Japanese automakers and their suppliers are short and remarkably imprecise, essentially committing the parties only to work together to resolve difficulties as they emerge. Indeed, they do not even specify prices, which instead are renegotiated on a regular basis. From the hold-up perspective, the prospect of frequent renegotiations over the prices of parts that are not yet even designed would certainly seem problematic.

The key to making this system work is obviously the long-term, repeated nature of the interaction.[4] Although supply contracts are nominally year-by-year, the shared understanding is that the chosen supplier will have the business until the model is redesigned, which lasts typically four or five years. Moreover, the expectation is that the firms will continue to do business together indefinitely. There has been very little turnover of Japanese auto parts suppliers: over a recent eleven-year period, only three firms out of roughly 150 ceased to be members of *kyohokai*, the association of first-level Toyota suppliers (Asanuma, 1989).

The familiar logic of repeated games, that future rewards and punishments motivate current behavior, supports the on-going dealings.[5] An attempted hold-up would presumably bring severe future penalties. As importantly, the amount of future business awarded to a supplier is linked to ratings of supplier performance. The auto companies carefully monitor supplier behavior – including cost reductions, quality levels and improvements, general cooperativeness, and so on – and frequent redesigns allow them to punish and reward performance on an on-going basis. In this sense, supplier relationships in Japan are potentially *less*, not more, locked in than in the traditional U.S. model, where at the

---

[3] Interestingly, Toyota followed U.S. practice in supplying the dies used by at least some of the suppliers to its Kentucky assembly plant (Milgrom and Roberts, 1993).

[4] Taylor and Wiggins (1997) argue that these long-term relations are also the means used in the Japanese system to solve moral hazard problems with respect to quality.

[5] Baker et al. (1997) [Ed.: published as Baker, Gibbons and Murphy 2002] present a formal analysis of the choice between external and internal procurement, taking into account the important fact that long-term relational contracts can be maintained both within a firm as well as across firms.

corresponding point in the value chain, the supplier is typically an in-house division or department.

Having a small number of suppliers is crucial to the Japanese system. It reduces the costs of monitoring and increases the frequency of transacting, both of which strengthen the force of reputation. Also, the rents that are generated in the production process do not have to be shared too widely, providing the source for significant future rewards. This logic underlies the normal "two-supplier system" used at Toyota. There is more than one supplier to permit comparative performance evaluation, to allow shifting of business as a reward or punishment, to provide insurance against mishaps, and perhaps to limit the hold-up power of each supplier, but the number is not chosen to minimize hold-ups.

The relationship is marked by rich information sharing, including both schedules of production plans necessary for just-in-time inventory management and also details of technology, operations and costs. The automakers also assist the suppliers in improving productivity and lowering costs: technical support engineers are a major part of the automakers' purchasing staff, and they spend significant amounts of time at the suppliers' facilities. All this in turn means that potential information asymmetries are reduced, which presumably facilitates both performance evaluation and the pricing negotiations.[6]

Perhaps the major problem in the system may be that the automakers are inherently too powerful and thus face too great a temptation to misbehave opportunistically. Indeed, many Japanese observers of the system have interpreted it in terms of the automakers' exploitation of their power. One counterbalance to this power asymmetry is the supplier association, which facilitates communication among the suppliers and ensures that if the auto company exploits its power over one, all will know and its reputation will be damaged generally. This raises the cost of misbehavior. In this regard, the fact that Toyota itself organized an association of the leading suppliers for its Kentucky assembly plant is noteworthy (Milgrom and Roberts, 1993).

An alternative solution to this imbalance would be for the automaker to own the dies, as in the United States. Here a property rights explanation may be useful: under this arrangement, the supplier would not have the same incentives to maintain the dies, since it must be very hard to contract over the amount of wear and tear and its prevention.[7]

---

[6] Strikingly, as automobile electronics have become more sophisticated and a greater part of the cost of a car, Toyota has ceased to rely exclusively on its former sole supplier, Denso, and has developed its own in-house capabilities in this area. Arguably, this was to overcome information asymmetries and their associated costs (Ahmadjian and Lincoln, 1997). In contrast, see the discussion of the effects of Ford's complete reliance on Lear for developing seats for the redesigned 1997 Taurus (Walton, 1997).

[7] See Segal and Whinston (1997) for a model in the property rights spirit that is relevant to these issues.

The boundaries of the firm revisited

Mini-mills, exclusive sourcing and inside contracting

Another significant shift in the organization of production is illustrated by Nucor, the most successful steel maker in the United States over the past 20 years. Nucor operates mini-mills, which use scrap (mainly car bodies) as raw material for steel production. After an initial technological breakthrough, Nucor started to expand aggressively (Ghemawat, 1995). The strategy required much capital, and to save on capital outlays, Nucor decided to outsource its entire procurement of steel scrap. Traditionally, mini-mills had integrated backwards, partly to secure an adequate supply of raw material and partly because sourcing entails substantial know-how and so was considered "strategically critical." Chaparral Steel, another big mini-mill operator, continues to be integrated backwards, for instance.

In a break with the tradition, Nucor decided to make a single firm, the David J. Joseph Company (DJJ), its sole supplier of scrap. Total dependence on a single supplier would seem to carry significant hold-up risks, but for more than a decade, this relationship has been working smoothly and successfully. Unlike in the Japanese subcontracting system, there are certain contractual supports. Prices are determined by a cost-plus formula to reflect market conditions, and an "evergreen" contract specifies that the parties have to give advance warning (about half a year in advance) if they intend to terminate the relationship. Even so, there is plenty of room for opportunism. Despite transparent cost accounting (essentially, open books), DJJ can misbehave, since realized costs need not be the same as potential costs. Asset specificity remains significant even with the six-month warning period, since a return to traditional sourcing and selling methods would be quite disruptive and expensive for both sides. Indeed, one reason why the partnership has been working so well may be the high degree of mutual dependence: Nucor's share of DJJ's scrap business is estimated to be over 50 percent.

The success of Nucor's organizational model has led other mini-mills to emulate and refine it. In England, Co Steel has gone as far as relying on its sole supplier to make ready-to-use "charges," the final assemblage of materials to go into the steel-making ovens. The production technology for charges is quite complicated: about 20–30 potential ingredients go into each mixture, with the mix depending on the desired properties of the final product, and big cost savings can be had by optimizing the use of the different inputs. This activity entails much know-how and requires extensive information exchange with the steel plant to match inputs with final product demand. The charges must be prepared by the supplier on Co Steel's premises, both for logistical reasons and to facilitate information sharing. In transaction cost economics, such a cheek-by-jowl situation would be an obvious candidate for integration. Yet, the industry is moving in the direction of disintegration in the belief that specialization will

161

save on costs by eliminating duplicate assets, streamlining the supply chain, and providing better incentives for the supplier through improved accountability.

Related experiments of "inside contracting" include Volkswagen's new car manufacturing plant in Brazil, where the majority of the production workers in the factory are employees, not of Volkswagen, but of subcontractors that provide and install components and systems on the cars as they move along the line. It is too early to tell whether other firms will return to inside contracting, which used to be quite common in the United States up to World War I (Buttrick, 1952), and whether such a move will be successful. But evidently, even potentially large hold-up problems have not deterred recent experimentation.

Airline alliances

Another illustration of close coordination without ownership is provided by airline alliances, which have proliferated in recent years. Coordinating flight schedules to take advantage of economies of scope requires the parties to resolve an intricate set of issues, particularly ones related to complex "yield management" decisions on how to allocate seats across different price categories and how to shift prices as the flight date approaches. Information and contracting problems abound, and it is hardly surprising that tensions occasionally surface. For instance, KLM and Northwest Airlines recently ran into a dispute that had to be resolved by dismantling their cross-ownership structure. But interestingly, this did not prevent KLM and Northwest from deepening their commitment to their North Atlantic alliance by agreeing to eliminate, over a period of years, all duplicate support operations in the United States and Europe. With the completion of this deal, KLM and Northwest have made themselves extraordinarily interdependent in one of the most profitable segments of their business. A 13-year exclusive contract, with an "evergreen" provision requiring a three-year warning before pull-out, is the main formal protection against various forms of opportunism, but undoubtedly the real safeguard comes from the sizable future rents that can be reaped by continued good behavior.

Why don't the two airlines instead integrate? Regulations limiting foreign ownership and potential government antitrust objections are a factor, as may be tax considerations. However, an explanation we have been given is that airline cultures (and labor unions) are very strong and merging them is extremely difficult. Pilot seniority is a particularly touchy issue.

Contractual assets and network influence

In property rights theory, the boundaries of the firm are identified with the ownership of assets, but in the real world, control over assets is a more subtle matter. "Contractual assets" can often be created rather inexpensively to serve some of the same purposes that the theory normally assigns to ownership: to provide levers that give bargaining power and thereby enhance investment incentives. What we have in mind here are contracts that allocate decision rights much like ownership; for instance, exclusive dealing contracts such as Nucor's, or licensing agreements of various kinds. Such "governance contracts" are powerful vehicles for regulating market relationships. With increased disintegration, governance contracts seem to have become more nuanced and sophisticated. They place firms at the center of a network of relationships, rather than as owners of a clearly defined set of capital assets.

. . .

Microsoft and the web of inter-firm relations centered around it provide another illustration. The stock market values Microsoft at around $250 billion, which is more than $10 million per employee. Surely very little of this is attributable to its ownership of physical assets. Instead, by leveraging its control over software standards, using an extensive network of contracts and agreements that are informal as well as formal and that include firms from small start-ups to Intel, Sony and General Electric, Microsoft has gained enormous influence in the computer industry and beyond. We are not experts on Microsoft's huge network of relationships, but it seems clear that the traditional hold-up logic does poorly in explaining how the network has developed and what role it serves. If one were to measure asset specificity simply in terms of separation costs, the estimates for breaking up some of the relationships – say, separating Intel from Microsoft – would likely be large. Yet these potential losses do not seem to cause any moves in the direction of ownership integration.

A similar pattern can be observed in the biotechnology industry (Powell, 1996). As in the computer industry, the activities of the different parties are highly inter-related, with different firms playing specialized roles in the development and marketing of different products. Most firms are engaged in a large number of partnerships; for instance, in 1996 Genentech was reported to have 10 marketing partnerships, 20 licensing arrangements, and more than 15 formal research collaborations (Powell, p. 205). Significant relationship-specific investments are made by many parties, and potential conflicts must surely arise after these investments are in place. Yet the system works, thanks to creative contractual assets – patents and licensing arrangements being the oldest and most ingenious – but also to the force of reputation in a market that is rather transparent, because of the close professional relationships among the researchers.

163

Firm boundaries are responsive to more than investment incentives

The examples above make clear that there are many alternatives to integration when one tries to solve hold-up problems. The examples also suggest that ownership may be responsive to problems other than underinvestment in specific assets. Speaking broadly, the problems relate to contractual externalities of various kinds, of which hold-ups are just one.

Resolving agency problems

An example of how agency issues can affect the boundaries of an organization is whether a firm employs its sales force directly, or whether it uses outside sales agents. The best-known example here involves electronic parts companies, some of which hire their own sales agents while others sell through separate supply companies (Andersen, 1985; Andersen and Schmittlein, 1984). Originally, Andersen (1985) appears to have expected that the observed variation in this choice would relate to the degree of asset specificity; for example, the extent to which investment by sales people with knowledge about products was specific to a particular company. Instead, measurement costs and agency concerns turned out to be central. An employee sales force is used when individual performance is difficult to measure and when non-selling activities (like giving customer support or gathering information about customers' needs) are important to the firm; otherwise, outside companies are used.

Holmstrom and Milgrom (1991a, 1994) rationalize this pattern with a model of multi-task agency, in which sales people carry out three tasks: making current sales, cultivating long-term customer satisfaction, and gathering and relaying information on customer needs. If the latter two activities are important and if the three activities compete for the agent's time, then the marginal rewards to improved performance on each must be comparable in strength; otherwise, the ill-paid activities will be slighted. Because performance in non-selling activities is arguably hard to measure, it may be best to provide balanced, necessarily lower-powered incentives for all three activities.

Offering weak incentives to an outside sales agent can be problematic, however, because the agent may then divert all effort to selling other firms' products that come with stronger rewards for sales. With an employee, this problem can be handled with a salary and a low commission rate, because the employee's outside activities are more easily constrained and promotion and other broader incentives can be used within the firm to influence the agent's behavior.[8] This

---

[8] For a further discussion of the idea that low-powered incentives are a major virtue of firm organization and can help explain firm boundaries, see Holmstrom (1996).

logic also explains why outside agents commonly receive higher commission rates than does an inside sales force.

A less familiar illustration of how ownership responds to agency concerns comes from multi-unit retail businesses. Some of these businesses are predominantly organized though traditional franchise arrangements, in which a manufacturer contracts with another party to sell its products in a dedicated facility, as in gasoline retailing. Others, including fast-food restaurants, hotels and pest-control services, are organized in what is called "business concept" franchising. The franchiser provides a brand name and usually other services like advertising, formulae and recipes, managerial training and quality control inspections, collecting a fee from the franchisee in return, but the physical assets and production are owned and managed by the franchisee. Sometimes franchisers (like McDonald's) own and operate a number of outlets themselves. Finally, other businesses are commonly organized with a single company owning all the multiple outlets and hiring the outlet managers as employees. Examples are grocery supermarkets and department stores. What accounts for such differences?

It is hard to see how the specificity of the assets – real estate, cash registers, kitchens and inventories – differs between supermarkets and restaurants in such a way that transactions cost arguments would lead to the observed pattern. Indeed, the assets involved are often not very specific at all. Alternatively, applying the Hart-Moore property rights model here would involve identifying non-contractible investments that are unavailable to the other party if the franchise agreement is terminated or the store manager's employment should end. Noncontractible investments by the center in building the brand might qualify on the one hand, but in many cases, it is hard to see what the investments of the operator might be. For example, a fast-food restaurant manager might invest in training the workers and building a clientele, but these investments would presumably still be effective even if the manager were replaced by another. Further, these should also be investments that vary across cases in such a way that it is more important to provide the strong incentives of ownership to the manager of the outlet in one case and to the central party in the other.[9]

An alternative approach based on the need to offer incentives for effort has been proposed by Maness (1996). This approach begins by noting that any elements of the retail outlet's financial costs that are sufficiently difficult to measure must accrue to the owner of the outlet as residual claimant, because they cannot be passed by contract to another party. Suppose then that all costs are non-contractible in this sense; that is, since the level or appropriateness of various costs cannot be well-monitored from outside, such costs cannot be part of an agreed-upon contract. Then, the only possibility for payments from the owner to the other party is on the basis of revenues. Indeed, actual franchise

---

[9] See Lutz (1995) for a formal model of franchising along these lines.

fees are almost always based on revenues and not on costs (Maness, p. 102) and incentive pay for employee managers is also often based on sales. In such a structure, the employee-manager has no direct incentive to control costs under central ownership, while the franchiser has no incentives for cost-reduction under local ownership. Because the efforts of either party might affect costs, this creates a potential inefficiency. The solution is to lodge ownership with the party to whom it is most important to give incentives for cost control. Maness then argues that cost control in a fast-food operation is more influenced by the local manager's efforts at staffing, training, controlling waste and the like, while costs in supermarkets are most influenced by the inventory and warehousing system, which can be centrally managed. Thus, an explanation emerges for the observed patterns: ownership is assigned to give appropriate incentives for cost control.

A more complex example involves gasoline retailing in the United States and Canada, which has been studied by Shepard (1993) and Slade (1996), respectively. They document a variety of contractual arrangements that are used in each country between the gasoline refining company and the station operator and, in the United States, significant variation in ownership of the station. While the physical assets used in gasoline retailing are quite specific to that use, a station can be switched from one brand to another with a little paint and new signs. Consequently, neither study attempted to explain the variation in contractual and ownership arrangements in terms of specific assets and hold-up.

Both studies find that the observed patterns are consistent with the arrangements being chosen to deal with problems of inducing effort and its allocation among tasks. These arrangements differ over the strengths of the incentives given to sell gasoline and other, ancillary services like repairs, car washes, or convenience store items. In turn, these ancillary services differ in the ease and accuracy of performance measurement. The observed patterns were generally consistent with their being selected to provide appropriately balanced incentives. For example, Shepard's (1993) work notes that in repair services, effort is hard to measure and, more importantly, monitoring the realized costs and revenues by the refiner may be tricky. This should make it less likely that the refinery will own the station and employ the operator and more likely that an arrangement will be adopted where the operator is residual claimant on sales of all sorts, either owning the station outright or leasing it from the refiner on a long-term basis. This is what the data show. In Slade's (1996) data, the presence of repair did not affect the ownership of the station (essentially all the stations were refiner-owned). It did, however, favor leasing arrangements, where the operator is residual claimant on all sales, and diminished the likelihood of commission arrangements, which would offer unbalanced incentives because the operator is residual claimant on non-gasoline business but is paid only a small commission on gasoline sales. The presence of full service rather than just self-serve gasoline sales also favors moving away from the company-owned model, since it matches the returns to relationship-building with the costs, which are borne by the local operator.[10] However, adding a convenience store actually increases the likelihood of using company-owned and -operated stations in the U.S. data, which goes against this logic unless one assumes that monitoring of such sales is relatively easy.

Considering a broad variety of retailing businesses more generally, LaFontaine and Slade (1997) document that the contractual and ownership arrangements that are used are responsive to agency considerations.

. . .

Knowledge transfers and common assets

Information and knowledge are at the heart of organizational design, because they result in contractual and incentive problems that challenge both markets and firms. Indeed, information and knowledge have long been understood to be different from goods and assets commonly traded in markets. In light of this, it is surprising that the leading economic theories of firm boundaries have paid almost no attention to the role of organizational knowledge.[11] The subject certainly deserves more scrutiny.

One of the few economic theory papers to discuss knowledge and firm boundaries is Arrow (1975), who argued that information transmission between upstream and downstream firms may be facilitated by vertical integration. As we saw in the examples of Nucor and the case of Japanese subcontracting, however, this type of information transfer may actually work fairly well even without vertical integration. More significant problems are likely to emerge when a firm comes up with a better product or production technology. Sharing this knowledge with actual or potential competitors would be socially efficient and could in principle enrich both parties, but the dilemma is how to pay for the trade. Until the new ideas have been shown to work, the potential buyer is unlikely to want to pay a lot. Establishing the ideas' value, however, may require giving away most of the relevant information for free. Again, repeated

---

[10] A hold-up story is consistent with the fact that the presence of repair services favors dealer ownership over leasing arrangements in the U.S. data: a lessee who invests in building a clientele for repair work might worry that the refining company will raise the lease payments to appropriate the returns from this investment. This argument, however, does not do much to explain the pattern in the Canadian data, where the refiners own all the stations. One might also attempt to apply this logic to the choice between company-owned and leased stations by arguing that if the company owns the station it cannot motivate the employee-manager to invest in building a clientele because it will appropriate all the returns. However, this argument is not compelling without explaining how firms in other industries succeed in motivating their employees to undertake similar investments.

[11] In contrast, researchers outside economic theory have made much of the role of knowledge. See, for instance, Teece et al. (1994).

interactions can help here; in fact, even competing firms engage in continuous information exchange on a much larger scale than commonly realized. A common example is the extensive use of benchmarking, in which the costs of particular processes and operations are compared between firms. But when big leaps in knowledge occur, or when the nature of the knowledge transfer will involve ongoing investments or engagements, the issues become more complex. A natural option in that case is to integrate. Any claims about the value of knowledge are then backed up by the financial responsibility that comes with pairing cash flow and control rights.[12]

We think that knowledge transfers are a very common driver of mergers and acquisitions and of horizontal expansion of firms generally, particularly at times when new technologies are developing or when learning about new markets, technologies or management systems is taking place. Given the current level of merger and acquisition activity, and the amount of horizontal rather than vertical integration, it seems likely that many industries are experiencing such a period of change. The trend towards globalization of businesses has put a special premium on the acquisition and sharing of knowledge in geographically dispersed firms.

. . .

The problem with knowledge transfers can be viewed as part of the more general problem of free-riding when independent parties share a common asset. If bargaining is costly, the situation is most easily solved by making a single party responsible for the benefits as well as the costs of using the asset. Brand-names are another example of common assets that typically need to be controlled by a single entity.

Concluding remarks

It seems to us that the theory of the firm, and especially work on what determines the boundaries of the firm, has become too narrowly focused on the hold-up problem and the role of asset specificity. Think of arraying the set of coordination and motivation problems that the firm solves along one dimension of a matrix, and the set of instruments it has available along the other. Put the provision of investment incentives in column one and ownership-defined boundaries in row one. Let an element of the matrix be positive if the corresponding instrument is used to solve the corresponding problem, and zero

---

[12] Stuckey (1983), in his extraordinary study of the aluminum industry, reports that knowledge transfer was an important driver of joint ventures.

otherwise. So there is certainly a positive entry in row one, column one: ownership does affect incentives for investment. We have argued, however, that both the first column and the first row have many other positive elements; ownership boundaries serve many purposes and investment incentives are provided in many ways.

. . .

The property rights approach, with its emphasis on incentives driven by ownership, may be a good starting point. . . . But this approach also needs to expand its horizon and recognize that power derives from other sources than asset ownership and that other incentive instruments than ownership are available to deal with the joint problems of motivation and coordination. We do not believe that a theory of the firm that ignores contracts and other substitutes for ownership will prove useful for empirical studies. The world is replete with alternative instruments and, as always, the economically interesting action is at the margin of these substitutions.

PART III

The employment relation, the human factor, and internal organization

CHAPTER 13

Production, information costs, and economic organization

ARMEN ALCHIAN AND HAROLD DEMSETZ

Armen Alchian is Professor Emeritus at the University of California, Los Angeles. See also the chapter by Alchian with Benjamin Klein and Robert Crawford.

Harold Demsetz was born in Chicago, Illinois, in 1930. He received a Ph.D. in economics at Northwestern University in 1959. This article was written during his last months at the University of Chicago and his first months at the University of California, Los Angeles, where he has been Professor of Economics since 1971 and is now Professor of Economics, Emeritus.

The mark of a capitalistic society is that resources are owned and allocated by such nongovernmental organizations as firms, households, and markets. Resource owners increase productivity through cooperative specialization and this leads to the demand for economic organizations which facilitate cooperation. When a lumber mill employs a cabinetmaker, cooperation between specialists is achieved within a firm, and when a cabinetmaker purchases wood from a lumberman, the cooperation takes place across markets (or between firms). Two important problems face a theory of economic organization – to explain the conditions that determine whether the gains from specialization and cooperative production can better be obtained within an organization like the firm, or across markets, and to explain the structure of the organization.

It is common to see the firm characterized by the power to settle issues by fiat, by authority, or by disciplinary action superior to that available in the conventional market. This is delusion. The firm does not own all its inputs. It has no power of fiat, no authority, no disciplinary action any different in the slightest degree from ordinary market contracting between any two people. I can "punish" you only by withholding future business or by seeking redress in the courts for any failure to honor our exchange agreement. That is exactly all that any employer can do. He can fire or sue, just as I can fire my grocer by stopping purchases from him or sue him for delivering faulty products. What

Reprinted with minor abridgements from Armen Alchian and Harold Demsetz, "Production, Information Costs, and Economic Organization," *The American Economic Review,* 62 (1972): 777–95, by permission of the publisher.

then is the content of the presumed power to manage and assign workers to various tasks? Exactly the same as one little consumer's power to manage and assign his grocer to various tasks. The single consumer assigns his grocer to the task of obtaining whatever the customer can induce the grocer to provide at a price acceptable to both parties. That is precisely all that an employer can do to an employee. To speak of managing, directing, or assigning workers to various tasks is a deceptive way of noting that the employer continually is involved in renegotiation of contracts on terms that must be acceptable to both parties. Telling an employee to type this letter rather than to file that document is like my telling a grocer to sell me this brand of tuna rather than that brand of bread. I have no contract to continue to purchase from the grocer and neither the employer nor the employee is bound by any contractual obligations to continue their relationship. Long-term contracts between employer and employee are not the essence of the organization we call a firm. My grocer can count on my returning day after day and purchasing his services and goods even with the prices not always marked on the goods – because I know what they are – and he adapts his activity to conform to my directions to him as to what I want each day . . . he is not my employee.

Wherein then is the relationship between a grocer and his employee different from that between a grocer and his customers? It is in a *team* use of inputs and a centralized position of some party in the contractual arrangements of *all* other inputs. It is the *centralized contractual agent in a team productive process* – not some superior authoritarian directive or disciplinary power. Exactly what is a team process and why does it induce the contractual form, called the firm? These problems motivate the inquiry of this paper.

I. The metering problem

The economic organization through which input owners cooperate will make better use of their comparative advantages to the extent that it facilitates the payment of rewards in accord with productivity. If rewards were random, and without regard to productive effort, no incentive to productive effort would be provided by the organization; and if rewards were negatively correlated with productivity the organization would be subject to sabotage. Two key demands are placed on an economic organization – metering input productivity and metering rewards.[1]

Metering problems sometimes can be resolved well through the exchange of products across competitive markets, because in many situations markets yield

---

[1] Meter means to measure and also to apportion. One can meter (measure) output and one can also meter (control) the output. We use the word to denote both; the context should indicate which.

a high correlation between rewards and productivity. If a farmer increases his output of wheat by 10 percent at the prevailing market price, his receipts also increase by 10 percent. This method of organizing economic activity meters the *output directly*, reveals the marginal product and apportions the *rewards* to resource owners in accord with that direct measurement of their outputs. The success of this decentralized, market exchange in promoting productive specialization requires that changes in market rewards fall on those responsible for changes in *output*.[2]

The classic relationship in economics that runs from marginal productivity to the distribution of income implicitly *assumes* the existence of an organization, be it the market or the firm, that allocates rewards to resources in accord with their productivity. The problem of economic organization, the economical means of metering productivity and rewards, is not confronted directly in the classical analysis of production and distribution. Instead, that analysis tends to assume sufficiently economic – or zero cost – means, as if productivity automatically created its reward. We conjecture the direction of causation is the reverse – the specific system of rewarding which is relied upon stimulates a particular productivity response. If the economic organization meters poorly, with rewards and productivity only loosely correlated, then productivity will be smaller; but if the economic organization meters well, productivity will be greater. What makes metering difficult and hence induces means of economizing on metering costs?

---

[2] A producer's wealth would be reduced by the present capitalized value of the future income lost by loss of reputation. Reputation, i.e., credibility, is an asset, which is another way of saying that reliable information about expected performance is both a costly and a valuable good. For acts of God that interfere with contract performance, both parties have incentives to reach a settlement akin to that which would have been reached if such events had been covered by specific contingency clauses. The reason, again, is that a reputation for "honest" dealings – i.e., for actions similar to those that would probably have been reached had the contract provided this contingency – is wealth.

Almost every contract is open-ended in that many contingencies are uncovered. For example, if a fire delays production of a promised product by A to B, and if B contends that A has not fulfilled the contract, how is the dispute settled and what recompense, if any, does A grant to B? A person uninitiated in such questions may be surprised by the extent to which contracts permit either party to escape performance or to nullify the contract. In fact, it is hard to imagine any contract, which, when taken solely in terms of its stipulations, could not be evaded by one of the parties. Yet that is the ruling, viable type of contract. Why? Undoubtedly the best discussion that we have seen on this question is by Stewart Macaulay (1963).

There are means not only of detecting or preventing cheating but also for deciding how to allocate the losses or gains of unpredictable events or quality of items exchanged. Sales contracts contain warranties, guarantees, collateral, return privileges and penalty clauses for specific nonperformance. These are means of assignment of *risks* of losses of cheating. A lower price without warranty – an "as is" purchase – places more of the risk on the buyer while the seller buys insurance against losses of his "cheating." On the other hand, a warranty or return privilege or service contract places more risk on the seller with insurance being bought by the buyer.

II. Team production

Two men jointly lift heavy cargo into trucks. Solely by observing the total weight loaded per day, it is impossible to determine each person's marginal productivity. With team production it is difficult, solely by observing total output, to either define or determine *each* individual's contribution to this output of the cooperating inputs. The output is yielded by a team, by definition, and it is not a *sum* of separable outputs of each of its members. Team production of Z involves at least two inputs, X_i and X_j, with $\partial^2 Z/\partial X_i \partial X_j \neq 0$.[3] The production function is *not* separable into two functions each involving only inputs X_i or only inputs X_j. Consequently, there is no *sum* of Z of two separable functions to treat as the Z of the team production function. (An example of a *separable* case is $Z_i = aX_i^2$ and $Z_j = bX_j^2$, and $Z = Z_i + Z_j$. This is not team production.) There exist production techniques in which the Z obtained is greater than if X_i and X_j had produced separable Z. Team production will be used if it yields an output enough larger than the sum of separable production of Z to cover the costs of organizing and disciplining team members – the topics of this paper.[4]

Usual explanations of the gains from cooperative behavior rely on exchange and production in accord with the comparative advantage specialization principle with separable additive production. However, as suggested above there is a source of gain from cooperative activity involving working as a *team*, wherein individual cooperating inputs do not yield identifiable, separate products which can be *summed* to measure the total output. For this cooperative productive activity, here called "team" production, measuring *marginal* productivity and making payments in accord therewith is more expensive by an order of magnitude than for separable production functions.

Team production, to repeat, is production in which (1) several types of resources are used and (2) the product is not a sum of separable outputs of each cooperating resource. An additional factor creates a team organization problem – (3) not all resources used in team production belong to one person.

We do not inquire into why all the jointly used resources are not owned by one person, but instead into the types of organization, contracts, and informational and payment procedures used among owners of teamed inputs. With respect to the one-owner case, perhaps it is sufficient merely to note that (a) slavery is prohibited, (b) one might assume risk aversion as a reason for one person's not borrowing enough to purchase all the assets or sources of services rather than renting them, and (c) the purchase–resale spread may be so large that costs

---

[3] The function is separable into additive functions if the cross partial derivative is zero, i.e., if $\partial^2 Z/\partial X_i \partial X_j = 0$.

[4] With sufficient generality of notation and conception, this team production function could be formulated as a case of the generalized production function interpretation given by our colleague, E. A. Thompson (1970).

of short-term ownership exceed rental costs. Our problem is viewed basically as one of organization among different people, not of the physical goods or services, however much there must be selection and choice of combination of the latter.

How can the members of a team be rewarded and induced to work efficiently? In team production, marginal products of cooperative team members are not so directly and separably (i.e., cheaply) observable. What a team offers to the market can be taken as the marginal product of the team but not of the team members. The costs of metering or ascertaining the marginal products of the team's members is what calls forth new organizations and procedures. Clues to each input's productivity can be secured by observing *behavior* of individual inputs. When lifting cargo into the truck, how rapidly does a man move to the next piece to be loaded, how many cigarette breaks does he take, does the item being lifted tilt downward toward his side?

If detecting such behavior were costless, neither party would have an incentive to shirk, because neither could impose the cost of his shirking on the other (if their cooperation was agreed to voluntarily). But since costs must be incurred to monitor each other, each input owner will have more incentive to shirk when he works as part of a team than if his performance could be monitored easily or if he did not work as a team. If there is a net increase in productivity available by team production, net of the metering cost associated with disciplining the team, then team production will be relied upon rather than a multitude of bilateral exchange of separable individual outputs.

Both leisure and higher income enter a person's utility function.[5] Hence, each person should adjust his work and realized reward so as to equate the marginal rate of substitution between leisure and production of real output to his marginal rate of substitution in consumption. That is, he would adjust his rate of work to bring his demand prices of leisure and output to equality with their true costs. However, with detection, policing, monitoring, measuring, or metering costs, each person will be induced to take more leisure, because the effect of relaxing on *his realized* (reward) rate of substitution between output and leisure will be less than the effect on the *true* rate of substitution. His realized cost of leisure will fall more than the true cost of leisure, so he "buys" more leisure (i.e., more nonpecuniary reward).

If his relaxation cannot be detected perfectly at zero cost, part of its effects will be borne by others in the team, thus making *his* realized cost of relaxation less than the true total cost to the team. The difficulty of detecting such actions permits the private costs of his actions to be less than their full costs. Since each person responds to his private realizable rate of substitution (in production)

[5] More precisely: "if anything other than pecuniary income enters his utility function." Leisure stands for all nonpecuniary income for simplicity of exposition.

rather than the true total (i.e., social) rate, and so long as there are costs for other people to detect his shift toward relaxation, it will not pay (them) to force him to readjust completely by making him realize the true cost. Only enough efforts will be made to equate the marginal gains of detection activity with the marginal costs of detection; and that implies a lower rate of productive effort and more shirking than in a costless monitoring, or measuring, world.

In a university, the faculty use office telephones, paper, and mail for personal uses beyond strict university productivity. The university administrators could stop such practices by identifying *the* responsible person in each case, but they can do so only at higher costs than administrators are willing to incur. The extra costs of identifying each party (rather than merely identifying the presence of such activity) would exceed the savings from diminished faculty "turpitudinal peccadilloes." So the faculty is allowed some degree of "privileges, perquisites, or fringe benefits." And the total of the pecuniary wages paid is lower because of this irreducible (at acceptable costs) degree of amenity-seizing activity. Pay is lower in pecuniary terms and higher in leisure, conveniences, and ease of work. But still every person would prefer to see detection made more effective (if it were somehow possible to monitor costlessly) so that he, as part of the now more effectively producing team, could thereby realize a higher pecuniary pay and less leisure. If everyone could, at zero cost, have his reward-realized rate brought to the true production possibility real rate, all could achieve a more preferred position. But detection of the responsible parties is costly; that cost acts like a tax on work rewards.[6] Viable shirking is the result.

What forms of organizing team production will lower the cost of detecting "performance" (i.e., marginal productivity) and bring personally realized rates of substitution closer to true rates of substitution? Market competition, in principle, could monitor some team production. (It already *organizes* teams.) Input owners who are not team members can offer, in return for a smaller share of the team's rewards, to replace excessively (i.e., overpaid) shirking members. Market competition among potential team members would determine team membership and individual rewards. There would be no team leader, manager, organizer, owner, or employer. For such decentralized organizational control to work, outsiders, possibly after observing each team's total output, can speculate about their capabilities as team members and, by a market competitive process, revised teams with greater productive ability will be formed and sustained. Incumbent members will be constrained by threats of replacement by outsiders

---

[6] Do not assume that the sole result of the cost of detecting shirking is one form of payment (more leisure and less take home money). With several members of the team, each has an incentive to cheat against each other by engaging in more than the average amount of such leisure if the employer can not tell at zero cost which employee is taking more than average. As a result the total productivity of the team is lowered. Shirking detection costs thus change the form of payment and also result in lower total rewards. Because the cross partial derivatives are positive, shirking reduces other people's marginal products.

offering services for lower reward shares or offering greater rewards to the other members of the team. Any team member who shirked in the expectation that the reduced output effect would not be attributed to him will be displaced if his activity is detected. Teams of productive inputs, like business units, would evolve in apparent spontaneity in the market – without any central organizing agent, team manager, or boss.

But completely effective control cannot be expected from individualized market competition for two reasons. First, for this competition to be completely effective, new challengers for team membership must know where, and to what extent, shirking is a serious problem, i.e., know they can increase net output as compared with the inputs they replace. To the extent that this is true it is probably possible for existing fellow team members to recognize the shirking. But, by definition, the detection of shirking by observing team output is costly for team production. Secondly, assume the presence of detection costs, and assume that in order to secure a place on the team a new input owner must accept a smaller share of rewards (or a promise to produce more). Then his incentive to shirk would still be at least as great as the incentives of the inputs replaced, because he still bears less than the entire reduction in team output for which he is responsible.

III. The classical firm

One method of reducing shirking is for someone to specialize as a monitor to check the input performance of team members.[7] But who will monitor the monitor? One constraint on the monitor is the aforesaid market competition offered by other monitors, but for reasons already given, that is not perfectly effective. Another constraint can be imposed on the monitor: give him title to the net earnings of the team, net of payments to other inputs. If owners of cooperating inputs agree with the monitor that he is to receive any residual product above prescribed amounts (hopefully, the marginal value products of the other inputs), the monitor will have an added incentive not to shirk as a monitor. Specialization in monitoring plus reliance on a residual claimant status will reduce shirking, but additional links are needed to forge the firm of classical economic theory. How will the residual claimant monitor the other inputs?

---

[7] What is meant by performance? Input energy, initiative, work attitude, perspiration, rate of exhaustion? Or output? It is the latter that is sought – the *effect* or output. But performance is nicely ambiguous because it suggests both input and output. It is *nicely* ambiguous because as we shall see, sometimes by inspecting a team member's input activity we can better judge his output effect, perhaps not with complete accuracy but better than by watching the output of the *team*. It is not always the case that watching input activity is the only or best means of detecting, measuring, or monitoring output effects of each team member, but in some cases it is a useful way. For the moment the word performance glosses over these aspects and facilitates concentration on other issues.

We use the term *monitor* to connote several activities in addition to its disciplinary connotation. It connotes measuring output performance, apportioning rewards, observing the input behavior of inputs as means of detecting or estimating their marginal productivity and giving assignments or instructions in what to do and how to do it. (It also includes, as we shall show later, authority to terminate or revise contracts.) Perhaps the contrast between a football coach and team captain is helpful. The coach selects strategies and tactics and sends instructions about what plays to utilize. The captain is essentially an observer and reporter of the performance at close hand of the members. The latter is an inspector-steward and the former a supervisor-manager. For the present all these activities are included in the rubric "monitoring." All these tasks are, in principle, negotiable across markets, but we are presuming that such market measurement of marginal productivities and job reassignments are not so cheaply performed for team production. And in particular our analysis suggests that it is not so much the costs of spontaneously negotiating contracts in the markets among groups for team production as it is the detection of the performance of individual members of the team that calls for the organization noted here.

The specialist *who receives the residual rewards* will be the monitor of the members of the team (i.e., will manage the use of cooperative inputs). The monitor earns his residual through the reduction in shirking that he brings about, not only by the prices that he agrees to pay the owners of the inputs, but also by observing and directing the actions or uses of these inputs. *Managing or examining the ways to which inputs are used in team production is a method of metering the marginal productivity of individual inputs to the team's output.*

To discipline team members and reduce shirking, the residual claimant must have power to revise the contract terms and incentives of *individual* members without having to terminate or alter every other input's contract. Hence, team members who seek to increase their productivity will assign to the monitor not only the residual claimant right but also the right to alter individual membership and performance on the team. Each team member, of course, can terminate his own membership (i.e., quit the team), but only the monitor may unilaterally terminate the membership of any of the other members without necessarily terminating the team itself or his association with the team; and he alone can expand or reduce membership, alter the mix of membership, or sell the right to be the residual claimant-monitor of the team. It is this entire bundle of rights: (1) to be a residual claimant, (2) to observe input behavior, (3) to be the central party common to all contracts with inputs, (4) to alter the membership of the team, and (5) to sell these rights, that defines the *ownership* (or the employer) of the *classical* (capitalist, free-enterprise) firm. The coalescing of these rights has arisen, our analysis asserts, because it resolves the shirking-information problem of team production better than does the noncentralized contractual arrangement.

The relationship of each team member to the *owner* of the firm (i.e., the party common to all input contracts *and* the residual claimant) is simply a "quid pro quo" contract. Each makes a purchase and sale. The employee "orders" the owner of the team to pay him money in the same sense that the employer directs the team member to perform certain acts. The employee can terminate the contract as readily as can the employer, and long-term contracts, therefore, are not an essential attribute of the firm. Nor are "authoritarian," "dictational," or "fiat" attributes relevant to the conception of the firm or its efficiency.

In summary, two necessary conditions exist for the emergence of the firm on the prior assumption that more than pecuniary wealth enter utility functions: (1) It is possible to increase productivity through team-oriented production, a production technique for which it is costly to directly measure the marginal outputs of the cooperating inputs. This makes it more difficult to restrict shirking through simple market exchange between cooperating inputs. (2) It is economical to estimate marginal productivity by observing or specifying input behavior. The simultaneous occurrence of both these preconditions leads to the contractual organization of inputs, known as the *classical capitalist firms* with (a) joint input production, (b) several input owners, (c) one party who is common to all the contracts of the joint inputs, (d) who has rights to renegotiate any input's contract independently of contracts with other input owners, (e) who holds the residual claim, and (f) who has the right to sell his central contractual residual status.[8]

Other theories of the firm

At this juncture, as an aside, we briefly place this theory of the firm in the contexts of those offered by Ronald Coase and Frank Knight.[9] Our view of the firm is not necessarily inconsistent with Coase's; we attempt to go further and identify refutable implications. Coase's penetrating insight is to make more of the fact that markets do not operate costlessly, and he relies on the cost of using markets to *form* contracts as his basic explanation for the existence of firms. We do not disagree with the proposition that, *ceteris paribus*, the higher is the cost of transacting across markets the greater will be the comparative advantage of organizing resources within the firm; it is a difficult proposition to disagree with or to refute. We could with equal ease subscribe to a theory of the firm based on the cost of managing for surely it is true that, *ceteris paribus*, the lower is the cost of managing the greater will be the comparative advantage of organizing resources within the firm. To move the theory forward, it is necessary to know what is meant by a firm and to explain the circumstances under which the

---

[8] Removal of (b) converts a capitalist proprietary firm to a socialist firm.

[9] Recognition must also be made to the seminal inquiries by Morris Silver and Richard Auster (1969) and by H. B. Malmgren (1961).

cost of "managing" resources is low relative to the cost of allocating resources through market transaction. The conception of and rationale for the classical firm that we propose takes a step down the path pointed out by Coase toward that goal. Consideration of team production, team organization, difficulty in metering outputs, and the problem of shirking are important to our explanation but, so far as we can ascertain, not in Coase's. Coase's analysis insofar as it had heretofore been developed would suggest open-ended contracts but does not appear to imply anything more – neither the residual claimant status nor the distinction between employee and subcontractor status (nor any of the implications indicated below). And it is not true that employees are generally employed on the basis of long-term contractual arrangements any more than on a series of short-term or indefinite length contracts.

The importance of our proposed additional elements is revealed, for example, by the explanation of why the person to whom the control monitor is responsible receives the residual, and also by our later discussion of the implications about the corporation, partnerships, and profit sharing. These alternative forms for organization of the firm are difficult to resolve on the basis of market transaction costs only. Our exposition also suggests a definition of the classical firm – something crucial that was heretofore absent.

In addition, sometimes a technological development will lower the cost of market transactions while, at the same time, it expands the role of the firm. When the "putting out" system was used for weaving, inputs were organized largely through market negotiations. With the development of efficient central sources of power, it became economical to perform weaving in proximity to the power source and to engage in team production. The bringing in of weavers surely must have resulted in a reduction in the cost of negotiating (forming) contracts. Yet, what we observe is the beginning of the factory system in which inputs are organized within a firm. Why? The weavers did not simply move to a common source of power that they could tap like an electric line, purchasing power while they used their own equipment. Now team production in the joint use of equipment became more important. The measurement of marginal productivity, which now involved interactions between workers, especially through their joint use of machines, became more difficult though contract negotiating cost was reduced, while managing the *behavior* of inputs became easier because of the increased centralization of activity. The firm as an organization expanded even though the cost of transactions was reduced by the advent of centralized power. The same could be said for modern assembly lines. Hence the emergence of central power sources expanded the scope of productive activity in which the firm enjoyed a comparative advantage as an organizational form.

Some economists, following Knight, have identified the bearing of risks of wealth changes with the director or central employer without explaining why that is a viable arrangement. Presumably, the more risk-averse inputs

182

become employees rather than owners of the classical firm. Risk averseness and uncertainty *with regard to the firm's fortunes* have little, if anything, to do with our explanation although it helps to explain why all resources in a team are not owned by one person. That is, the role of risk taken in the sense of absorbing the windfalls that buffet the firm because of unforeseen competition, technological change, or fluctuations in demand are not central to our theory, although it is true that imperfect knowledge and, therefore, risk, in *this* sense of risk, underlie the problem of monitoring team behavior. We deduce the system of paying the manager with a residual claim (the equity) from the desire to have efficient means to reduce shirking so as to make team production economical and not from the smaller aversion to the risks of enterprise in a dynamic economy. We conjecture that "distribution-of-risk" is not a valid rationale for the *existence* and organization of the *classical* firm.

Although we have emphasized team production as creating a costly metering task and have treated team production as an essential (necessary?) condition for the firm, would not other obstacles to cheap metering also call forth the same kind of contractual arrangement here denoted as a firm? For example, suppose a farmer produces wheat in an easily ascertained quantity but with subtle and difficult to detect quality variations determined by how the farmer grew the wheat. A vertical integration could allow a purchaser to control the farmer's behavior in order to more economically estimate productivity. But this is not a case of joint or team production, unless "information" can be considered part of the product. (While a good case could be made for that broader conception of production, we shall ignore it here.) Instead of forming a firm, a buyer can contract to have his inspector on the site of production, just as home builders contract with architects to supervise building contracts; that arrangement is not a firm. Still, a firm might be organized in the production of many products wherein no team production or jointness of use of separately owned resources is involved.

This possibility rather clearly indicates a broader, or complementary, approach to that which we have chosen. (1) As we do in this paper, it can be argued that the firm is the particular policing device utilized when joint team production is present. If other sources of high policing costs arise, as in the wheat case just indicated, some other form of contractual arrangement will be used. Thus to each source of informational cost there may be a different type of policing and contractual arrangement. (2) On the other hand, one can say that where policing is difficult across markets, various forms of contractual arrangements are devised, but there is no reason for that known as the firm to be uniquely related or even highly correlated with team production, as defined here. It might be used equally probably and viably for other sources of high policing cost. We have not intensively analyzed other sources, and we can only note that our current and readily revisable conjecture is that (1) is valid, and has motivated us in our current endeavor. In any event, the test of the theory advanced here is to see whether the conditions we have identified are necessary for firms to have long-run viability rather than merely births with high infant mortality. Conglomerate firms or collections of separate production agencies into one owning organization can be interpreted as an investment trust or investment diversification device – probably Knight's interpretation. A holding company can be called a firm, because of the common association of the word firm with any ownership unit that owns income sources. The term firm as commonly used is so turgid of meaning that we cannot hope to explain every entity to which the name is attached in common or even technical literature. Instead, we seek to identify and explain a particular contractual arrangement induced by the cost of information factors analyzed in this paper.

IV. Types of firms

A. Profit-sharing firms

Explicit in our explanation of the capitalist firm is the assumption that the cost of *managing* the team's inputs by a central monitor, who disciplines himself because he is a residual claimant, is low relative to the cost of metering the marginal outputs of team members.

If we look within a firm to see who monitors – hires, fires, changes, promotes, and renegotiates – we should find him being a residual claimant or, at least, one whose pay or reward is more than any others correlated with fluctuations in the residual value of the firm. They more likely will have options or rights or bonuses than will inputs with other tasks.

An implicit "auxiliary" assumption of our explanation of the firm is that the cost of team production is increased if the residual claim is not held entirely by the central monitor. That is, we assume that if profit sharing had to be relied upon for *all* team members, losses from the resulting increase in central monitor shirking would exceed the output gains from the increased incentives of other team members not to shirk. If the optimal team size is only two owners of inputs, then an equal division of profits and losses between them will leave each with stronger incentives to reduce shirking than if the optimal team size is large, for in the latter case only a smaller percentage of the losses occasioned by the shirker will be borne by him. Incentives to shirk are positively related to the optimal size of the team under an equal profit-sharing scheme.[10]

---

[10] While the degree to which residual claims are centralized will affect the size of the team, this will be only one of many factors that determine team size, so as an approximation, we can treat team size as exogenously determined. Under certain assumptions about the shape of the "typical" utility function, the incentive to avoid shirking with unequal profit-sharing can be measured by the Herfindahl index.

The preceding does not imply that profit sharing is never viable. Profit sharing to encourage self-policing is more appropriate for small teams. And, indeed, where input owners are free to make whatever contractual arrangements suit them, as generally is true in capitalist economies, profit sharing seems largely limited to partnerships with a relatively small number of *active*[11] partners. Another advantage of such arrangements for smaller teams is that it permits more effective reciprocal monitoring among inputs. Monitoring need not be entirely specialized.

Profit sharing is more viable if small team size is associated with situations where the cost of specialized management of inputs is large relative to the increased productivity potential in team effort. We conjecture that the cost of managing team inputs increases if the productivity of a team member is difficult to correlate with his behavior. In "artistic" or "professional" work, watching a man's activities is not a good clue to what he is actually thinking or doing with his mind. While it is relatively easy to manage or direct the loading of trucks by a team of dock workers where input activity is so highly related in an obvious way to output, it is more difficult to manage and direct a lawyer in the preparation and presentation of a case. Dock workers can be directed in detail without the monitor himself loading the truck, and assembly line workers can be monitored by varying the speed of the assembly line, but detailed direction in the preparation of a law case would require in much greater degree that the monitor prepare the case himself. As a result, artistic or professional inputs, such as lawyers, advertising specialists, and doctors, will be given relatively freer reign with regard to individual behavior. If the management of inputs is relatively costly, or ineffective, as it would seem to be in these cases, but, nonetheless if team effort is more productive than separable production with exchange across markets, then there will develop a tendency to use profit-sharing schemes to provide incentives to avoid shirking.[12]

B. Socialist firms

We have analyzed the classical proprietorship and the profit-sharing firms in the context of free association and choice of economic organization. Such organizations need not be the most viable when political constraints limit the forms of organization that can be chosen. It is one thing to have profit sharing when professional or artistic talents are used by small teams. But if political or

[11] The use of the word *active* will be clarified in our discussion of the corporation, which follows below.
[12] Some sharing contracts, like crop sharing, or rental payments based on gross sales in retail stores, come close to profit sharing. However, it is gross output sharing rather than profit sharing. We are unable to specify the implications of the difference. We refer the reader to S. N. S. Cheung (1969).

tax or subsidy considerations induce profit-sharing techniques when these are not otherwise economically justified, then additional management techniques will be developed to help reduce the degree of shirking.

For example, most, if not all, firms in Jugoslavia are owned by the employees in the restricted sense that all share in the residual. This is true for large firms and for firms which employ nonartistic, or nonprofessional, workers as well. With a decay of political constraints, most of these firms could be expected to rely on paid wages rather than shares in the residual. This rests on our auxiliary assumption that general sharing in the residual results in losses from enhanced shirking by the monitor that exceed the gains from reduced shirking by residual-sharing employees. If this were not so, profit sharing with employees should have occurred more frequently in Western societies where such organizations are neither banned nor preferred politically. Where residual sharing by employees is politically imposed, as in Jugoslavia, we are led to expect that some management technique will arise to reduce the shirking by the central monitor, a technique that will not be found frequently in Western societies since the monitor retains all (or much) of the residual in the West and profit sharing is largely confined to small, professional-artistic team production situations. We do find in the larger scale residual-sharing firms in Jugoslavia that there are employee committees that can recommend (to the state) the termination of a manager's contract (veto his continuance) with the enterprise. We conjecture that the workers' committee is given the right to recommend the termination of the manager's contract precisely because the general sharing of the residual increases "excessively" the manager's incentive to shirk.[13]

C. The corporation

All firms must initially acquire command over some resources. The corporation does so primarily by selling promises of future returns to those who (as creditors or owners) provide financial capital. In some situations resources can be acquired in advance from consumers by promises of future delivery (for example, advance sale of a proposed book). Or where the firm is a few artistic or professional persons, each can "chip in" with time and talent until the sale of services brings in revenues. For the most part, capital can be acquired more cheaply if many (risk-averse) investors contribute small portions to a large investment. The economies of raising large sums of equity capital in this

---

[13] Incidentally, investment activity will be changed. The inability to capitalize the investment value as "take-home" private property *wealth* of the members of the firm means that the benefits of the investment must be taken as annual income by those who are employed at the time of the income. Investment will be confined more to those with shorter life and with higher rates or payoffs if the alternative of investing is paying out the firm's income to its employees to take home and use as private property. For a development of this proposition, see the papers by Eirik Furubotn and Svetozar Pejovich (1972), and by Pejovich (1969).

way suggest that modifications in the relationship among corporate inputs are required to cope with the shirking problem that arises with profit sharing among large numbers of corporate stockholders. One modification is limited liability, especially for firms that are large relative to a stockholder's wealth. It serves to protect stockholders from large losses no matter how they are caused.

If every stock owner participated in each decision in a corporation, not only would large bureaucratic costs be incurred, but many would shirk the task of becoming well informed on the issue to be decided, since the losses associated with unexpectedly bad decisions will be borne in large part by the many other corporate shareholders. More effective control of corporate activity is achieved for most purposes by transferring decision authority to a smaller group, whose main function is to negotiate with and manage (renegotiate with) the other inputs of the team. The corporate stockholders retain the authority to revise the membership of the management group and over major decisions that affect the structure of the corporation or its dissolution.

As a result a new modification of partnerships is induced – the right to sale of corporate shares without approval of any other stockholders. Any share holder can remove his wealth from control by those with whom he has differences of opinion. Rather than try to control the decisions of the management, which is harder to do with many stockholders than with only a few, unrestricted salability provides a more acceptable escape to each stockholder from continued policies with which he disagrees.

Indeed, the policing of managerial shirking relies on across-market competition from new groups of would-be managers as well as competition from members within the firm who seek to displace existing management. In addition to competition from outside and inside managers, control is facilitated by the temporary congealing of share votes into voting blocs owned by one or a few contenders. Proxy battles or stock-purchases concentrate the votes required to displace the existing management or modify managerial policies. But it is more than a change in policy that is sought by the newly formed financial interests whether of new stockholders or not. It is the capitalization of expected future benefits into stock prices that concentrates on the innovators the wealth gains of their actions if they own large numbers of shares. Without capitalization of future benefits, there would be less incentive to incur the costs required to exert informed decisive influence on the corporation's policies and managing personnel. Temporarily, the structure of ownership is reformed, moving away from diffused ownership into decisive power blocs, and this is a transient resurgence of the classical firm with power again concentrated in those who have title to the residual.

In assessing the significance of stockholders' power it is not the usual diffusion of voting power that is significant but instead the frequency with which voting congeals into decisive changes. Even a one-man owned company may have a long term with just one manager – continuously being approved by the owner. Similarly, a dispersed voting power corporation may be also characterized by a long-lived management. The question is the probability of replacement of the management if it behaves in ways not acceptable to a majority of the stockholders. The unrestricted salability of stock and the transfer of proxies enhances the probability of decisive action in the event current stockholders or any outsider believes that management is not doing a good job with the corporation. We are not comparing the corporate responsiveness to that of a single proprietorship; instead, we are indicating features of the corporate structure that are induced by the problem of delegated authority to manager-monitors.[14]

---

[14] Instead of thinking of shareholders as joint *owners*, we can think of them as investors, like bondholders, except that the stockholders are more optimistic than bondholders about the enterprise prospects. Instead of buying bonds in the corporation, thus enjoying smaller risks, shareholders prefer to invest funds with a greater realizable return if the firm prospers as expected, but with smaller (possibly negative) returns if the firm performs in a manner closer to that expected by the more pessimistic investors. The pessimistic investors, in turn, regard only the bonds as likely to pay off.

If the entrepreneur-organizer is to raise capital on the best terms to him, it is to his advantage, as well as that of prospective investors, to recognize these differences in expectations. The residual claim on earnings enjoyed by shareholders does not serve the function of enhancing their efficiency as monitors in the general situation. The stockholders are "merely" the less risk-averse or the more optimistic member of the group that finances the firm. Being more optimistic than the average and seeing a higher mean value future return, they are willing to pay more for a certificate that allows them to realize gain on their expectations. One method of doing so is to buy claims to the distribution of returns that "they see" while bondholders, who are more pessimistic, purchase a claim to the distribution that they see as more likely to emerge. Stockholders are then comparable to warrant holders. They care not about the voting rights (usually not attached to warrants); they are in the same position in so far as voting rights are concerned as are bondholders. The only difference is in the probability distribution of rewards and the terms on which they can place their bets.

If we treat bondholders, preferred and convertible preferred stockholders, and common stockholders and warrant holders as simply different classes of investors – differing not only in their risk averseness but in their beliefs about the probability distribution of the firm's future earnings, why should stockholders be regarded as "owners" in any sense distinct from the other financial investors? The entrepreneur-organizer, who let us assume is the chief operating officer and sole repository of control of the corporation, does not find his authority residing in common stockholders (except in the case of a take over). Does this type of control make any difference in the way the firm is conducted? Would it make any difference in the kinds of behavior that would be tolerated by competing managers and investors (and we here deliberately refrain from thinking of them as owner-stockholders in the traditional sense?)

Investment old timers recall a significant incidence of nonvoting common stock, now prohibited in corporations whose stock is traded on listed exchanges. (Why prohibited?) The entrepreneur in those days could hold voting shares while investors held nonvoting shares, which in every other respect were identical. Nonvoting share holders were simply investors devoid of ownership connotations. The control and behavior of inside owners in such corporations has never, so far as we have ascertained, been carefully studied. For example, at the simplest level of interest, does the evidence indicate that nonvoting shareholders fared any worse because of not having voting rights? Did owners permit the nonvoting holders the normal return available to voting shareholders? Though evidence is prohibitively expensive to obtain, it is remarkable that voting and nonvoting shares sold for essentially identical prices, even during some proxy battles. However, our casual evidence deserves no more than interest-initiating weight.

D. Mutual and nonprofit firms

The benefits obtained by the new management are greater if the stock can be purchased and sold, because this enables *capitalization* of anticipated future improvements into present *wealth* of new managers who bought stock and created a larger capital by their management changes. But in nonprofit corporations, colleges, churches, country clubs, mutual savings banks, mutual insurance companies, and "coops," the future consequences of improved management are not capitalized into present wealth of stockholders. (As if to make more difficult that competition by new would-be monitors, multiple shares of ownership in those enterprises cannot be bought by one person.) One should therefore, find greater shirking in nonprofit, mutually owned enterprises. (This suggests that nonprofit enterprises are especially appropriate in realms of endeavor where more shirking is desired and where redirected uses of the enterprise in response to market-revealed values is less desired.)

E. Partnerships

Team production in artistic or professional intellectual skills will more likely be by partnerships than other types of team production. This amounts to market-organized team activity and to a non-employer status. Self-monitoring partnerships, therefore, will be used rather than employer–employee contracts, and these organizations will be small to prevent an excessive dilution of efforts through shirking. Also, partnerships are more likely to occur among relatives or long-standing acquaintances, not necessarily because they share a common utility function, but also because each knows better the other's work characteristics and tendencies to shirk.

One more point. The facade is deceptive. Instead of nonvoting shares, today we have warrants, convertible preferred stocks all of which are solely or partly "equity" claims without voting rights, though they could be converted into voting shares.

In sum, is it the case that the stockholder–investor relationship is one emanating from the *division* of *ownership* among several people, or is it that the collection of investment funds from people of varying anticipations is the underlying factor? If the latter, why should any of them be thought of as the owners in whom voting rights, whatever they may signify or however exercisable, should reside in order to enhance efficiency? Why voting rights in any of the outside, participating investors?

Our initial perception of this possibly significant difference in interpretation was precipitated by Henry Manne (1967). A reading of his paper makes it clear that it is hard to understand why an investor who wishes to back and "share" in the consequences of some new business should necessarily have to acquire voting power (i.e., power to change the manager-operator) in order to invest in the venture. In fact, we invest in some ventures in the hope that no other stockholders will be so "foolish" as to try to toss out the incumbent management. We want him to have the power to stay in office, and for the prospect of sharing in his fortunes we buy nonvoting common stock. Our willingness to invest is enhanced by the knowledge that we can act legally via fraud, embezzlement and other laws to help assure that we outside investors will not be "milked" beyond our initial discounted anticipations.

F. Employee unions

Employee unions, whatever else they do, perform as monitors for employees. Employers monitor employees and similarly employees monitor an employer's performance. Are correct wages paid on time and in good currency? Usually, this is extremely easy to check. But some forms of employer performance are less easy to meter and are more subject to employer shirking. Fringe benefits often are in non-pecuniary, contingent form; medical, hospital, and accident insurance, and retirement pensions are contingent payments or performances partly in *kind* by employers to employees. Each employee cannot judge the character of such payments as easily as money wages. Insurance is a contingent payment – what the employee will get upon the contingent event may come as a disappointment. If he could easily determine what other employees had gotten upon such contingent events he could judge more accurately the performance by the employer. He could "trust" the employer not to shirk in such fringe contingent payments, but he would prefer an effective and economic monitor of those payments. We see a specialist monitor – the union employees' agent – hired by them and monitoring those aspects of employer payment most difficult for the employees to monitor. Employees should be willing to employ a specialist monitor to administer such hard-to-detect employer performance, even though their monitor has incentives to use pension and retirement funds not entirely for the benefit of employees.

V. Team spirit and loyalty

Every team member would prefer a team in which no one, not even himself, shirked. Then the true marginal costs and values could be equated to achieve more preferred positions. If one could enhance a common interest in nonshirking in the guise of a team loyalty or team spirit, the team would be more efficient. In those sports where team activity is most clearly exemplified, the sense of loyalty and team spirit is most strongly urged. Obviously the team is better, with team spirit and loyalty, because of the reduced shirking – not because of some other feature inherent in loyalty or spirit as such.[15]

[15] *Sports Leagues*: Professional sports contests among teams is typically conducted by a *league* of teams. We assume that sports consumers are interested not only in absolute sporting skill but also in skills *relative* to other teams. Being slightly better than opposing teams enables one to claim a major portion of the receipts; the inferior team does not release resources and reduce costs, since they were expected in the play of contest. Hence, absolute skill is developed beyond the equality of marginal investment in sporting skill with its true social marginal value product. It follows there will be a tendency to overinvest in training athletes and developing teams. "Reverse shirking" arises, as budding players are induced to overpractice hyperactively relative to the social marginal value of their enhanced skills. To prevent overinvestment, the teams seek an agreement with each other to restrict practice, size of teams, and even pay of the team members (which reduces incentives of young people to overinvest in developing skills). Ideally, if all the contestant teams were owned by

190

Corporations and business firms try to instill a spirit of loyalty. This should not be viewed simply as a device to increase profits by *over*working or misleading the employees, nor as an adolescent urge for belonging. It promotes a closer approximation to the employees' potentially available true rates of substitution between production and leisure and enables each team member to achieve a more preferred situation. The difficulty, of course, is to create economically that team spirit and loyalty. It can be preached with an aura of moral code of conduct – a morality with literally the same basis as the ten commandments – to restrict our conduct toward what we would choose if we bore our full costs.

VI. Kinds of inputs owned by the firm

To this point the discussion has examined why firms, as we have defined them, exist? That is, why is there an owner-employer who is the common party to contracts with other owners of inputs in team activity? The answer to that question should also indicate the kind of the jointly used resources likely to be owned by the central-owner-monitor and the kind likely to be hired from people who are not team-owners. Can we identify characteristics or features of various inputs that lead to their being hired or to their being owned by the firm?

How can residual-claimant, central-employer-owner demonstrate ability to pay the other hired inputs the promised amount in the event of a loss? He can pay in advance or he can commit wealth sufficient to cover negative residuals. The latter will take the form of machines, land, buildings, or raw materials committed to the firm. Commitments of labor wealth (i.e., human wealth), given the property rights in people, is less feasible. These considerations suggest that residual claimants – owners of the firm – will be investors of resalable capital equipment in the firm. The goods or inputs more likely to be invested, than

one owner, overinvestment in sports would be avoided, much as ownership of common fisheries or underground oil or water reserve would prevent overinvestment. This hyperactivity (to suggest the opposite of shirking) is controlled by the league of teams, wherein the league adopts a common set of constraints on each team's behavior. In effect, the teams are no longer really owned by the team owners but are supervised by them, much as the franchisers of some product. They are not full-fledged owners of their business, including the brand name, and cannot "do what they wish" as franchises. Comparable to the franchiser, is the league commissioner or conference president, who seeks to restrain hyperactivity, as individual team supervisors compete with each other and cause external diseconomies. Such restraints are usually regarded as anticompetitive, antisocial, collusive-cartel devices to restrain free open competition and reduce players' salaries. However, the interpretation presented here is premised on an attempt to avoid hyperinvestment in team sports production. Of course, the team operators have an incentive, once the league is formed and restraints are placed on hyperinvestment activity, to go further and obtain the private benefits of monopoly restriction. To what extent overinvestment is replaced by monopoly restriction is not yet determinable; nor have we seen an empirical test of these two competing, but mutually consistent interpretations. (This interpretation of league-sports activity was proposed by Earl Thompson (1970) and formulated by Michael Canes (1970)). Again, athletic teams clearly exemplify the specialization of monitoring with captains and coaches; a captain detects shirkers while the coach trains and selects strategies and tactics. Both functions may be centralized in one person.

rented, by the owners of the enterprise, will have higher resale values relative to the initial cost and will have longer expected use in a firm relative to the economic life of the good.

But beyond these factors are those developed above to explain the existence of the institution known as the firm – the costs of detecting output performance. When a durable resource is used it will have a marginal product and a depreciation. Its use requires payment to cover at least use-induced depreciation; unless that user cost is specifically detectable, payment for it will be demanded in accord with *expected* depreciation. And we can ascertain circumstances for each. An indestructible hammer with a readily detectable marginal product has zero user cost. But suppose the hammer were destructible and that careless (which is easier than careful) use is more abusive and causes greater depreciation of the hammer. Suppose in addition the abuse is easier to detect by observing the way it is used than by observing only the hammer after its use, or by measuring the output scored from a hammer by a laborer. If the hammer were rented and used in the absence of the owner, the depreciation would be greater than if the use were observed by the owner and the user charged in accord with the imposed depreciation. (Careless use is more likely than careful use – if one does not pay for the greater depreciation.) An absentee owner would therefore ask for a higher rental price because of the higher *expected* user cost than if the item were used by the owner. The expectation is higher because of the greater difficulty of observing specific user cost, by inspection of the hammer after use. Renting is therefore in this case more costly than owner use. This is the valid content of the misleading expressions about ownership being more economical than renting – ignoring all other factors that may work in the opposite direction, like tax provision, short-term occupancy, and capital risk avoidance.

Better examples are tools of the trade. Watch repairers, engineers, and carpenters tend to own their own tools especially if they are portable. Trucks are more likely to be employee owned rather than other equally expensive team inputs because it is relatively cheap for the driver to police the care taken in using a truck. Policing the use of trucks by a nondriver owner is more likely to occur for trucks that are not specialized to one driver, like public transit busses.

The factor with which we are concerned here is one related to the costs of monitoring not only the gross product performance of an input but also the abuse or depreciation inflicted on the input in the course of its use. If depreciation or user cost is more cheaply detected when the owner can see its use than by only seeing the input before and after, there is a force toward owner use rather than renting. Resources whose user cost is harder to detect when used by someone else tend on this count to be owner-used. Absentee ownership, in the lay language, will be less likely. Assume momentarily that labor service cannot be performed in the absence of its owner. The labor owner can more cheaply monitor any abuse of himself than if somehow labor services could be provided without the labor owner observing its mode of use or knowing what was happening. Also his incentive to abuse himself is increased if he does not own himself.[16]

The similarity between the preceding analysis and the question of absentee landlordism and of sharecropping arrangements is no accident. The same factors which explain the contractual arrangements known as a firm help to explain the incidence of tenancy, labor hiring, or sharecropping.[17]

VII. Firms as a specialized market institution for collecting, collating, and selling input information

The firm serves as a highly specialized surrogate market. Any person contemplating a joint-input activity must search and detect the qualities of available joint inputs. He could contact an employment agency, but that agency in a small town would have little advantage over a large firm with many inputs. The employer, by virtue of monitoring many inputs, acquires special superior information about their productive talents. This aids his *directive* (i.e., market hiring) efficiency. He "sells" his information to employee-inputs as he aids them in ascertaining good input combinations for team activity. Those who work as employees or who rent services to him are using him to discern

---

[16] Professional athletes in baseball, football, and basketball, where athletes having sold their source of service to the team owners upon entering into sports activity, are owned by team owners. Here the team owners must monitor the athletes' physical condition and behavior to protect the team owners' wealth. The athlete has *less* (not, *no*) incentive to protect or enhance his athletic prowess since capital value changes have less impact on his own wealth and more on the team owners. Thus, some athletes sign up for big initial bonuses (representing present capital value of future services). Future salaries are lower by the annuity value of the prepaid "bonus" and hence the athlete has *less* to lose by subsequent abuse of his athletic prowess. Any decline in his subsequent service value would in part be borne by the team owner who owns the players' future service. This does not say these losses of future salaries have no effect on preservation of athletic talent (we are not making a "sunk cost" error). Instead, we assert that the preservation is reduced, not eliminated, because the amount of loss of wealth suffered is smaller. The athlete will spend less to maintain or enhance his prowess thereafter. The effect of this revised incentive system is evidenced in comparisons of the kinds of attention and care imposed on the athletes at the "expense of the team owner" in the case where athletes' future service are owned by the team owner with that where future labor service values are owned by the athlete himself. Why athletes' future athletic services are owned by the team owners rather than being hired is a question we should be able to answer. One presumption is cartelization and monopsony gains to team owners. Another is exactly the theory being expounded in this paper – costs of monitoring production of athletes; we know not on which to rely.

[17] The analysis used by Cheung (1969) in explaining the prevalence of sharecropping and land tenancy arrangements is built squarely on the same factors – the costs of detecting output performance of jointly used inputs in team production and the costs of detecting user costs imposed on the various inputs if owner used or if rented.

superior combinations of inputs. Not only does the director-employer "decide" what each input will produce, he also estimates which heterogeneous inputs will work together jointly more efficiently, and he does this in the context of a privately owned market for forming teams. The department store is a firm and is a superior private market. People who shop and work in one town can as well shop and work in a privately owned firm.

This marketing function is obscured in the theoretical literature by the assumption of homogeneous factors. Or it is tacitly left for individuals to do themselves via personal market search, much as if a person had to search without benefit of specialist retailers. Whether or not the firm arose because of this efficient information service, it gives the director-employer more knowledge about the productive talents of the team's inputs, and a basis for superior decisions about efficient or profitable combinations of those heterogeneous resources.

In other words, opportunities for profitable team production by inputs already within the firm may be ascertained more economically and accurately than for resources outside the firm. Superior combinations of inputs can be more economically identified and formed from resources already used in the organization than by obtaining new resources (and knowledge of them) from the outside. Promotion and revision of employee assignments (contracts) will be preferred by a firm to the hiring of new inputs. To the extent that this occurs there is reason to expect the firm to be able to operate as a conglomerate rather than persist in producing a single product. Efficient production with heterogeneous resources is a result not of having *better* resources but in *knowing more accurately* the relative productive performances of those resources. Poorer resources can be paid less in accord with their inferiority; greater accuracy of knowledge of the potential and actual productive actions of inputs rather than having high productivity resources makes a firm (or an assignment of inputs) profitable.[18]

---

[18] According to our interpretation, the firm is a specialized surrogate for a market for team use of inputs; it provides superior (i.e., cheaper) collection and collation of knowledge about heterogeneous resources. The greater the set of inputs about which knowledge of performance is being collated within a firm the greater are the present costs of the collation activity. Then, the larger the firm (market) the greater the attenuation of monitor control. To counter this force, the firm will be divisionalized in ways that economize on those costs – just as will the market be specialized. So far as we can ascertain, other theories of the reasons for firms have no such implications.

   In Japan, employees by custom work nearly their entire lives with one firm, and the firm agrees to that expectation. Firms will tend to be large and conglomerate to enable a broader scope of input revision. Each firm is, in effect, a small economy engaging in "intranational and international" trade. Analogously, Americans expect to spend their whole lives in the United States, and the bigger the country, in terms of variety of resources, the easier it is to adjust to changing tastes and circumstances. Japan, with its lifetime employees, should be characterized more by large, conglomerate firms. Presumably, at some size of the firm, specialized knowledge about inputs becomes as expensive to transmit across divisions of the firms as it does across markets to other firms.

VIII. Summary

While ordinary contracts facilitate efficient specialization according to comparative advantage, a special class of contracts among a group of joint inputs to a team production process is commonly used for team production. Instead of multilateral contracts among all the joint inputs owners, a central common party to a set of bilateral contracts facilitates efficient organization of the joint inputs in team production. The terms of the contracts form the basis of the entity called the firm – especially appropriate for organizing team production processes.

Team productive activity is that in which a union, or joint use, of inputs yields a larger output than the sum of the products of the separately used inputs. This team production requires – like all other production processes – an assessment of marginal productivities if efficient production is to be achieved. Nonseparability of the products of several differently owned joint inputs raises the cost of assessing the marginal productivities of those resources or services of each input owner. Monitoring or metering the productivities to match marginal productivities to costs of inputs and thereby to reduce shirking can be achieved more economically (than by across market bilateral negotiations among inputs) in a firm.

The essence of the classical firm is identified here as a contractual structure with: (1) joint input production, (2) several input owners, (3) one party who is common to all the contracts of the joint inputs, (4) who has rights to renegotiate any input's contract independently of contracts with other input owners, (5) who holds the residual claim, and (6) who has the right to sell his central contractual residual status. The central agent is called the firm's owner and the employer. No authoritarian control is involved; the arrangement is simply a contractual structure subject to continuous renegotiation with the central agent. The contractual structure arises as a means of enhancing efficient organization of team production. In particular, the ability to detect shirking among owners of jointly used inputs in team production is enhanced (detection costs are reduced) by this arrangement and the discipline (by revision of contracts) of input owners is made more economic.

Testable implications are suggested by the analysis of different types of organizations – nonprofit, proprietary for profit, unions, cooperatives, partnerships, and by the kinds of inputs that tend to be owned by the firm in contrast to those employed by the firm.

We conclude with a highly conjectural but possibly significant interpretation. As a consequence of the flow of information to the central party (employer), the firm takes on the characteristic of an efficient market in that information about the productive characteristics of a large set of specific inputs is now more cheaply available. Better recombinations or new uses of resources can be more efficiently ascertained than by the conventional search through the general market. In this sense inputs compete with each other within and via a firm rather than solely across markets as conventionally conceived. Emphasis on interfirm competition obscures intrafirm competition among inputs. Conceiving competition as the *revelation and exchange* of knowledge or information about qualities, potential uses of different inputs in different potential applications indicates that the firm is a device for enhancing competition among sets of input resources as well as a device for more efficiently rewarding the inputs. In contrast to markets and cities which can be viewed as publicly or nonowned market places, the firm can be considered a privately owned market; if so, we could consider the firm and the ordinary market as competing types of markets, competition between private proprietary markets and public or communal markets. Could it be that the market suffers from the defects of communal property rights in organizing and influencing uses of valuable resources?

CHAPTER 14

Contested exchange: new microfoundations for the political economy of capitalism

SAMUEL BOWLES AND HERBERT GINTIS

Samuel Bowles was born in 1939 in New Haven, Connecticut. He received a Ph.D. in economics at Harvard University in 1965. When this article was published, he was Professor of Economics at the University of Massachusetts at Amherst, where he is now Professor of Economics, Emeritus. He also currently serves as the Arthur Spiegel Research Professor at the Santa Fe Institute and as Professor of Economics at the University of Siena.

Herbert Gintis was born in 1940 in Philadelphia, Pennsylvania. He received a Ph.D. in economics at Harvard University in 1969. When this article was published, he was Professor of Economics at the University of Massachusetts at Amherst, where he is now Professor of Economics, Emeritus. He also currently serves as Professor of Economics at the Central European University in Budapest.

Though conflicts of interest are central to economic reasoning, they are addressed in an artificial and misleading way in the conventional neoclassical model. This treatment is apparent in the following quote from the distinguished economist Abba Lerner:

An economic transaction is a solved political problem. Economics has gained the title of queen of the social sciences by choosing *solved* political problems as its domain.[1]

Exchanges may be solved political problems where contracts are comprehensive and enforceable at no cost to the exchanging parties. We use the term *exogenous claim enforcement* to refer to this type of comprehensive and third party (generally state) regulation of contracts; it tends to occur where the transaction is transparent in the sense that the characteristics of the goods or services exchanged are readily determined, and hence contractual transgressions are readily detected and redressed, often by resort to the courts.

Excerpted from Samuel Bowles and Herbert Gintis, "Contested Exchange: New Microfoundations for the Political Economy of Capitalism," *Politics and Society*, 18, no. 2 (June 1990): 165–222, with minor amendments by the authors. Reprinted with permission of Sage Publications.
[1] Lerner (1972).

Where some aspect of the object of exchange is so complex or difficult to monitor that comprehensive contracts are not feasible or enforceable by a third party, however, exogenous claim enforcement does not obtain, and the exchange is *not* a solved political problem. By comparison with the transparency of the exogenously enforceable exchange, these exchanges are characterized by opacity: Some aspect of the good or service exchanged is not readily determined. Far from being a special case, the absence of exogenous claim enforcement is quite general; the two critical exchanges of the capitalist economy – the labor and the capital markets – provide, as we will see, the archetypal examples.

In these cases which we take to be quite general, we have a *problem of agency*: In an exchange between agents A and B, B can take actions that are harmful or beneficial to A's interests, and which cannot be precluded or guaranteed by contractual agreement. Where a problem of agency exists, the *de facto* terms of an exchange result in part from the sanctions, surveillance, and other enforcement activities adopted by the parties to the exchange themselves. We refer to this process of regulation of the contract by the parties to the contract as *endogenous claim enforcement*.

A transaction characterized by both an agency problem and endogenous claim enforcement is termed a *contested exchange*. More formally, consider agent A who engages in an exchange with agent B. We call the exchange *contested* when B's good or service possesses an attribute that is valuable to A, is costly for B to provide, and yet is not fully specified in a costlessly enforceable contract.

Our key claim is that the most important exchanges in a capitalist economy are contested and that in these exchanges endogenous enforcement gives rise to a well-defined set of power relations among voluntarily participating agents even in the absence of collusion or other obstacles to perfect *competition.*

We take as uncontroversial the following *sufficient condition for the exercise of power*. Let us accept the assertion that, *for A to have power over B, it is sufficient that, by imposing or threatening to impose sanctions on B, A is capable of affecting B's actions in ways that further A's interests while B lacks this capacity with respect to A.* Because in Walrasian equilibrium the cost to B of foregoing an exchange with A is zero (B is free to deal with C on identical terms), A cannot affect B's well-being by terminating the exchange. Thus in the competitive equilibrium of a Walrasian economy, no sanctions may be imposed through the private actions of noncolluding agents. Whence flows Alchian's and Demsetz's belief that one can walk away from one's employer or creditor with as little concern as one crosses the street to shop at one supermarket rather than another.

Paul Samuelson's famous assertion "in a perfectly competitive market it really doesn't matter who hires whom; so let capital hire labor"[2] follows

[2] Samuelson (1957).

198

trivially. For the *boss* has no more authority over the workers than conversely (they all have none), and there is no real decision-making authority to relocate. A worker-run firm would be constrained by competition simply to replicate the structure and functioning of the capitalist firm. By a simple extension of this argument, the traditional democratic and socialist critiques of the fragmentation of tasks, deskilling, and other aspects of work experience, technology, and the division of labor in capitalist production may be shown to be without foundation. Work may be unpleasant, but a socialist economy would offer the same unless it chose to sacrifice productive efficiency.

The relationship between wage labor and capital is a contested exchange because while the worker's time can be contracted for, the amount and quality of actual work done generally cannot. The relationship of borrower to lender or of owner to the management of a firm is also a contested exchange because, while the repayment schedule of the loan can be contracted for, this is not true of the actions of the borrower that will determine the possibility of repayment. Exogenous enforcement will generally be absent and exchanges will be contested when there is no relevant third party (as when A and B are sovereign states), when the contested attribute can be measured only imperfectly or at considerable cost (work effort, for example, or the degree of risk assumed by a firm's management), when the relevant evidence is not admissible in a court of law (such as an agent's eye witness but unsubstantiated experience), when there is no possible means of redress (for example, when the liable party is bankrupt), or when the number of contingencies concerning future states of the world relevant to the exchange preclude writing a fully specified contract.

In such cases the *ex post* terms of exchange are determined by the monitoring and sanctioning mechanisms instituted by A to induce B to provide the desired level of the contested attribute. We shall here stress one extremely important endogenous enforcement mechanism: *contingent renewal*. This obtains when A elicits performance from B by promising to renew the contract in future periods if satisfied and to terminate the contract if not. For instance, a manager may promise a worker reemployment contingent upon satisfactory performance or a lender may offer a borrower a short-term loan with the promise of rolling over the loan contingent upon the borrower's prudent business behavior.

The labor market is a case in point. An employment relationship is established when, in return for a wage, the worker agrees to submit to the authority of the employer. The worker's promise to bestow an adequate level of effort and care upon the tasks assigned, even if offered, is legally unenforceable. At the level of effort expected by management, work is subjectively costly for the worker to provide, valuable to the employer, and costly to measure. The manager–worker relationship thus is a contested exchange. The endogenous enforcement mechanisms of the enterprise, not the state, are thus responsible

199

for ensuring the delivery of any particular level of labor services per hour of labor time supplied.[3]

A simple model of the manager–worker relationship will illuminate the archetypal contested exchange. Our objective is to identify the aspects of the labor market and the labor process that determine the terms of exchange: the wage rate and the intensity of labor. Let e represent the level of work effort provided by employee B. We assume effort is costly for B to provide above some minimal level $\bar{e}$. B's employer, A, knows that B will choose e in response to both the cost of supplying effort and the penalty employer A will impose if dissatisfied with B's performance. The penalty imposed by A is the nonrenewal of employment – that is, dismissing the worker. Of course the employer may choose not to terminate the worker if the cost associated with the termination (demoralization or ill will among fellow workers, a work-to-rule slowdown, a strike, or simply the search and training costs of replacement) are excessive.

The level of work intensity is chosen in a proximate sense by the worker. But in choosing, the worker must consider both short- and long-term costs and benefits; working less hard now, for example, means more on-the-job leisure now and a probability of no job and hence less income later. To take into account this time dimension, we will consider the worker's job as an asset, the value of which depends in part on the worker's effort level.

We define the *value of employment*, $v(w)$, as the discounted present value of the worker's future income stream taking account of the probability that the worker will be dismissed; for obvious reasons it is an increasing function of the current wage rate w. We define the employee's *fallback position, z,* as the present value of future income for a person whose job is terminated – perhaps the present value of a future stream of unemployment benefits, the present value of some other job, or more likely a sequence of the two weighted by the expected duration of unemployment. Then A's threat of dismissal is credible only if $v(w) > z$. We call $v(w) - z$, the difference between the value of employment and the fallback position, z, the *employment rent* or the cost of job loss. We term this a *rent* as it represents a payment above and beyond the income of an identical employee without the job.[4] Workers who receive employment rents are not indifferent to losing their job (their cost of job loss is not zero).

Employment rents accorded to workers in labor markets are a particularly important case of the more general category, *enforcement rents*, which arise in

---

[3] The analysis presented in this section is developed in Gintis (1976); Bowles (1985); Gintis and Ishikawa (1987); and Bowles and Gintis (1993a, 1993b).

[4] It is thus similar to the rents in the theory of rent-seeking behavior (Buchanan et al., 1980) except for the important difference that contested exchange rents arise through the *lack* of effective state intervention while rent-seeking literature focuses on state intervention as the source of rents.

all cases of competitively determined contested exchange under conditions of contingent renewal. Our objective will be to show that employment rents – and more generally, enforcement rents – will exist in a competitive equilibrium of a contested exchange.

A sufficiently low wage would make the job no more desirable to the worker than a spell of unemployment followed by a job search and another job. Let $\bar{w}$ be this wage that equates $v(w)$ and z. This wage rate implies a zero employment rent, hence the absence of effective sanctions by the employer, and thus induces the worker's freely chosen effort level, $\bar{e}$, the "whistle-while-you-work labor intensity." We term $\bar{w}$ the *reservation wage*. At any wage less than $\bar{w}$ the worker will refuse employment or quit if employed. The level of $\bar{w}$ depends obviously on the worker's relative enjoyment of leisure and work, the level and coverage of unemployment benefits, the expected duration of unemployment for a terminated worker, the loss of seniority associated with moving to a new job, and the availability of other income. In the Walrasian model, the equilibrium wage must be the reservation wage; otherwise workers could not be indifferent between their current transaction and their next best alternative.

We assume A has a monitoring system such that B's performance will be found adequate with a probability f, which depends positively on B's level of effort. If this effort level is found to be inadequate, B is dismissed with probability $1 - p$ (that is, is the probability that the worker found to be working inadequately will *not* be dismissed). It is the link between effort and the likelihood of job retention that induces B to provide effort above $\bar{e}$.[5]

To elicit greater effort than $\bar{e}$, A is obliged to offer a wage greater than $\bar{w}$, balancing the cost of paying the larger wage against the benefits associated with B's greater effort induced by a higher cost of job loss. For any given wage, the worker will determine how hard to work by trading the marginal disutility of additional effort against the effect that additional effort has on the probability of retaining the job and thus continuing to receive the employment rent. Noting that the fallback position z is exogenous to the exchange, we may write B's best response to w, which we call the *labor extraction function*, simply as $e = e(w)$. In the neighborhood of the competitive equilibrium, e increases with w, though at a diminishing rate, or $e_w > 0$, $e_{ww} < 0$.[6]

---

[5] More complete models allow an endogenous selection by A of an optimal schedule of dismissal probabilities and an optimal choice of the level of surveillance underlying the function $f(e)$ (Bowles, 1985; Gintis and Ishikawa, 1987). We lose little, however, by assuming that the probability of detection is exogenously given as a function of effort.

[6] The single and double subscripts, respectively, indicate first and second derivatives of the function e. The labor extraction function can be derived as follows. Let $u = u(w, e)$ be B's utility function, and assume $u_w > 0$, $u_e < 0$ for $(w, e) > (\bar{w}, \bar{e})$. In the simplest case, where the worker is dismissed if detected not working (that is, $p = 0$), B's value of employment is then

$$v = \{u(w, e) + f(e)v + (1 - f(e)z\}/(1 + \rho),$$

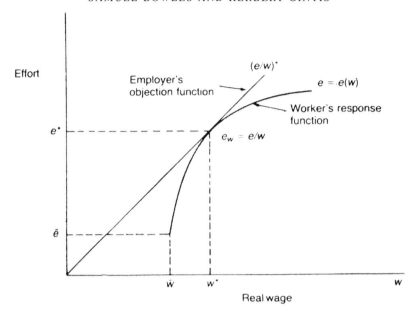

Figure 14.1. Optimal wages and labor intensity.

The equilibrium wage and effort level illustrated in Figure 14.1 is determined as follows. Agent A knows B's best response schedule, $e(w)$, so once A selects the wage, the level of effort that will be performed is known with certainty. Agent A then optimizes – maximizes profits or, what is equivalent in this model, minimizes costs – *given the response schedule of B*. Contingent renewal equilibria are thus Stackelberg equilibria, where agent A is a Stackelberg leader, making a take it or leave it offer to B, the Stackelberg follower.[7]

where ρ is the employee's rate of time preference: B receives $u(w, e)$ this period plus the present value v if retained, which occurs with probability $f(e)$, and plus the present value z if dismissed, which occurs with probability $1 - f(e)$. Assuming for simplicity that income and the disutility of effort are both evaluated at the end of the period, the whole expression is discounted to the present by the factor $1/(1 + \rho)$. Solving for v, we obtain

$$v = (u(w, e) - \rho z)/(1 - f(e) + \rho) + z,$$

where the first term on the right-hand side is obviously the employment rent, $v - z$, or *value of employment = employment rent + fallback position*. The $e(w)$ schedule then results from B's choosing e to maximize v for given w, taking the schedule $f(e)$ as given. The resulting first order condition, to equate u_e to $-f_e(v - z)$, expresses the tradeoff mentioned in the text.

[7] This asymmetry between leader and follower that is absent in the Walrasian equilibrium. In the latter both agents make offers, and only offers (those that clear markets) are accepted. A Stackelberg equilibrium (see von Stackelberg, 1934 and Sonnenschein, 1987) is one in which the leader, A, has no incentive to change strategy given the offer curve (response function) of the follower B, and B has no incentive to change strategy given that followed by A. B gains no strategic advantage by

The solution to A's optimum problem is to set w such that $e_w = e/w$, or the marginal effect on effort of a wage increase equals the average effort provided per unit of wage cost.[8] This solution yields the equilibrium effort level e^* and wage w^*, shown in Figure 14.1. The ray $(e/w)^*$ is one of the employer's isolabor cost loci: All points on this ray have the same effort per wage dollar, and the employer is hence indifferent amongst them. Its slope is e^*/w^*. Steeper rays are obviously preferred by the employer.

Two important results are apparent. First, $e^* > \bar{e}$, so B provides a level of effort greater than would have been the case in the absence of the enforcement rent and the employer's monitoring system; and second, $w^* > \bar{w}$, so B receives a wage greater than the reservation wage. The first result indicates that A's enforcement strategy is effective; the second indicates that the labor market does not clear in competitive equilibrium: Workers holding jobs are not indifferent to losing them, and there are identical workers either involuntarily unemployed or employed in less desirable positions.

Both results are of course at variance with the Walrasian model, which can be seen to be a limiting case of contested exchange that obtains when there is either an absence of a conflict of interest between employer and employee over effort or a costless means by which A can enforce a specific level of effort. The first of these conditions can be represented in Figure 14.1 by hypothetically increasing $\bar{e}$, the level of effort B supplied independently of the wage. This might occur, for example, if work norms were to change so as to favor greater work effort. Alternatively, $\bar{e}$ might rise, for example, if the employer had some other means of extracting effort, for example, through physical punishment. At some point $\bar{e}/\bar{w}$ may exceed e_w, implying that the optimal solution for A is simply to pay $\bar{w}$ and accept the effort level $\bar{e}$.[9]

The second Walrasian case may be illustrated by *flattening out* the best response schedule $e(w)$, so the level of effort does not vary significantly with the enforcement rent. This might occur, for example, if workers were so rich that they were indifferent to additional income. At some point we again arrive at the corner solution at $(\bar{e}, \bar{w})$, implying the Walrasian result: The employer offers a wage equal to the reservation wage $\bar{w}$, abandons the attempt to apply enforcement rent sanctions to the employee, and accepts the effort level $\bar{e}$.

Perhaps significantly, the Walrasian result can be seen to require either the unalienated or perhaps conformist norm-following Stakhanovite (the first case) or the income-satiated worker who cannot be manipulated by the wage

---

considering A's response function since A will choose a single cost-minimizing wage no matter what B does. (Strictly speaking B is also optimizing with respect to A's response function. In this case, however, A's response function is simply a vertical line in (e, w) space, as A's action cannot be influenced by B's choices.)

[8] This is the first order condition for the problem: Select w so as to maximize $e(w)/w$.

[9] A similar result obtains if the reservation wage $\bar{w}$ is decreased sufficiently, provided $\bar{e} > 0$.

carrot (the second case). In either case, the labor process would not then be a contested exchange, the labor market would clear in equilibrium, and no agent could sanction any other. Our sufficient condition for the exercise of power would thus not obtain. One might reasonably suspect, nonetheless, that in at least the first case the exercise of power is implicated, perhaps in the prior socialization of the worker to accept hard work as a norm or the effectiveness of employer sanctions unrelated to income. We regard both cases as unrealistic: Workers are not indifferent to additional income, and they would not choose the profit-maximizing level of effort in the absence of employer sanctions.

If one were rightly to dismiss on empirical grounds either the Stakhanovite or income-satiated worker routes back to the Walrasian model of clearing markets, however, one might equally charge that our representation of the labor process and labor market fails to capture important aspects of actually existing capitalism and particularly the social nature of the work process and the welfare state. By stressing the carrot of high wages and the stick of dismissal we do not, however, abstract from other possibly important aspects of the regulation of work such as conformism, good will, and pride in work, for these determine the position of the labor extraction function. Does not the welfare state and collective bargaining offer workers some protection from job termination and a minimum living standard when unemployed? True, but the degree of worker security from firing and unemployment insurance are integral parts of the model (reflected in p and z respectively). Indeed one of the advantages of the model is that it allows an analysis of the economic effects of the welfare state that goes considerably beyond the standard treatments of the effects of taxes and transfers on the supply of factors of production and on individual saving behavior.[10]

Short-side power in the production process

Does employer A have power over worker B? Given the sufficient condition for the exercise of power, the answer is surely yes: A may use the threat of sanction to cause B to act in A's interest, and the converse is not true. First, A may dismiss B, reducing B's present value to z. Hence A can apply sanctions to B. Second, A can use sanctions to elicit a preferred level of effort from B and thus to further A's interests.[11] Finally, while B may be capable of applying sanctions to A (for example, B may be capable of burning down A's factory),

[10] For example, as p approaches 1 (complete job security) or unemployment insurance coverage is extended such that z approaches v, the effectiveness of a dismissal based labor extraction system is eroded. See Bowles and Gintis (1982a) and Bowles and Gintis (1982b).

[11] A game theorist might object that the threat to dismiss the worker is not credible so long as the dismissal imposes costs upon the employer (for example, costs of search and training). Clearly, however, if the firm's overall contingent renewal strategy is profit maximizing, and if shirking and dismissal are observed by other workers, a shirking worker must be dismissed to maintain the credibility of the employer's threat.

B cannot use this capacity to induce A to choose a different wage or to refrain from dismissing B should A desire to do so. Should B make A a take-it-or-leave-it offer to work at a higher than equilibrium wage or should B threaten to apply sanctions unless A offers a higher wage, A would simply reject the offer and hire another worker. For as we have seen in the previous section, in equilibrium there will exist unemployed workers identical to B who would prefer to be employed. Thus A has power over B.

This model can be extended to include many agents and firms in a system of general economic equilibrium, making explicit the centrality of nonclearing markets to contested exchange equilibrium. In particular, because such an equilibrium exhibits positive enforcement rents, it entails by definition involuntary unemployment as well. The existence of agents who are involuntarily without employment (or with less desirable employment than B) follows from the strict inequality $v(w) > z$: If B enjoys an employment rent, there must be another otherwise identical agent, C, who would be willing to fill B's position at the going, or even at a lower, wage.[12] Moreover, should C promise A to work as hard as B for a lower wage, the offer will rightly be disbelieved and hence rejected by A. The reason is that, other than their employment status, B and C are identical; A knows exactly how much effort is forthcoming for a given employment rent and has already selected a cost-minimizing wage. Agent C is thus involuntarily unemployed in equilibrium so A's threat to replace B is credible.[13]

Models in which markets fail to clear have traditionally been viewed as disequilibrium theories. In the contested exchange model, however, nonclearing markets are characteristic of competitive equilibrium defined in the standard manner: No actor is capable of improving his or her position by altering a variable over which he or she has control. Employers have no interest in changing the wage offered, employed workers have no interest in changing the level of effort supplied, and workers in search of a job can do nothing but await an offer at the equilibrium wage.

The employer's power is thus related to his or her favorable position in a nonclearing market. We say that the employer A, who can purchase any desired amount of labor and hence is not quantity constrained, is on the *short side* of

[12] Such agents, rather than being unemployed, may simply prefer B's position to their own at the going wage. The point is that they are quantity constrained: They would prefer to sell more of their services at the going rate but are unable to (unless B is dismissed).

[13] Does A have power over C? The negative sanction that A may impose on B (withdrawal of the employment rent) is exactly equal to a positive sanction that A might offer or refuse to extend to C. If A refuses to hire C in order to maintain a racially homogeneous workplace, for instance, we might say that A has furthered his or her interests (gratification of racial prejudice) and A has sanctioned C (refused to offer the employment rent). By contrast to the relationship of A to B, however, the sanction is incidental to the furthering of A's interests. Thus A does not have power over C in our sense.

the market. Where excess supply exists – as in the labor market – the demand side is the short side and conversely.[14] Suppliers of labor are on the *long side* of the market. When contingent renewal is operative and where the institutional environment is such that the threat of sanctions by the short sider may be instrumental to furthering his or her interests, the principle of short-side power holds: Agents on the short side of the market will have power over agents on the long side with whom they transact.[15] Long-side agents are of two types: those such as B who succeed in finding an employer and thus receive a rent that constrains them to accept the employer's authority and those such as C who fail to make a transaction and hence are rationed out of the market. We will sometimes refer to agents such as B as long-side transactors and those such as C as quantity constrained.

Three aspects of this result deserve to be noted. First, it might appear that A has expressed a preference for power and has simply traded away some money – the enforcement rent – to gain power. But while real world employers may act this way, it is quite unnecessary for our result: A is assumed to be indifferent to the nature of the authority relationship per se and is simply maximizing profits.

Second, it might be thought that A has intentionally generated the unemployment necessary for the maintenance of his or her short-side power. It is true that the employer's profit maximizing strategy, when it is adopted by all other employers, results in the existence of unemployed workers and that other wage-setting rules would not have this result. But we have assumed that the employer treats the level of unemployment, which figures in the determination of the workers' fallback position, z, as exogenous for the simple reason that no employer acting singly can determine the level of aggregate employment.[16]

Third, it may be argued that B has power over A, if not in our formal sense then in the sense that B has the capacity to induce A to offer an employment rent over and above the amount needed to induce B to enter into the transaction. But B's advantage does not stem from B's *power* in the sense of a capacity that can be strategically deployed towards furthering one's interests. To see this,

---

[14] More generally, the short side of an exchange is located where the total amount of desired transactions is least; the demand side, if there is excess supply; and the supply side, if there is excess demand (Benassy, 1982).

[15] Note that being on the short side of a nonclearing market does not *in itself* ensure that an agent has short-side power. Since such a market does not clear, short sider A can indeed impose sanction on long sider B. A, however, need not have the ability to use this capacity in any way to affect B's behavior. Consumers buying on glutted markets present an example of agents whose short-side location does not confer short-side power (unless they collude).

[16] If employers act collectively, of course, a quite different picture emerges, as the contested exchange model demonstrates the interests of employers in the existence of unemployment and suggests that they might use their influence on the state to foster macroeconomic policies to maintain adequate levels of unemployment. An interpretation of recent U.S. macroeconomic policy along these lines is presented in Bowles, Gordon, and Weisskopf (1989). A parallel treatment of the collective action of workers is presented in Bowles and Boyer (1990).

note that A's power to dismiss B is a credible threat, while B can put forth no credible threat whatever. Rather than attributing the fact that B receives a wage in excess of the reservation wage to "B's power over A," we might better say that the employment rent derives from B's autonomy, that is from the inability of A costlessly to determine B's level of effort. The rent is a cost to A of exercising power over B.[17]

We may summarize these results in the form of two propositions:

Proposition 1 (short-side power): A competitive equilibrium of a system of contested exchanges may allocate power to agents on the short side of nonclearing markets.

Proposition 2 (the politics of production): Those in positions of decision-making authority in capitalist firms occupy locations on the short side of the labor market and exercise power over employees.

Let us not overstate these results. Not all contested exchanges give rise to short-side power. We analyzed an important case of contested exchange where contingent renewal strategies of endogenous enforcement are adopted by agents on one side of the market and where the short-side agents have the strategic capacity to act as Stackelberg leaders and thus to make use of their advantageous short-side location. But there may be other important cases in which our sufficient condition for the exercise of power do not obtain. Where no costlessly enforceable contracts can be written at all, for example, both agents may engage in endogenous enforcement activities, both may receive enforcement rents, and each may thus effectively pursue their interests by threatening to sanction the other. An employer facing a group of organized workers where the cost of replacing workers is high is an example of such bilateral power.[18]

---

[17] A fourth possible objection is that the employment rent could be recouped by the employer by requiring that workers post a bond – that is, to transfer a sum of money to the employer as a condition of employment, in effect paying the employer for the job. Since the present value of the job exceeds the present value of being unemployed, potential employees might be willing to post such a bond to gain access to the job. Because bonding will generally be profit enhancing for the employer, our abstraction from bonding on empirical grounds cannot be motivated theoretically within the framework of our models. But if bonding is used, its availability to workers is likely to be related to their holdings of property. Thus were we to take account of bonding, the importance of wealth in the market for managers and labor would be considerably enhanced. Reasons for the absence of bonding are explored by Eaton and White (1982); Akerlof and Katz (1988); Dickens, Katz, Lang, and Summers (1989); and Bowles and Gintis (1990b).

[18] See Aoki (1984) and Williamson (1985). We doubt, however, the substantive symmetry between employers and workers on empirical grounds. A terminated worker experiences a significant reduction in net wealth, roughly equivalent to a year's income, following termination. By contrast, in all but the smallest firms, the loss inflicted upon the firm in the form of search, recruitment, and training costs is a very small percentage of net profits (Bowles and Gintis 1990b and Mitchell and Kimball 1982).

Second, we have located power in the economy, but we have not shown that the exercise of this power is socially consequential. Indeed is it not inconceivable that, while short-side agents in labor markets exercise power over long-side transactors, there are no feasible alternative institutional arrangements that would yield superior outcomes. Rendering economic power democratically accountable is an important political project only if the exercise of power has socially consequential effects. While demonstrating this point is far from trivial, we think that the power of short siders does make a difference in both moral and political senses and have explored the implications of democratic accountability.

We may extract two less obvious results from the contested exchange model of the labor process and labor market. The first concerns Milton Friedman's claim that labor market discrimination and competitive equilibrium are incompatible.

In a contested exchange framework, discriminatory hiring practices may be an equilibrium employer strategy: Paying identical workers different wages (according to race, for example) will be profitable if it contributes to racial divisions that make cooperation among workers more difficult and hence lowers the cost of identifying and terminating a nonworking employee. Because all workers receive wages above their reservation wage, paying some less than others is not precluded as it is in the Walrasian model by the lower wage workers withdrawing their labor supply. If we identify as *primary jobs* the higher-paying positions into which one racial group is hired and as *secondary jobs* the lower-paying positions into which the other is hired, the labor market then includes in addition to employed and unemployed, the new category of *job-rationed* workers: agents who may be employed in one job category but are excluded from employment in another category for which they are qualified. A discriminated-against worker employed in a secondary position is thus job-rationed in the sense of being a long sider with a contract (a type B agent) with respect to the secondary market but a long sider without a contract (a type C agent) with respect to the primary job market.

The efficacy of cooperation among workers is obviously critical to this argument. But how might collusion among workers benefit workers at the expense of their employers? Most obviously a unified work force could threaten to strike if even a single worker is terminated. Of course under competitive assumptions the striking workers could be replaced, but the search, recruitment, and training costs of an entire workforce might deter the termination of any but the most recalcitrant on-the-job loafer. If racial hiring practices impede collusion among workers and if they are not costly on other grounds, they will be an equilibrium strategy for the employer who as a Stackelberg leader will design wage and working conditions packages with racial disunity as an objective and make these as take-it-or-leave-it offers to prospective employees.

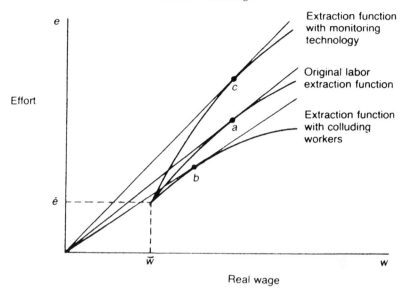

Figure 14.2. The effects of worker collusion and monitoring technologies on the labor extraction equilibrium (a, b, and c are the three equilibria corresponding to the three extraction functions).

Formally, an increase in collusion will raise p, the probability of *not* being terminated if observed not working up to standard. This in turn will have the effect of reducing the optimal amount of effort offered at each wage rate, yielding a downward rotation around point $(\bar{w}, \bar{e})$ of the labor extraction function as shown in Figure 14.2. The result, necessarily, is a fall in e/w, or what is the same thing, an increase in labor costs per unit of effective labor done. An analogous downward shift in the extraction function might take place if collusion among workers made the detection of nonworking workers more difficult or more costly, perhaps by workers refusing to cooperate with the surveillance system of the employer, giving false reports on the work activities of fellow workers, and the like. We thus have:

Proposition 3 (divide and rule): The competitive equilibrium of a contested exchange economy may exhibit racial, gender, and other forms of labor market discrimination among otherwise identical workers.

It is worth noting that Proposition 3 relies on the constitutive as well as the contested nature of the exchange process: The structure of wages provides a basis for feelings of solidarity or antagonism.

Our last labor market result concerns the social determination of technology or what might be termed the shaping of the forces of production by the social

209

relations of production.[19] The production system entailed by our model includes a production function, which describes the transformation of inputs into outputs, and a labor extraction function, which describes the manner in which the firm acquires work from employees whose time it has purchased on the labor market. Thus far we have assumed that the choice of the technologies that make up the production function is unrelated to the endogenous enforcement of claims arising in the labor market. But technologies differ markedly in their impact on the enforcement problem facing employers; some, like the assembly line, computerized point-of-sale terminals, or centralized word processing systems, make the detection of a laggard worker by a nonworker relatively simple while others, like team production methods, make the production process considerably more opaque to outsiders.

Thus the choice of technology will influence the cost of monitoring the work process and, for any given cost level the probability, that a nonworking worker will be detected. Formally the choice of a technology that yields an easily monitored production process may be represented as an upwards rotation of the labor extraction function, as shown in Figure 14.2. The result is a saving on the cost of extracting labor from labor power that in the technical choice decision will be compared with the possibly greater production cost of the new technology stemming from its possibly lesser efficiency in transforming inputs into outputs. Thus the efficiency of a technology in transforming inputs into outputs does not determine the course of technical change, and the choice of technique may be inefficient in the sense that production systems may be selected for their capacity to police the labor process despite their relative ineffectiveness in producing goods and services. We thus can assert:

Proposition 4 (capitalist technology): Where claim enforcement is endogenous, the profit-maximizing choice of production technologies will be made in light of both the efficiency with which technologies transform inputs into outputs and their efficacy in enforcing contested claims; the resulting technologies, though cost minimizing, will generally not be efficient.

Thus the technologies in use (and possibly technological research) will be influenced by the structure of the enforcement environments and enforcement instruments available. Because these are determined in important measure by the social institutions governing everything from civil liberties through

---

[19] Our model here is obviously inspired by, but is a drastic simplification of, primarily historical and institutionalist arguments presented in the now vast literature initiated by Marglin's treatment of this problem (1974). For a more extended contested exchange treatment of technical change with some historical examples, see Bowles (1988).

bankruptcy law to the welfare state, we may expect social institutions and production relations in particular to influence technical choice in ways unrelated to the standard arguments concerning price and income effects.[20]

Our analysis of the employment relationship and labor markets may be extended in two ways. First, it is well known that markets are allocation mechanisms, promoting movements to and along an exogenously defined production possibility frontier. But markets are also disciplinary mechanisms, altering the supplies of inputs and technologies alike and thus shifting the production possibility frontier. Just as allocative efficiency is a sensible normative standard for economic institutions, we may reasonably inquire to what extent and under what conditions markets provide efficient disciplining mechanisms.

Second, enforcement capacities are a determinant of institutional evolution. Like markets, all important economic institutions have consequences for the enforcement of claims arising from exchange. The evolution of such institutions responds to the changing technologies of enforcement no less than to the changing technologies of production and demographic shifts stressed in the standard treatment by neoclassical economic historians.[21] The workings and larger consequences of economically important institutions (schooling and the welfare state come to mind) may also be fruitfully analyzed from the standpoint of their effects on endogenous enforcement environments.[22]

---

[20] Analogous reasoning applies to the choice of which goods to produce. According to a number of economic historians, for example, the production of some products – like sugar – present relatively few endogenous enforcement problems while others – tobacco, for example – depend heavily on subtle variations in the quality of care that are highly costly to extract from a resistant workforce. Ortiz (1963) used this argument to construct a powerful interpretation of the modern history of Cuba. Nilsson (1989) has analyzed product-related enforcement effects in an incisive critique of the neoclassical theory of comparative advantage and international specialization.

[21] Here North's recent work (1981) represents a major contribution to the post-Walrasian theory of institutional structure and evolution (see also Levi [1988] and Pagano [1988]), while his earlier work is closer to the Walrasian tradition.

[22] Failure to analyze the effect of schooling on the labor market enforcement environment was our main critique of human capital theory. See Bowles and Gintis (1975); and Bowles and Gintis (1976). On the effect of the welfare state on enforcement environments see Bowles and Gintis (1982a); Bowles and Gintis (1982b); and Schor and Bowles (1987).

CHAPTER 15

Understanding the employment relation:
the analysis of idiosyncratic exchange

OLIVER WILLIAMSON, MICHAEL WACHTER,
AND JEFFREY HARRIS

Oliver Williamson is the Edgar F. Kaiser Professor, Emeritus, of Business Administration, Economics, and Law at the University of California, Berkeley. See also the previous chapters by Williamson.

Michael Wachter was born in New York City in 1943. He received a Ph.D. in economics from Harvard University in 1970. When this paper was published, he was Associate Professor of Economics at the University of Pennsylvania. He is currently William B. Johnson Professor of Law and Economics and Director of the Institute for Law and Economics at the University of Pennsylvania.

Jeffrey Harris was born in 1948. He earned an M.D. and a Ph.D. in economics from the University of Pennsylvania in 1974 and 1975, respectively. At the time this paper was published, he was a Resident in Medicine at Massachusetts General Hospital. Since 1982, he has taught at the Massachusetts Institute of Technology, where he is currently Professor of Economics. He is also a practicing internist at a community health center in Pawtucket, Rhode Island.

This paper is concerned with jobs for which nontrivial job-specific skills and task-specific knowledge evolve, in a learning by doing fashion, during the course of a worker's employment. Otherwise qualified but inexperienced workers can not be regarded as the equivalent of job incumbents under such circumstances. The underlying factors that give rise to job idiosyncrasies and the contractual properties of four alternative contracting modes for jobs of this kind are evaluated with the assistance of what we refer to as the "organizational failures framework." Individualistic contracting modes of the contingent claims contracting, spot contracting, and authority relation types are examined. The implied demands on the rationality limits of human actors are shown to be severe and the associated costs of adapting to changing job and market

Reprinted with abridgments from Oliver Williamson, Michael Wachter, and Jeffrey Harris, "Understanding the Employment Relation: The Analysis of Idiosyncratic Exchange," *The Bell Journal of Economics*, 6 (1975): 250–78. Copyright © 1975. Reprinted with permission of the Rand Corporation. (A variant of this paper also appears as Chapter 4 of Williamson's *Markets and Hierarchies: Analysis and Antitrust Implications*. New York: The Free Press, 1975.)

circumstances are shown to be considerable for jobs of the idiosyncratic kind. Collectivizing the employment agreement alleviates these conditions in that it serves to economize on transaction costs by relieving bounds on rationality and attenuating opportunism. The upshot is that "internal labor markets," which others have interpreted in mainly noneconomic terms, can be supplied with an efficiency rationale – additionally if not instead.

. . .

2. Background

. . .

Conventional treatments – indivisibilities

Indivisibilities of both physical capital and informational types are said to lead to the substitution of internal for market organization. The former involves scale economies associated with physical assets and is reasonably familiar. Larger scale units, provided they are utilized at design capacity, permit lower average costs to be realized. The group may thus be formed so as to assure that utilization demands will be sufficient.

Somewhat less familiar are the indivisibilities associated with information. Radner observes in this connection that "the acquisition of information often involves a 'set up cost'; i.e., the resources needed to obtain the information may be independent of the scale of the production process in which the information is used."[1] Consequently, groups may also be formed so as to economize on information costs.

That there are economies of either of these types to be realized, however, does not clearly imply, as a technological imperative, collective organization. Thus, technologically speaking, there is nothing that prevents one individual from procuring the physical asset in requisite size to realize the economies in question and contracting to supply the services of this asset to all of the members of the group. Similarly, there is no technological bar that prevents one individual from assuming the information gathering and dissemination function. All parties, suppliers of the specialized services and users alike, could be independent, yet scale economies of both types could be fully realized. If, therefore, such specialization fails to materialize, it is not because monopoly ownership of the physical assets and information services in question is impeded in technological respects. Rather, the problems are to be traced to transactional difficulties that predictably attend market exchange in these circumstances.

---

[1] Radner (1970), p. 457.

Accordingly, the incentive to collectivize activities for which indivisibilities are large in relation to the market is ultimately of a transactional kind.

Conventional treatments – nonseparabilities

Alchian and Demsetz[2] contend that normal sales relationships are supplanted by an employment relation on account of nonseparabilities. The standard example is the manual loading of freight into a truck by two men, both of whom must work coordinately to lift the cargo in question. The inability to impute marginal products to each man on the basis of observed output is what, in Alchian and Demsetz' scheme of things, warrants hierarchical organization. A "boss" is introduced who monitors the work of both, thereby checking malingering and yielding a larger team output.

We agree, but make two further points. First, it is not the nonseparability by itself that occasions the problem. Rather it is this in conjunction with what we shall refer to below as "opportunism" and a condition of "information impactedness" that poses the difficulties. Absent these transactional considerations, the purported metering problems associated with nonseparability vanish. Second, and more important, we contend that most tasks are separable in the sense that – provided that successive stages of production are in balance – it is possible to sever the connection between stages by introducing buffer inventories.

Consider Adam Smith's pin-making example.[3] Pin manufacture involved a series of technologically distinct operations (wire straightening, cutting, pointing, grinding, etc.). In principle, each of these activities could be performed by an independent specialist and work passed from station to station by contract. Autonomous contracting would be facilitated, moreover, by introducing buffer inventories at each station, since coordination requirements and hence contractual complexity would thereby be reduced. Each worker could then proceed at his own pace, subject only to the condition that he maintain his buffer inventory at some minimum level. A series of independent entrepreneurs rather than a group of employees, each subject to an authority relation, could thus perform the tasks in question.

Transaction costs militate against such an organization of tasks, however. For one thing, it may be possible to economize on buffer inventories by designating someone to act as a coordinator,[4] which entails, albeit in limited degree, a shift toward hierarchy. But more germane to our purposes here are the economies attributable to the structure of internal labor markets – provided that the jobs in question are idiosyncratic in nontrivial degree. The ways in which the structured bargaining features of internal labor markets permit such economies

[2] Alchian and Demsetz (1972).   [3] Smith (1937), p. 457.
[4] For a discussion of some of the ways in which buffer inventory savings can be realized, see Williamson (1964a), pp. 1454–5.

to be realized are developed below. We nevertheless take this opportunity to emphasize that small numbers exchange relations *evolve* much more frequently than is usually acknowledged, and that the prospect of costly haggling among autonomous agents is a consequence. The interesting institutional design question that is thereby posed is how can such haggling be attenuated? Examining the structural bargaining attributes of alternative contracting modes is plainly relevant in this connection.

Small numbers – general

Arrow illustrates the problem of small numbers exchange with the lighthouse example. Indivisibility is no problem, since the light can be either on or off. He furthermore abstracts from uncertainty, by assuming that the lighthouse keeper knows exactly when each ship will need its services, and assumes that exclusion is possible since only one ship will be within lighthouse range at any one time. A trading problem nevertheless arises, because "there would be only one buyer and one seller and no competitive forces to drive the two of them into competitive equilibrium."[5] As will be evident, this condition, together with the stipulation that the firm is confronted with changing internal and market circumstances, is what we mainly rely on to explain the employment relation.

Small numbers – task idiosyncrasies

Doeringer and Piore describe idiosyncratic tasks in the following way:[6]

Almost every job involves some specific skills. Even the simplest custodial tasks are facilitated by familiarity with the physical environment specific to the workplace in which they are being performed. The apparently routine operation of standard machines can be importantly aided by familiarity with the particular piece of operating equipment. . . . In some cases workers are able to anticipate trouble and diagnose its source by subtle changes in the sound or smell of the equipment. Moreover, performance in some production or managerial jobs involves a team element, and a critical skill is the ability to operate effectively with the given members of the team. This ability is dependent upon the interaction skills of the personalities of the members, and the individual's work "skills" are specific in the sense that skills necessary to work on one team are never quite the same as those required on another.

Hayek describes the consequences of idiosyncrasy as follows:[7]

. . . practically every individual has some advantage over all others in that he possesses unique information of which beneficial use might be made, but of which use can be made only if the decisions depending on it are left to him or are made with his active

---

[5] Arrow (1969), p. 58.   [6] Doeringer and Piore (1971), pp. 15–16.
[7] Hayek (1945), pp. 521–2.

cooperation. We need to remember only how much we have to learn in any occupation after we have completed our theoretical training, how big a part of our working life we spend learning particular jobs, and how valuable an asset in all walks of life is knowledge of people, of local conditions, and special circumstances.

More generally, task idiosyncrasies can arise in at least four ways: (1) equipment idiosyncrasies, due to incompletely standardized, albeit common, equipment, the unique characteristics of which become known through experience; (2) process idiosyncrasies, which are fashioned or "adopted" by the worker and his associates in specific operating contexts; (3) informal team accommodations, attributable to mutual adaptation among parties engaged in recurrent contact but which are upset, to the possible detriment of group performance, when the membership is altered; and (4) communication idiosyncrasies with respect to information channels and codes that are of value only within the firm. Given that "technology is [partly] unwritten and that part of the specificity derives from improvements which the work force itself introduces, workers are in a position to perfect their monopoly over the knowledge of the technology should there be an incentive to do so."[8]

Training for idiosyncratic jobs ordinarily takes place in an on-the-job context. Classroom training is unsuitable both because the *uniqueness* attributes associated with particular operations, machines, the work group, and, more generally, the atmosphere of the workplace may be impossible to replicate in the classroom, and because job incumbents, who are in possession of the requisite skills and knowledge with which the new recruit or candidate must become familiar, may be unable to describe, demonstrate, or otherwise impart this information except in an operational context.[9] Teaching by doing thus facilitates the learning by doing process. Where such uniqueness and teaching attributes are at all important, specific exposure in the workplace at some stage becomes essential. Outsiders who lack specific experience can thus achieve parity with insiders only by being hired and incurring the necessary start up costs.

The success of on-the-job training is plainly conditional on the information disclosure attitudes of incumbent employees. Both individually and as a group, incumbents are in possession of a valuable resource (knowledge) and can be expected to reveal it fully and candidly only in exchange for value. The way the employment relation is structured turns out to be important in this connection. The danger is that incumbent employees will hoard information to their personal advantage and engage in a series of bilateral monopolistic exchanges with the management – to the detriment of both the firm and other employees as well.

An additional feature of these tasks not described above but nevertheless important to an understanding of the contractual problems associated with

[8] Doeringer and Piore (1971), p. 84.   [9] See Doeringer and Piore (1971), p. 20.

the employment relation is that the activity in question is subject to periodic disturbance by environmental changes.[10] Shifts in demand due to changes in the prices of complements or substitutes or to changes in consumer incomes or tastes occur; relative factor price changes appear; and technological changes of both product design and production technique types take place. Successive adaptations to changes of each of these kinds are typically needed if efficient production performance is to be realized. In addition, life cycle changes in the workforce occur which occasion turnover, upgrading, and continuous training. The tasks in question are thus to be regarded in moving equilibrium terms. Put differently, they are not tasks for which a once-for-all adaptation by workers is sufficient, thereafter to remain unchanged.

. . .

4. Individualistic bargaining models

Four types of individualistic contracting modes can be distinguished:[11] (1) contract now for the specific performance of x in the future; (2) contract now for the delivery of x_i contingent on event e_i obtaining in the future; (3) wait until the future materializes and contract for the appropriate (specific) x at the time; and (4) contract now for the right to select a specific x from within an admissible set X, the determination of the particular x to be deferred until the future. Simon's study of the employment relation[12] treats contracts of the first type, which he characterizes as sales contracts, as the main alternative to the so-called authority relation (type 4). This, however, is unfortunate because type 1 contracts, being rigid, are singularly unsuited to permit adaptation in response to changing internal and market circumstances. By contrast, contingent claims contracts

---

[10] Omitted from the discussion of the framework in this paper is a systems related condition referred to as "atmosphere." Failure to include atmosphere does not imply that we think it unimportant. But the concept is somewhat difficult to explicate in what is already a rather long paper.

[11] Lest the ensuing discussion of autonomous bargaining modes be thought to be contrived and/or unnecessary, since "everyone knows" such bargaining modes are inapposite, we make the following observations. First, though it is widely recognized that complex contingent claims contracting is infeasible (e.g., Radner notes that the Arrow-Debreu contracting model "requires that the economic agents possess capabilities of imagination and calculation that exceed reality by many orders of magnitude" (1970, p. 457), the reasons for this are rarely fully spelled out – either in general or, even less, with respect to labor market contracting). We attempt to rectify this condition in Section 4 below. Second, as our discussion of Alchian and Demsetz below reveals, it is plainly not the case that everyone appreciates that idiosyncratic tasks need to be distinguished from tasks in general and that sequential spot contracting is singularly unsuited for jobs of the idiosyncratic kind. Third, so as to correct the widely held belief that the authority relation represents a well defined alternative to "normal" market contracting (as recently illustrated by Arrow's (1974, pp. 25, 63–64) reliance on Simon's treatment of the authority relation), we think it important that the ambiguities of the authority relation be exposed.

[12] Simon (1957), pp. 183–195.

(type 2) and sequential spot sales contract (type 3) both permit adaptation. If complexity/uncertainty is held to be a central feature of the environment with which we are concerned, which it is, the deck is plainly stacked against contracts of type 1 from the outset. Accordingly, type 1 contracts will hereafter be disregarded.

Contingent claims contracts. Suppose that the efficient choice of x on each date depends on how the future unfolds. Suppose furthermore that the parties are instructed to negotiate a once-for-all labor contract in which the obligations of both employer and employee are fully stipulated at the outset. A complex contingent claims contract would then presumably result. The employer would agree to pay a particular wage now in return for which the employee agrees to deliver stipulated future services of a contingent kind, the particular services being dependent upon the circumstances which eventuate.

Contracting problems of several kinds can be anticipated. First, can the complex contract be written? Second, even if it can, is a meaningful agreement between the parties feasible? Third, can such agreements be implemented in a low cost fashion? The issues posed can all usefully be considered in the context of the framework sketched out above.

The feasibility of writing complex contingent claims contracts reduces fundamentally to a bounded rationality issue. The discussion by Feldman and Kanter of complex decision trees is instructive in this connection:[13]

For even moderately complex problems . . . the entire decision trees cannot be generated. There are several reasons why this is so: one is the size of the tree. The number of alternative paths in complex decision problems is very large. . . . A second reason is that in most decision situations, unlike chess, neither the alternative paths nor a rule for generating them is available. . . . A third reason is the problem of estimating consequences. . . . For many problems, consequences of alternatives are difficult, if not impossible to estimate. The comprehensive decision model is not feasible for most interesting decision problems.

Plainly, the complex labor agreements needed to describe the idiosyncratic tasks in question are of this kind. Not only are changing market circumstances (product demand, rivalry, factor prices, technological conditions, and the like) impossibly complex to enumerate, but the appropriate adaptations thereto cannot be established with any degree of confidence *ex ante*. Changing life cycle conditions with respect to the internal labor force compound the complexities.

The enumeration problems referred to are acknowledged by Meade in his discussion of contingent claims contracts: "When environmental uncertainties are so numerous that they cannot all be considered . . . or, what comes perhaps

---

[13] Feldman and Kanter (1965), p. 615.

to much the same thing, when any particular environmental risks are so hard to define and to distinguish from each other that it is impossible to base a firm betting or insurance contract upon the occurrence or nonoccurrence of any of them, then for this reason alone it is impossible to have a system of contingency . . . markets."[14] But for bounded rationality, Meade's concerns with excessive numbers, undefinable risks, and indistinguishable events would vanish.

But suppose, *arguendo*, that exhaustive complex contracts could be written at reasonable expense. Would such contracts be acceptable to the parties? We submit that a problem of incomprehensibility will frequently arise and impede reaching agreement. At least one of the parties, probably the worker, will be unable meaningfully to assess the implications of the complex agreement to which he is being asked to accede. Sequential contracting, in which experience permits the implications of various contingent commitments to be better understood, is thus apt to be favored instead.

Assume, however, that *ex ante* understanding poses no bar to contracting. *Ex post* enforcement issues then need to be addressed. First, there is the problem of declaring what state of the world has obtained. Meade's remarks that contingent claims contracts are infeasible in circumstances where it is impossible, on the contract execution date, "to decide precisely enough for the purposes of a firm legal contract" what state of the world has eventuated bear on this.[15] While it is easy to agree with Meade's contentions, we think it noteworthy to observe that, were it not for opportunism and information impactedness, the impediments to contracting to which he refers vanish. Absent these conditions, the responsibility for declaring what state of the world had obtained could simply be assigned to the "best informed" party. Once he has made the determination, the appropriate choice of x is found by consulting the contract. Execution then follows directly.

It is hazardous, however, to permit the best informed party unilaterally to make state of the world declarations where opportunism can be anticipated. If the worker is not indifferent between supplying services of type x_j rather than x_k, and if the declaration of the state of the world were to be left to him, he will be inclined, when circumstances permit, to represent the state of the world in terms most favorable to him. Similar problems are to be expected for those events for which the employer is thought to be the best informed party and unilaterally declares, from among a plausible set, which e_i has eventuated.[16] Moreover,

---

[14] Meade (1971), p. 183.   [15] Meade (1971), p. 183.

[16] The issue here is somewhat more subtle, however. The employer, when he assumes the role of the best informed party, will not wish to declare a false state of the world *unless,* at the time he got the worker to agree to a wage w, he represented to the worker that services of type x_i would be called for when even e_i obtained when in fact x_i' services, which the worker dislikes, yield a greater e_i gain. The worker, being assured that he would be called on to perform x, ne_i' services only when the unlikely even e_i' occurred, agreed to a lower wage than he would have if he realized that an x_i'

mediation by a third party is no answer since, by assumption, an information impactedness condition prevails with respect to the observations in question.

Finally, even were it that state of the world issues could be settled conclusively at low cost, there is still the problem of execution. Did the worker really supply x_i in response to condition e_i, as he should, or did he (opportunistically) supply x_j instead? If the latter, how does the employer show this in a way that entitles him to a remedy? These are likewise information impactedness issues. Problems akin to moral hazard are posed.

Ordinarily, bounded rationality renders the description of once-for-all contingent claims' employment contracts strictly in-feasible. Occasions to examine the negotiability and enforcement properties of such contracts thus rarely develop. It is sufficient for our purposes here, however, merely to establish that problems of any of these kinds impair contingent claims contracting. In consideration of these difficulties, alternatives to the once-for-all supply relation ought presumably to be examined.

Sequential spot contracts. Alchian and Demsetz take the position that it is delusion to characterize the relation between employer and employee by reference to fiat, authority, or the like. Rather, it is their contention that the relation between an employer and his employee is identical to that which exists between a shopper and his grocer in fiat and authority respects[17]:

The single consumer can assign his grocer to the task of obtaining whatever the customer can induce the grocer to provide at a price acceptable to both parties. That is precisely all that an employer can do to an employee. To speak of managing, directing, or assigning workers to various tasks is a deceptive way of noting that the employer continually is involved in renegotiation of contracts on terms that must be acceptable to both parties. . . . Long term contracts between employer and employee are not the essence of the organization we call a firm.

Implicit in their argument, we take it, is an assumption that the transition costs associated with employee turnover are negligible. Employers, therefore, are able easily to adapt to changing market circumstances by filling jobs on a spot market basis. Although job incumbents may continue to hold jobs for a considerable period of time, and may claim to be subject to an authority relationship, all that they are essentially doing is continuously meeting bids for their jobs in the spot market. This is option number three, among the contracting alternatives described at the beginning of this section, done repeatedly.

That adaptive, sequential decision-making can be effectively implemented in sequential spot labor markets which satisfy the low transition cost assumption

---

response would be called for in both e_i and e_i' situations because the employer will falsely declare e_i to be e_i' so as to get x_i' performed.

[17] Alchian and Demsetz (1972), p. 777.

(as some apparently do, e.g., migrant farm labor),[18] without posing issues that differ in kind from the usual grocer – customer relationship, seems uncontestable. We submit, however, that many jobs do not satisfy this assumption. In particular, the tasks of interest here are not of this primitive variety. Where tasks are idiosyncratic, in nontrivial degree, the worker – employer relationship is no longer contractually equivalent to the usual grocer – customer relationship and the feasibility of sequential spot market contracting breaks down.

Whereas the problems of contingent claims contracts were attributed to bounded rationality and opportunism conditions, sequential spot contracts are principally impaired only by the latter. (Bounded rationality poses a less severe problem because no effort is made to describe the complex decision tree from the outset. Instead, adaptations to uncertainty are devised as events unfold.) Wherein does opportunism arise and how is sequential spot contracting impaired?

Recall from the discussion of opportunism in Section 3 that opportunism poses a contractual problem only to the extent that it appears in a small numbers bargaining context. Otherwise, large numbers bidding effectively checks opportunistic inclinations and competitive outcomes result. The problem with the tasks in question is that while large numbers bidding conditions obtain at the outset, before jobs are first assigned and the work begun, the idiosyncratic nature of the work experience effectively destroys parity at the contract renewal interval. Incumbents who enjoy nontrivial advantages over similarly qualified but inexperienced bidders are well situated to demand some fraction of the cost savings which their idiosyncratic experience has generated.

One possible adaptation is for employers to avoid idiosyncratic technologies and techniques in favor of more well-standardized operations. Although least-cost production technologies are sacrificed in the process, pecuniary gains may nevertheless result since incumbents realize little strategic advantage over otherwise qualified but inexperienced outsiders. Structuring the initial bidding in such a way as to permit the least-cost technology and techniques to be employed without risking untoward contract renewal outcomes is, however, plainly to be preferred. Two possibilities warrant consideration: (1) extract a promise from each willing bidder at the outset that he will not use his idiosyncratic knowledge and experience in a monopolistic way at the contract renewal interval; or (2) require incumbents to capitalize the prospective monopoly gains that each will accrue and extract corresponding lump-sum payments from winning bidders at the outset.

The first of these can be dismissed as utopian. It assumes that promises not to behave opportunistically are either self-enforcing or can be enforced in the courts. Self-enforcement is tantamount to denying that human agents are prone

---

[18] See Doeringer and Piore (1971), pp. 4–5; also Kerr (1954). p. 95.

to be opportunists, and fails for want of reality testing. Enforcement of such promises by the courts is likewise unrealistic. Neither case by case litigation nor simple rule-making disposition of the issues is feasible. Litigation on the merits of each case is prohibitively costly, while rules to the effect that "all workers shall receive only competitive wages" fail because courts cannot, for information impactedness reasons, determine whether workers put their energies and inventiveness into the job in a way which permits task-specific cost savings to be fully realized – in which case disaffected workers can counter such rules by withholding effort.

The distinction between consummate and perfunctory cooperation is important in this connection. Consummate cooperation is an affirmative job attitude – to include the use of judgment, filling gaps, and taking initiative in an instrumental way.[19] Perfunctory cooperation, by contrast, involves job performance of a minimally acceptable sort. Incumbents, who through experience have acquired task-specific skills, need merely to maintain a slight margin over the best available inexperienced candidate (whose job attitude, of necessity, is an unknown quantity). The upshot is that workers, by shifting to a perfunctory performance mode, are in a position to "destroy" idiosyncratic efficiency gains. Reliance on preemployment promises as a means by which to deny workers from participating in such gains is accordingly self-defeating.

Consider therefore the second alternative in which, though worker participation in realized cost savings is assumed to be normal, workers are required to submit lump-sum bids for jobs at the outset. Assuming that large numbers of applicants are qualified to bid for these jobs at the outset, will such a scheme permit employers fully to appropriate the expected, discounted value of future cost savings by awarding the job to whichever worker offers to make the highest lump-sum payment?

Such a contracting scheme amounts to long-term contracting in which many of the details of the agreement are left unspecified. As might be anticipated, numerous problems are posed. For one thing, it assumes that workers are capable of assessing complex future circumstances in a sophisticated way and of making a determination of what the prospective gains are. Plainly, a

---

[19] Consummate cooperation involved working in a fully functional, undistorted mode. Efforts are not purposefully withheld; neither is behavior of a knowingly inapt kind undertaken. Blau and Scott are plainly concerned with the difference between perfunctory and consummate cooperation in the following passage (1962, p. 140):

the contract obligates employees to perform only a set of duties in accordance with minimum standards and does not assure their striving to achieve optimum performance . . . [L]egal authority does not and cannot command the employee's willingness to devote his ingenuity and energy to performing his tasks to the best of his ability. . . . It promotes compliance with directives and discipline, but does not encourage employees to exert effort, to accept responsibilities, or to exercise initiative.

serious bounded rationality issue is raised. Second, even if workers had the competence to complete such an exercise, it is seriously to be doubted that they could raise the funds, if their personal assets were deficient, to make the implied full valuation bids. As Malmgren has observed, in a somewhat different but nevertheless related context, "some [individuals] will see opportunities, but be unable to communicate their own information and expectations favorably to bankers, and thus be unable to acquire finance, or need to pay a higher charge for the capital borrowed."[20] The communication difficulties referred to are due to language limitations (attributable to bounded rationality) that the parties experience. That bankers are unwilling to accept the representations of loan-seekers at face value is because of the risks of opportunism.

Third, and crucially, the magnitude of the estimated future gains to be realized by workers often depends not merely on exogenous events and/or activities that each worker fully controls but also on the posture of coworkers and the posture of the employer. Problems with coworkers arise if, despite steady state task separability, the consent or active cooperation of workers who interface with the task in question must be secured each time an adaptation is proposed. This effectively means that related sets of workers must enter bids as teams, which complicates the bidding scheme greatly and offers opportunities for free-riding. Problems also arise if gains cannot be realized independently of the decisions taken by management with respect, for example, to the organization of production, complementary new asset acquisitions, equipment repair policy, etc. Lump sum bidding is plainly hazardous where workers are entering bids on life cycle earnings streams that are repeatedly exposed to re-bargaining.[21]

Finally, but surely of negligible importance in relation to the issues already raised, there is the question of efficient risk bearing: which party is best situated to bear the risks of future uncertainties, individual workers or the firm? That individual workers may be poorly suited to bear such risks and, as a group, can pool risks only with difficulty, seems evident and further argues against the bidding scheme proposed.

Transactional difficulties thus beset both contingent claims and sequential spot market contracting for the idiosyncratic tasks of interest in this chapter. Consider therefore the so-called authority relation as the solution to the contracting problems in question.

---

[20] Malmgren (1961), p. 46.

[21] There is the related problem of comparing the bids of workers who have different age, health, and other characteristics. Possibly this could be handled by stipulating that winners have claims to jobs in perpetuity, so that a job can be put up for rebidding by the estate of a worker who dies or retires. Such rebidding, however, is hazardous if the new worker must secure anew the cooperation of his colleagues. Established workers are then in a position strategically to appropriate some of the gains. (This assumes that coalition asymmetries exist which favor old workers in relation to the new.)

The authority relation. Simon has made one of the few attempts to assess the employment relation formally. Letting B designate the employer (or boss), W be the employee (or worker), and x be an element in the set of possible behavior patterns of W, he defines an authority relation as follows:[22]

We will say that B exercises *authority* over W if W permits B to select x. That is, W accepts authority when his behavior is determined by B's decision. In general, W will accept authority only if x_0, the x chosen by B, is restricted to some subset (W's "area of acceptance") of all the possible values.

An employment contract is then said to exist whenever W agrees to accept the authority of B in return for which B agrees to pay W a stated wage.[23]

Simon then asks when will such an employment relationship be preferred to a sales contract, and offers the following two conjectures:[24]

(1) W will be willing to enter into an employment contract with B only if it does not matter to him "very much" which x (within the agreed upon area of acceptance) B will choose, or if W is compensated in some way for the possibility that B will choose x that is not desired by W (i.e., that B will ask W to perform an unpleasant task).

(2) It will be advantageous to B to offer W added compensation for entering into an employment contract if B is unable to predict with certainty, at the time the contract is made, which x will be the optimum one, from his standpoint. That is, B will pay for the privilege of postponing, until some time after the contract is made, the selection of x.

He then goes on to develop a formal model in which he demonstrates that the employment contract commonly has attractive properties, under conditions of uncertainty, *provided that the alternatives are* (1) the promise of a particular x in exchange for a given wage w (what he considers to be the sales contract option), or (2) a set of X from which a particular x will subsequently be chosen in exchange for a given wage w' (the employment contract option).

Put differently, the deterministic sales contract is shown to be inferior to an incompletely specified employment relation in which W and B do not agree on all terms *ex ante*, but "agree to agree later" – or better, "agree to tell and be told." But plainly the terms are rigged from the outset. As noted previously, the particular type of sales contract to which Simon refers in attempting to establish the rationale for an authority relation is the only one of the three types of sales contracts described at the beginning of this section that lacks for adaptability in response to changing market circumstances. Since employment contracts of both the contingent claims and sequential spot marketing kinds are

---

[22] Simon (1957), p. 184.   [23] See Simon (1957), p. 184.   [24] Simon (1957), p. 185.

not similarly flawed, a better test of the authority relation would be to compare it with either of these instead.

Simon's modeling apparatus, unfortunately, does not lend itself to such purposes. It is simply silent with respect to the efficiency properties of alternative contracts in which adaptability is featured. Not only is it unable to discriminate between the authority relation, contingent claims contract, and spot market contracting in adaptability respects, but Simon's model fails to raise transaction cost issues of the types described here.

This is not, however, to suggest that the authority relation has nothing to commend it. To the contrary, such a relation does not require that the complex decision tree be generated in advance, and thus does not pose the severe bounded rationality problems to which the contingent claims contracting model is subject. The authority relation also, presumably, reduces the frequency with which contracts must be negotiated in comparison with the sequential spot contracting mode. Adaptations in the small can be costlessly accomplished under an authority relation because such changes, to the worker, do not matter "very much."

Assuming, however, that the parties are prospectively joined in a long-term association and the jobs in question are of the idiosyncratic kind, most of the problems of sequential spot contracting still need to be faced. Thus how are wage and related terms of employment to be adjusted through time in response to either small, but cumulative, or large, discrete changes in the data? What happens when hitherto unforeseen and unforeseeable contingencies eventuate? How are differences between the parties regarding state of the world determinations, the definition of the task, and job performance to be reconciled? Substantially all of the problems that are posed by idiosyncratic tasks in the sequential spot contracting mode appear, we submit, under the authority relation as well.

5. The efficiency implications of internal labor market structures

The upshot is that none of the above contracting schemes has acceptable properties for tasks of the idiosyncratic variety. Contingent claims contracting[25] fails principally on account of bounded rationality. Spot market contracting[26] is impaired by first mover advantages and problems of opportunism. The authority relation[27] is excessively vague and, ultimately, is confronted with the same types of problems as is spot market contracting. Faced with this result, the question of alternative contracting schemes naturally arises. Can more effective schemes be designed? Do more efficient contracting modes exist?

---

[25] See Meade (1971), Chapter 10. [26] See Alchian and Demsetz (1972), p. 777.
[27] See Simon (1957), pp. 183–95.

225

Our analysis here is restricted to the latter of these questions, which we answer in the affirmative. Although we do not contend that the internal labor market structures which we describe are optimally efficient with respect to idiosyncratic tasks, we think it significant that their efficiency properties have been little noted or understated by predominantly nonneoclassical interpretations of these markets in the past.

Our assessment of the efficiency implications of internal labor market structures is in three parts. The occasion for and purposes of collective organization are sketched first. The salient structural attributes of internal labor markets are then described and the efficiency implications of each, expressed in terms of the language of the organizational failures framework, are indicated. Several caveats follow.

Collective organization. To observe that the pursuit of perceived individual interests can sometimes lead to defective collective outcomes is scarcely novel. Schelling has treated the issue extensively in the context of the "ecology of micromotives."[28] The individual in each of his examples is both small in relation to the system – and thus his behavior, by itself, has no decisive influence on the system – and is unable to appropriate the collective gains that would obtain were he voluntarily to forego individual self-interest seeking. Schelling then observes that the remedy involves collective action. An enforceable social contract which imposes a cooperative solution on the system is needed.[29]

Although it is common to think of collective action as state action, this is plainly too narrow. As Arrow and Schelling[30] emphasize, both private collective action (of which the firm, with its hierarchical controls, is an example) and norms of socialization are also devices for realizing cooperative solutions. The internal labor market, we contend, is usefully interpreted in this same spirit.

Thus, although it is in the interest of each worker, bargaining individually or as a part of a small team, to acquire and exploit monopoly positions, it is plainly not in the interest of the *system* that employees should behave in this way. Opportunistic bargaining not only itself absorbs real resources, but efficient adaptations will be delayed and possibly foregone altogether. What this suggests, accordingly, is that the employment relation be transformed in such a way that systems concerns are made more fully to prevail and the following objectives are realized: (1) bargaining costs are made lower, (2) the internal wage structure is rationalized in terms of objective task characteristics, (3) consummate rather than perfunctory cooperation is encouraged, and (4) investments of idiosyncratic types, which constitute a potential source of monopoly, are undertaken without risk of exploitation. For the reasons and in

---

[28] Schelling (1971).   [29] See Schelling (1971), p. 69.
[30] See Arrow (1969), p. 62, and Schelling (1971), p. 69.

the ways developed below, internal labor markets can have, and some do have, the requisite properties to satisfy this prescription.[31]

Structural attributes and their efficiency consequences

Wage bargaining. A leading difficulty with individual contracting schemes where jobs are idiosyncratic is that workers are strategically situated to bargain opportunistically. The internal labor market achieves a fundamental transformation by shifting to a system where wage rates attach mainly to jobs rather than to workers. Not only is individual wage bargaining thereby discouraged, but it may even be legally foreclosed.[32] Once wages are expressly removed from individual bargaining, there is really no occasion for the worker to haggle over the incremental gains that are realized when adaptations of degree are proposed by the management. The incentives to behave opportunistically, which infect individual bargaining schemes, are correspondingly attenuated.

Moreover, not only are affirmative incentives lacking, but there are disincentives, of group disciplinary and promotion ladder types, which argue against resistance to authority on matters that come within the range customarily covered by the authority relation.[33] Promotion ladder issues are taken up in conjunction with the discussion of ports of entry below; consider, therefore, group disciplinary effects.

Barnard observes in this connection:[34]

Since the efficiency of organization is affected by the degree to which individuals assent to orders, denying the authority of an organization communication is a threat to the interests of all individuals who derive a net advantage from their connection with the organization, unless the orders are unacceptable to them also. Accordingly, at any given time there is among most of the contributors an active personal interest in the maintenance of the authority of all orders which to them are within the zone of indifference. The maintenance of this interest is largely a function of informal organization.

[31] Commons' discussion with Sidney Hillman concerning the transformation of membership attitudes among the Amalgamated Clothing Workers illustrates some of the systems attributes of collective agreements (1970, p. 130):

Ten years after World War I, I asked Sidney Hillman... why his members were less revolutionary than they had been when I knew them twenty-five years before in the sweatshop... Hillman replied, "They know now that they are citizens of the industry. They know that they must make the corporation a success on account of their own jobs." They were citizens because they had an arbitration system which gave them security against arbitrary foreman. They had an unemployment system by agreement with firm which gave them security of earnings. This is an illustration of the meaning of part-whole relations.

[32] See Summers (1969), pp. 538, 573.

[33] Authority relation is used here in the *qualified* short-run sense suggested in our discussion of Simon in Section 4 above.

[34] Barnard (1962), p. 169.

The application of group pressures thus combines with promotional incentives to facilitate adaptations in the small.[35] Even individuals who have exhausted their promotional prospects can thereby be induced to comply. System interests are made more fully to prevail. This concern with viability possibly explains the position taken in labor law that those orders which are ambiguous with respect to, and perhaps even exceed, the scope of authority, are to be fulfilled first and disputed later.[36]

Contractual incompleteness/arbitration. Internal labor market agreements are commonly reached through collective bargaining. Cox observes in this connection that the collective bargaining agreement should be understood as an instrument of government as well as an instrument of exchange: "the collective agreement governs complex, many-sided relations between large numbers of people in a going concern for very substantial periods of time."[37] Provision for unforeseeable contingencies is made by writing the contract in general and flexible terms and supplying the parties with a special arbitration machinery: "One simply cannot spell out every detail of life in an industrial establishment, or even of that portion which both management and labor agree is a matter of mutual concern."[38] Such contractual incompleteness is an implicit concession to bounded rationality. Rather than attempt to anticipate all bridges that might conceivably be faced, which is impossibly ambitious and excessively costly, bridges are crossed as they appear.

But however attractive adaptive, sequential decision making is in bounded rationality respects, admitting gaps into the contract also poses hazards: where parties are not indifferent with respect to the manner in which gaps are to be filled, fractious bargaining or litigation commonly results. It is for the purpose of forestalling worst outcomes of this kind that the special arbitration apparatus is devised.

Important differences between commercial and labor arbitration are to be noted in this connection. For one thing, "the commercial arbitrator finds facts – did the cloth meet the sample – while the labor arbitrator necessarily pours meaning into the general phrases and interstices of a document."[39] In addition, the idiosyncratic practices of the firm and its employees also constitute "shop

---

[35] Of course informal organization does not cooperate exclusively in the context of a collectivized wage bargain. Autonomous bargainers, however, are ordinarily expected to behave in autonomous ways. The extent to which group powers serve as a check on challenges to authority is accordingly much weaker where the individual mode prevails (see March and Simon, 1958, pp. 59, 66). By contrast, the individual in the collectivized system who refuses to accede to orders on matters that fall within the customarily defined zone of acceptance is apt to be regarded as cantankerous or malevolent, since there is no private pecuniary gain to be appropriated, and will be ostracized by his peers.

[36] See Summers (1969), pp. 538, 573.   [37] Cox (1958), p. 22.
[38] Cox (1958), p. 23.   [39] Cox (1958), p. 23.

law" and, to the labor arbitrator, are essential background for purposes of understanding a collective agreement and interpreting its intent.[40]

In the language of Section 3, the creation of such a special arbitration apparatus serves to overcome information impactedness, in that the arbitrator is able to explore the facts in greater depth and with greater sensitivity to idiosyncratic attributes of the enterprise than could judicial proceedings. Furthermore, once it becomes recognized that the arbitrator is able to apprise himself of the facts in a discerning and low-cost way, opportunistic misrepresentations of the data are discouraged as well.

Grievances. Also of interest in relation to the above is the matter of who is entitled to activate the arbitration machinery when an individual dispute arises. Cox takes the position that[41]

> ... giving the union control over all claims arising under the collective agreement comports so much better with the functional nature of a collective bargaining agreement. ... Allowing an individual to carry a claim to arbitration whenever he is dissatisfied with the adjustment worked out by the company and the union ... discourages the kind of day-to-day cooperation between company and union which is normally the mark of sound industrial relations – a relationship in which grievances are treated as problems to be solved and contracts are only guideposts in a dynamic human relationship. When ... the individual's claim endangers group interests, the union's function is to resolve the competition by reaching an accommodation or striking a balance.

The practice described by Cox of giving the union control over arbitration claims plainly permits group interests, whence concern for system viability, to supersede individual interests, thereby curbing small numbers opportunism.

Internal promotion/ports of entry. Acceding to authority on matters that fall within the zone of acceptance[42] merely requires that the employee respond in a minimally acceptable, even perfunctory way. This may be sufficient for tasks that are reasonably well structured. In such circumstances, the zeal with which an instruction to "do this" or "do that" is discharged may have little effect on

---

[40] Cox (1958), p. 24.

[41] Cox (1958), p. 24. We are informed that this practice is changing and offer three comments in this regard. First, institutional change does not always promote efficiency outcomes; backward steps will sometimes occur – possibly because the efficiency implications are not understood. Second, relegating control to the union as to whether a grievance is to be submitted to arbitration can sometimes lead to capricious results. Disfavored workers can be unfairly disadvantaged by those who control the union decision-making machinery. Some form of appeal may therefore be a necessary corrective. Third, that workers are given rights to bring grievances on their own motion does not imply that this will happen frequently. Grievances that fail to secure the support of peers are unlikely to be brought unless they represent egregious conditions on which the grievant feels confidently he will prevail. The bringing of trivial grievances not only elicits the resentment of peers but impairs the grievant's standing when more serious matters are posed.

[42] The zone of acceptance is discussed in the quotation from Barnard in Section 5 above.

the outcome. As indicated, however, consummate cooperation is valued for the tasks of interest here. But how is cooperation of this more extensive sort to be realized?

A simple answer is to reward cooperative behavior by awarding incentive payments on a transaction-specific basis. The employment relation would then revert to a series of haggling encounters over the nature of the quid pro quo, however, and would hardly be distinguishable from a sequential spot contract. Moreover, such payments would plainly violate the nonindividualistic wage bargaining attributes of internal labor markets described above.

The internal promotion practices in internal labor markets are of special interest in this connection. Access to higher level positions on internal promotion ladders is not open to all comers on an unrestricted basis. Rather, as part of the internal incentive system, higher level positions (of the prescribed kinds)[43] are filled by promotion from within whenever this is feasible. This practice, particularly if it is followed by other enterprises to which the worker might otherwise turn for upgrading opportunities, ties the interests of the worker to the firm in a continuing way.[44] Given these ties, the worker looks to internal promotion as the principal means of improving his position.[45]

The practice of restricting entry to lower level jobs and promoting from within has interesting experience-rating implications. It permits firms to protect themselves against low productivity types, who might otherwise successfully represent themselves to be high productivity applicants, by bringing employees in at low level positions and then upgrading them as experience warrants.[46] Furthermore, employees who may have been incorrectly upgraded but later have been "found out," and hence barred from additional internal promotions, are unable to move to a new organization without penalty.[47] Were unpenalized lateral moves possible, workers might, considering the problems of accurately

---

[43] For a discussion, see Doeringer and Piore (1971), pp. 42–47.

[44] Since access to idiosyncratic types of jobs is limited by requiring new employees to accept a lower job at the bottom of promotion ladders, individuals can usually not shift laterally between firms without cost: "employees in nonentry jobs in one enterprise often have access only to entry-level jobs in other enterprises. The latter will often pay less than those which the employees currently hold" (Doeringer and Piore, 1971, p. 78).

[45] Assuming that unit costs are equalized across rival enterprises (as a condition of competitive viability), the internal wage structure will be everywhere lower, including port of entry wages, if straight seniority is adopted.

[46] For a more general discussion of the special powers of internal organization in auditing and experience rating respects, see Williamson (1975). The treatment in the text is keyed to an efficiency interpretation of the Doeringer and Piore (1971) discussion of ports of entry limitation.

[47] Agents seeking transfer may have gotten ahead in an organization by error. Experiencing rating, after all, is a statistical inference process and is vulnerable to "Type II" error. When a mistake has been discovered and additional promotions are not forthcoming, the agent might seek transfer in the hope that he can successfully disguise his true characteristics in the new organization and thereby secure further promotions. Alternatively, the agent may have been promoted correctly, but changed his work attitudes subsequently – in which case further promotion is denied. Again, he might seek transfer in the hope of securing additional promotion in an organization that, because

transmitting productivity valuations between firms, be able to disguise their true productivity attributes from new employers sufficiently long to achieve additional promotions. Restricting access to low level positions serves to protect the firm against exploitation by opportunistic types who would, if they could, change jobs strategically for the purpose of compounding errors between successive independent organizations.

Were it, however, that markets could equally well perform these experience-rating functions, the port of entry restrictions described would be unnecessary. The (comparative) limitations of markets in experience-rating respects accordingly warrant attention. The principal impediment to effective interfirm experience-rating is one of communication.[48] By comparison with the firm, markets lack a rich and common rating language. The language problem is particularly severe where the judgments to be made are highly subjective. The advantages of hierarchy in these circumstances are especially great if those who are the most familiar with an agent's characteristics, usually his immediate supervisor, also do the experience-rating. The need to rationalize subjective assessments that are confidently held but, by reason of bounded rationality, difficult to articulate is reduced. Put differently, interfirm experience-rating is impeded in information impactedness respects.

Reliance on internal promotion has affirmative incentive properties in that workers can anticipate that differential talent and degrees of cooperativeness will be rewarded. Consequently, although the attachment of wages to jobs rather than to individuals may result in an imperfect correspondence between wages and marginal productivity at ports of entry, productivity differentials will be recognized over time and a more perfect correspondence can be expected for higher level assignments in the internal labor market job hierarchy.

. . .

of the difficulty of interfirm communication about agent characteristics, is less able to ascertain his true characteristics initially.

[48] Interfirm experience-rating may also suffer in veracity respects, since firms may choose deliberately to mislead rivals. The major impediment, however, is one of communication.

CHAPTER 16

Multitask principal–agent analyses: incentive contracts, asset ownership, and job design

BENGT HOLMSTROM AND PAUL MILGROM

Bengt Holmstrom is the Paul A. Samuelson Professor of Economics at the Massachusetts Institute of Technology. See also the chapter by Holmstrom and Roberts.

Paul Milgrom is the Shirley R. and Leonard W. Ely, Jr., Professor of Humanities and Science and Professor of Economics at Stanford University. See also the chapter by Milgrom and Roberts.

1. Introduction

In the standard economic treatment of the principal–agent problem, compensation systems serve the dual function of allocating risks and rewarding productive work. A tension between these two functions arises when the agent is risk averse, for providing the agent with effective work incentives often forces him to bear unwanted risk. Existing formal models that have analyzed this tension, however, have produced only limited results.[1] It remains a puzzle for this theory that employment contracts so often specify fixed wages and more generally that incentives within firms appear to be so muted, especially compared to those of the market. Also, the models have remained too intractable to effectively address broader organizational issues such as asset ownership, job design, and allocation of authority.

In this article, we will analyze a principal–agent model that (i) can account for paying fixed wages even when good, objective output measures are available and agents are highly responsive to incentive pay; (ii) can make recommendations and predictions about ownership patterns even when contracts can take full account of all observable variables and court enforcement is perfect;

Excerpted from Bengt Holmstrom and Paul Milgrom, "Multitask Principal–Agent Analyses: Incentive Contracts, Asset Ownership, and Job Design," *Journal of Law, Economics, and Organization* 7 (1991): 24–52, with permission of Oxford University Press.
[1] Some of the predictive weaknesses of standard agency models are discussed in the surveys by MacDonald, Hart and Holmstrom, and Baker, Jensen, and Murphy.

(iii) can explain why employment is sometimes superior to independent contracting even when there are no productive advantages to specific physical or human capital and no financial market imperfections to limit the agent's borrowings; (iv) can explain bureaucratic constraints; and (v) can shed light on how tasks get allocated to different jobs.

The distinguishing mark of our model is that the principal either has several different tasks for the agent or agents to perform, or the agent's single task has several dimensions to it. Some of the issues raised by this modeling are well illustrated by the current controversy over the use of incentive pay for teachers based on their students' test scores. Proponents of the system, guided by a conception very like the standard one-dimensional incentive model, argue that these incentives will lead teachers to work harder at teaching and to take greater interest in their students' success. Opponents counter that the principal effect of the proposed reform would be that teachers would sacrifice such activities as promoting curiosity and creative thinking and refining students' oral and written communication skills in order to teach the narrowly defined basic skills that are tested on standardized exams. *It would be better, these critics argue, to pay a fixed wage without any incentive scheme than to base teachers' compensation only on the limited dimensions of student achievement that can be effectively measured.*[2]

Multidimensional tasks are ubiquitous in the world of business. As simple examples, production workers may be responsible for producing a *high volume* of *good quality* output, or they may be required both to produce output and to care for the machines they use. In the first case, if volume of output is easy to measure but the quality is not, then a system of piece rates for output may lead agents to increase the volume of output at the expense of quality. Or, if quality can be assured by a system of monitoring or by a robust product design, then piece rates may lead agents to abuse shared equipment or to take inadequate care of it. In general, when there are multiple tasks, incentive pay serves not only to allocate risks and to motivate hard work, it also serves to direct the allocation of the agents' attention *among* their various duties. This represents the first fundamental difference between the multidimensional theory and the more common one-dimensional principal–agent models.

There is a second fundamental difference as well, and it, too, can be illustrated by reference to the problem of teaching basic skills: If the task of teaching basic skills could be separated from that of teaching higher-level thinking, then

---

[2] As a concrete illustration of the distortions that testing can cause, in 1989 a ninth-grade teacher in Greenville, South Carolina, was caught having passed answers to questions on the statewide tests of basic skills to students in her geography classes in order to improve her performance rating (*Wall Street Journal*, November 2, 1989).

these tasks could be carried out by different teachers at different times during the day. Similarly, in the example of the production worker, when the care and maintenance of a productive asset can be separated from the use of that asset in producing output, the problem that a piece-rate system would lead to inadequate care can be mitigated or even eliminated. In general, in multitask principal–agent problems, *job design is an important instrument for the control of incentives*. In the standard model, when each agent can engage in only one task, the grouping of tasks into jobs is not a relevant issue.

Our formal modeling of these issues utilizes our linear principal–agent model (Holmstrom and Milgrom, 1987), mainly specialized to the case where the agent's costs depend only on the *total* effort or attention the agent devotes to all of his tasks. This modeling assures that an increase in an agent's compensation in any one task will cause some reallocation of attention away from other tasks. First, we show that an optimal incentive contract can be to pay a fixed wage independent of measured performance, just as the opponents of incentives based on educational testing have argued. More generally, the desirability of providing incentives for any one activity decreases with the difficulty of measuring performance in any other activities that make competing demands on the agent's time and attention. This result may explain a substantial part of the puzzle of why incentive clauses are so much less common than one-dimensional theories would predict.

Second, we specialize our model to the case where the unmeasurable aspect of performance is how the value of a productive asset changes over time. The difficulties of valuing assets are well recognized, and the vast majority of accounting systems value assets using fixed depreciation schedules based on historical costs, deviating from this procedure only in exceptional circumstances. Under these conditions, when the principal owns the returns from the asset, the optimal incentive contract will provide only muted incentives for the agent to produce output, in order to mitigate any abuse of the asset or any substitution of effort away from asset maintenance. However, when the agent owns the asset returns, the optimal incentive contract will provide more intensive incentives to engage in production, in order to alleviate the reverse problem that the agent may use the asset too cautiously or devote too much attention to its care and improvement. This analysis supports Williamson's observation that "high-powered" incentives are more common in market arrangements than within firms, without relying on any assumptions about specific investments. Moreover, it provides a rudimentary theory of ownership, according to which the conditions that favor the agent owning the assets are (i) that the agent is not too risk averse, (ii) that the variance of asset returns is low, and (iii) that the variance of measurement error in other aspects of the agent's performance is low. Thus, it emphasizes measurement cost as an important determinant of integration in contrast to the leading approaches, which stress asset specificity.[3]

. . .

Third, we explore how a firm might optimally set policies limiting personal business activities on company time. Again, it is not just the characteristics of the "outside activities" themselves that determine whether these activities should be permitted. We find that outside activities should be most severely restricted when performance in the tasks that benefit the firm – the "inside activities" – are hard to measure and reward. Thus, a salesperson whose pay is mostly in the form of commissions will optimally be permitted to engage in more personal activities during business hours than a bureaucrat who is paid a fixed wage, because the commissions direct the salesperson toward inside activities in a way that cannot be duplicated for the bureaucrat. Our theory also predicts that home office work should be accompanied by a stronger reliance on performance-based pay incentives, a prediction that seems to fit casual observation.

Our analysis of restrictions on outside activities underscores the fact that incentives for a task can be provided in two ways: either the task itself can be rewarded or the marginal opportunity cost for the task can be lowered by removing or reducing the incentives on competing tasks. Constraints are substitutes for performance incentives and are extensively used when it is hard to assess the performance of the agent. We believe this opens a new avenue for understanding large-scale organization. It also offers an alternative interpretation of the Anderson–Schmittlein evidence. It is inefficient to let a salesperson, whose performance is poorly measured, divert his time into commission selling of competing products. If the employer has an advantage in restricting the employees' other activities, as both Simon and Coase have argued, then problems with measuring sales performance will lead to employing an in-house sales force.

Finally, we obtain a series of results in the theory of job design, using a model in which the employer can divide responsibility for many small tasks between two agents and can determine how performance in each task will be compensated. The resulting optimization problem is a fundamentally nonconvex one, and we have had to make some extra assumptions to keep the analysis

---

[3] Alchian and Demsetz argued that monitoring difficulties account for the formation of firms, but their theory was subsequently rejected in favor of the view that asset specificity and *ex post* bargaining problems drive integration (Grossman and Hart; Williamson). We are reintroducing measurement cost as a key factor but in a way that differs from the original Alchian–Demsetz theory. In particular, we do not argue that owners can better monitor the workforce. Our approach is more closely related to Barzel's work.

tractable. Nevertheless, the results we obtain seem intriguing and suggestive. First, we find that each task should be made the responsibility of just one agent. To our knowledge, this the first formal derivation in the incentive literature of the principle of unity of responsibility, which underlies the theory of hierarchy. Second, we find that tasks should be grouped into jobs in such a way that the tasks in which performance is most easily measured are assigned to one worker and the remaining tasks are assigned to the other worker. This conclusion squares nicely with the intuition that it is the *differences* between the measurability of quantity and quality in production, or of the so-called basic skills and higher-order thinking skills in education, that make those incentive problems difficult. The theory indicates that even when the agents have identical *ex ante* characteristics, the principal should still design their jobs to have measurement characteristics that differ as widely as possible. The principal should then provide more intensive incentives and require more work effort from the jobholder whose performance is more easily measured.

Our results are variations on the general theme of second best, which stresses that when prices cannot allocate inputs efficiently, then optimal incentives will typically be provided by subsidizing or taxing all inputs. For instance, Greenwald and Stiglitz, in a vivid metaphor, point out the value of a government subsidy for home fire extinguishers, since homeowners with fire insurance have too little incentive to invest in all forms of fire prevention and to fight fires once they have started. This mechanism has been most extensively analyzed in the theory of optimal taxation and in welfare theory.

However, the study of interdependencies among incentives and the use of instruments other than compensation to alleviate incentive problems have entered agency analyses more recently. Lazear argues that where cooperation among workers is important, we should expect to see less wage differentiation, that is, "lower-powered" incentives. Holmstrom and Ricart i Costa have observed how a firm's capital budgeting policy, including the hurdle rate and the way the firm assesses idiosyncratic risks, can affect the willingness of risk-averse managers to propose risky investment projects. Milgrom and Milgrom and Roberts have studied how organizational decision processes affect the allocation of effort between politicking and directly productive work. Farrell and Shapiro show that a price clause may be worse than no contract at all, because it reduces incentives to supply quality; this is similar to our result that it may be optimal to provide no quantity incentives when quality is poorly measured.

Some articles containing related ideas have been developed contemporaneously. Itoh (1991), in an analysis complementary to ours, studies conditions under which an employer might induce workers to work separately on their tasks, and those in which it is best for them to spend some effort helping one another. Laffont and Tirole show that concerns for quality help explain the use of cost plus contracting in procurement. Baker investigates a model in which observable proxies of marginal product are imperfect in a way that causes the agent to misallocate effort across contingencies and therefore leads to incentives that are not as powerful as standard theory would suggest. Minahan reports a result on task separation that suggests a job design similar to ours but based on a different argument, as we will later explain.

The remainder of this article is organized as follows. In Section 2, we recapitulate our basic principal–agent theory, upon which the entire analysis is based. In Section 3, we specialize the analysis to the case where the agent's costs depend only on the total attention supplied and prove the various propositions about the optimality of fixed wages, the factors determining the assignment of ownership, and the optimal limits on outside business activities. In Section 4, we consider restrictions on private tasks. In Section 5, we offer a summary and suggest directions in which this line of research can be taken.

. . .

3. Allocation incentives for effort and attention

3.1 The effort and attention allocation model

We now move to a group of models in which the agent's effort or attention is a homogeneous input that can be allocated among tasks however the agent likes. We shall suppose that effort in the various tasks is perfectly substitutable in the agent's cost function. More formally, we suppose that the agent chooses a vector $t = (t_1, \ldots, t_m)$ at a personal (strictly convex) cost $C(t_1 + \cdots + t_m)$, leading to expected profits $B(t)$ and generating signals $x(t) = \mu(t) + \epsilon$. Then, if the agent increases the amount of time or attention devoted to one activity, the marginal cost of attention to the other activities will grow larger.

Contrary to most earlier principal–agent models, we shall not suppose that all work is unpleasant. . . . A worker on the job may take pleasure in working up to some limit; incentives are only required to encourage work beyond that limit. Formally, we assume that there is some number $\bar{t} > 0$ such that $C(t) \leq 0$ for $t \leq \bar{t}$ and $C(\bar{t}) = 0$. This is important, because it means that contracts that provide for fixed wages may still elicit some effort, though more may be elicited by providing positive incentives. It also means that there is a range of effort allocations among which the agent is indifferent and willing to follow the principal's preference.

3.2 Missing incentive clauses in contracts

One of the most puzzling and troubling failures of incentive models has been their inability to account for the paucity of explicit incentive provisions in actual contracts. For example, it is surprisingly uncommon in contracts for home remodeling to incorporate explicit incentives for timely completion of construction, even though construction delays arise frequently and can be profoundly disruptive to the homeowner. There can be little doubt that such clauses could be written into the contracts; similar clauses are common in commercial construction contracts. We shall argue that these facts can best be understood as a result of the greater standardization of commercial construction and the consequent ability of commercial buyers to specify and monitor quality standards. The innovation in our analysis is that our explanation of the presence or absence of the timely completion clause lies in an examination of the principal's ability to monitor *other aspects* of the agent's performance.[4]

Thus, suppose that some desirable attributes of the contractor's performance (such as courtesy, attention to detail, or helpful advice) are unmeasurable but are enhanced by attention t_1 spent on that activity, while other aspects of quality (such as timely completion) are measurable (perhaps imperfectly) and enhanced by attention t_2 devoted to this second activity. Supposing that the measured quality is one dimensional, we may write $\mu(t_1,t_2) = \mu(t_2), x = \mu + \epsilon$. As we have seen, the agent's efficient compensation contract pays an amount $S = \alpha x + \beta$.

Suppose that the overall value of the job to the homeowner is determined by the function $B(t_1,t_2)$. To model the idea that the first activity is "very important" and that both activities are valuable, we assume that B is increasing and that $B(0,t_2) = 0$, for all $t_2 \geq 0$.

Proposition 1. For the home contractor model specified in the last paragraph, the efficient linear compensation rule pays a fixed wage and contains no incentive component ($\alpha = 0$), even if the contractor is risk neutral.

. . .

The ideas that underlie this analysis have many applications. For example, piece rates are relatively rare in manufacturing and, where they are used, they are frequently accompanied by careful attention to monitoring the quality of the work. Our analysis indicates that if quality were poorly measured, it would be expensive or impossible to maintain good quality while using a piece-rate scheme. Similarly, where individuals spend part of their efforts on individual projects and part on team production, and assuming that individual contributions to the team effort are difficult to assess, it would be dangerous to provide incentives for good performance on the individual projects. The

---

[4] Another plausible explanation is that home construction contracts are frequently changed to reflect design modifications, and timely completion clauses would be nullified by these changes.

problem, of course, is that individuals may shift their attention from the team activity where their individual contributions are poorly measured to the better measured and well-compensated individual activity. For this reason, piece-rate schemes may be especially dysfunctional in large hierarchies.

3.3 "Low-powered incentives" in firms

A similar model can be used to explain Williamson's observation that the incentives offered to employees in firms are generally "low-powered" compared to the "high-powered" incentives offered to independent contractors. Like Williamson, we distinguish employees from independent contractors by the condition of asset ownership: Employees use and develop assets that are owned by others while contractors use and develop their own assets.

Once again, the heart of our modeling is our assumption that there are multiple activities to be undertaken and that the allocation of time and attention between them is crucial. Thus, let the expected gross profit from the enterprise be the sum of two parts, $B(t_1) + V(t_2)$, where B represents the expected net receipts and V the expected change in the net asset value. We assume that B and V are increasing, concave, and twice continuously differentiable and that $B(0) = V(0) = 0$. The actual change in asset value, $V + \epsilon_v$, accrues to whomever owns the asset. Assets are notoriously hard to value (that is why accountants generally use historical cost as a valuation basis), so we assume that there is no performance indicator for the asset enhancement activity t_2. The primary activity t_1 is to produce output for sale in the current period: its indicator is $x = \mu(t_1) + \epsilon_x$, where μ is increasing and concave. We assume that ϵ_x and ϵ_v are independent.

We consider two alternative organizational modes – *contracting*, in which the change in asset value accrues to the agent, and *employment*, in which the change in asset value accrues to the firm or principal. The crucial difference between these lies in the incentives for the agent to engage in the two kinds of activities. To focus on the most interesting case, we will assume that it is highly desirable to induce the agent to devote a positive amount of effort to both activities. Let

$$\pi^1 = \underset{t_1}{\text{Max}}\ B(t_1) - C(t_1),$$

$$\pi^2 = \underset{t_2}{\text{Max}}\ V(t_2) - C(t_2),$$

$$\pi^{12} = \underset{t_1}{\text{Max}}\ B(t_1) + V(\bar{t} - t_1) - C(\bar{t}).$$

Proposition 2. Assume that $\pi^{12} \geq \text{Max}(\pi^1, \pi^2)$. Then, the optimal employment contract always entails paying a fixed wage ($\alpha = 0$). Whenever the independent contracting relation is optimal, it involves "high-powered incentives" ($\alpha > 0$). Furthermore, there exist values of the parameters r, σ_v^2, σ_x^2 [ed.: risk aversion and the variances associated with V and x, respectively] for which employment contracts are optimal and others for which independent contracting is optimal. If employment contracting is optimal for some fixed parameters $(r, \sigma_v^2, \sigma_x^2)$, then it is also optimal for higher values of these parameters. Similarly, if independent contracting is optimal, then it is also optimal for lower values of these parameters.

. . .

[A] piece of evidence consistent with our model comes from the fast-food industry. Firms such as McDonald's and Burger King own about 30% of their stores and franchise the rest. The difference in incentives between franchisees and owner-managed firms is striking. Franchisees pay royalties that are at most 10% of sales, corresponding to at least a 90% commission, whereas managers of company-owned stores typically receive no explicit incentives either on profit or sales (Krueger, 1991; Brickley and Dark, 1987). The difference in incentives is all the more remarkable, considering how similar the two types of stores are in all other aspects. According to our theory, the discontinuous shift in residual returns $[V(t_2)]$ associated with franchising and the attendant shift in attention toward long-term asset values and cost containment, forces the franchise contract to increase short-term incentives sharply. Or, looked upon the other way, short-term incentives for employed managers must be muted to prevent them from allocating their attention away from important, but hard to measure, asset values.

4. Limits on outside activities

Our previous analysis emphasizes the importance of studying the full range of the agent's activities for analyzing incentives. If activities interact in the agent's cost function, incentive strength can be predicted only once the agent's whole portfolio of tasks is known. An equally important implication is that the principal can influence the agent's incentives by choosing the agent's portfolio of tasks. In the next section, we will study the optimal allocation of tasks between two agents. In this section, we consider how the principal might try to manage the agent's access to outside (private) activities.

Even casual observation makes it clear that the rules governing outside activities depend on the job. It is a commonplace observation that employees in "responsible positions" are allowed more freedom of action than other employees and that they use that freedom in part to pursue personally beneficial activities. To analyze the issues that this observation raises, we begin with the assumption that it is easier for an employer to exclude an activity entirely than to monitor it and limit its extent. For example, a rule against personal telephone calls during business hours is found in many offices and seems to be motivated in part by its ease of enforcement compared, say, to a rule that limits the percentage of business hours devoted to personal calls to 2%. Although generalizations about employment all seem to have exceptions, a common feature of employment contracts is that the employer has authority to restrict the employee's outside activities during business hours, and sometimes after hours as well.

Assume then that the agent has a finite pool $K = \{1, \ldots, N\}$ of potential activities, which the principal can control only by exclusion. The returns to these tasks, which we will refer to as the agent's *personal business* for short, are assumed nonstochastic and to benefit the agent alone (in principle, these tasks could benefit the principal, too, but the analytics would be more complicated). The principal controls the agent's personal business by allowing the agent to engage only in a subset of tasks $A \subset K$. Within the *set of allowable tasks, A*, the agent can engage in as much or as little personal business as he pleases, but none outside A. To focus on the interactions between the agent's workplace activities and personal business, we represent workplace activities simply as a single task in which performance is imperfectly measured.

. . .

[Proposition 4.] (ii) If it becomes easier to measure the agent's performance (σ^2 decreases), or the agent becomes less risk averse (r decreases), then the agent's marginal reward will be raised and his personal business activities will be less curtailed.

. . .

[Thus], there will be more constraints on an agent's activities in situations where performance rewards are weak because of measurement problems. The rigid rules and limits that characterize bureaucracy, in this view, constitute an optimal response to difficulties in measuring and rewarding performance. Among the "personal business" activities that bureaucracies try to limit are collusion (Tirole; Holmstrom and Milgrom, 1990; Itoh, 1989) and influence activities (Milgrom; Milgrom and Roberts). The restrictions on trade between employees that Holmstrom and Milgrom (1990) recommend and the restrictions on communications that Milgrom and Roberts propose are examples of optimal exclusion of activities that would be permitted or perhaps even encouraged in a first-best world.

. . .

5. Allocating tasks between two agents

In the single-agent model, the commission rates α_i serve three purposes: they allocate risk, motivate work, and direct the agent's efforts among his various activities. A trade-off arises when these objectives are in conflict with each other: Optimal risk sharing may be inconsistent with motivating work, and motivating hard work may distort the agent's allocation of efforts across tasks. Among the instruments available to the principal to alleviate these problems are job restructuring and relative performance evaluation: The former allows the principal to reduce the distortions in how attention is allocated among activities, while the latter enables the principal to lower the cost of incentives by using a more sensitive measure of actual performance.

5.1 Optimal groupings of tasks into jobs

Here we initiate the study of how incentive considerations might affect the grouping of tasks into jobs. We use a model that eliminates other important effects, such as differences among the agents and complementarities among task assignments. There are two identical agents, indexed $i = 1,2$, who allocate their attention across a continuum of tasks indexed by $k \in [0,1]$. Let $t_i(k)$ denote the attention agent i devotes to task k. We assume that the two agents can share a task and that their labor inputs are perfect substitutes. Thus, profit $B(t)$ is a function of the total time vector $t \equiv \{t(k): k \in [0,1]\}$, where $t(k) = t_1(k) + t_2(k)$. Likewise, the performance signal from task k, $\mu(t(k),k)$, only depends on the total attention $t(k)$ devoted to it. The error variance of task k is $\sigma^2(k) > 0$ and the errors are assumed independent.

. . .

Proposition 5. In the model described above, it is never optimal for the two agents to be jointly responsible for any task k.

. . .

This proposition reflects our earlier observation that providing incentives for an agent in any task incurs a fixed cost as the agent assumes some nontrivial fraction of the risk associated with that task (or its measurement). Since we have assumed that the tasks are small relative to the agent's capabilities, assigning joint responsibility for any task would incur two fixed costs unnecessarily. As the proof demonstrates, if one begins with an arrangement in which some tasks are shared, it is possible to split the same tasks among the agents without affecting either the total effort required of either agent or the total effort allocated to any task. This rearrangement makes it possible to eliminate some of each agent's responsibilities [setting $\alpha_i(k) = 0$], thereby reducing the risk that the agent must bear and so increasing the total surplus of the three parties.

Having established that each task will be assigned to just one employee, we next turn to the issue of how the tasks will be grouped. With this in mind, it is convenient to redefine our variables. We reinterpret $\alpha_i(k)$ to be the *hypothetical* commission rate that the principal would need to pay in order to elicit the desired level of effort $t(k)$ from agent i if he were assigned task k.

. . .

Proposition 6. Suppose that the two agents devote different amounts of total attention to their tasks (i.e., $\bar{t}_1 \leq \bar{t}_2$). Then, tasks are optimally assigned in this model so that all the hardest-to-monitor tasks are undertaken by agent 1 and all the easiest-to-monitor tasks are undertaken by agent 2. That is, agent 1 is assigned all the tasks k for which $\rho(k) \geq \rho$, and agent 2 is assigned all those with $\rho(k) < \rho$, where ρ is defined in (23) [ed.: as an indicator of task measurability].

. . .

These results provide, in purely incentive-theoretic terms, an account of how activities might be grouped, with some employees specializing in activities that are hard to monitor and others in activities that are easily monitored. Separating tasks according to their measurability characteristics [$\rho(k)$] allows the principal to give strong incentives for tasks that are easy to measure without fearing that the agent will substitute efforts away from other, harder-to-measure tasks. The present model oversimplifies these issues by assuming that there are no restrictions on how the principal may group tasks. In the case of piece rates discussed in Section 3, it might not be possible to separate the tasks of providing high output from those of providing high quality: The worker might always be able to substitute speed for attention to details. Nevertheless, the results of Proposition 6 are suggestive.

. . .

243

6. Conclusion

The problem of providing incentives to agents and employees is far more intricate than is represented in standard principal–agent models. The performance measures upon which rewards are based may aggregate highly disparate aspects of performance into a single number and omit other aspects of performance that are essential if the firm is to achieve its goals. Commonly, the principal–agent problem boils down to this: Given a highly incomplete set of performance measures and a highly complex set of potential responses from the agent, how can the agent be motivated to act in the social interest?

Our approach emphasizes that incentive problems must be analyzed in totality; one cannot make correct inferences about the proper incentives for an activity by studying the attributes of that activity alone. Moreover, the range of instruments that can be used to control an agent's performance in one activity is much wider than just deciding how to pay for performance. One can also shift ownership of related assets, vary restrictions on the ways a job can be done, vary limits and incentives for competing activities, group related tasks into a single job, and so on.

In a related article (Holmstrom and Milgrom, 1991b), we study the simultaneous use of various instruments for controlling agents to derive new, testable results from the theory of organization. Our emphasis there is on how cross-sectional variations in the parameters that determine the optimal design of jobs, the optimal intensity of incentives, and the optimal allocation of ownership lead to covariations among endogenous variables that are similar to the patterns we find in actual firms.

Most past models of organization focus only on one instrument at a time for determining incentives and a single activity to be motivated. Newer theories, such as ours, that explicitly recognize connections between instruments and activities, offer new promise to explain the richer patterns of actual practice.

CHAPTER 17

Work motivation

TRUMAN BEWLEY

Truman Bewley was born in 1941 in Bridgeport, Connecticut. In 1970 and 1971, he received a Ph.D. in economics and a Ph.D. in mathematics, respectively, both from the University of California at Berkeley. Since 1983, he has served as the Alfred Cowles Professor of Economics in Yale University's Department of Economics.

During 1992 and 1993, I undertook a field study in the Northeast of the United States to learn why wages and salaries seldom fall during recessions.[1] I interviewed more than 330 business people, labor leaders, counselors of unemployed workers, labor market intermediaries (headhunters), labor lawyers, and management consultants. The purpose of the study was exploratory; much of my effort went into the search for hypotheses rather than tests of specific ones. For this reason, I did not require informants to answer a fixed list of questions, but informed them of the purpose of the study and invited them to tell me what they thought was relevant. I intervened only occasionally to seek clarification, show interest, or nudge the discussion in new directions.

Only after informants had spoken at length did I ask specific questions to cover points that interested me. I usually avoided asking about economic theories until the end of interviews. Such questions sometimes stopped conversation, because the theories seemed naive and the questions led respondents to try to think like an economist, rather than to explain their world concretely in their own terms. Some business people refused such open-ended interviews, probably because they feared that while talking loosely they might say something that would embarrass them or hurt their company. I concluded that low response rates might make a random sample unrepresentative. (I had much less difficulty gaining the cooperation of the other types of respondents.) Most interviews with business people were obtained through personal contacts or by telephoning people and persuading them to cooperate. Often, people I interviewed arranged further interviews.

Excerpted from Truman Bewley, "Work Motivation," *The Federal Reserve Bank of St. Louis Review*, 81, 3 (May/June 1999): 35–50. Reprinted with the permission of the Federal Reserve Bank of St. Louis.

[1] The results of the study are reported in a book, entitled *Why Wages Don't Fall During a Recession*, to be published by Harvard University Press in 1999.

I strove to avoid sample bias by holding interviews in a large and diverse set of companies as well as by using many distinct avenues of approach to gain access to them. Using these methods, I avoided talking to people from only a few circles of friends. The companies represented a broad spectrum of industries and a full range of sizes and financial conditions. Some were bankrupt, many were shrinking and experiencing heavy layoffs, and some were growing rapidly. Some had been founded only recently, while most were well-established. Some were unionized, whereas many had no union presence. Some were public corporations and others were closely held or family-owned. I made a point of finding businesses that had cut or frozen pay during the recession. There were few such; most firms continued to grant regular raises. My method did not yield a valid opinion survey nor reliable statistics on the incidence of various business practices. I believe, however, that I gathered valuable information about what happens in the labor market during a recession and what business people and labor leaders think about layoffs and pay cuts.

The explanation of wage rigidity given by more than 275 business people and labor leaders I interviewed was based on views of worker motivation that deviate from the standard model. In this paper, I formulate a somewhat speculative model of work motivation stimulated by what I heard. The model incorporates ideas from psychology into the utility-maximizing framework of economics.

Wage rigidity and morale

In this section, I will summarize what I heard in interviews, giving the reasons for wage rigidity explained to me by business people and labor leaders. In the first instance, the resistance to pay reduction came from managers, not from workers, though it was anticipated employee discontent that motivated management to oppose pay cuts. The discontent, usually described as poor morale, would not necessarily be expressed openly. Nonetheless, business people believed it could be harmful enough to cause monetary losses that would exceed the savings from a pay cut.

The downward rigidity of the pay of existing and of newly hired employees have separate explanations. The reason almost all managers gave for not cutting the pay of existing employees was concern about morale. New employees would probably object little if, before they applied for their jobs, pay rates for new hires had fallen by no more than the pay of existing employees in the same jobs. New employees, in contrast, feel it is inequitable to be paid according to a scale lower than the one that applied to colleagues that were hired earlier. For this reason, downward pay rigidity for new hires exists only because the pay of existing employees is rigid. The pay of new hires is usually downwardly flexible when co-workers do not have enough contact with each other to know each other's pay. This circumstance arises typically when labor turnover is high and when a large fraction of the employees work part-time on schedules that seldom overlap. Typical examples are floor crews in fast-food restaurants and in supermarkets.

Good morale means many things in industry: a willingness to cooperate with company objectives, a sense of common purpose consistent with the firm's goals, enthusiasm for the job, happiness, toleration of unpleasantness, moral behavior, and mutual trust. Business people value good morale because it reduces labor turnover, makes it easier to recruit good workers, and increases the productivity of the existing work force. The increase in productivity arises not so much because employees work harder at assigned tasks that are monitored, but because workers do the right thing even when no one is watching. They do extra things without instruction, make suggestions for improvements, help each other, and share information with each other and with superiors. Good morale is thought to be especially important for productivity in jobs where it is difficult to monitor performance, where good performance requires imagination and creativity, and where workers must deal with customers. Morale is important in the latter case, because employees handle customers better when cheerful.

The morale of existing employees is hurt by pay cuts because of what may be called the insult effect and the standard of living effect. The latter occurs because lower living standards distract and aggravate workers and cause them to blame the company for the difficult adaptation to lower incomes. The insult effect occurs because workers associate pay with self-worth and recognition of their value to the company. Many workers receive regular increases, grow used to them, and interpret them as recognition of loyalty and good performance. Hence, a pay cut is interpreted as a signal of dissatisfaction with employees, even if everyone's pay is reduced. These effects apply to both real and nominal pay reduction, though the effects of an abrupt nominal cut are stronger than those of a slow decline in the purchasing power of pay.

Another reason a pay cut is interpreted as an affront is that it is viewed as unfair, because the company takes something away while giving nothing in return. A pay cut is not felt to be insulting if management can convince workers that the reduction is justified; that is, if it prevents a large number of layoffs. Pay cuts typically occur when a business is in danger of closing or has trouble competing in product markets. In these circumstances, workers usually accept cuts. Such circumstances are rare, however. A central fact of life for most businesses is that pay rates have little impact on total employment. That is, in most firms the elasticity of demand for labor is small. Pay cuts are more common among firms where this elasticity is high.

Business people and labor leaders were confident they usually could convince employees, with some effort, that pay cuts were justified, if indeed they were. I was told that workers refuse to believe what they are told about company difficulties only when management has a reputation for duplicity, when relations between management and union representatives are bad, or when workers recoil from facing reality. I found little support for the many theories of wage rigidity based on information asymmetries, and, in particular, theories based on the assumption that management cannot persuade workers that low profits or competitive conditions require pay reduction. The general thrust of what was said was that normally information flows freely enough within businesses so that most employees know when their company is in trouble. In some small- and medium-sized companies, the workers may know this before management does, because it is low-level employees who take orders and keep accounts, and gossip spreads quickly.

Nevertheless, asymmetries of information underlie the explanation of wage rigidity. Morale is important for productivity because management finds it prohibitively expensive to monitor employees closely. For this reason, companies rely on workers to do what they are supposed to do without being told, even when supervisors are unlikely to check up on them or never do so. Workers are likely to be so cooperative only if they have good morale.

Though employees expect to share in company success through pay increases, they do not expect to share in its losses by having their pay reduced. Adjusting to lower income is too painful for workers to endure relative to the sacrifices made by company owners, and pay cuts raise the awkward issue of the disparity between the incomes of workers and owners.

Morale is fragile and can be destroyed quickly by matters more minor than pay cuts. It can be hurt by any form of unfair or inequitable treatment by management, where the standards of fairness, especially regarding pay differentials, are often determined by company or industry traditions rather than by absolute standards of justice.

Good morale normally takes a long time to build. It is fostered by:

- Frank, but good, relations between subordinates and superiors;
- Prospects for economic security and progress within the company;
- Recognition and reward of contributions to the company;
- Good explanations of the social contribution of the company's products; and
- Good explanations of a worker's role in the production process.

Collective activities within the company, such as charity drives and company picnics, also improve morale, as does almost anything that encourages workers to think of people other than themselves.

Morale is hurt by threats, such as threats of being fired if performance is substandard. Though companies fire some workers, it is thought to be a bad business practice to have people work in a negative, menacing atmosphere. Just this style of management is sometimes used, however, with low-level and low-paid labor doing short-term jobs that are easily monitored. Firing is most useful for ridding an organization of scoundrels and ne'er-do-wells rather than as a way of motivating ordinary workers to perform. Positive incentives and an optimistic atmosphere encourage performance more effectively than do threats. Most workers want to do well and will do so, if given the opportunity, and if they understand what they are supposed to do. Furthermore, many people enjoy their work.[2] A sense of pride, duty, and accomplishment can make even disagreeable jobs bearable. Nevertheless, strict discipline is necessary for good morale, for if some workers are allowed to get away with slacking, those who work hard feel they are being treated inequitably.

What has been said is a fair summary, I believe, of the dominant views of business people and labor leaders. I now turn to the problem of formulating these ideas in ways that may be useful for economic theory.

Interpretation of morale

Good morale has three components:

- Identification with the organization or internalization of its objectives,
- Good moods, and
- Trust and mutual affinity among members of the organization.

A person may be judged to have internalized the objectives of their organization if they act to advance its interests without specific instructions and without any possibility of being monitored and rewarded. Identification is manifested by internalizing the organization's objectives as well as by actions that demonstrate membership and by expressing feelings of belonging. Moods are states of mind that affect work habits and the pleasure or displeasure derived from work. Cooperation within an organization is fostered by a network of trusting relationships among employees. Cooperation may not be directed toward helping the organization, however, unless members accept its objectives. Though the social network is an important component of morale, it is not hurt by pay cutting, so I give it little attention.[3]

Identity and internalization

It is clear that human beings have the capacity to identify with organizations and to internalize codes of behavior and the interests of others. Experimentally, it is easy to induce people to identify with a group and to act in its interests

---

[2] Juster (1985) found in a survey that ordinary people preferred work to activities associated with leisure.

[3] Some industrial psychologists measure morale as the existence of effective groups (Blum, 1956, pp. 163–69).

(Tajfel, 1970, and Turner, 1987). Children show empathy for others at a young age and learn to internalize social and moral rules (Gleitman, 1995, pp. 550–58). It is impossible to know whether the capacities for empathy, morality, and group identity are accidental or if long ago they evolved in humanity because they increased chances of survival, nor do we need to know the answer to this question. What is important is that the capacities exist.

A psychological theory of organizational identity should describe its function or purpose and the mental mechanism of which it is a part. Identity, in general, is a person's image of who they are. One advantage of identity is that it simplifies mental processes by summarizing a person's goals and providing a set of rules for how to behave. A great deal of what we do mentally is done unconsciously or semi-consciously. Conscious mental operations are slow, though adaptable. Unconscious ones are rapid, though restricted to learned routines. Thus, it is hard to learn to play the piano or to speak a foreign language, but, once those skills are learned, they occur smoothly and with only general conscious direction. Identity includes many such mental subroutines. For instance, it would be nearly impossible to function socially if we constantly weighed self-interest against collective advantage. These calculations are replaced, in most cases, by rules about how we should behave, who are our friends or foes, and what we should expect of them. Those rules are all part of identity. In summary, the function of identity is to make mental activity more efficient, and identity's mental mechanism is a set of unconscious goals and mental subroutines.

An additional advantage to an individual of group identification is that it contributes to his or her sense of being powerful, valuable, important, and wanted. A sense of self-worth is needed by people because it gives them a reason to survive and promote their own interests. Without a sense of worth and the power to shape their own lives, people can be incapacitated by what psychologists call learned helplessness (Gleitman, 1995, pp. 133–35).

An obvious benefit of group identity is that it makes it easier to work with other people, which is important because most productive human activities require cooperation. This benefit does not explain morale's fragility, however. Its function may be to protect individual self-interest. Though commitment to a group helps overcome prisoner's dilemma or free-rider problems arising in cooperative activity, the same sense of responsibility exposes individuals to exploitation. It is useful to have a system that balances private and group advantage, and conventional standards of fairness offer an orderly way of accomplishing this. These establish rules of reciprocation among group members and between them and the organization, and the duties specified by these rules are accepted by members when they agree emotionally to join. Perhaps the brittleness of morale is a self-protective reflex provoked by violation of fairness standards. Reading a psychology textbook, such as Gleitman (1995), makes it clear that many parts of the nervous system operate through offsetting pairs of activating and inhibiting signals. The teetering between group commitment and indignant rebellion may reflect just such a pairing that is built into the psyche.

It remains to be explained why unjustified pay cuts impair identification with the employer. A superficial answer, given earlier, is that they are regarded as unfair. Fairness specifies rules of reciprocation and workers receive nothing in exchange for a pay cut that saves few jobs. It might be that in a different world, workers would view wages and salaries coolly as fluctuating market prices and would accept price declines as a normal part of business life, just as salespeople accept large income fluctuations. Most people do not think this way. I was told many times that workers do not view themselves as commodities and inevitably interpret pay cuts as statements about how satisfied the company is with them, because, in their experience, pay increases signal appreciation of workers' contribution.

Mood, work effort, and its disutility

Managers and labor leaders did not usually speak of jobs as disagreeable, but assumed that employees liked to work. They said that one of the bad effects of layoff was loss of the pleasure of working and of social contacts on the job. If, in the standard model of work, however, we assume that effort brings positive rather than negative utility, then people should work hard, even if they have no financial incentive to do so. This implication conflicts with common sense. Though volunteer labor makes important contributions to society, it is hard to imagine that it would succeed in producing ordinary economic output. Other phenomena that are inconsistent with the usual model of work effort are the importance of mood to job performance and satisfaction from work. I was told that bad moods are distracting and that they increase fatigue, discomfort, and accidents.

In order to make sense of these observations, it may be helpful to consider an analogy with a lion hunting an antelope. In chasing an antelope, the lion expends energy, loses time, and risks injury. These costs must be weighed against the probability of catching the prey and the pleasure of eating it. Imagine that the lion unconsciously, or half consciously, weighs the costs against the benefits before deciding whether to chase his prey and before choosing the level of physical effort to expend on the pursuit. Once he makes his decision, the lion's mind automatically adjusts his mood and level of nervous and physical arousal to handle the effort required. If the lion decides not to go after the antelope, he will not be aroused. He will feel lazy and may find running uncomfortable. In contrast, if he decides to try for a kill, he will be mobilized, excited, and will probably be exhilarated by the effort. Given this decision, he will consciously decide how much effort to put into the hunt and how to go about it. We may

251

imagine that the lion's unconscious mind chooses the mood and level of arousal so that his conscious mind chooses an effort level that optimizes a utility that is unconscious. This unconscious utility depends on the probability of success, energy expenditure, and risk of injury. The lion's unconscious choice of mood may be constrained by his preexisting state of mind. If he just lost his wives to a rival, he may be discouraged and not feel like hunting, whereas if he is a hopeful young bachelor, he may feel vigorous.

Another illuminating analogy may be that of a virtuoso pianist. For an appreciative and sensitive audience, she will probably play at her best and love doing so. If she hears snores and catcalls, she will no doubt feel her fingers stiffen, stumble, and hate playing.

It is important, in my opinion, to recognize that mood automatically adjusts to fit the perceived net benefits of tasks. I believe it is general human experience that capacities to act and perceptions of pain or pleasure depend on circumstances. Danger stimulates us to fight or flee. Anger makes us ignore pain and danger. Though deprivation of life's necessities causes us discomfort and unhappiness, we get used to prolonged hardship, probably so that we can cope with the unavoidable misery. Soldiers and prisoners living in frightful conditions eventually cheer up and joke about their state, though, of course, they are not happy. It is a mistake to separate the disutility of labor from the utility of its reward, or to imagine that labor is normally perceived as disagreeable. The utilities of labor and its reward interact.

CHAPTER 18

Worker participation

JOHN PENCAVEL

John Pencavel was born in London in 1943. He received his Ph.D. in economics from Princeton University in 1969. Since that year, he has taught at Stanford University, where he is currently the Levin Professor in the Department of Economics.

How labor markets differ from consumer markets

(From chapter 1)

For a number of reasons, the exchange of labor is quite different from the exchanges that individuals engage in as consumers, and therefore the take-it-or-leave-it approach to labor markets is unsatisfactory as a model of how workplace transactions ought to be conducted. First, unlike transactions involving consumer goods and services, exchanges involving labor services cannot be disembodied from the individuals supplying them. The sellers of labor services must deliver these services themselves. This means that workers care not only about how much they are paid but also about many nonmonetary aspects of their jobs: Who will they work with? How hard are they expected to work? What things may they refuse to do? Who will be their supervisors? The answers to these questions profoundly affect the value of the job to a worker.

Second, the labor market is distinguished from the consumer market by the different dimensions to the exchange of labor services. Workers supply not only their time but also their effort, their cooperation, and a subset of their liberties to management. The typical supervisor has the authority to direct a worker to a number of different tasks, activities that are almost never specified in advance. In most cases, the specification of the labor contract – precisely what duties the worker is supposed to undertake, with what diligence, and for what duration – is difficult to outline. Hence it is left vague and is incomplete. Even if a written statement were drawn up that listed the work to be done in various circumstances, it would leave lots of opportunity for disputing whether the contract had

Excerpted from John Pencavel, *Worker Participation: Lessons from the Worker Co-Ops of the Pacific Northwest*. New York: Russell Sage Foundation, 2001. Reprinted with the permission of the Russell Sage Foundation, 112 East 64th Street, New York, NY 10021.

been adhered to. By its very character, the exchange of labor services precludes uncomplicated contracts under which a well-defined payment is specified for a well-defined job.

Third, long-term relationships are apt to develop between a worker and an employer. Because a worker finds a job with a particular employer difficult to assess until actually doing the job, and because an employer finds the quality of a worker difficult to determine before the job is performed, workers and employers sample one another. Tacitly, they contract for a period of time in which to determine the value of the match. It is not surprising that turnover is highest among workers who have been employed for only a short while. This is a reflection of the difficulty in assessing the quality of the match before actually experiencing it. When a valuable match has been made, the worker and employer remain with each other, and long-term contracts emerge.

Fourth, among such long-tenure employees, the employer-worker match includes an element of "rent": the worker's wage with this employer is better than his or her best available alternative wage from another employer; at the same time, this worker is paid a wage that is less than the cost to management of employing a replacement worker. In this situation, the employer views a new worker as only an imperfect substitute for an existing worker, and the worker assesses other job possibilities as inferior to his or her current employment. The worker embodies specific skills or attributes that make him or her a more valuable employee to the current employer than to another company. Because the worker's productivity is higher in the current company than it would be in another company, and because the employer cannot replace the worker with a new employee who embodies the same attributes, the relationship between this worker and this employer has an idiosyncratic element. There is something distinctive and nonreproducible about the current match between a worker and an employer.

Thus the terms of the implicit contract are somewhat arbitrary. The employee's compensation has both a lower and an upper bound, and where the pay settles within these bounds is unclear. The lower bound is set by what the worker could get elsewhere: the value of the job to the employee cannot be less than what could be obtained in another company, or else the employee would quit. The upper bound is set by the firm's expected cost of hiring and training a new employee. If the employee's compensation exceeded this cost, the firm would find it more profitable to replace the employee with a new hire. In some cases, the bounds will be narrow, in which case there will be little latitude in setting the wage. In other cases, the bounds will be wide, and the discretionary element in wage setting will be considerable.

Where the terms of the contract will settle within these bounds will be determined by bargaining between the employer and the worker, although it has often been surmised that, in most instances, the employer has the upper hand in this bargaining setting. This is because in the event of bargaining breaking down and the employment relationship is discontinued, the loss to the employer is relatively small (that is, the cost to an employer of replacing a single worker assumes a small fraction of his total costs), whereas the worker's entire livelihood may be at stake. This greater vulnerability of the worker to the termination of the employment relationship gives the employer an advantage in bargaining. Of course, unless the workers are organized in a labor union, the bargaining is typically tacit, not explicit. However, this does not mean that the relationship is not one of bargaining, only that the bargaining outcome is close to what the employer specifies.

For these reasons, labor markets tend to have characteristics that set them apart from the markets for commodities and for physical and financial assets. These characteristics imply that the take-it-or-leave-it process by which commodities are allocated in markets for private consumer goods may not be well suited to the incomplete contracts that typify labor markets.

Workplace public goods

In the market for private consumer goods, consumers reveal their preferences by "exiting" (that is, ceasing consuming) the market for commodities they do not care for and by "entering" (that is, embarking on consuming) the market for commodities they prefer. In this way, through spending patterns, consumers' preferences are signaled to firms, inducing firms to tailor their production in response to these exit and entry cues. The exit mechanism of preference revelation operates less effectively in markets in which the costs of switching are high and when information about alternative options is incomplete.[1] Thus, for example, few would advocate dispensing with local elections on the ground that the best way to register dissatisfaction with the policies followed by the local government is to live elsewhere. Some migration is surely motivated by the search for a more attractive local jurisdictions. However, the opportunity to voice one's preferences for local government policies through elections and speaking out at meetings is, at the very least, a useful complement to voting with one's feet.[2]

The situation within a workplace is somewhat analogous to that of local government in that important public goods components are present in both

---

[1] The distinction between "exit" and "voice" as options for registering dissatisfaction with a situation derives from Albert Hirschman (1970). The distinction is applied to labor markets by Richard Freeman (1976).

[2] The standard reference to the situation in which the movement of people across communities addresses problems regarding the provision of public goods by local governments is Charles Tiebout (1956). For a skeptical argument of the effectiveness of mobility as a revelation device for public goods preferences, see Joseph Stiglitz (1977).

venues. For example, when a workplace is made safer, the benefit is provided not to a single worker but to all workers in that workplace; usually, one worker's safety cannot be enhanced without also enhancing the safety of the neighboring worker. The public goods parallel is also present when there are important interdependencies among workers: many firms require conformity among workers in the length of the workday and the scheduling of breaks. Such synchronization dictates that the operation of the workplace cannot be tailored to the heterogeneous preferences of individual workers, just as the different elements of an assembly line cannot run at different speeds. A third example of workplace public goods relates to each company's rules and conventions for dealing with employee grievances. Just as the legal system enforces the rights of all citizens when it rules on a particular case, so a grievance system that operates within a firm shapes the rights of all workers in that firm. Although these public goods are not extended to all workers in the economy, they are locally universal to one workplace.

A firm could determine the preferences of its workers for the length of the workday and the pace at which the assembly line operates by trying different schedules and speeds and observing the corresponding rate at which its employees quit the enterprise. Although it might be difficult for the firm to draw inferences from these patterns of turnover, quit rates are likely to provide some useful information. This information about workers' preferences can be augmented by direct communication with the workers.

Worker participation

If the efficient operation of the firm calls for mechanisms that elicit the "voice" of employees on workplace public goods questions, why don't employers supply these mechanisms voluntarily? In fact, many employers do set up mechanisms that solicit from workers information about their preferences and their recommendations for improvements in the organization of production. Sometimes these preferences are delivered individually, as when a worker raises an issue with a supervisor or drops a note in a suggestion box. Other mechanisms are collective and take the form of employee involvement committees, assemblies, briefing groups, and labor unions. In this way, many workers in the United States are already involved in fashioning their work environments. However, when workers are asked about the extent of their power to voice their opinions about the workplace, they generally reply that these mechanisms are inadequate.[3] The U.S. economy may be effective in satisfying consumers' demands for private goods, but it appears to be less successful in satisfying

---

[3] The Worker Representation and Participation Study, conducted in 1994, asked employees about their influence and involvement in a set of eight workplace decisions; 53 percent of those responding reported having less involvement than they want (Freeman and Rogers 1999).

employees' demands for a vigorous voice in shaping their work environments. Why is there an underprovision of these voice mechanisms?

First, employers tend to be suspicious that the activities of these voice mechanisms will not be restricted to issues that enhance productivity but will become a means to reallocate the organization's rents away from the firm's owners and toward production labor. After all, the mission of conventional firms is to maximize profits for their owners, not to maximize productivity. Hence employers fear that participatory schemes such as health and safety committees are apt to stray from their task of improving the efficiency of the organization and become embroiled in a struggle over the division of the rents.

A second reason for the inadequacy of voice mechanisms at the workplace derives from the very nature of the public goods they are designed to produce. Because public goods have the character of being nonexclusive – that is, if a public good is provided to one person, it is available to all people – each person has an incentive to conceal his or her true valuation of this good in the hope that others will pay for provision of the public good. In this case, a single worker will "free ride" on other people's willingness to pay. Because all workers tend to conceal their true valuations and are attracted by the possibility of free riding, the result is a chronic underprovision of public goods in the workplace.

Consider a situation in which a number of workers are agitating to press the employer to institute a grievance system. Individual workers hope this agitation will succeed because they will benefit from the presence of a grievance system. However, a single worker hopes this success will come about without calling on his or her own efforts. Workers will be inclined to direct their energies in the pursuit of their individual private goods, not public goods. The private incentives to keep silent and to free ride on the activities of others are even greater when an employer has the power and authority to punish those who agitate for such workplace public goods. Hence public goods tend to be produced in inadequate amounts.

The meager participation of employees in regulating their work environments means that these workplaces are remarkably oligarchic structures. Usually, important decisions are made by a relatively small number of managers, who involve workers in these issues only in a casual and haphazard way. In those instances when workers do participate, the extent and manner of worker participation are usually determined by management. When and insofar as it is in the interests of the managers to permit workers to participate in shaping their work environments, then some degree of worker participation will emerge, but it is largely by the grace of managers, not the result of workers exercising some right to participation.

How can this limited degree of worker participation be justified? The rejection of "exit" as a valid response to an authoritarian local government rests on several considerations, but one is that exit may require citizens to undertake considerable costs to uproot themselves and change residence, something that many would regard as unfair and probably inefficient.[4] The same point applies to workers for whom exit is the only available option in response to an unsatisfactory work environment. Indeed, in an economy composed of many authoritarian firms, a worker's sole option is to exit one firm and join another where he or she also lacks voice. If public goods supplied by local governments are judged to require voice mechanisms for the expression of residents' preferences in addition to the take-it-or-leave-it variety, why doesn't the provision of public goods by workplaces also require such mechanisms for the expression of workers' preferences in addition to the take-it-or-leave-it type?[5]

One answer has been the claim that hierarchically managed firms outperform other types of enterprises. Indeed, it is sometimes argued, a market economy has the feature that, if any other management system were more efficient than the oligarchical system, this other system would now be dominant. This is a powerful argument because it maintains that, in effect, the loss in output and consumption that would result from permitting workers a voice in shaping their environment is too high a price to pay and that society has accepted the undemocratic nature of most business enterprises because the conventional system delivers the goods.

This book concerns this response. It takes up not the ethical questions of worker participation but rather the positive issue of the comparative performance of companies in which workers have a significant voice. There are many ways to evaluate this important issue. My method here is to describe two case studies. No single study is definitive, but the particular case studies here are at least instructive. I analyze a polar case of worker participation in which the workers' voice is expected to be loud and clear: this occurs when the workers not only participate in managing the workplace but also own it.

---

[4] Imagine your city is run by a small group of people who refuse to offer themselves up for election on the argument that, if the city's citizens disapprove of their lot, they may move and live elsewhere. Most of us would determine that the absence of "voice" in local government violates basic notions of fair representation. Yet an analogous argument is applied to rationalize the inability of workers to voice their preferences within the capitalist firm. Hence, the political scientist Robert Dahl (1985, 115) maintains that "like a state, . . . a firm can also be viewed as a political system in which relations of power exist between governments and the governed. If so, is it not appropriate to insist that the relationship between governors and governed should satisfy the criteria of the democratic process – as we properly insist in the domain of the state?"

[5] On this, I cannot resist quoting Leland Stanford, the founder and namesake of the university for which I work. After amassing a fortune, Stanford became a strong believer in worker-owned cooperatives, reasoning that "cooperation is merely an extension to the industrial life of our people of our great political system of self-government. That government itself is founded upon the great doctrine of the consent of the governed, and has as its corner stone in the memorable principle that men are endowed with inalienable rights. This great principle has a clearly defined place in cooperative organization" (quoted in Altenberg 1990, 12).

Worker participation

In this book I take up the principal empirical issues regarding "enterprise democracy" or worker cooperatives: the productive efficiency and long-run viability of such organizations; the degree to which they reduce "alienation" in the workplace and adversarial relations among different groups; the extent to which the cooperative firm's important decisions are determined by an active and involved workplace citizenry rather than by a narrow, entrenched oligarchy; and the responses of such enterprises to external shocks to which they must make some accommodation. The political argument for worker co-ops and worker participation will be more difficult to maintain if co-ops are shown to be inefficient and wasteful production units or if they are run not by the broad mass of workers but by a small, privileged elite. It is to assess the empirical content of these issues that this book is devoted. Before these questions are taken up, however, we must first consider the meaning of the management and ownership of companies.

. . .

Labor and capital in the worker co-ops of the Pacific Northwest

(From chapter 2)

The Pacific Northwest has been home to at least two major groups of worker co-ops. One of these is the plywood industry, the U.S. manufacturing industry in which worker ownership and management have extended most widely over the past eighty years. At this time, however, the plywood co-ops may well be in their twilight. The first plywood co-op, the Olympia Veneer Company, was established in 1921. After a successful experience, it was sold to the United States Plywood Corporation in 1954, when more than one-quarter of all plywood production in the Pacific Northwest was coming from the co-ops (and when all U.S. plywood was being produced in the Northwest). Today only three plywood co-ops are in operation: Hardel Mutual Plywood and Hoquiam Plywood, in Washington, and Linnton Plywood, in Oregon. The plywood co-ops no longer constitute a prominent feature of the industry, and their presence today looks more idiosyncratic. Thus we are able to appraise the full life cycle of the plywood co-ops – from their beginnings following the First World War to their virtual demise today.

The plywood co-ops of the Pacific Northwest provide a perfect case study to use in examining many of the issues raised in the research on worker-owned and worker-managed firms. First, the cooperative mills come close to the ideal of cooperative forms of production. All workers are paid the same hourly rate, so divisions among workers on the basis of pay do not exist. All the owners are workers, and most of the workers are owners. A fusion between those who supply labor and those who supply capital is close to being achieved. Virtually all the mills hire workers who are not owners, although nonowner workers have usually constituted a minority (often a small minority) of all workers. Some of the nonmember workers are people who anticipate being owners or who are on probation for membership.

Each plywood co-op member owns one share (and usually only one share) in his firm. The shares trade in open markets, though co-ops often require a probationary period of employment for any new member. A co-op's workers hold regular meetings during which the company's general policies are discussed. The board of directors is made up of worker-members who are selected by a vote of all members. Because turnover of board members is high, the formation of a small oligarchy of active worker-members tends to be avoided.

These features imply that the plywood co-ops have the qualities often deemed necessary to constitute meaningful cooperative ownership and management: in each co-op, participation in decision making on the major issues facing the organization is high, and task divisions among the worker-members are relatively unimportant. As one close observer has written, "The producer cooperatives in the American plywood industry are substantially democratized work settings, as close as we have come in the United States to worker self-management in industrial enterprises" (Greenberg 1986, 25).

An additional feature of the Pacific Northwest plywood industry that makes it an attractive study subject is that conventional capitalist firms also operate in the industry. Unlike much of the research on worker-owned firms, which compares the activities of worker co-ops and capitalist firms operating in different industries, the plywood industry affords the opportunity to compare capitalist and cooperative firms in the same industry at the same time in the same place. Moreover, although some of the plywood mills are owned by the large timber corporations, no firm produces more than a small fraction of total output. A compelling case can be made that the price of plywood and the price of logs (the mills' principal raw-material input) are outside the control of (or exogenous to) each of the plywood firms. Because the demand for plywood derives from the demand for new construction, which is highly volatile, plywood and log prices are also volatile; consequently the economic environment of the plywood mills generates substantial shocks requiring some form of adjustment. The plywood industry is an excellent setting in which to determine whether co-ops adjust to price shocks differently from capitalist firms. In this way, the structure of the plywood industry makes the study of the cooperative organization in the industry especially appealing.

. . .

Productivity

(From chapter 3)

. . .

Because of their similar size, the most convincing comparison is that between the co-ops and the unionized mills for which output is simulated at their actual levels of inputs. The simple average of the proportionate differences between the co-ops and unionized mills' outputs is 13.5 percent. This is not a trivial difference. It is as if the workers in the co-ops could go on vacation for an extra seven weeks a year and still produce in total output what the unionized firms would have produced for that year. The comparisons of the co-ops with the classical firms suggest that the co-ops are also superior in efficiency to the classical firms, although the substantially different levels of inputs and outputs between the two groups of mills make comparisons more hazardous.

What is the source of this difference in productivity? The surveys suggest that a co-op's worker-owners are more industrious and that, as has already been mentioned, the co-op mills operate with fewer supervisors than the conventional mills. Greenberg (1986, 49) reports that "the shareholders individually manage themselves and each other. Filled with a sense of responsibility for the enterprise as a whole, they work in a manner that is sufficiently diligent and responsible as to require little outside supervision. If coordination becomes necessary, or some members are not contributing in a way that other members consider appropriate, groups of worker-shareholders will tend to act as collective supervisors on the job."

. . .

Worker participation in workplace governance

(From chapter 4)

The experiences of the co-ops in the Pacific Northwest testify to the difficulty that such organizations face: they are intrinsically risky enterprises, and often their very structure may contain incentives for their own evolution, or degeneration, to capitalist firms. Yet at the same time, the experiences of the co-ops attest to the fact that they can be durable organizations that appeal to many workers. Their appeal is based on a number of qualities: they offer an opportunity for workers to participate in shaping the environments in which they earn their livings; they offer much more security against cyclical layoffs than conventional firms; and they are typically no less efficient, and probably more efficient, than capitalist firms.[6] Can these benefits be extended to workers in other organizations by some sort of structural reforms?...

...

... The authors of the Workplace Representation and Participation Survey of 1994 undertake some analysis of the effects of worker participation and group compensation methods on a number of outcomes, including work effort and indicators of productivity. Their consistent findings are that employee involvement programs are invariably positively associated with desirable outcomes (such as greater work effort and higher productivity), whereas measures of performance pay are less robustly associated with these outcomes. Indeed, performance pay seems to be associated with these desirable outcomes only when employee involvement programs are in place. All this supports the notion that there are benefits to performance pay compensation methods, but these benefits are largely contingent on the presence of programs of worker participation. By contrast, desirable effects of worker participation are not conditional on the presence of performance pay. Hence, though there are benefits to pay mechanisms related to group performance, the key variable is worker participation.

This should come as no surprise to academics. Imagine working in a university in which the design of the curriculum, the courses that each faculty member teaches, and the scholastic standards determining the awarding of degrees are determined by the "managers" who have not and do not undertake any teaching or scholarship. Imagine also that, if enrollment in any department's courses suddenly drops, that department's faculty are promptly laid off. Would this system lead to a university with a curriculum and course structure that is efficient from the point of view of either research or teaching, and would it be a gratifying place to teach and study? In fact, the American university is a good example of an organization in which a subset of the workers participates extensively in determining its operation and design. Most universities are organized in such a way that many issues are determined at a highly decentralized level and the university's principal administrative officers are drawn from the ranks of the faculty.

...

The importance for productivity of mechanisms fostering worker participation and the role of complementary aspects of work organization are frequent

---

[6] Recall that the plywood co-ops have been found to be more efficient producers than capitalist firms (especially the unionized plywood firms). I surmise that this greater productivity arises from the greater work effort of the worker-owners, which manifests itself in greater value added (that is, a higher output per raw material input).

conclusions of contemporary research. An excellent example of this type of work is the study by Casey Ichniowski, Kathryn Shaw, and Giovanna Prennushi (1997) of thirty-six steel-finishing plants. Variations among the plants in the nature of the product are small, yet there are distinct differences in workplace production methods. "Traditional" production involves narrow job classifications, training by on-the-job learning exclusively, the absence of work teams, close supervision by foremen, communication entirely through formal grievance systems, and incentive aspects of earnings in which the quantity of steel produced plays a large role. "Innovative" production is characterized by extensive communication between workers and managers, the organization of workers into teams, off-site training programs, the rotation of jobs, employment security, and incentive aspects of earnings in which the quality of work undertaken also figures. Using the fraction of total scheduled hours lost because of unscheduled line stops as an indicator of productivity, Ichniowski and colleagues find that the innovative production system yielded about 7 percent higher productivity than the traditional system. Individual elements of innovative production had little effect on productivity. The productivity benefits were in evidence when the components were combined. In other words, they were highly complementary.

A number of other studies suggest that this examination of steel-finishing plants is by no means unrepresentative (see, for example, the studies in Ichniowski et al. 2000). . . .

. . .

[I]n a 1994 national survey of more than twenty-four hundred workers, Richard Freeman and Joel Rogers (1999) found that 63 percent of respondents sought more influence in decisions at their workplace. For every class of worker, a gap existed between the influence workers believed they exerted on their work life and the influence they would have liked to have. Workers expressed a desire for greater individual and collective representation at the workplace, but they believed their management resisted workers' attempts to seek a voice. Indeed, managers confirmed this impression.

When given a choice among different types of workplace organizations, the vast majority of workers selected something that is run jointly by employees and management over an organization run by employees alone. The difficulty is that this organizational form is certainly not encouraged by current U.S. labor laws and, indeed, is probably illegal if it discusses issues that are by law reserved for collective bargaining. In other words, workers have modest aspirations for their involvement in workplace governance, yet the law stifles innovation of the sort of organizational form that would allow the expression of these aspirations. As is clear from this examination of the activities of

263

the worker-managed enterprises of the Pacific Northwest, there are gains to be had in allowing firms and workers to design different forms of representative organizations that involve workers in effective decision making within the workplace; and, consequently, there are also benefits to amending current labor law to permit them to do so.

. . .

PART IV

Finance and the control of the firm

CHAPTER 19

Mergers and the market for corporate control

HENRY MANNE

Henry Manne was born in 1928 in New Orleans, Louisiana. He received a J.D. at the University of Chicago in 1952 and a J.S.D. at Yale University in 1966. He was Professor at George Washington University Law School when this paper was published. In 1986, he became Dean of the School of Law at George Mason University, where he is currently Professor, Emeritus.

The corporate-control market

The conventional approach to a merger problem takes corporations merely as decision-making units or firms within the classical market framework. This approach dictates a ban on many horizontal mergers almost by definition. The basic proposition advanced in this paper is that the control of corporations may constitute a valuable asset, that this asset exists independent of any interest in either economies of scale or monopoly profits, that an active market for corporate control exists, and that a great many mergers are probably the result of the successful workings of this special market.

Basically this paper will constitute an introduction to a study of the market for corporation control. The emphasis will be placed on the antitrust implications of this market, but the analysis to follow has important implications for a variety of economic questions. Perhaps the most important implications are those for the alleged separation of ownership and control in large corporations. So long as we are unable to discern any control relationship between small shareholders and corporate management, the thrust of Berle and Means's famous phrase remains strong. But, as will be explained below, the market for corporate control gives to these shareholders both power and protection commensurate with their interest in corporate affairs.

A fundamental premise underlying the market for corporate control is the existence of a high positive correlation between corporate managerial efficiency

Excerpted from Henry Manne, "Mergers and the Market for Corporate Control," *Journal of Political Economy*, 73 (1965): 110–20. Copyright © 1965. Reprinted with the permission of the University of Chicago Press.

and the market price of shares of that company.[1] As an existing company is poorly managed – in the sense of not making as great a return for the shareholders as could be accomplished under other feasible managements – the market price of the shares declines relative to the shares of other companies in the same industry or relative to the market as a whole. This phenomenon has a dual importance for the market for corporate control.

In the first place, a lower share price facilitates any effort to take over high-paying managerial positions. The compensation from these positions may take the usual forms of salary, bonuses, pensions, expense accounts, and stock options. Perhaps more important, it may take the form of information useful in trading in the company's shares; or, if that is illegal, information may be exchanged and the trading done in other companies' shares. But it is extremely doubtful that the full compensation recoverable by executives for managing their corporations explains more than a small fraction of outsider[2] attempts to take over control. Takeovers of corporations are too expensive generally to make the "purchase" of management compensation an attractive proposition.[3]

It is far more likely that a second kind of reward provides the primary motivation for most takeover attempts. The market price of shares does more than measure the price at which the normal compensation of executives can be "sold" to new individuals. Share price, or that part reflecting managerial efficiency, also measures the potential capital gain inherent in the corporate stock. The lower the stock price, relative to what it could be with more efficient management, the more attractive the takeover becomes to those who believe

---

[1] The claim of a positive correlation between managerial efficiency and the market price of shares would seem at first blush to raise an empirical question. In fact, however, the concept of corporate managerial efficiency, with its overtones of an entrepreneurial function, is one for which there are no objective standards. But there are compelling reasons, apart from empirical data, for believing that this correlation exists. Insiders, those who have the most reliable information about corporate affairs, are strongly motivated financially to perform a kind of arbitrage function for their company's stock. That is, given their sense of what constitutes efficient management, they will cause share prices to rise or decline in accordance with that standard. The contention is often made that stock-market prices are not accurate gauges, since far more trades take place without reliable information than with it. But there is reason to believe that intelligence rather than ignorance ultimately determines the course of individual share prices. Stock-market decisions tend to be of the one-out-of-two-alternatives variety, such as buy or not buy, hold or sell, or put or call. To the extent that decisions on these questions are made by shareholders or potential shareholders operating without reliable information, over a period of time the decisions will tend to be randomly distributed and the effect will therefore be neutral. Decisions made by those with a higher degree of certainty will to that extent not meet a canceling effect since they will not be made on a random basis. Over some period of time it would seem that the average market price of a company's shares must be the "correct" one.

[2] "Outsider" here refers to anyone not presently controlling the affairs of the corporation, even though it may include one or more individuals on the corporation's board of directors.

[3] To the extent that executive compensation increases with higher share prices, the takeover is most attractive at the time when it is also most expensive. Indeed, the danger of a takeover may account for managers' voluntarily decreasing their compensation when the company's share price is down.

that they can manage the company more efficiently. And the potential return from the successful takeover and revitalization of a poorly run company can be enormous.

Additional leverage in this operation can be obtained by borrowing the funds with which the shares are purchased, although American commercial banks are generally forbidden to lend money for this purpose. A comparable advantage can be had from using other shares rather than cash as the exchange medium. Given the fact of special tax treatment for capital gains, we can see how this mechanism for taking over control of badly run corporations is one of the most important "get rich quick" opportunities in our economy today.

But the greatest benefits of the takeover scheme probably inure to those least conscious of it. Apart from the stock market, we have no objective standard of managerial efficiency. Courts, as indicated by the so-called business-judgment rule, are loath to second-guess business decisions or remove directors from office. Only the takeover scheme provides some assurance of competitive efficiency among corporate managers and thereby affords strong protection to the interests of vast numbers of small, noncontrolling shareholders. Compared to this mechanism, the efforts of the SEC and the courts to protect shareholders through the development of a fiduciary duty concept and the shareholder's derivative suit seem small indeed. It is true that sales by dissatisfied shareholders are necessary to trigger the mechanism and that these shareholders may suffer considerable losses. On the other hand, even greater capital losses are prevented by the existence of a competitive market for control.[4]

. . .

[4] Unfortunately, the suppression of this market would be the consequence of proposals made by several writers in the field. For a review and a criticism of this literature, see Henry G. Manne, (1962), 399–432. For another defense of this market, see Harry G. Johnson (1963), pp. xvii–xviii.

CHAPTER 20

Agency problems and the theory of the firm

EUGENE FAMA

Eugene Fama was born in 1939 in Boston, Massachusetts. He received a Ph.D. in business from the University of Chicago in 1964. When this paper was published, he was Theodore O. Yntema Professor of Finance in the Graduate School of Business at the University of Chicago. He is currently Robert R. McCormick Distinguished Service Professor of Finance in the same school.

Economists have long been concerned with the incentive problems that arise when decision making in a firm is the province of managers who are not the firm's security holders.[1] One outcome has been the development of "behavioral" and "managerial" theories of the firm which reject the classical model of an entrepreneur, or owner-manager, who single-mindedly operates the firm to maximize profits, in favor of theories that focus more on the motivations of a manager who controls but does not own and who has little resemblance to the classical "economic man." Examples of this approach are Baumol (1959), Simon (1959), Cyert and March (1963), and Williamson (1964b).

More recently the literature has moved toward theories that reject the classical model of the firm but assume classical forms of economic behavior on the part of agents within the firm. The firm is viewed as a set of contracts among factors of production, with each factor motivated by its self-interest. Because of its emphasis on the importance of rights in the organization established by contracts, this literature is characterized under the rubric "property rights." Alchian and Demsetz (1972) and Jensen and Meckling (1976b) are the best examples. The antecedents of their work are in Coase (1937, 1960).

The striking insight of Alchian and Demsetz (1972) and Jensen and Meckling (1976b) is in viewing the firm as a set of contracts among factors of production. In effect, the firm is viewed as a team whose members act from self-interest but realize that their destinies depend to some extent on the survival of the team in its competition with other teams. This insight, however, is not carried

Reprinted with abridgements from Eugene Fama, "Agency Problems and the Theory of the Firm," *Journal of Political Economy*, 88 (1980): 288–307. Copyright © 1980. Reprinted with the permission of the University of Chicago Press.

[1] Jensen and Meckling (1976b) quote from Adam Smith (1937 [1776]). The modern literature on the problem dates back at least to Berle and Means (1932).

far enough. In the classical theory, the agent who personifies the firm is the entrepreneur who is taken to be both manager and residual risk bearer. Although his title sometimes changes – for example, Alchian and Demsetz call him "the employer" – the entrepreneur continues to play a central role in the firm of the property rights literature. As a consequence, this literature fails to explain the large modern corporation in which control of the firms is in the hands of managers who are more or less separate from the firm's security holders.

The main thesis of this paper is that separation of security ownership and control can be explained as an efficient form of economic organization within the "set of contracts" perspective. We first set aside the typical presumption that a corporation has owners in any meaningful sense. The attractive concept of the entrepreneur is also laid to rest, at least for the purposes of the large modern corporation. Instead, the two functions usually attributed to the entrepreneur, management and risk bearing, are treated as naturally separate factors within the set of contracts called a firm. The firm is disciplined by competition from other firms, which forces the evolution of devices for efficiently monitoring the performance of the entire team and of its individual members. In addition, individual participants in the firm, and in particular its managers, face both the discipline and opportunities provided by the markets for their services, both within and outside of the firm.

The irrelevance of the concept of ownership of the firm

To set a framework for the analysis, let us first describe roles for management and risk bearing in the set of contracts called a firm. Management is a type of labor but with a special role – coordinating the activities of inputs and carrying out the contracts agreed among inputs, all of which can be characterized as "decision making." To explain the role of the risk bearers, assume for the moment that the firm rents all other factors of production and that rental contracts are negotiated at the beginning of each production period with payoffs at the end of the period. The risk bearers then contract to accept the uncertain and possibly negative difference between total revenues and costs at the end of each production period.

When other factors of production are paid at the end of each period, it is not necessary for the risk bearers to invest anything in the firm at the beginning of the period. Most commonly, however, the risk bearers guarantee performance of their contracts by putting up wealth *ex ante*, with this front money used to purchase capital and perhaps also the technology that the firm uses in its production activities. In this way the risk-bearing function is combined with ownership of capital and technology. We also commonly observe that the joint functions of risk bearing and ownership of capital are repackaged and sold in different proportions to different groups of investors. For example, when front money is raised by issuing both bonds and common stock, the bonds involve a combination of risk bearing and ownership of capital with a low amount of risk bearing relative to the combination of risk bearing and ownership of capital inherent in the common stock. Unless the bonds are risk free, the risk-bearing function is in part borne by the bondholders, and ownership of capital is shared by bondholders and stockholders.

However, ownership of capital should not be confused with ownership of the firm. Each factor in a firm is owned by somebody. The firm is just the set of contracts covering the way inputs are joined to create outputs and the way receipts from outputs are shared among inputs. In this "nexus of contracts" perspective, ownership of the firm is an irrelevant concept. Dispelling the tenacious notion that a firm is owned by its security holders is important because it is a first step toward understanding that control over a firm's decisions is not necessarily the province of security holders. The second step is setting aside the equally tenacious role in the firm usually attributed to the entrepreneur.

Management and risk bearing: a closer look

The entrepreneur (manager–risk bearer) is central in both the Jensen–Meckling and Alchian–Demsetz analyses of the firm. For example, Alchian–Demsetz state: "The essence of the classical firm is identified here as a contractual structure with: (1) joint input production, (2) several input owners, (3) one party who is common to all the contracts of the joint inputs, (4) who has the right to renegotiate any input's contract independently of contracts with other input owners, (5) who holds the residual claim, and (6) who has the right to sell his central contractual residual status. The central agent is called the firm's owner and the employer" (1972, p. 794).

To understand the modern corporation, it is better to separate the manager, the agents of points 3 and 4 of the Alchian–Demsetz definition of the firm, from the risk bearer described in points 5 and 6. The rationale for separating these functions is not just that the end result is more descriptive of the corporation, a point recognized in both the Alchian–Demsetz and Jensen–Meckling papers. The major loss in retaining the concept of the entrepreneur is that one is prevented from developing a perspective on management and risk bearing as separate factors of production, each faced with a market for its services that provides alternative opportunities and, in the case of management, motivation toward performance.

Thus, any given set of contracts, a particular firm, is in competition with other firms, which are likewise teams of cooperating factors of production. If there is a part of the team that has a special interest in its viability, it is not obviously the risk bearers. It is true that if the team does not prove viable, factors like labor and management are protected by markets in which rights

272

to their future services can be sold or rented to other teams. The risk bearers, as residual claimants, also seem to suffer the most direct consequences from the failings of the team. However, the risk bearers in the modern corporation also have markets for their services – capital markets – which allow them to shift among teams with relatively low transaction costs and to hedge against the failings of any given team by diversifying their holdings across teams.

Indeed, portfolio theory tells us that the optimal portfolio for any investor is likely to be diversified across the securities of many firms.[2] Since he holds the securities of many firms precisely to avoid having his wealth depend too much on any one firm, an individual security holder generally has no special interest in personally overseeing the detailed activities of any firm. In short, efficient allocation of risk bearing seems to imply a large degree of separation of security ownership from control of a firm.

On the other hand, the managers of a firm rent a substantial lump of wealth – their human capital – to the firm, and the rental rates for their human capital signaled by the managerial labor market are likely to depend on the success or failure of the firm. The function of management is to oversee the contracts among factors and to ensure the viability of the firm. For the purposes of the managerial labor market, the previous associations of a manager with success and failure are information about his talents. The manager of a firm, like the coach of any team, may not suffer any immediate gain or loss in current wages from the current performance of his team, but the success or failure of the team impacts his future wages, and this gives the manager a stake in the success of the team.

The firm's security holders provide important but indirect assistance to the managerial labor market in its task of valuing the firm's management. A security holder wants to purchase securities with confidence that the prices paid reflect the risks he is taking and that the securities will be priced in the future to allow him to reap the rewards (or punishments) of his risk bearing. Thus, although an individual security holder may not have a strong interest in directly overseeing the management of a particular firm, he has a strong interest in the existence of a capital market which efficiently prices the firm's securities. The signals provided by an efficient capital market about the values of a firm's securities are likely to be important for the managerial labor market's revaluations of the firm's management.

We come now to the central question. To what extent can the signals provided by the managerial labor market and the capital market, perhaps along with other market-induced mechanisms, discipline managers? We first discuss, still in general terms, the types of discipline imposed by managerial labor markets,

---

[2] Detailed discussions of portfolio models can be found in Fama and Miller (1972, chaps. 6 and 7), Jensen (1972), and Fama (1976, chaps. 7 and 8).

both within and outside of the firm. We then analyze specific conditions under which this discipline is sufficient to resolve potential incentive problems that might be associated with the separation of security ownership and control.

The viability of separation of security ownership and control of the firm: general comments

The outside managerial labor market exerts many direct pressures on the firm to sort and compensate managers according to performance. One form of pressure comes from the fact that an ongoing firm is always in the market for new managers. Potential new managers are concerned with the mechanics by which their performance will be judged, and they seek information about the responsiveness of the system in rewarding performance. Moreover, given a competitive managerial labor market, when the firm's reward system is not responsive to performance the firm loses managers, and the best are the first to leave.

There is also much internal monitoring of managers by managers themselves. Part of the talent of a manager is his ability to elicit and measure the productivity of lower managers, so there is a natural process of monitoring from higher to lower levels of management. Less well appreciated, however, is the monitoring that takes place from bottom to top. Lower managers perceive that they can gain by stepping over or shirking less competent managers above them. Moreover, in the team or nexus of contracts view of the firm, each manager is concerned with the performance of managers above and below him since his marginal product is likely to be a positive function of theirs. Finally, although higher managers are affected more than lower managers, all managers realize that the managerial labor market uses the performance of the firm to determine each manager's outside opportunity wage. In short, each manager has a stake in the performance of the managers above and below him and, as a consequence, undertakes some amount of monitoring in both directions.

All managers below the very top level have an interest in seeing that the top managers choose policies for the firm which provide the most positive signals to the managerial labor market. But by what mechanism can top management be disciplined? Since the body designated for this function is the board of directors, we can ask how it might be constructed to do its job. A board dominated by security holders does not seem optimal or endowed with good survival properties. Diffuse ownership of securities is beneficial in terms of an optimal allocation of risk bearing, but its consequence is that the firm's security holders are generally too diversified across the securities of many firms to take much interest in a particular firm.

If there is competition among the top managers themselves (all want to be the boss of bosses), then perhaps they are the best ones to control the board of directors. They are most directly in the line of fire from lower managers when the markets for securities and managerial labor give poor signals about the performance of the firm. Because of their power over the firm's decisions, their market-determined opportunity wages are also likely to be most affected by market signals about the performance of the firm. If they are also in competition for the top places in the firm, they may be the most informed and responsive critics of the firm's performance.

Having gained control of the board, top management may decide that collusion and expropriation of security holder wealth are better than competition among themselves. The probability of such collusive arrangements might be lowered, and the viability of the board as a market-induced mechanism for low-cost internal transfer of control might be enhanced, by the inclusion of outside directors. The latter might best be regarded as professional referees whose task is to stimulate and oversee the competition among the firm's top managers. In a state of advanced evolution of the external markets that buttress the corporate firm, the outside directors are in their turn disciplined by the market for their services which prices them according to their performance as referees. Since such a system of separation of security ownership from control is consistent with the pressures applied by the managerial labor market, and since it likewise operates in the interests of the firm's security holders, it probably has good survival properties.[3]

This analysis does not imply that boards of directors are likely to be composed entirely of managers and outside directors. The board is viewed as a market-induced institution, the ultimate internal monitor of the set of contracts called a firm, whose most important role is to scrutinize the highest decision makers within the firm. In the team or nexus of contracts view of the firm, one cannot rule out the evolution of boards of directors that contain many different factors of production (or their hired representatives), whose common trait is that their marginal products are affected by those of the top decision makers. On the other hand, one also cannot conclude that all such factors will naturally show up on boards since there may be other market-induced institutions, for example, unions, that more efficiently monitor managers on behalf of specific factors. All one can say is that in a competitive environment lower-cost sets of monitoring mechanisms are likely to survive. The role of the board in this framework is to provide a relatively low-cost mechanism for replacing or reordering top managers; lower cost, for example, than the mechanism provided by an outside

---

[3] Watts and Zimmerman (1978) provide a similar description of the market-induced evolution of "independent" outside auditors whose function is to certify and, as a consequence, stimulate the viability of the set of contracts called the firm. Like the outside directors, the outside auditors are policed by the market for their services which prices them in large part on the basis of how well they resist perverting the interests of one set of factors (e.g., security holders) to the benefit of other factors (e.g., management). Like the professional outside director, the welfare of the outside auditor depends largely on "reputation."

takeover, although, of course, the existence of an outside market for control is another force which helps to sensitize the internal managerial labor market.

The perspective suggested here owes much to, but is nevertheless different from, existing treatments of the firm in the property rights literature. Thus, Alchian (1969) and Alchian and Demsetz (1972) comment insightfully on the disciplining of management that takes place through the inside and outside markets for managers. However, they attribute the task of disciplining management primarily to the risk bearers, the firm's security holders, who are assisted to some extent by managerial labor markets and by the possibility of outside takeover. Jensen and Meckling (1976b) likewise make control of management the province of the firm's risk bearers, but they do not allow for any assistance from the managerial labor market. Of all the authors in the property-rights literature, Manne (1965, 1967) is most concerned with the market for corporate control. He recognizes that with diffuse security ownership, management and risk bearing are naturally separate functions. But for him, disciplining management is an "entrepreneurial job" which in the first instance falls on a firm's organizers and later on specialists in the process of outside takeover.

When management and risk bearing are viewed as naturally separate factors of production, looking at the market for risk bearing from the viewpoint of portfolio theory tells us that risk bearers are likely to spread their wealth across many firms and so not to be interested in directly controlling the management of any individual firm. Thus, models of the firm, like those of Alchian–Demsetz and Jensen–Meckling, in which the control of management falls primarily on the risk bearers, are not likely to allay the fears of those concerned with the apparent incentive problems created by the separation of security ownership and control. Likewise, Manne's approach, in which the control of management relies primarily on the expensive mechanism of an outside takeover, offers little comfort. The viability of the large corporation with diffuse security ownership is better explained in terms of a model where the primary disciplining of managers comes through managerial labor markets, both within and outside of the firm, with assistance from the panoply of internal and external monitoring devices that evolve to stimulate the ongoing efficiency of the corporate form, and with the market for outside takeovers providing discipline of last resort.

The viability of separation of security ownership and control: details

The preceding is a general discussion of how pressure from managerial labor markets helps to discipline managers. We now examine somewhat more specifically conditions under which the discipline imposed by managerial labor markets can resolve potential incentive problems associated with the separation of security ownership and control of the firm.

To focus on the problem we are trying to solve, let us first examine the situation where the manager is also the firm's sole security holder, so that there is clearly no incentive problem. When he is sole security holder, a manager consumes on the job, through shirking, perquisites, or incompetence, to the point where these yield marginal expected utility equal to that provided by an additional dollar of wealth usable for consumption or investment outside of the firm. The manager is induced to make this specific decision because he pays directly for consumption on the job; that is, as manager he cannot avoid a full *ex post* settling up with himself as security holder.

In contrast, when the manager is no longer sole security holder, and in the absence of some form of full *ex post* settling up for deviations from contract, a manager has an incentive to consume more on the job than is agreed in his contract. The manager perceives that, on an *ex post* basis, he can beat the game by shirking or consuming more perquisites than previously agreed. This does not necessarily mean that the manager profits at the expense of other factors. Rational managerial labor markets understand any shortcomings of available mechanisms for enforcing *ex post* settling up. Assessments of *ex post* deviations from contract will be incorporated into contracts on an *ex ante* basis; for example, through an adjustment of the manager's wage.

Nevertheless, a game which is fair on an *ex ante* basis does not induce the same behavior as a game in which there is also *ex post* settling up. Herein lie the potential losses from separation of security ownership and control of a firm. There are situations where, with less than complete *ex post* settling up, the manager is induced to consume more on the job than he would like, given that on average he pays for his consumption *ex ante*.

Three general conditions suffice to make the wage revaluation imposed by the managerial labor market a form of full *ex post* settling up which resolves the managerial incentive problem described above. The first condition is that a manager's talents and his tastes for consumption on the job are not known with certainty, are likely to change through time, and must be imputed by managerial labor markets at least in part from information about the manager's current and past performance. Since it seems to capture the essence of the task of managerial labor markets in a world of uncertainty, this assumption is no real restriction.

The second assumption is that managerial labor markets appropriately use current and past information to revise future wages and understand any enforcement power inherent in the wage revision process. In short, contrary to much of the literature on separation of security ownership and control, we impute efficiency or rationality in information processing to managerial labor markets. In defense of this assumption, we note that the problem faced by managerial labor markets in revaluing the managers of a firm is much entwined with the problem faced by the capital market in revaluing the firm itself. Although we do not understand all the details of the process, available empirical evidence (e.g., Fama, 1976, chaps. 5 and 6) suggests that the capital market generally makes rational assessments of the value of the firm in the face of imprecise and uncertain information. This does not necessarily mean that information processing in managerial labor markets is equally efficient or rational, but it is a warning against strong presumption to the contrary.

The final and key condition for full control of managerial behavior through wage changes is that the weight of the wage revision process is sufficient to resolve any potential problems with managerial incentives. In this general form, the condition amounts to assuming the desired result. More substance is provided by specific examples.

. . .

Example: stochastic processes for marginal products

The next example of *ex post* settling up through the wage revision process is somewhat more formal than that described above. We make specific assumptions about the stochastic evolution of a manager's measured marginal product and about how the managerial labor market uses information from the process to adjust the manager's future wages – in a manner which amounts to precise, full *ex post* settling up for the results of past performance.

Suppose the manager's measured marginal product for any period t is composed of two terms: (i) an expected value, given his talents, effort exerted during t, consumption of perquisites, etc.; and (ii) random noise. The random noise may in part result from measurement error, that is, the sheer difficulty of accurately measuring marginal products when there is team production, but it may also arise in part from the fact that effort exerted and talent do not yield perfectly certain consequences. Moreover, because of the uncertain evolution of the manager's talents and tastes, the expected value of his marginal product is itself a stochastic process. Specifically, we assume that the expected value, $\bar{z}_t$, follows a random walk with steps that are independent of the random noise, ϵ_t, in the manager's measured marginal product, z_t. Thus, the measured marginal product,

$$z_t = \bar{z}_t + \epsilon_t, \tag{1}$$

is a random walk plus white noise. For simplicity, we also assume that this process describes the manager's marginal product both in his current employment and in the best alternative employment.

The characteristics (parameters) of the evolution of the manager's marginal product depend to some extent on endogenous variables like effort and perquisites consumed, which are not completely observable. Our purpose is

278

to set up the managerial labor market so that the wage revision process resolves any potential incentive problems that may arise from the endogeneity of z_t in a situation where there is separation of security ownership and control of the firm.

Suppose next that risk bearers are all risk neutral and that 1-period market interest rates are always equal to zero. Suppose also that managerial wage contracts are written so that the manager's wage in any period t is the expected value of his marginal product, $\bar{z}_t$, conditional on past measured values of his marginal product, with the risk bearers accepting the noise ϵ_t, in the *ex post* measurement of the marginal product. We shall see below that this is an optimal arrangement for our risk-neutral risk bearers. However, it is not necessarily optimal for the manager if he is risk averse. A risk-averse manager may want to sell part of the risk inherent in the uncertain evolution of his expected marginal product to the risk bearers, for example, through a long-term wage contract.

We avoid this issue by assuming that, perhaps because of the more extreme moral hazard problems in long-term contracts (remember that $\bar{z}_t$ is in part under the control of the manager) and the contracting costs to which these moral hazard problems give rise, simple contracts in which the manager's wage is reset at the beginning of each period are dominant, at least for some nontrivial subset of firms and managers.[4] If we could also assume away any remaining moral hazard (managerial incentive) problems, then with risk-averse managers, risk-neutral risk bearers, and the presumed fixed recontracting period, the contract which specifies *ex ante* that the manager will be paid the current expected value of his marginal product dominates any contract where the manager also shares the *ex post* deviation of his measured marginal product from its *ex ante* expected value (see, e.g., Spence and Zeckhauser, 1971).

However, contracts which specify *ex ante* that the manager will be paid the current expected value of his marginal product seem to leave the typical moral hazard problem that arises when there is less than complete *ex post* enforcement of contracts. The noise ϵ_t in the manager's marginal product is borne by the risk bearers. Once the manager's expected marginal product $\bar{z}_t$ ($=$ his current wage) has been assessed, he seems to have an incentive to consume more perquisites and provide less effort than are implied in $\bar{z}_t$.

A mechanism for *ex post* enforcement is, however, built into the model. With the expected value of the manager's marginal product wandering randomly

---

[4] Institutions like corporations, that are subject to rapid technological change with a large degree of uncertainty about future managerial needs, may find that long-term managerial contracts can only be negotiated at high cost. On the other hand, institutions like governments, schools, and universities may be able to forecast more reliably their future needs for managers (and other professionals) and so may be able to offer long-term contracts at relatively low cost. These institutions can then be expected to attract the relatively risk-averse members of the professional labor force, while the riskier employment offered by corporations attracts those who are willing to accept shorter-term contracts.

through time, future assessments of expected marginal products (and thus of wages) will be determined in part by ϵ_t, the deviation of the current measured marginal product from its *ex ante* expected value. In the present scenario, where $\bar{z}_t$ is assumed to follow a random walk, Muth (1960) has shown that the expected value of the marginal product evolves according to

$$\bar{z}_t = \bar{z}_{t-1} + (1 - \phi)\epsilon_{t-1}, \tag{2}$$

where the parameter ϕ ($0 < \phi < 1$) is closer to zero the smaller the variance of the noise term in the marginal product equation (1) relative to the variance of the steps in the random walk followed by the expected marginal product.

In fact, the process by which future expected marginal products are adjusted on the basis of past deviations of marginal products from their expected values leads to a precise form of full *ex post* settling up. This is best seen by writing the marginal product z_t in its inverted form, that is, in terms of past marginal products and the current noise. The inverted form for our model, a random walk embedded in random noise is

$$z_t = (1 - \phi)z_{t-1} + \phi(1 - \phi)z_{t-2} + \phi^2(1 - \phi)z_{t-3} + \cdots + \epsilon_t, \tag{3}$$

so that

$$\bar{z}_t = (1 - \phi)z_{t-1} + \phi(1 - \phi)z_{t-2} + \phi^2(1 - \phi)z_{t-3} + \cdots \tag{4}$$

(see, e.g., Nelson, 1973, chap. 4; or Muth, 1960).

For our purposes, the interesting fact is that, although he is paid his *ex ante* expected marginal product, the manager does not get to avoid his *ex post* marginal product. For example, we can infer from (4) that z_{t-1} has weight $1 - \phi$ in $\bar{z}_t$; then it has weight $\phi(1 - \phi)$ in $\bar{z}_{t+1}$, $\phi^2(1 - \phi)$ in $\bar{z}_{t+2}$, and so on. In the end, the sum of the contributions of z_{t-1} to future expected marginal products, and thus to future wages, is exactly z_{t-1}. With zero interest rates, this means that the risk bearers simply allow the manager to smooth his marginal product across future periods at the going opportunity cost of all such temporal wealth transfers. As a consequence, the manager has no incentive to try to bury shirking or consumption of perquisites in his *ex post* measured marginal product.

Since the managerial labor market is presumed to understand the weight of the wage revision process, which in this case amounts to precise full *ex post* settling up, any potential managerial incentive problems in the separation of risk bearing, or security ownership, from control are resolved. The manager can contract for and take an optimal amount of consumption on the job. The wage set *ex ante* need not include any allowance for *ex post* incentives to deviate from the contract since the wage revision process neutralizes any such incentives. Note, moreover, that the value of ϕ in the wage revision process described by (4) determines how the observed marginal product of any given period is subdivided and spread across future periods; but whatever the value of ϕ, the given marginal product is fully accounted for in the stream of future wages. Thus, it is now clear what was meant by the earlier claim that although the parameter ϕ in the process generating the manager's marginal product is to some extent under his control, this is not a matter of particular concern to the managerial labor market.

A somewhat evident qualification is in order. The smoothing process described by (4) contains an infinite number of terms, whereas any manager has a finite working life. For practical purposes, full *ex post* settling up is achieved as long as the manager's current marginal product is "very nearly" fully absorbed by the stream of wages over his future working life. This requires a value of ϕ in (4) which is sufficiently far from 1.0, given the number of periods remaining in the manager's working life. Recall that ϕ is closer to 1.0 the larger the variance of the noise in the manager's measured marginal product relative to the variance of the steps of the random walk taken by the expected value of his marginal product. Intuitively, when the variance of the noise term is large relative to that of the changes in the expected value, the current measured marginal product has a weak signal about any change in the expected value of the marginal product, and the current marginal product is only allocated slowly to expected future marginal products.

Some extensions

Having qualified the analysis, let us now indicate some ways in which it is robust to changes in details of the model.

1. More complicated models for the manager's marginal product.

The critical ingredient in enforcing precise full *ex post* settling up through wage revisions on the basis of reassessments of expected marginal products is that when the marginal product and its expected value are expressed in inverted form, as in (3) and (4), the sum of the weights on past marginal products is exactly 1.0. This will be the case (see, e.g., Nelson, 1973, chap. 4) whenever the manager's marginal product conforms to a nonstationary stochastic process, but the changes from period to period in the marginal product conform to some stationary ARMA (mixed autoregressive moving average) process. The example summarized in equations (1)–(4) is the interesting but special case where the expected marginal product follows a random walk so that the differences of the marginal product are a stationary, first-order moving average process. The general case allows the expected value of the marginal product to follow any more complicated nonstationary process which has the property that the differences of the marginal product are stationary, so that the marginal product and its expected value can be expressed in inverted form as

$$z_t = \pi_1 z_{t-1} + \pi_2 z_{t-2} + \cdots + \epsilon_t \tag{5}$$

$$\bar{z}_t = \pi_1 z_{t-1} + \pi_2 z_{t-2} + \cdots \tag{6}$$

with

$$\sum_{i=1}^{\infty} \pi_i = 1. \tag{7}$$

These can be viewed as the general conditions for enforcing precise full *ex post* settling through the wage revision process when the manager's wage is equal to the current expected value of his marginal product.[5]

· · ·

---

[5] When $\bar{z}_t$ follows a stationary process, the long-run average value toward which the process always tends will eventually be known with near perfect certainty. Thus, the case of a stationary expected marginal product is of little interest, at least for the purpose of *ex post* settling up enforced by the wage revision process.

CHAPTER 21

Theory of the firm: managerial behavior, agency costs, and ownership structure

MICHAEL JENSEN AND WILLIAM MECKLING

Michael Jensen was born in 1939 in Rochester, New York. He received a Ph.D. in finance from the University of Chicago in 1968. When this paper was published, he was Associate Professor at the University of Rochester. Since 1989, he has taught at the Graduate School of Business Administration, Harvard University, where he is currently the Jesse Isidor Straus Professor of Business Administration, Emeritus.

William Meckling (1921–1998) was born in McKeesport, Pennsylvania. He received an M.B.A. degree at the University of Denver in 1947 and did postgraduate work at the University of Chicago from 1949 to 1952. When this paper was published, he was Dean of the Graduate School of Management, University of Rochester.

The directors of such [joint stock] companies, however, being the managers rather of other people's money than of their own, it cannot well be expected that they should watch over it with the same anxious vigilance with which the partners in a private copartnery frequently watch over their own. Like the stewards of a rich man, they are easily apt to consider attention to small matters as not for their master's honour and very easily give themselves a dispensation from having it. Negligence and profusion, therefore, must always prevail, more or less, in the management of the affairs of such a company.

Adam Smith, *The Wealth of Nations*, 1776, Cannan Edition
(Modern Library, New York, 1937), p. 700.

1. Introduction and summary

1.1. Motivation of the paper

In this paper we draw on recent progress in the theory of (1) property rights, (2) agency, and (3) finance to develop a theory of ownership structure[1] for the

Reprinted in abridged form from Michael Jensen and William Meckling, "Theory of the Firm: Managerial Behavior, Agency Costs and Ownership Structure," *The Journal of Financial Economics*, 3 (1976): 305–60, by permission of the publisher.

[1] We do not use the term "capital structure" because that term usually denotes the relative quantities of bonds, equity, warrants, trade credit, etc., which represent the liabilities of a firm. Our theory implies there is another important dimension to this problem – namely the relative amounts of ownership claims held by insiders (management) and outsiders (investors with no direct role in the management of the firm).

firm. In addition to tying together elements of the theory of each of these three areas, our analysis casts new light on and has implications for a variety of issues in the professional and popular literature such as the definition of the firm, the "separation of ownership and control," the "social responsibility" of business, the definition of a "corporate objective function," the determination of an optimal capital structure, the specification of the content of credit agreements, the theory of organizations, and the supply side of the completeness of markets problem.

Our theory helps explain:

1. why an entrepreneur or manager in a firm which has a mixed financial structure (containing both debt and outside equity claims) will choose a set of activities for the firm such that the total value of the firm is *less* than it would be if he were the sole owner and why this result is independent of whether the firm operates in monopolistic or competitive produce or factor markets;

2. why his failure to maximize the value of the firm is perfectly consistent with efficiency;

3. why the sale of common stock is a viable source of capital even though managers do not literally maximize the value of the firm;

4. why debt was relied upon as a source of capital before debt financing offered any tax advantage relative to equity;

5. why preferred stock would be issued;

6. why accounting reports would be provided voluntarily to creditors and stockholders, and why independent auditors would be engaged by management to testify to the accuracy and correctness of such reports;

7. why lenders often place restrictions on the activities of firms to whom they lend, and why firms would themselves be led to suggest the imposition of such restrictions;

8. why some industries are characterized by owner-operated firms whose sole outside source of capital is borrowing;

9. why highly regulated industries such as public utilities or banks will have higher debt equity ratios for equivalent levels of risk than the average nonregulated firm;

10. why security analysis can be socially productive even if it does not increase portfolio returns to investors.

1.2. Theory of the firm: an empty box?

While the literature of economics is replete with references to the "theory of the firm," the material generally subsumed under that heading is not a theory of the firm but actually a theory of markets in which firms are important actors. The firm is a "black box" operated so as to meet the relevant marginal conditions with respect to inputs and outputs, thereby maximizing profits, or more accurately, present value. Except for a few recent and tentative steps, however, we have no theory which explains how the conflicting objectives of the individual participants are brought into equilibrium so as to yield this result. The limitations of this black box view of the firm have been cited by Adam Smith and Alfred Marshall, among others. More recently, popular and professional debates over the "social responsibility" of corporations, the separation of ownership and control, and the rash of reviews of the literature on the "theory of the firm" have evidenced continuing concern with these issues.[2]

A number of major attempts have been made during recent years to construct a theory of the firm by substituting other models for profit or value maximization; each attempt motivated by a conviction that the latter is inadequate to explain managerial behavior in large corporations.[3] Some of these reformulation attempts have rejected the fundamental principle of maximizing behavior as well as rejecting the more specific profit maximizing model. We retain the notion of maximizing behavior on the part of all individuals in the analysis to follow.[4]

1.3. Property rights

An independent stream of research with important implications for the theory of the firm has been stimulated by the pioneering work of Coase and extended by Alchian, Demsetz, and others.[5] A comprehensive survey of this literature is

[2] Reviews of this literature are given by Peterson (1965), Alchian (1965, 1968), Machlup (1967), Shubik (1970), Cyert and Hedrick (1972), Branch (1973), Preston (1975).

[3] See Williamson (1964b, 1970, 1975), Marris (1964), Baumol (1959), Penrose (1958), and Cyert and March (1963). Thorough reviews of these and other contributions are given by Machlup (1961) and Alchian (1965).

Simon (1955) developed a model of human choice incorporating information (search) and computational costs which also has important implications for the behavior of managers. Unfortunately, Simon's work has often been misinterpreted as a denial of maximizing behavior and misused, especially in the marketing and behavioral science literature. His later use of the term "satisficing" (Simon, 1959) has undoubtedly contributed to this confusion because it suggests rejection of maximizing behavior rather than maximization subject to costs of information and of decision making.

[4] See Meckling (1976) for a discussion of the fundamental importance of the assumption of resourceful, evaluative, maximizing behavior on the part of individuals in the development of theory. Klein (1976) takes an approach similar to the one we embark on in this paper in his review of the theory of the firm and the law.

[5] See Coase (1937, 1959, 1960), Alchian (1965, 1968), Alchian and Kessel (1962), Demsetz (1967), Alchian and Demsetz (1972), Monsen and Downs (1965), Silver and Auster (1969), and McManus (1975).

given by Furubotn and Pejovich (1972). While the focus of this research has been "property rights,"[6] the subject matter encompassed is far broader than that term suggests. What is important for the problems addressed here is that specification of individual rights determines how costs and rewards will be allocated among the participants in any organization. Since the specification of rights is generally effected through contracting (implicit as well as explicit), individual behavior in organizations, including the behavior of managers, will depend upon the nature of these contracts. We focus in this paper on the behavioral implications of the property rights specified in the contracts between the owners and managers of the firm.

1.4. Agency costs

Many problems associated with the inadequacy of the current theory of the firm can also be viewed as special cases of the theory of agency relationships in which there is a growing literature.[7] This literature has developed independently of the property rights literature even though the problems with which it is concerned are similar; the approaches are in fact highly complementary to each other.

We define an agency relationship as a contract under which one or more persons (the principal(s)) engage another person (the agent) to perform some service on their behalf which involves delegating some decision making authority to the agent. If both parties to the relationship are utility maximizers there is good reason to believe that the agent will not always act in the best interests of the principal. The *principal* can limit divergences from his interest by establishing appropriate incentives for the agent and by incurring monitoring costs designed to limit the aberrant activities of the agent. In addition in some situations it will pay the *agent* to expend resources (bonding costs) to guarantee that he will not take certain actions which would harm the principal or to ensure that the principal will be compensated if he does take such actions. However, it is generally impossible for the principal or the agent at zero cost to ensure that the agent will make optimal decisions from the principal's viewpoint. In most agency relationships the principal and the agent will incur positive monitoring and bonding costs (nonpecuniary as well as pecuniary), and in all there will be some divergence between the agent's decisions[8] and those decisions which would maximize the welfare of the principal. The dollar equivalent of the reduction in welfare experienced by the principal due to this divergence is

---

[6] Property rights are of course human rights, i.e., rights which are possessed by human beings. The introduction of the wholly false distinction between property rights and human rights in many policy discussions is surely one of the all time great semantic flimflams.

[7] Cf. Berhold (1971), Ross (1973, 1974), Wilson (1968, 1969), and Heckerman (1975).

[8] Given the optimal monitoring and bonding activities by the principal and agent.

also a cost of the agency relationship, and we refer to this latter cost as the "residual loss." We define *agency costs* as the sum of:

1. the monitoring expenditures by the principal,[9]
2. the bonding expenditures by the agent,
3. the residual loss.

Note also that agency costs arise in any situation involving cooperative effort (such as the coauthoring of this paper) by two or more people even though there is no clear cut principal–agent relationship. Viewed in this light it is clear that our definition of agency costs and their importance to the theory of the firm bears a close relationship to the problem of shirking and monitoring of team production which Alchian and Demsetz (1972) raise in their paper on the theory of the firm.

Since the relationship between the stockholders and manager of a corporation fit the definition of a pure agency relationship, it should be no surprise to discover that the issues associated with the "separation of ownership and control" in the modern diffuse ownership corporation are intimately associated with the general problem of agency. We show below that an explanation of why and how the agency costs generated by the corporate form are born leads to a theory of the ownership (or capital) structure of the firm.

Before moving on, however, it is worthwhile to point out the generality of the agency problem. The problem of inducing an "agent" to behave as if he were maximizing the "principal's" welfare is quite general. It exists in all organizations and in all cooperative efforts – at every level of management in firms,[10] in universities, in mutual companies, in cooperatives, in governmental authorities and bureaus, in unions, and in relationships normally classified as agency relationships such as are common in the performing arts and the market for real estate. The development of theories to explain the form which agency costs take in each of these situations (where the contractual relations differ significantly) and how and why they are born will lead to a rich theory

---

[9] As it is used in this paper the term *monitoring* includes more than just measuring or observing the behavior of the agent. It includes efforts on the part of the principal to "control" the behavior of the agent through budget restrictions, compensation policies, operating rules, etc.

[10] As we show below, the existence of positive monitoring and bonding costs will result in the manager of a corporation possessing control over some resources which he can allocate (within certain constraints) to satisfy his own preferences. However, to the extent that he must obtain the cooperation of others in order to carry out his tasks (such as divisional vice presidents) and to the extent that he cannot control their behavior perfectly and costlessly, they will be able to appropriate some of these resources for their own ends. In short, there are agency costs generated at every level of the organization. Unfortunately, the analysis of these more general organizational issues is even more difficult than that of the "ownership and control" issue because the nature of the contractual obligations and rights of the parties are much more varied and generally not as well specified in explicit contractual arrangements. Nevertheless, they exist and we believe that extensions of our analysis in these directions show promise of producing insights into a viable theory of organization.

of organizations which is now lacking in economics and the social sciences generally. We confine our attention in this paper to only a small part of this general problem – the analysis of agency costs generated by the contractual arrangements between the owners and top management of the corporation.

Our approach to the agency problem here differs fundamentally from most of the existing literature. That literature focuses almost exclusively on the normative aspects of the agency relationship, that is, how to structure the contractual relation (including compensation incentives) between the principal and agent to provide appropriate incentives for the agent to make choices which will maximize the principal's welfare given that uncertainty and imperfect monitoring exist. We focus almost entirely on the positive aspects of the theory. That is, we assume individuals solve these normative problems, and given that only stocks and bonds can be issued as claims, we investigate the incentives faced by each of the parties and the elements entering into the determination of the equilibrium contractual form characterizing the relationship between the manager (i.e., agent) of the firm and the outside equity and debt holders (i.e., principals).

1.5. Some general comment on the definition of the firms

Ronald Coase (1937) in his seminal paper on "The Nature of the Firm" pointed out that economics had no positive theory to determine the bounds of the firm. He characterized the bounds of the firm as that range of exchanges over which the market system was suppressed and resource allocation was accomplished instead by authority and direction. He focused on the cost of using markets to effect contracts and exchanges and argued that activities would be included within the firm whenever the costs of using markets were greater than the costs of using direct authority. Alchian and Demsetz (1972) object to the notion that activities within the firm are governed by authority, and correctly emphasize the role of contracts as a vehicle for voluntary exchange. They emphasize the role of monitoring in situations in which there is joint input or team production.[11] We sympathize with the importance they attach to monitoring, but we believe the emphasis which Alchian–Demsetz place on joint input production is too narrow and therefore misleading. Contractual relations are the essence of the firm, not only with employees but with suppliers, customers, creditors, etc. The problem of agency costs and monitoring exists for all of these contracts, independent

---

[11] They define the classical capitalist firm as a contractual organization of inputs in which there is "(a) joint input production, (b) several inputs owners, (c) one party who is common to all the contracts of the joint inputs, (d) who has rights to renegotiate any input's contract independently of contracts with other input owners, (e) who holds the residual claim, and (f) who has the right to sell his contractual residual status."

of whether there is joint production in their sense; i.e., joint production can explain only a small fraction of the behavior of individuals associated with a firm. A detailed examination of these issues is left to another paper.

It is important to recognize that most organizations are simply *legal fictions*[12] *which serve as a nexus for a set of contracting relationships among individuals.* This includes firms; nonprofit institutions such as universities, hospitals, and foundations; mutual organizations such as mutual savings banks and insurance companies; and cooperatives; some private clubs; and even governmental bodies such as cities, states and the Federal government; government enterprises such as TVA, the Post Office, transit systems, etc.

The private corporation or firm is simply one form of *legal fiction which serves as a nexus for contracting relationships and which is also characterized by the existence of divisible residual claims on the assets and cash flows of the organization which can generally be sold without permission of the other contracting individuals.* While this definition of the firm has little substantive content, emphasizing the essential contractual nature of firms and other organizations focuses attention on a crucial set of questions – why particular sets of contractual relations arise for various types of organizations, what the consequences of these contractual relations are, and how they are affected by changes exogenous to the organization. Viewed this way, it makes little or no sense to try to distinguish those things which are "inside" the firm (or any other organization) from those things that are "outside" of it. There is in a very real sense only a multitude of complex relationships (i.e., contracts) between the legal fiction (the firm) and the owners of labor, material, and capital inputs and the consumers of output.[13]

Viewing the firm as the nexus of a set of contracting relationships among individuals also serves to make it clear that the personalization of the firm implied by asking questions such as "what should be the objective function of the firm," or "does the firm have a social responsibility" is seriously misleading. *The firm is not an individual.* It is a legal fiction which serves as a focus for a complex process in which the conflicting objectives of individuals (some of whom may "represent" other organizations) are brought into equilibrium within a framework of contractual relations. In this sense the "behavior" of the firm is like the behavior of a market, i.e., the outcome of a complex equilibrium

---

[12] By legal fiction we mean the artificial construct under the law which allows certain organizations to be treated as individuals.

[13] For example, we ordinarily think of a product as leaving the firm at the time it is sold, but implicitly or explicitly such sales generally carry with them continuing contracts between the firm and the buyer. If the product does not perform as expected the buyer often can and does have a right to satisfaction. Explicit evidence that such implicit contracts do exist is the practice we occasionally observe of specific provision that "all sales are final."

process. We seldom fall into the trap of characterizing the wheat or stock market as an individual, but we often make this error by thinking about organizations as if they were persons with motivations and intentions.[14]

1.6. An overview of the paper

We develop the theory in stages. Sections 2 and 4 provide analyses of the agency costs of equity and debt, respectively. These form the major foundation of the theory. Section 3 poses some unanswered questions regarding the existence of the corporate form of organization and examines the role of limited liability. Section 5 provides a synthesis of the basic concepts derived in sections 2–4 into a theory of the corporate ownership structure which takes account of the trade-offs available to the entrepreneur-manager between inside and outside equity and debt. Some qualifications and extensions of the analysis are discussed in section 6, and section 7 contains a brief summary and conclusions.

2. The agency costs of outside equity

2.1. Overview

In this section we analyze the effect of outside equity on agency costs by comparing the behavior of a manager when he owns 100 percent of the residual claims on a firm to his behavior when he sells off a portion of those claims to outsiders. If a wholly owned firm is managed by the owner, he will make operating decisions which maximize his utility. These decisions will involve not only the benefits he derives from pecuniary returns but also the utility generated by various nonpecuniary aspects of his entrepreneurial activities such as the physical appointments of the office, the attractiveness of the secretarial staff, the level of employee discipline, the kind and amount of charitable contributions, personal relations ("love," "respect," etc.) with employees, a larger than optimal computer to play with, purchase of production inputs from

---

[14] This view of the firm points up the important role which the legal system and the law play in social organizations, especially the organization of economic activity. Statutory law sets bounds on the kinds of contracts into which individuals and organizations may enter without risking criminal prosecution. The police powers of the state are available and used to enforce performance of contracts or to enforce the collection of damages for nonperformance. The courts adjudicate conflicts between contracting parties and establish precedents which form the body of common law. All of these government activities affect both the kinds of contracts executed and the extent to which contracting is relied upon. This in turn determines the usefulness, productivity, profitability, and viability of various forms of organization. Moreover, new laws as well as court decisions often can and do change the rights of contracting parties *ex post*, and they can and do serve as a vehicle for redistribution of wealth. An analysis of some of the implications of these facts is contained in Jensen and Meckling (1976a) and we shall not pursue them here.

friends, etc. The optimum mix (in the absence of taxes) of the various pecuniary and nonpecuniary benefits is achieved when the marginal utility derived from an additional dollar of expenditure (measured net of any productive effects) is equal for each nonpecuniary item and equal to the marginal utility derived from an additional dollar of after tax purchasing power (wealth).

If the owner-manager sells equity claims on the corporation which are identical to his (i.e., share proportionately in the profits of the firm and have limited liability), agency costs will be generated by the divergence between his interest and those of the outside shareholders, since he will then bear only a fraction of the costs of any nonpecuniary benefits he takes out in maximizing his own utility. If the manager owns only 95 percent of the stock, he will expend resources to the point where the marginal utility derived from a dollar's expenditure of the firm's resources on such items equals the marginal utility of an additional 95 cents in general purchasing power (i.e., *his* share of the wealth reduction) and not one dollar. Such activities, on his part, can be limited (but probably not eliminated) by the expenditure of resources on monitoring activities by the outside stockholders. But as we show below, the owner will bear the entire wealth effects of these expected costs so long as the equity market anticipates these effects. Prospective minority shareholders will realize that the owner-manager's interests will diverge somewhat from theirs, hence the price which they will pay for shares will reflect the monitoring costs and the effect of the divergence between the manager's interest and theirs. Nevertheless, ignoring for the moment the possibility of borrowing against his wealth, the owner will find it desirable to bear these costs as long as the welfare increment he experiences from converting his claims on the firm into general purchasing power[15] is large enough to offset them.

As the owner-manager's fraction of the equity falls, his fractional claim on the outcomes falls and this will tend to encourage him to appropriate larger amounts of the corporate resources in the form of perquisites. This also makes it desirable for the minority shareholders to expend more resources in monitoring his behavior. Thus, the wealth costs to the owner of obtaining additional cash in the equity markets rise as his fractional ownership falls.

We shall continue to characterize the agency conflict between the owner-manager and outside shareholders as deriving from the manager's tendency to appropriate perquisites out of the firm's resources for his own consumption. However, we do not mean to leave the impression that this is the only or even the most important source of conflict. Indeed, it is likely that the most important conflict arises from the fact that as the manager's ownership claim falls, his

---

[15] For use in consumption, for the diversification of his wealth, or more importantly, for the financing of "profitable" projects which he could not otherwise finance out of his personal wealth. We deal with these issues below after having developed some of the elementary analytical tools necessary to their solution.

incentive to devote significant effort to creative activities such as searching out new profitable ventures falls. He may, in fact, avoid such ventures simply because it requires too much trouble or effort on his part to manage or to learn about new technologies. Avoidance of these personal costs and the anxieties that go with them also represent a source of on the job utility to him and it can result in the value of the firm being substantially lower than it otherwise could be.

2.2. A simple formal analysis of the sources of agency costs of equity and who bears them

In order to develop some structure for the analysis to follow, we make two sets of assumptions. The first set (permanent assumptions) are those which shall carry through almost all of the analysis in section 2–5. The effects of relaxing some of these are discussed in section 6. The second set (temporary assumptions) are made only for expositional purposes and are relaxed as soon as the basic points have been clarified.

Permanent assumptions

P.1. All taxes are zero.

P.2. No trade credit is available.

P.3. All outside equity shares are nonvoting.

P.4. No complex financial claims such as convertible bonds or preferred stock or warrants can be issued.

P.5. No outside owner gains utility from ownership in a firm in any way other than through its effect on his wealth or cash flows.

P.6. All dynamic aspects of the multiperiod nature of the problem are ignored by assuming there is only one production–financing decision to be made by the entrepreneur.

P.7. The entrepreneur-manager's money wages are held constant throughout the analysis.

P.8. There exists a single manager (the peak coordinator) with ownership interest in the firm.

Temporary assumptions

T.1. The size of the firm is fixed.

T.2. No monitoring or bonding activities are possible.

T.3. No debt financing through bonds, preferred stock, or personal borrowing (secured or unsecured) is possible.

T.4. All elements of the owner-manager's decision problem involving portfolio considerations induced by the presence of uncertainty and the existence of diversifiable risk are ignored.

Define:

X $=$ $\{x_1, x_2, \ldots, x_n\} =$ vector of quantities of all factors and activities within the firm from which the manager derives nonpecuniary benefits;[16] the x_i are defined such that this marginal utility is positive for each of them;

$C(X)$ $=$ total dollar cost of providing any given amount of these items;

$P(X)$ $=$ total dollar value to the firm of the productive benefits of X;

$B(X)$ $=$ $P(X) - C(X) =$ net dollar benefit to the firm of X ignoring any effects of X on the equilibrium wage of the manager.

Ignoring the effects of X on the manager's utility and therefore on his equilibrium wage rate, the optimum levels of the factors and activities X are defined by X^* such that

$$\frac{\partial B\,(X^*)}{\partial X^*} = \frac{\partial P\,(X^*)}{\partial X^*} - \frac{\partial C\,(X^*)}{\partial X^*} = 0$$

Thus for any vector $X \geq X^*$ (i.e., where at least one element of X is greater than its corresponding element of X^*), $F \equiv B(X^*) - B(X) > 0$ measures the dollar cost to the firm (net of any productive effects) of providing the increment $X - X^*$ of the factors and activities which generate utility to the manager. We assume henceforth that for any given level of cost to the firm, F, the vector of factors and activities on which F is spent are those, $\hat{X}$, which yield the manager maximum utility. Thus $F \equiv B(X^*) - B(\hat{X})$.

We have thus far ignored in our discussion the fact that these expenditures on X occur through time and therefore there are trade-offs to be made across time as well as between alternative elements of X. Furthermore, we have ignored the fact that the future expenditures are likely to involve uncertainty (i.e., they are subject to probability distributions) and therefore some allowance must be made for their riskiness. We resolve both of these issues by defining C, P, B, and F to be the *current market values* of the sequence of probability distributions on the period by period cash flows involved.[17]

Given the definition of F as the current market value of the stream of manager's expenditures on nonpecuniary benefits we represent the constraint which a single owner-manager faces in deciding how much nonpecuniary income he will extract from the firm by the line $\bar{V}F$ in Figure 21.1. This is analogous to a budget constraint. The market value of the firm is measured along the vertical axis and the market value of the manager's stream of expenditures on nonpecuniary benefits, F, are measured along the horizontal axis. $0\bar{V}$ is the value of

[16] Such as office space, air conditioning, thickness of the carpets, friendliness of employee relations, etc.

[17] And again we assume that for any given market value of these costs, F, to the firm, the allocation across time and across alternative probability distribution is such that the manager's current expected utility is at a maximum.

MARKET VALUE OF THE STREAM OF MANAGER'S EXPENDITURES
ON NON-PECUNIARY BENEFITS

Figure 21.1. The value of the firm (V) and the level of nonpecuniary benefits consumed (F) when the fraction of outside equity is $(1 - \alpha)V$, and U_1 ($j = 1, 2, 3$) represents owner's indifference curves between wealth and nonpecuniary benefits.

the firm when the amount of nonpecuniary income consumed is zero. By definition $\bar{V}$ is the maximum market value of the cash flows generated by the firm for a given money wage for the manager when the manager's consumption of nonpecuniary benefits are zero. At this point all the factors and activities within the firm which generate utility for the manager are at level X^* defined above. There is a different budget constraint $\bar{V}F$ for each possible scale of the firm (i.e., level of investment, I) and for alternative levels of money wage, W, for the manager. For the moment we pick an arbitrary level of investment (which we assume has already been made) and hold the scale of the firm constant at this level. We also assume that the manager's money wage is fixed at the level W^* which represents the current market value of his wage contract[18] in the optimal compensation package which consists of both wages, W^*, and nonpecuniary benefits, F^*. Since one dollar of current value of nonpecuniary benefits

[18] At this stage when we are considering a 100% owner-managed firm the notion of a "wage contract" with himself has no content. However, the 100% owner-managed case is only an expositional device used in passing to illustrate a number of points in the analysis, and we ask the reader to bear with us briefly while we lay out the structure for the more interesting partial ownership case where such a contract does have substance.

withdrawn from the firm by the manager reduces the market value of the firm by \$1, by definition, the slope of $\bar{V}F$ is -1.

The owner-manager's tastes for wealth and nonpecuniary benefits is represented in Figure 21.1 by a system of indifference curves, U_1, U_2, etc.[19] The indifference curves will be convex as drawn as long as the owner-manager's marginal rate of substitution between nonpecuniary benefits and wealth diminishes with increasing levels of the benefits. For the 100 percent owner-manager, this presumes that there are not perfect substitutes for these benefits available on the outside, i.e., to some extent they are job specific. For the fractional owner-manager this presumes the benefits cannot be turned into general purchasing power at a constant price.[20]

When the owner has 100 percent of the equity, the value of the firm will be V^* where indifference curve U_2 is tangent to VF, and the level of nonpecuniary benefits consumed is F^*. If the owner sells the entire equity but remains as manager, and if the equity buyer can, at zero cost, force the old owner (as manager) to take the same level of nonpecuniary benefits as he did as owner, then V^* is the price the new owner will be willing to pay for the entire equity.[21]

---

[19] The manager's utility function is actually defined over wealth and the future time sequence of vectors of quantities of nonpecuniary benefits, X_t. Although the setting of his problem is somewhat different, Fama (1970, 1972) analyzes the conditions under which these preferences can be represented as a derived utility function defined as a function of the money value of the expenditures (in our notation F) on these goods conditional on the prices of goods. Such a utility function incorporates the optimization going on in the background which define $\hat{X}$ discussed above for a given F. In the more general case where we allow a time series of consumption, $\hat{X}_t$, the optimization is being carried out across both time and the components of X_t for fixed F.

[20] This excludes, for instance, (a) the case where the manager is allowed to expend corporate resources on anything he pleases, in which case F would be a perfect substitute for wealth; or (b) the case where he can "steal" cash (or other marketable assets) with constant returns to scale – if he could, the indifference curves would be straight lines with slope determined by the fence commission.

[21] Point D defines the fringe benefits in the optimal pay package since the value to the manager of the fringe benefits F^* is greater than the cost of providing them as is evidenced by the fact that U_2 is steeper to the left of D than the budget constraint with slope equal to -1.

That D is indeed the optimal pay package can easily be seen in this situation since if the conditions of the sale to a new owner specified that the manager would receive no fringe benefits after the sale, he would require a payment equal to V_3 to compensate him for the sacrifice of his claims to V^* and fringe benefits amounting to F^* (the latter with total value to him of $V_3 - V^*$). But if $F = 0$, the value of the firm is only $\bar{V}$. Therefore, if monitoring costs were zero, the sale would take place at V^* with provision for a pay package which included fringe benefits of F^* for the manager.

This discussion seems to indicate there are two values for the "firm," V_3 and V^*. This is not the case if we realize that V^* is the value of the right to be the residual claimant on the cash flows of the firm and $V_3 - V^*$ is the value of the managerial rights, i.e., the right to make the operating decisions which include access to F^*. There is at least one other right which has value which plays no formal role in the analysis as yet – the value of the control right. By control right we mean the right to hire and fire the manager, and we leave this issue to a future paper.

In general, however, we would not expect the new owner to be able to enforce identical behavior on the old owner at zero costs. If the old owner sells a fraction of the firm to an outsider, he, as manager, will no longer bear the full cost of any nonpecuniary benefits he consumes. Suppose the owner sells a share of the firm, $1 - \alpha$, $(0 < \alpha < 1)$ and retains for himself a share, α. If the prospective buyer believes that the owner-manager will consume the same level of nonpecuniary benefits as he did as full owner, the buyer will be willing to pay $(1 - \alpha)V^*$ for a fraction $(1 - \alpha)$ of the equity. Given that an outsider now holds a claim to $(1 - \alpha)$ of the equity, however, the *cost* to the owner-manager of consuming \$1 of nonpecuniary benefits in the firm will no longer be \$1. Instead, it will be $\alpha \times \$1$. If the prospective buyer actually paid $(1 - \alpha)V^*$ for his share of the equity, and if thereafter the manager could choose whatever level of nonpecuniary benefits he liked, his budget constraint would be V_1P_1 in Figure 21.1 and has a slope equal to $-\alpha$. Including the payment the owner receives from the buyers as part of the owner's postsale wealth, his budget constraint V_1P_1, must pass through D, since he can if he wishes have the same wealth and level of nonpecuniary consumption he consumed as full owner.

But if the owner-manager is free to choose the level of perquisites, F, subject only to the loss in wealth he incurs as a part owner, his welfare will be maximized by increasing his consumption of nonpecuniary benefits. He will move to point A where V_1P_1 is tangent to U_1, representing a higher level of utility. The value of the firm falls from V^* to V^0, i.e., by the amount of the cost to the firm of the increased nonpecuniary expenditures, and the owner-manager's consumption of nonpecuniary benefits rises from F^* to F^0.

If the equity market is characterized by rational expectations the buyers will be aware that the owner will increase his nonpecuniary consumption when his ownership share is reduced. If the owner's response function is known or if the equity market makes unbiased estimates of the owner's response to the changed incentives, the buyer will not pay $(1 - \alpha)V^*$ for $(1 - \alpha)$ of the equity.

Theorem. For a claim of the firm of $(1 - \alpha)$ the outsider will pay only $(1 - \alpha)$ times the value he expects the firm to have given the induced change in the behavior of the owner-manager.

Proof. For simplicity we ignore any element of uncertainty introduced by the lack of perfect knowledge of the owner-manager's response function. Such uncertainty will not affect the final solution if the equity market is large as long as the estimates are rational (i.e., unbiased) and the errors are independent across firms. The latter condition assures that this risk is diversifiable and therefore equilibrium prices will equal the expected values.

Let W represent the owner's total wealth after he has sold a claim equal to $1 - \alpha$ of the equity to an outsider. W has two components. One is the payment, S_0, made by the outsider for $1 - \alpha$ of the equity; the rest, S_i, is the value of the owner's (i.e., insider's) share of the firm, so that W, the owner's wealth, is given by

$$W = S_0 + S_i = S_0 + \alpha V(F, \alpha),$$

where $V(F, \alpha)$ represents the value of the firm given that the manager's fractional ownership share is α and that he consumes perquisites with current market value of F. Let $V_2 P_2$, with a slope of $-\alpha$, represent the trade-off the owner-manager faces between nonpecuniary benefits and his wealth after the sale. Given that the owner has decided to sell a claim $1 - \alpha$ of the firm, his welfare will be maximized when $V_2 P_2$ is tangent to some indifference curve such as U_3 in Figure 21.1. A price for a claim of $(1 - \alpha)$ on the firm that is satisfactory to both the buyer and the seller will require that this tangency occur along $\bar{V}F$, i.e., that the value of the firm must be V'. To show this, assume that such is not the case – that the tangency occurs to the left of the point B on the line $\bar{V}F$. Then, since the slope of $V_2 P_2$ is negative, the value of the firm will be larger than V'. The owner-manager's choice of this lower level of consumption of nonpecuniary benefits will imply a higher value both to the firm as a whole and to the fraction of the firm $(1 - \alpha)$ which the outsider has acquired; that is, $(1 - \alpha)V' > S_0$. From the owner's viewpoint, he has sold $1 - \alpha$ of the firm for less than he could have, given the (assumed) lower level of nonpecuniary benefits he enjoys. On the other hand, if the tangency point B is to the right of the line $\bar{V}F$, the owner-manager's higher consumption of nonpecuniary benefits means the value of the firm is less than V', and hence $(1 - \alpha)V(F, \alpha) < S_0 = (1 - \alpha)V'$. The outside owner then has paid more for his share of the equity than it is worth. S_0 will be a mutually satisfactory price if and only if $(1 - \alpha)V' = S_0$. But this means that the owner's postsale wealth is equal to the (reduced) value of the firm V', since

$$W = S_0 + \alpha V' = (1 - \alpha) V' + \alpha V' = V'. \tag{Q.E.D.}$$

The requirement that V^* and F' fall on $\bar{V}F$ is thus equivalent to requiring that the value of the claim acquired by the outside buyer be equal to the amount he pays for it and conversely for the owner. *This means that the decline in the total value of the firm* $(V^* - V')$ *is entirely imposed on the owner-manager.* His total wealth after the sale of $(1 - \alpha)$ of the equity is V', and the decline in his wealth is $V^* - V'$.

The distance $V^* - V$ is the reduction in the market value of the firm engendered by the agency relationship and is a measure of the "residual loss" defined earlier. In this simple example the residual loss represents the total agency costs engendered by the sale of outside equity because monitoring and bonding activities have not been allowed. The welfare loss the owner incurs is less than the residual loss by the value to him of the increase in nonpecuniary benefits $(F' - F^*)$. In Figure 21.1 the difference between the intercepts on the Y axis of the two indifference curves U_2 and U_3 is a measure of the owner-manager's welfare loss due to the incurrence of agency costs,[22] and he would sell such a claim only if the increment in welfare he achieves by using the cash amounting to $(1 - \alpha)V'$ for other things was worth more to him than this amount of wealth.

$$\ldots$$

2.4. The role of monitoring and bonding activities in reducing agency costs

In the above analysis we have ignored the potential for controlling the behavior of the owner-manager through monitoring and other control activities. In practice it is usually possible by expending resources to alter the opportunity the owner-manager has for capturing nonpecuniary benefits. These methods include auditing, formal control systems, budget restrictions, and the establishment of incentive compensation systems which serve to more closely identify the manager's interests with those of the outside equity holders, etc. Figure 21.2 portrays the effects of monitoring and other control activities in the simple situation portrayed in Figure 21.1. Figures 21.1 and 21.2 are identical except for the curve BCE in Figure 21.2 which depicts a "budget constraint" derived when monitoring possibilities are taken into account. Without monitoring, and with outside equity of $(1 - \alpha)$, the value of the firm will be V' and nonpecuniary expenditures F'. By incurring monitoring costs, M, the equity holders can restrict the manager's consumption of perquisites to amounts less than F'. Let $F(M, \alpha)$ denote the maximum perquisites the manager can consume for alternative levels of monitoring expenditures, M, given his ownership share, α. We assume that increases in monitoring reduce F and reduce it at a decreasing rate, i.e., $\partial F/\partial M < 0$ and $\partial^2 F/\partial M^2 > 0$.

Since the current value of expected future monitoring expenditures by the outside equity holders reduce the value of any given claim on the firm to them dollar for dollar, the outside equity holders will take this into account in determining the maximum price they will pay for any given fraction of the firm's equity. Therefore, given positive monitoring activity, the value of the firm is given by $V = \bar{V} - F(M, \alpha) - M$, and the locus of these points for various levels of M and for a given level of α lie on the line BCE in Figure 21.2. The vertical difference between the $\bar{V}F$ and BCE curves is M, the current market value of the future monitoring expenditures.

---

[22] The distance $V^* - V'$ is a measure of what we will define as the gross agency costs. The distance $V_3 - V_4$ is a measure of what we call net agency costs, and it is this measure of agency costs which will be minimized by the manager in the general case where we allow investment to change.

Figure 21.2. The value of the firm (V) and level of nonpecuniary benefits (F) when outside equity is $(1 - \alpha)$, U_1, U_2, U_3 represent owner's indifference curves between wealth and nonpecuniary benefits, and monitoring (or bonding) activities impose opportunity set BCE as the tradeoff constraint facing the owner.

If it is possible for the outside equity holders to make these monitoring expenditures and thereby to impose the reductions in the owner-manager's consumption of F, he will voluntarily enter into a contract with the outside equity holders which gives them the rights to restrict his consumption of non-pecuniary items to F''. He finds this desirable because it will cause the value of the firm to rise to V''. Given the contract, the optimal monitoring expenditure on the part of the outsiders, M, is the amount $D - C$. The entire increase in the value of the firm that accrues will be reflected in the owner's wealth, but his welfare will be increased by less than this because he forgoes some nonpecuniary benefits he previously enjoyed.

If the equity market is competitive and makes unbiased estimates of the effects of the monitoring expenditures on F and V, potential buyers will be indifferent between the following two contracts:

(i) Purchase of a share $(1 - \alpha)$ of the firm at a total price of $(1 - \alpha)V'$ and no rights to monitor or control the manager's consumption of perquisites.

299

(ii) Purchase of a share $(1 - \alpha)$ of the firm at a total price of $(1 - \alpha)V''$ and the right to expend resources up to an amount equal to $D - C$ which will limit the owner-manager's consumption of perquisites to F.

Given contract (ii) the outside shareholders would find it desirable to monitor to the full rights of their contract because it will pay them to do so. However, if the equity market is competitive the total benefits (net of the monitoring costs) will be capitalized into the price of the claims. Thus, not surprisingly, the owner-manager reaps all the benefits of the opportunity to write and sell the monitoring contract.

An analysis of bonding expenditures. We can also see from the analysis of Figure 21.2 that it makes no difference who actually makes the monitoring expenditures – the owner bears the full amount of these costs as a wealth reduction in all cases. Suppose that the owner-manager could expend resources to guarantee to the outside equity holders that he would limit his activities which cost the firm F. We call these expenditures "bonding costs," and they would take such forms as contractual guarantees to have the financial accounts audited by a public accountant, explicit bonding against malfeasance on the part of the manager, and contractual limitations on the manager's decisionmaking power (which impose costs on the firm because they limit his ability to take full advantage of some profitable opportunities as well as limiting his ability to harm the stockholders while making himself better off).

If the incurrence of the bonding costs were entirely under the control of the manager and if they yielded the same opportunity set BCE for him in Figure 21.2, he would incur them in amount $D - C$. This would limit his consumption of perquisites to F'' from F', and the solution is exactly the same as if the outside equity holders had performed the monitoring. The manager finds it in his interest to incur these costs as long as the net increments in his wealth which they generate (by reducing the agency costs and therefore increasing the value of the firm) are more valuable than the perquisites given up. This optimum occurs at point C in both cases under our assumption that the bonding expenditures yield the same opportunity set as the monitoring expenditures. In general, of course, it will pay the owner-manager to engage in bonding activities and to write contracts which allow monitoring as long as the marginal benefits of each are greater than their marginal cost.

2.5. Pareto optimality and agency costs in
manager-operated firms

In general we expect to observe both bonding and external monitoring activities, and the incentives are such that the levels of these activities will satisfy the conditions of efficiency. They will not, however, result in the firm being run in a manner so as to maximize its value. The difference between V^*, the efficient solution under zero monitoring and bonding costs (and therefore zero agency costs), and V'', the value of the firm given positive monitoring costs, are the total gross agency costs defined earlier in the introduction. These are the costs of the "separation of ownership and control" which Adam Smith focused on in the passage quoted at the beginning of this paper and which Berle and Means (1932) popularized 157 years later. The solutions outlined above to our highly simplified problem imply that agency costs will be positive as long as monitoring costs are positive – which they certainly are.

The reduced value of the firm caused by the manager's consumption of perquisites outlined above is "nonoptimal" or inefficient only in comparison to a world in which we could obtain compliance of the agent to the principal's wishes at zero cost or in comparison to a *hypothetical* world in which the agency costs were lower. But these costs (monitoring and bonding costs and "residual loss") are an unavoidable result of the agency relationship. Furthermore, since they are borne entirely by the decision maker (in this case the original owner) responsible for creating the relationship, he has the incentives to see that they are minimized (because he captures the benefits from their reduction). Furthermore, these agency costs will be incurred only if the benefits to the owner-manager from their creation are great enough to outweigh them. In our current example these benefits arise from the availability of profitable investments requiring capital investment in excess of the original owner's personal wealth.

In conclusion, finding that agency costs are nonzero (i.e., that there are costs associated with the separation of ownership and control in the corporation) and concluding therefore that the agency relationship is nonoptimal, wasteful, or inefficient is equivalent in every sense to comparing a world in which iron ore is a scarce commodity (and therefore costly) to a world in which it is freely available at zero resource cost, and concluding that the first world is "nonoptimal" – a perfect example of the fallacy criticized by Coase (1964) and what Demsetz (1969) characterizes as the "Nirvana" form of analysis.[23]

2.6. Factors affecting the size of the divergence from ideal maximization

The magnitude of the agency costs discussed above will vary from firm to firm. It will depend on the tastes of managers, the ease with which they can exercise

---

[23] If we could establish the existence of a feasible set of alternative institutional arrangements which would yield net benefits from the reduction of these costs, we could legitimately conclude the agency relationship engendered by the corporation was not Pareto optimal. However, we would then be left with the problem of explaining why these alternative institutional arrangements have not replaced the corporate form of organization.

their own preferences as opposed to value maximization in decision making, and the costs of monitoring and bonding activities.[24] The agency costs will also depend upon the cost of measuring the manager's (agent's) performance and evaluating it, the cost of devising and applying an index for compensating the manager which correlates with the owner's (principal's) welfare, and the cost of devising and enforcing specific behavioral rules or policies. Where the manager has less than a controlling interest in the firm, it will also depend upon the market for managers. Competition from other potential managers limits the costs of obtaining managerial services (including the extent to which a given manager can diverge from the idealized solution which would obtain if all monitoring and bonding costs were zero). The size of the divergence (the agency costs) will be directly related to the cost of replacing the manager. If his responsibilities require very little knowledge specialized to the firm, if it is easy to evaluate his performance, and if replacement search costs are modest, the divergence from the ideal will be relatively small and vice versa.

The divergence will also be constrained by the market for the firm itself, i.e., by capital markets. Owners always have the option of selling their firm, either as a unit or piecemeal. Owners of manager-operated firms can and do sample the capital market from time to time. If they discover that the value of the future earnings-stream to others is higher than the value of the firm to them given that it is to be manager-operated, they can exercise their right to sell. It is conceivable that other owners could be more efficient at monitoring or even that a single individual with appropriate managerial talents and with sufficiently large personal wealth would elect to buy the firm. In this latter case the purchase by such a single individual would completely eliminate the agency costs. If there were a number of such potential owner-manager purchasers chasers (all with talents and tastes identical to the current manager), the owners would receive in the sale price of the firm the full value of the residual claimant rights including the capital value of the eliminated agency costs plus the value of the managerial rights.

Monopoly, competition, and managerial behavior. It is frequently argued that the existence of competition in product (and factor) markets will constrain the behavior of managers to idealized value maximization, i.e., that monopoly in product (or monopsony in factor) markets will permit larger divergences from value maximization.[25] Our analysis does not support this hypothesis.

---

[24] The monitoring and bonding costs will differ from firm to firm depending on such things as the inherent complexity and geographical dispersion of operations, the attractiveness of perquisites available in the firm (consider the mint), etc.

[25] "Where competitors are numerous and entry is easy, persistent departures from profit maximizing behavior inexorably leads to extinction. Economic natural selection holds the stage. In these circumstances, the behavior of the individual units that constitute the supply side of the product market is essentially routine and uninteresting and economists can confidently predict industry behavior without being explicitly concerned with the behavior of these individual units. When

The owners of a firm with monopoly power have the same incentives to limit divergences of the manager from value maximization (i.e., the ability to increase their wealth) as do the owners of competitive firms. Furthermore, competition in the market for managers will generally make it unnecessary for the owners to share rents with the manager. The owners of a monopoly firm need only pay the supply price for a manager.

Since the owner of a monopoly has the same wealth incentives to minimize managerial costs as would the owner of a competitive firm, both will undertake that level of monitoring which equates the marginal cost of monitoring to the marginal wealth increment from reduced consumption of perquisites by the manager. Thus, the existence of monopoly will not increase agency costs.

Furthermore the existence of competition in product and factor markets will not eliminate the agency costs due to managerial control problems as has often been asserted [cf. Friedman (1970)]. If my competitors all incur agency costs equal to or greater than mine, I will not be eliminated from the market by their competition.

The existence and size of the agency costs depends on the nature of the monitoring costs, the tastes of managers for nonpecuniary benefits, and the supply of potential managers who are capable of financing the entire venture out of their personal wealth. If monitoring costs are zero, agency costs will be zero; or if there are enough 100 percent owner-managers available to own and run all the firms in an industry (competitive or not), then agency costs in that industry will also be zero.

. . .

the conditions of competition are relaxed, however, the opportunity set of the firm is expanded. In this case, the behavior of the firm as a distinct operating unit is of separate interest. Both for purposes of interpreting particular behavior within the firm as well as for predicting responses of the industry aggregate, it may be necessary to identify the factors that influence the firm's choices within this expanded opportunity set and embed these in a formal model." (Williamson, 1964b, p. 2).

CHAPTER 22

Organizational forms and investment decisions

EUGENE FAMA AND MICHAEL JENSEN

Eugene Fama is Professor of Finance in the Graduate School of Business at the University of Chicago. See also the previous paper by Fama.

Michael Jensen is the Jesse Isidor Straus Professor of Business Administration, Emeritus, at the Graduate School of Business Administration, Harvard University. See also the chapter by Jensen and Meckling.

1. Introduction

Different organizational forms are distinguished by the characteristics of their residual claims on net cash flows, for example, restrictions on the extent to which residual claimant status is separable from decision roles, or restrictions on the alienability of the residual claims. Different restrictions on residual claims imply different rules for optimal investment decisions. This paper analyzes the relations between characteristics of residual claims and investment decision rules in open and closed corporations, partnerships, proprietorships, financial mutuals, and nonprofits. Our purpose is to determine whether the decisions of each of these organizations can be modeled "as if" they come from the maximization of an objective function – for example, the value maximization rule of the financial economics literature. We focus on investment decisions, but the rules are applicable to all decisions. We ignore the effects of taxes.

We first analyze the investment decision rule implied by the common stock residual claims of open corporations. We compare this rule to the decision rules implied by the more restricted residual claims of proprietorships, partnerships, and closed corporations, and we discuss aspects of the choice of organizational form. Finally, we analyze the investment decision rules implied by the even more specialized residual claims of financial mutuals and nonprofits.

2. The decision rule implied by the common stock of open corporations

The least restricted residual claims in common use are the common stocks of large corporations. These residual claims have property rights in net cash flows

Excerpted from Eugene Fama and Michael Jensen, "Organizational Forms and Investment Decisions," *Journal of Financial Economics* 14 (1985): 101–119, by permission of the publisher.

for an indefinite horizon. They are separable in that stockholders are not required to have any other role in the organization. The residual claim of open corporations are also alienable without restriction. We call these organizations open corporations to distinguish them from closed corporations that are generally smaller and have residual claims that are largely restricted to decision agents.

The unrestricted nature of the residual claims of open corporations fosters the development of a capital market that specializes in pricing such claims and transferring them among investors at low cost. Suppose the capital market is perfectly competitive, that is, suppose there are perfect substitutes for the unrestricted residual claims of any open corporation, and both investors and open corporations are price takers in the capital market. Suppose also that unrestricted residual claims can be traded costlessly among investors and that the capital market is efficient or rational in the sense that the prices of residual claims correctly reflect available information. In this situation, a corporation's stockholders all agree that all decisions, including investments with payoffs in future periods, should be evaluated according to their contribution to the current market value of their residual claims. (See, for example, Fama, 1978).

The logic of the market value of maximum wealth rule is straightforward. The existence of perfect substitute securities that are always correctly priced and can be traded without transactions costs in a perfectly competitive market means the consumption streams that an investor can realize in future periods are constrained only by current wealth, that is, the market value of current and future resources. When the stream of payoffs implied by the wealth or value maximizing investment decisions of an open corporation does not correspond to an investor's optimal consumption stream, the capital market can be used to exchange residual claims in the corporation for other claims with the same market value but with a stream of payoffs that better matches the investor's desired consumption stream.

Because most residual claimants in open corporations have no direct role in the decision process, and because there are conflicts of interest with managers, there are agency problems between managers and residual claimants. As a consequence, an important investment choice in open corporations is the decision control process. As for other investment decisions, maximizing market value involves extending decision control mechanisms to the point where the incremental market value of improved decisions is just offset by the market value of the cost of improved decision control. This means some decisions that nominally reduce value will be taken when the cost of preventing them exceeds the value reduction they cause. It is obvious, but worth emphasizing, that market value reflects all costs, including agency costs – the costs incurred because contracts with decision agents are not costlessly written and enforced. These issues are discussed in detail in Jensen and Meckling (1976b) and Fama and Jensen (1983a, 1983b).

One can quarrel with the perfect capital market assumptions needed to obtain the conclusion that all investors prefer the market value rule for investment decisions by open corporations. However, this case is a useful point of reference for judging the effects of restrictions on residual claims on rules for investment decisions.

3. Decision rules implied by the restricted residual claims of proprietorships, partnerships, and closed corporations

Unlike the unrestricted common stock of open corporations, the residual claims of proprietorships, partnerships, and closed corporations are generally restricted to the organization's important decision agents. We are concerned with the effects of this restriction on investment decisions.

3.1. Proprietorship investment decisions under certainty

Many issues central to the analysis of investment decisions involve risk-bearing and agency problems that are somewhat artificial in a world of certainty. We begin the analysis with the certainty case because it allows simple derivation of many major results.

Consider a proprietorship faced with a two-period perfectly certain world and the investment opportunities summarized in Figure 22.1 by the function $F(K,P)$, where K is the amount of resources invested in the venture in period 1, and P indicates that the organizational form is a proprietorship. A proprietorship is an organization in which the primary decision agent holds 100% of the residual claim on net cash flows. Open corporations are distinguished from proprietorships by the outside ownership of residual claims.

Proprietorships and open corporations can finance with debt as well as residual claims. For the moment, we only consider unlevered proprietorships, which means the organization is financed entirely from the proprietor's wealth. This restriction is dropped shortly, without major effects, when we extend the analysis to partnerships and closed corporations in which there are multiple residual claimants. The certainty assumption is relaxed in section 3.3 where the capital structure issue is addressed.

At time 1 the proprietor puts up K_1 units of resources. His opportunities for transforming current resources into future resources through investment in plant, equipment, etc., are given by the function $F(K,P)$. The proprietor can also acquire resources at time 2 by buying the securities of open corporations. The capital market interest rate for such claims is r, and we continue to assume that they are traded without cost in a perfectly competitive capital market.

Figure 22.1. Investment decisions under certainty for two unlevered proprietorships....

Suppose the indifference curves, $A_j, j = 1, 2, \ldots$, represent the proprietor's tastes for combinations of resources consumed at time 1 and time 2. The proprietor optimally invests $K_1^* K_1$ within the proprietorship and $C_1^* K_1^*$ in the securities of open corporations. He then consumes C_1^A at time 1 and C_2^A at time 2. The proprietor stops investment within the proprietorship at $K_1^* K_1$ because further investment has a marginal return less than the rate of interest available on the securities of open corporations. An open corporation with investment opportunities summarized by the same function $F(K,P)$ would also invest $K_1^* K_1$ since this decision produces the maximum possible current wealth, W_1^*.

Although proprietor A in Figure 22.1 makes the same investment decision as an open corporation with the same opportunity set, a proprietor with tastes summarized by the indifference curves, $B_j, j = 1, 2, \ldots$, chooses to invest less. The essence of an unlevered proprietorship is that the proprietor is sole residual claimant. Thus, if proprietor B invests $K_1^* K_1$ internally at time 1, he cannot sell off part of the resulting claim to the payoff K_2^* generated at time 2. As a result, proprietor B maximizes utility by investing only the amount $C_1^B K_1$ which generates the resource combination (C_1^B, C_2^B) for consumption at time 1 and time 2.

Proprietor B's welfare would improve if he could borrow $K_1^* R_1^B$, of if he could reorganize as an open corporation, invest $K_1^* K_1$ internally, and then sell his residual claim for $K_1^* W_1^*$. However, as Jensen and Meckling (1979) and

307

Fama and Jensen (1983a,b) emphasize, differences in the contract structures of different organizational forms are likely to affect the costs of delivering products. Because alternative organizational forms involve different costs and thus different net payoffs for the same level of investment, the production or transformation function for a venture depends on organizational form. In Figure 22.1, the function $F(K,P)$ shows the maximum payoffs net of all costs that can be generated by an unlevered proprietorship at time 2 with different amounts of wealth invested internally at time 1. If the unlevered proprietorship is the optimal form of organization for the investment activities underlying Figure 22.1, the transformation function for the same venture undertaken by an open corporation (OC) might be $F(K,OC)$, which lies below the proprietorship transformation function.[1] Similarly, if proprietor B issues debt, conflicts of interest with debt holders lead to contracting and other agency costs that also cause the transformation function (not shown in Figure 22.1) to shift downward by an amount that depends on the amount of debt issued. We compare here only open corporations and unlevered proprietorships.

In our certain world the dominance of the proprietorship transformation function for the venture in Figure 22.1 can be thought of as due to higher contracting costs in open corporations associated with writing and administering contracts with external residual claimants and internal decision agents. In a world of uncertainty these costs would be balanced against the efficiencies in risk sharing allowed by the open corporate form. A realistic situation where the analysis in Figure 22.1 is relevant occurs when the personal human capital of the primary decision agent is the important resource in an organization. Because human capital is difficult to sell, the decision maker is in a situation like that of proprietor B who cannot sell residual claims on the project.

Proprietors like Mr. A evaluate investment opportunities according to the maximum wealth or market value rule because they also purchase claims for resources to be delivered at time 2 in the open capital market. The restriction of the proprietorship residual claim to an investor like Mr. A is not a binding constraint on his portfolio decisions. Thus, the market interest rate, r, on external investments provides the relevant opportunity cost for internal investments. On the other hand, a proprietor like Mr. B is not also a net investor in the outside capital market. The marginal rate of time preference implied by the slope of his indifference curve at (C_1^B, C_2^B) is higher than the market interest rate, r. Thus, it is rational for proprietor B to assign lower value to future resources

---

[1] Wolfson (1983) documents examples of the dependence of cost functions on organizational form in various forms of oil and gas limited partnerships. In particular, he provides evidence on how the choice of organizational form affects agency costs.

generated from internal investment than is implied by the market interest rate on the unrestricted common stocks of open corporations.

If "diversified" proprietors like Mr. A are sufficient to absorb all the proprietorships that exist in a general equilibrium, the market price for the rights to the transformation function $F(K,P)$ is $K_1 W_1^*$ and Mr. B sells his rights to the venture to a Mr. A type proprietor. After purchasing residual claims on open corporations in the amount $R_1^B W_1^*$, Mr. B then consumes R_1^B at time 1 and R_2^B at time 2 and achieves utility $B_3 > B_1$.

If "diversified" proprietors like Mr. A are not sufficient to absorb all the proprietorships that will exist in a general equilibrium, that is, if, like Mr. B, the marginal proprietor in the activity only invests internally, the market price for the transformation function $F(K,P)$ is less than $K_1 W_1^*$. Proprietors like Mr. B do not use the market value rule for decisions and they invest less than open corporations faced with the same investment opportunities.

3.2. Partnerships and closed corporations

The analysis extends to partnerships and closed corporations in which residual claims are again generally restricted to decision agents. If all residual claimants in these organizations also invest in the residual claims of open corporations, that is, if they have tastes similar to Mr. A in Figure 22.1, then in a world of certainty, partnerships and closed corporations make the same decisions as open corporations faced with the same investment opportunities. However, partnerships or closed corporations whose residual claimants have consumption preferences like Mr. B do not use the market value decision rule and invest less than an open corporation with the same opportunity set. A partnership or closed corporation with a mix of Mr. A's and Mr. B's, with differing demands for current vs. future resources, faces a difficult contracting problem in making investment decisions. Such conflicts over investment and payout policies are common, for example, in family corporations and partnerships. Unlike open corporations, where all residual claimants agree on the maximum wealth or market value rule for investment decisions, in partnerships and closed corporations, investment decision rules that satisfy the interests of all residual claimants require either that all residual claimants are "diversified" (like Mr. A in Figure 22.1) or that they have identical tastes.

The residual claims in partnerships and closed corporations are generally restricted to important decision agents and to outsiders acceptable to the important decision agents. The residual claims of these organizations generally specify rules for compensating residual claimants when they retire or otherwise leave the organization. The difficulties in designing valuation processes to substitute for the capital market that continuously revalues the unrestricted residual claim of open corporations means that partnerships and closed corporations will not generally follow the value maximizing decision rule. They will tend to underinvest in assets with long-term payoffs whose current values are not easily established.

We do not expect to see voluntary contractual restrictions on the alienability of residual claims in activities where the capital value problem described above is important, that is, where decisions present major opportunities to substitute between present and future cash flows. This occurs in activities optimally carried out with large quantities of long-term assets that are difficult to value and that are more efficiently purchased by residual claimants rather than rented, for example, plant and equipment, and reputation and goodwill that can be transferred from one generation of residual claimants to the next. For example, organizations in business and financial consulting, like brokerage houses and underwriters, that were partnerships with restricted residual claims are tending to reorganize as open corporations. We hypothesize that this is largely due to changes in the nature of these activities that increase capital value problems, for example, increased demand for wealth from residual claimants to purchase risky assets that are difficult to value, and pressure to transfer the rights to the net cash flows from such assets from one generation of residual claimants to the next.

In contrast, we hypothesize that when the important asset in an activity is the human capital of existing decision agents, the activity can be efficiently supplied by partnerships with restricted residual claims. This will be true when there are no important patents, specialized assets, or technologies to be passed from one generation of partners to the next. It will also be true when the reputation and goodwill that are important in some professional service activities, such as law, public accounting, and business consulting, are tied to the human capital currently in the organization. In such cases rather extreme restrictions on residual claims can survive. For example, professional partnership residual claims often limit a partner's rights in net cash flows to period of service in the organization. (See Fama and Jensen, 1983a.)

3.3. Choice of organizational form

Figure 22.2 shows a situation in which the contracting costs of the open corporate form are low enough relative to its advantages that it pays the proprietor, Mr. B, to organize the venture as an open corporation. In Figure 22.2, $F(K,OC)$ is the transformation function for an open corporation undertaking the venture. Mr. B realizes the amount $K_1 W^*_{OC}$ from sale to the corporation of his rights to the venture and $K^*_{OC} K_1$ is the value maximizing level of investment by the corporation. Mr. B achieves welfare level B_3 by purchasing shares of other open corporations amounting to $R^B_1 W^*_{OC}$ and consuming (R^B_1, R^B_2) at times 1 and 2.

310

Figure 22.2. Choice of organizational form and investment under certainty when the consumption preferences of the marginal proprietor make it desirable to incur the costs of the open corporate form of organization.

If Mr. B organized the venture as a proprietorship he would realize utility of $B_1 < B_3$ by investing $K_P^* K_1 < K_{OC}^* K_1$.[2]

The open corporate form is optimal for Mr. B in Figure 22.2 even though the corporate transformation function $F(K,OC)$ is everywhere below the proprietorship transformation function $F(K,P)$. Mr. B's strong preference for current consumption causes him to incur the costs associated with the open corporate form. The unrestricted alienability and separability of open corporate claims allow him to rearrange his consumption pattern by selling his claims in the capital market and devoting part or all of the proceeds to current consumption. Of course, the corporate firm is optimal for Mr. B only if there are no other potential proprietors willing to purchase his rights to the venture for more than $K_1 W_{OC}^*$. In particular, if the marginal proprietorship is "well diversified" like Mr. A, Mr. B will sell his rights to the venture to Mr. A for $K_1 W_1^* > K_1 W_{OC}^*$.

---

[2] If Mr. B both manages the corporation and owns shares in it, the corporate opportunity set $F(K,OC)$ depends on Mr. B's stock ownership fraction. Figure 22.2 portrays the polar case in which he sells off all his claims on the corporation. Jensen and Meckling (1976b) analyze the intermediate cases in which the proprietor maintains both management and stock ownership interests in the corporation.

311

While the optimal corporate investment level $K_{OC}^* K_1$ in Figure 22.2 maximizes value, $K_1 W_{OC}^*$, conditional on choice of the corporate organizational form, this is obviously not equivalent to the value, $K_1 W_1^*$, that could be obtained (at investment level $K_P^{**} K_1$) if the transformation function $F(K,P)$ applied to open corporations as well as to proprietorships. The distance, $W_{OC}^* W_1^*$, is what Jensen and Meckling (1976b, p. 320) define to be the gross agency costs of the corporate form, the difference between the maximum value attainable if the proprietorship production function were available to the open corporation and the maximum value attainable from the production function actually available to the corporation.

The transformation function for a proprietorship does not always dominate that for an open corporation. This is illustrated in Figure 22.3 [ed.: not shown here] where scale economies cause the transformation function for the open corporation to cross that for the proprietorship. Moreover, in an uncertain world the gains from specialization of risk-bearing and decision functions discussed in Fama and Jensen (1983a) can become so large with increasing scale that the open corporate form dominates the proprietorship. In general at each point in time there is a set of transformation functions for each venture, one for each possible organizational form.

At various stages in the life of a venture it may be best carried out under different organizational forms. For example, it might first be organized as a proprietorship and then, with increasing demands for financing risky investments, converted to a partnership or a closed corporation, and then to an open corporation. At a later time, conditions can indicate reconversion to a closed corporation, partnership, or even proprietorship form.

. . .

CHAPTER 23

The rise in managerial stock ownership*

CLIFFORD G. HOLDERNESS, RANDALL S. KROSZNER, AND DENNIS P. SHEEHAN

Clifford G. Holderness was born in Springfield, Massachusetts, in 1952. He received his B.A. and J.D. at Stanford University in 1974 and 1977, respectively, then earned his M.Sc. in economics at the London School of Economics in 1978. When this article was published, he was on the faculty of Boston College's Carroll School of Management, where he is currently Professor of Finance.

Randall S. Kroszner was born in 1962 in Englewood, New Jersey. He received a Ph.D. in economics from Harvard University in 1990. When this article was published, he was Associate Professor of Economics in the Graduate School of Business at the University of Chicago, where he is now the Norman R. Bobins Professor of Economics at the Booth School of Business. He served as a Member of the President's Council of Economic Advisors from 2001 to 2003 and as Member of the Board of Governors of the Federal Reserve System from 2006 to 2009.

Dennis P. Sheehan was born in 1951 in Newport, Rhode Island. He received a Ph.D. in economics from the University of California, Berkeley, in 1981. When this article was published, he was the Virginia and Louis Benzak Professor of Finance in the Smeal College of Business at Pennsylvania State University, where he now serves as the Associate Dean of MBA Programs.

Much of the vast research on corporate control over the past 30 years as well as many of the policy recommendations that have found their way into the securities law over the past 60 years are premised on the separation of ownership from control in public corporations. Thorstein Veblen first raised this issue in 1923 when he wrote of "absentee ownership" (Veblen, 1964). It was also the central concern of Adolf Berle and Gardiner Means in their

Reprinted with minor abridgments from Clifford G. Holderness, Randall S. Kroszner, and Dennis P. Sheehan, "The Rise in Managerial Stock Ownership," *Journal of Applied Corporate Finance,* 13, 3 (Fall 2000): 105–115. Reprinted with the permission of Blackwell Publishing.

*This is a shorter and less technical version of our paper entitled "Were the Good Old Days That Good? Changes in Managerial Stock Ownership Since the Great Depression," *Journal of Finance* 54, 1999, pp. 435–69. That paper won the Brattle Prize for the best paper in corporate finance published in the *Journal of Finance* in 1999.

C. G. HOLDERNESS, R. S. KROSZNER, AND D. P. SHEEHAN
hugely influential book *The Modern Corporation and Private Property* written in 1932. They warned that the separation of ownership and control "destroys the very foundation on which the economic order of the past three centuries has rested" and asserted that the "[d]ispersion in the ownership of separate enterprises . . . has already proceeded far, it is rapidly increasing, and appears to be an inevitable development" (Berle and Means, 1932) of the modern corporate system. More recently, academics such as Michael Jensen and Mark Roe have argued that a wide variety of tax incentives, antitrust policies, regulations, and political pressures, rather than anything inherent in capitalism, has led to the rise of what Roe calls "strong managers and weak owners.[1]

Although the premise of the separation of ownership from management plays such a central role, little, if any, evidence has been presented to support the proposition that managerial ownership has declined over time. We recently conducted a study that uses the earliest data available on ownership (published by the Securities and Exchange Commission in 1936) to investigate how the level of managerial ownership has changed since 1935. We compared a comprehensive cross-section of roughly 1,500 publicly traded U.S. firms in 1935 with a modern benchmark of more than 4,200 exchange-listed firms for 1995.

Contrary to the received wisdom, we found that managerial stock ownership is higher now than in 1935. The average percentage of common stock held by a firm's officers and directors as a group rose from 13% in 1935 to 21% in 1995. Median holdings doubled from 7% to 14%. Although the very largest firms had similar ownership percentages in both periods, a firm-size-weighted average was also higher in 1995 than 1935. In terms of real 1995 dollars, insider holdings were on average four times higher in 1995, rising from $18 million to $73 million, and this increase occurred across all firm sizes.

We examined two possible causes of this increase in managerial ownership. First, we explored whether managerial ownership has increased because, as some finance scholars have suggested, other mechanisms to control agency costs may have decreased. We found no evidence that insider ownership is substituting for alternative mechanisms such as incentive-based pay, monitoring by the board, the market for corporate control, or product-market competition. These mechanisms are all now in force with similar if not greater intensity as in 1935. This finding supports the view that alternative incentive devices must be balanced and will tend to increase or decrease in use simultaneously (Milgrom and Roberts, 1990b; Holmstrom and Milgrom, 1994).

The second hypothesis we investigated concerns how firm-specific characteristics associated with the costs and benefits of monitoring affect the level of

---

[1] See, for example, Jensen, 1989; Jensen, 1993; Roe, 1994.

managerial ownership. We found that most factors, such as firm size and regulation, had similar effects on managerial ownership in 1935 and 1995, so the monitoring costs and benefits for these factors do not appear to have changed over time.

Characteristics related to the volatility of the environment in which firms operated, however, had markedly different effects in the two periods. A general decline in volatility, coupled with innovations in financial markets and financial theory that have created greater hedging and diversification possibilities for both managers and firms (Merton, 1995; Stulz, 1996), have lowered the costs to managers of holding large equity stakes in their firms. Finance theory suggests that when risks outside the control of managers are reduced, firm performance becomes a less "noisy" measure of managers' quality and hence stock ownership becomes more cost-effective for solving the agency problem between managers and shareholders. This reduction in costs and increase in benefits of managerial ownership seems to offer at least a partial explanation of the increase in managerial ownership since 1935.

The data

To document the patterns of corporate ownership in the early part of this century, we used a rich but neglected data source from the Securities and Exchange Commission (SEC). The Securities and Exchange Act of 1934 mandates that any firm with equity registered on national securities exchanges must report the equity holdings of officers and directors to the SEC. The SEC collected and published these reports for shareholdings as of December 31, 1935.

This report, which is the earliest systematic evidence available on stock ownership, provides a comprehensive cross-section of the ownership structure for more than 1,500 publicly traded U.S. corporations. We supplemented these data with information from *Moody's*, the *Commercial and Financial Chronicle, Bank Quotation Record*, and the Center for Research in Securities Prices (CRSP). Firms that were not listed in these sources were dropped; our full 1935 sample consisted of 1,419 firms. The average firm had slightly more than ten officers and directors reporting their ownership stakes, so there were roughly 15,000 individual shareholding records in our 1935 database.

To understand how ownership has evolved, we compared our 1935 sample to a modern benchmark of 4,202 publicly traded firms in 1995. The data for these firms are from Compact Disclosure, a comprehensive and accurate database that contains information from proxy statements and annual reports on more than 5,600 U.S. companies traded on the NYSE, AMEX, and NASDAQ's National Market System (NMS). We supplemented these ownership data with information from *Moody's*, COMPUSTAT, and CRSP.

315

Consider some basic features of our 1935 and 1995 samples. We consider both the full sample, and the subsample of firms listed on the NYSE (651 firms in 1935 and 1,464 firms in 1995). For ease of comparison, we express the 1935 data in constant 1995 dollars using the GDP deflator, which rose roughly elevenfold during the 60-year period. On average, publicly traded firms were about four times larger in real terms in 1995 than in 1935, with the distribution being highly skewed in both periods. The mean ratio of debt to total value, where total value is long-term debt plus the market value of equity, has changed little since 1935. The mean and median market-to-book ratios were somewhat lower in 1935 than in 1995, reflecting the different states of the equity markets and investment opportunities during the two periods.

. . .

How has managerial ownership changed since 1935?

Contrary to the predictions of many scholars over the years, managerial stock ownership is higher now than when Berle and Means published their famous book. Table 1 compares the distribution of managerial ownership across publicly traded firms in 1935 and 1995. Stock ownership for officers and directors is defined as all common shares owned directly or indirectly, including stock options exercisable within 60 days. In the full sample of publicly traded firms, average equity ownership of officers and directors was 12.9% in 1935 and 21.1% in 1995. Median managerial holdings more than doubled from 6.5% to 14.4% between 1935 and 1995. If we restrict our comparison to firms listed on the NYSE, the average and median managerial ownership likewise increased from 8.6% to 12.2% for the mean and from 3.7% to 4.7% for the median. The differences between the 1935 and 1995 means and medians for both the full samples and the NYSE samples are all highly statistically significant.

In the managerial ownership statistics reported in Table 1, each firm received equal weight. On a value-weighted basis, with the total market value of each firm (equity plus long-term debt) as the weight, managerial stock ownership for the full sample increased from 4.2% in 1935 to 5.9% in 1995. This increase is statistically significant (p-value of 0.08) but is less pronounced because inside ownership tends to be inversely related to firm size (Demsetz and Lehn, 1985; Holderness and Sheehan, 1988).

Some scholars have suggested that the dollar value of holdings provides a better indication of a manager's incentives and willingness to bear risk than does the percentage value of holdings. Panel B of Table 1 shows that the average (inflation-adjusted) value of insiders' aggregate holdings roughly quadrupled from $17.9 million in 1935 to $73.0 million in 1995. The median value rose from $3.0 million to $16.2 million. The mean and median real dollar values

TABLE 1

PERCENTAGE AND REAL DOLLAR VALUE OF MANAGERIAL EQUITY OWNERSHIP
IN 1935 AND 1995*

		First Quartile	Median	Mean	Third Quartile
Panel A: Percentage Ownership					
Full sample:	1935	1.3	6.5	12.9	18.5
	1995	4.7	14.4	21.1	32.1
NYSE sample:	1935	0.8	3.7	8.6	11.7
	1995	1.4	4.7	12.2	16.2
Panel B: Real Dollar Value of Ownership					
Full sample:	1935	0.5	3.0	17.9	10.7
	1995	5.7	16.2	73.0	46.1
NYSE sample:	1935	0.8	5.4	32.0	21.2
	1995	9.4	30.7	131.2	92.1

* This table compares the mean, median, first quartile, and third quartile percentages (Panel A) and real dollar values (Panel B) of the total equity ownership of officers and directors for exchange-listed firms in 1935 and 1995. In Panel A, the percentage ownership is the sum of the common shares held (directly or indirectly) by officers and directors divided by the number of common shares outstanding. In Panel B, dollar value is the end-of-year stock price times the number of shares held, in millions of 1995 dollars.

grew by even larger amounts for NYSE firms. Once again, the difference between the 1935 and 1995 means and the difference between the medians are highly statistically significant.

Ownership and firm size

Table 2 shows how ownership percentages and the real dollar value of ownership varied with real firm size in 1935 and 1995. The first two columns of Table 2 report the real market value of the firm at the midpoint of each firm size decile for 1935 and 1995. The subsequent columns compare the mean and median ownership percentages (Panel A) and dollar values (Panel B) by size decile. For the nine smallest firm size deciles, both the mean and median managerial ownership percentages were higher in 1995 (Panel A of Table 2); each of these differences is, once again, highly statistically significant.

Measured in terms of real dollar values rather than percentages, mean and median managerial holdings were sharply and statistically significantly higher in 1995 for every size decile (Panel B of Table 2). The differences were greatest in the largest size deciles, suggesting that firm size increases faster than the percentage of managerial ownership falls across the deciles.

317

TABLE 2

PERCENTAGE AND REAL DOLLAR VALUE OF MANAGERIAL EQUITY
OWNERSHIP ACROSS DECILES OF THE MARKET VALUE OF THE
FIRM'S EQUITY FOR 1935 AND 1995*

Midpoint of Size Decile		Mean		Median	
1935	1995	1935	1995	1935	1995
Panel A: Percentage Ownership					
$3	$11	21.4	33.3	16.2	30.6
$8	$25	20.0	29.2	11.1	25.3
$16	$42	17.2	27.3	11.5	20.5
$24	$66	13.1	25.8	7.3	20.2
$41	$101	16.2	24.4	10.2	19.8
$63	$155	11.2	20.9	7.2	14.7
$104	$260	9.9	19.1	5.1	13.1
$186	$517	8.1	14.9	3.5	7.6
$399	$1,211	6.5	10.8	3.3	4.3
$1,538	$4,428	5.3	5.4	2.1	1.5
Panel B: Real Dollar Value of Ownership					
$3	$11	$0.6	$3.6	$0.4	$3.1
$8	$25	$1.7	$7.4	$0.9	$6.4
$16	$42	$2.6	$11.6	$1.6	$8.8
$24	$66	$3.2	$17.2	$1.9	$12.8
$41	$101	$6.6	$24.6	$4.4	$19.6
$63	$155	$7.0	$32.9	$4.9	$23.5
$104	$260	$10.6	$51.1	$5.8	$34.3
$186	$517	$15.0	$81.1	$6.4	$35.8
$399	$1,211	$26.4	$136.1	$13.7	$52.5
$1,538	$4,428	$104.9	$364.8	$29.9	$83.0

* This table compares 1935 and 1995 mean and median manageral stock ownership
percentages and dollar values for the full sample of exhange-listed firms broken
out by deciles of the market value of equity, calculated at end-of-year 1935 and
beginning-of-year 1995. Dollar values are in millions of 1995 dollars.

The largest firms

For firms in the largest size decile, however, the differences in the *percentage*
of managerial ownership were no longer statistically significant. The mean
percentage ownership for these firms was slightly higher and the median slightly
lower in 1995 than in 1935. . . .

To explore the change in ownership for the largest firms in more detail, we
examined ownership by the top officer rather than the managers as a group. The
result parallels our finding reported in Table 2 in which the mean percentage
of total managerial holdings for the largest firms was almost identical in 1935
and 1995 and the median percentage was slightly lower in 1995.

The rise in managerial stock ownership

In terms of the real dollar value of the holdings, however, we found that both the mean and median for the largest firms were much higher in 1995 than in 1935. . . . Thus, for the very largest firms, we found little difference in percentage ownership but much higher dollar values of ownership for 1995 versus 1935 for both CEOs and top managers as a group.

Robustness checks

To ensure that the increase in inside ownership we report in fact exists, we conducted a number of robustness checks. We found that 1935 and 1995 appear to be representative years for their respective periods as far as insider ownership is concerned. The publicly traded firms in our sample represent roughly the same fraction of all enterprises as well as the same size relative to GDP in the two sample periods. Insider reporting practices and requirements did not change between 1935 and 1995, nor did the number of persons reporting per firm. Common stock is the appropriate focus for both periods; preferred stock and debt were not a significant component of executive portfolios.

Stock ownership by insiders has increased in virtually every sector of the economy, so changes in the mix of industries between 1935 and 1995 did not appear to cause the increase in inside ownership. Differences in the ages of our firms also did not appear to be influencing our results. Finally, if we adjust for the length of managerial tenure (insiders' holdings tend to increase with their tenure), the increase in insider ownership since 1935 would be even greater than what is reflected in the summary statistics.

One robustness check that warrants a longer discussion is executive stock options. Until 1950, stock options were strongly tax-disfavored and so were virtually nonexistent in the 1935 sample period. Since the late 1980s, options grants have become increasingly frequent and now constitute a significant fraction of managerial compensation (Hall and Liebman, 1998).

The use of options, however, does not appear to have affected the overall level of insider ownership during the last quarter-century. . . . Insider ownership increased to its current level before the recent growth of executive stock option grants and does not appear to have fluctuated with their popularity.

. . .

Why has managerial stock ownership increased?

A variety of mechanisms other than insider ownership can perform the function of aligning managers' incentives with those of shareholders, including pay-for-performance contracts, an independent board of directors, debt, the market for corporate control, and competition in the product markets. If the relative costs of these different mechanisms have changed over time, the less costly ones should be substituted for the more costly ones. We examined whether the increase in insider ownership was accompanied by the decreasing use of any of these alternative control devices.

Incentive-Based Compensation. Linking the pay of top managers to firm performance provides a substitute for managerial stock holdings as a way to align the incentives of managers with owners. Previous research, however, has found lower pay-performance sensitivity for a sample of large industrial firms from 1933 to 1941 than in the 1980s and 1990s (Hadlock and Lumer, 1997). This finding persisted even after controlling for factors thought to affect management turnover, such as the composition of the board of directors and whether the top executive was a founder of the firm. These results imply that since the 1930s managerial ownership has not substituted for performance-based compensation.

Board Composition and Size. The board of directors can directly monitor the actions of managers and, if effective, can minimize inefficiency on the part of managers. Two factors that appear to influence the effectiveness of monitoring by directors are the proportion of outside directors (Weisbach, 1988; Kroszner and Rajan, 1997) and board size (Yermack, 1996). Two previous studies, one for the 1930s (Hadlock and Lumer, 1997) and one for the 1980s (Weisbach, 1988), found that the median percentage of outsiders on the boards of large publicly traded firms has remained stable at approximately 50%. We found that the average board had about eight members in both 1935 and 1995. Changes in board composition or size, consequently, do not appear to account for the changes in managerial ownership.

Leverage. Debt also can constrain managers because they must meet fixed interest obligations or risk triggering bankruptcy and losing their jobs (Jensen, 1986). If managerial ownership were substituting for leverage as a control device, we should observe a decline in firm indebtedness over time.... [T]his was not the case. The mean ratio of debt to debt-plus-equity was virtually unchanged between 1935 and 1995. The median debt ratio, however, has risen sharply since the 1930s because a larger fraction of publicly traded firms had no debt outstanding in 1935. Thus, there is no evidence of a general substitution of debt for insider ownership since 1935.

The Market for Corporate Control. The market for corporate control is far more active today than it was in the mid-1930s. Between 1933 and 1940, for example, the annual number of mergers was less than one-fifth of the yearly number in the late 1920s and the 1960s (Nelson, 1959; Golbe and White, 1988; Golbe and White, 1993). The market for corporate control was at an all-time high during the 1980s and continued to be more active in the 1990s than in the 1930s. The increase in insider ownership was thus not in response to any sort of weakness in the market for corporate control.

Product-Market Competition. Competition in a firm's output market can substitute for equity ownership as a disciplinary device on managers because inefficiently run firms will not survive (Hart, 1983). To explain the increase in managerial ownership by this means, product market competition would have to be falling over time. The aggregate concentration of production (measured by value added), as well as the proportion of income in the manufacturing sector that originated in industries in which the largest four enterprises accounted for more than half of the output in that industry, were both roughly stable over this period (Nutter, 1951; Scherer and Ross, 1990). Furthermore, U.S. firms today face much greater international competition than during the era of the Smoot-Hawley Tariff and the Great Depression. Imports as a share of GDP, for example, rose from 2.8% to 10.3% between 1935 and 1995. Since product market competition was at least as intense in 1995 as in 1935, this factor cannot account for the increase in managerial ownership during the period.

Summary. Incentive-alignment devices are used at least as much as, if not more than, in 1935. The rise in managerial ownership over time thus cannot be explained as the result of a substitution of ownership for other mechanisms used to solve the agency problem.

The complementary use of these instruments is consistent with the view of the firm that the use of alternative incentive devices should move in parallel. Because any particular device may reward one type of activity more than others, heavy reliance on one mechanism could lead a manager to focus on one task to the neglect of others. To maintain a balance among managers' responsibilities, i.e., to prevent "gaming" by managers, an increase in the intensity of one incentive mechanism should be accompanied by an increase in another. The growth of managerial ownership is thus part of a general rise in the use of many types of incentive-alignment devices in the modern corporation. Life has become more intense over the past several decades for those who lead American corporations.

Changes in the determinants of insider ownership

An alternative approach for understanding why managers' stock ownership has increased over time views ownership structure as the outcome of an optimization process that determines the most effective uses of control devices to maximize firm value.[2] Insider ownership, under this approach, varies

---

[2] See, for example, Harold Demsetz, "The structure of ownership and the theory of the firm," *Journal of Law and Economics* 26, 1983, pp. 375–90; Demsetz and Lehn (1985); Stacey Kole and Kenneth Lehn, "Deregulation and the adaptation of governance structure: The case of the U.S. airline industry," *Journal of Financial Economics*, 52, 1 (April 1999): 79–117; Himmelberg et al., 1999.

systematically across firms depending on characteristics of each firm that are related to the costs and benefits of insider ownership.[3]

To explore how these factors affected managerial ownership in 1935 and 1995, we regressed managerial stock ownership on five different firm characteristics.[4] First, because individual wealth constraints may affect the costs to managers of acquiring significant percentage holdings in large firms, we included firm size as an independent variable, measured as the log of the total market value of the firm (long-term debt plus market value of equity).

Next we included a measure of the volatility of the firm's operating environment (defined as the standard error from the market model estimated using monthly returns from the previous 60 months; we also included the square of the standard error to allow for a nonlinear relationship). Including volatility allows us to investigate the trade-off between the diversification costs to managers of holding a large fraction of their wealth in a risky security and the benefits to shareholders of incentive alignment when the costs of external monitoring presumably are high.[5] Third, we included the age of the firm (measured as the number of years since incorporation) to explore any life-cycle effect.

The fourth firm characteristic that might affect the costs and benefits of insider ownership is regulation (Demsetz and Lehn, 1985). A regulated firm has both shareholders and regulators to monitor management, so a regulatory agency may partially substitute for shareholders as a monitor (Kole and Lehn, 1999). In addition, the managers of regulated firms typically have less discretion precisely because regulation limits the firms' activities and opportunities. We tried to capture these effects by including three dummy variables that take the value of one if the firm is (i) a railroad, (ii) an electric or gas public utility, or (iii) in another regulated transportation or communications industry. One-digit SIC industry indicator variables were also included in all of the regressions.

---

[3] An alternative approach is to examine the impact of executive ownership on firm performance; see, for example, Randall Morck, Andrei Shleifer, and Robert Vishny, "Management ownership and market valuation: An empirical analysis," *Journal of Financial Economics* 20, 1988, pp. 293–315, and McConnell and Servaes (1990). We find a very similar relationship between the percentage of managerial ownership and performance, as measured by Tobin's Q, in 1935 to what Morck, Shleifer, and Vishny (1988) find in the modern data; see also Holderness, Kroszner, Sheehan, "Were the Good Old Days that Good? Changes in Managerial Stock Ownership Since the Great Depression," *Journal of Finance*, April 1999, 54, 435–469. Since this relationship does not appear to have changed over time, it does not help to explain the increase in managerial ownership since the 1930s.

[4] The dependent variable in our ordinary least squares regressions is the logistic transform of the percentage of ownership by officers and directors, that is, log[ownerships /(1 – ownership)]. None of our results change if we use log(ownership) as the dependent variable. Note that other researchers, notably Demsetz and Lehn (1985), cited earlier, have also used a logistic transform of ownership data.

[5] Other researchers have explored the benefits to highly volatile firms of relying on high insider ownership to address agency problems. See Demsetz and Lehn (1985), and Smith and Watts, 1992.

TABLE 3

RELATIONSHIP BETWEEN MANAGERIAL OWNERSHIP AND FIRM
CHARACTERISTICS IN 1935 AND 1995*

	1935	1995
Intercept	1.41	4.32
	(0.22)	(<0.01)
Log of Market Value	−0.20	−0.52
	(<0.01)	(<0.01)
Standard Error of Monthly Stock Returns	−7.20	−9.89
	(0.04)	(<0.01)
Standard Error of Returns Squared	8.00	−27.58
	(0.17)	(0.01)
Age of the Firm	−0.004	−0.002
	(0.39)	(0.06)
Public Utility Indicator	−3.35	−2.09
	(<0.01)	(<0.01)
Railroad Indicator	−2.82	0.17
	(<0.01)	(0.73)
Other Regulated Indicator	−2.98	−0.69
	(0.01)	(0.01)
Debt Ratio	−0.43	−1.00
	(0.27)	(<0.01)
Adjusted R2	0.21	0.38
p-value of F-statistic for the Regression	<0.01	<0.01

* This table presents the results of the regressions described in the text for 571 NYSE-listed
firms in 1935 and 1,370 NYSE-listed firms in 1995 (p-values are in parentheses under
each coefficient estimate). Firm size is measured as the log of the market value of equity.
Volatility is measured as the standard error from the market model estimated from January
1931 to December 1935 for 1935 and from January 1990 to December 1994 for 1995. Age
of the firm is the number of years since incorporation. Public Utility Indicator is one for SIC
code 49 and zero otherwise. Railroad Indicator is one for SIC code 40 and zero otherwise.
Other Regulated Indicator is one for SIC codes 41 through 48 and zero otherwise. Debt
ratio is the ratio of long-term debt to total firm value (equity plus debt). All regressions
include one-digit SIC industry indicator variables.

We included leverage as a final factor that might affect the level of managerial
ownership. Higher leverage, by allowing greater concentration of ownership,
permits managers to have more voting control for a given dollar value of their
investment in the firm (Stulz, 1988). Also, high leverage may be used to reduce
managerial discretion by constraining the free cash flow that managers might
spend on perquisites for themselves (Jensen, 1986). Because equity returns data
for the 1930s are available electronically only for NYSE firms, we restricted
both our 1935 and 1995 samples to firms listed on the NYSE. Table 3 presents
the regression results.

In both samples, insider ownership declines as firm size increases. The relationship was more pronounced in 1995 than in 1935, although it was statistically significant in both years. The presence of regulation (except for railroads in 1995) also lowers insider ownership in both periods, and the coefficients were statistically significant.

Firm age had a small, negative effect of similar magnitude in both 1935 and 1995, although the effect was not statistically significant in 1935. This provides evidence in favor of the ownership life-cycle hypothesis (whereby managerial ownership of public companies starts out high and falls as the firm ages) in 1995 and weak evidence of it in 1935. The debt ratio also had a negative effect on insider ownership in both periods. In 1995, however, the effect was twice as strong as in 1935 and was statistically significant. As Table 1 shows, firms are much larger today than in 1935. Our results are thus consistent with some degree of substitution between the use of managerial ownership and leverage in each cross-section, with a much larger effect in 1995.

The effect of volatility on managerial ownership, however, was starkly different in 1935 than in 1995. In 1935, an increase in volatility had a *negative* and statistically significant effect on ownership. In 1995, the effect of volatility on ownership was *positive* (although at a declining rate and becoming negative at higher levels of volatility) and statistically significant.

The greater volatility of the markets in the 1930s might account for the contrasting relationship between volatility and ownership and may also help to explain the lower levels of insider ownership during that period. The average monthly standard deviation of stock returns for the 1935 sample was roughly double that for 1995 sample (0.17 versus 0.09). The high variability would apply not only to financial wealth invested in the stock of the firm but also to managers' firm-specific human capital. Given the low managerial turnover during the 1930s (Hadlock and Lumer, 1997), a relatively larger component of managers' human capital may have been firm-specific then.

In addition, financial innovations have reduced the costs of hedging. A 1995 study suggested that the ability to diversify risks in both human and financial capital is much greater today than in the 1930s (Merton, 1995). Modern risk management techniques also can be used to reduce firm risks outside of managers' control. This permits performance to be a more precise signal of managerial competence and may enhance the willingness of managers to hold equity in their own firms (Stulz, 1996). Previous research, for example, has found a positive correlation between the extent of hedging at gold mining firms and managerial ownership (Tufano, 1996). The optimal response to lower volatility and more sophisticated hedging opportunities is for insiders to hold greater ownership stakes. Advances in financial theory and markets thus appear to have played a role in the rise in managerial ownership since the Great Depression.

The lower costs of holding larger stakes, however, may be a double-edged sword for management discipline. High managerial stock ownership could be used to entrench managers and reduce the probability of a takeover (Stulz, 1988). With a more active corporate control market today than in 1935, managers may have an incentive to raise their ownership stakes to achieve the same level of protection they once had. Innovations such as executive stock swaps (Bolster, Chance, and Rich, 1996) allow managers to maintain voting rights but hedge against movements in their own stock price, thereby reducing the cost to the managers of controlling a large voting bloc. On the other hand, if the corporate control market provides less discipline for the largest firms (because they are more difficult to take over), then this motivation for insiders to hold large equity stakes is attenuated. This could be part of the explanation for the similar low levels of percentage ownership in the largest firms across time.

Conclusion

Despite the widespread view from Berle and Means onward that ownership of firms is increasingly separated from managerial control of those firms, we find that managerial ownership of public corporations is markedly higher today than in 1935. Using a comprehensive sample of the 1,500 publicly traded firms in 1935 and a comparable sample of 4,200 firms in 1995, we find that managerial ownership has increased from an average of 13% in 1935 to 21% in 1995. In terms of real (1995) dollar values, average managerial ownership has increased from $18 million to $73 million.

A potential explanation for this rise is that greater reliance on managerial ownership has substituted for less reliance on other incentive alignment devices to discipline management. We find, however, just the opposite. The use of other corporate governance mechanisms, such as pay-for-performance and the market for corporate control, has stayed the same or increased over time. The top management of publicly traded corporations thus faces more intensive pressure from incentive-alignment devices today than earlier in the century.

An alternative explanation is that the relationships between firm-specific characteristics and the costs and benefits of using managerial ownership as a control device have changed over time. While most of the characteristics we examine have the same relationship to managerial ownership in both periods, the role of volatility is different. In 1935, managerial ownership is inversely related to firm volatility. In 1995, however, managerial ownership has a nonlinear relationship with volatility: managerial ownership is positively related to firm volatility at low and moderate levels of volatility but the relationship turns negative when firm volatility is high. The overall lower level of volatility today along with advances in capital markets and financial theory appear to have reduced the costs of managers holding large stakes in their firms. Changes in these external conditions that have reduced the cost of hedging, for example, have had an impact on the ownership structure of firms.

These results have implications for current policy issues concerning corporate governance. The effects of volatility and financial market development on the costs of insider ownership have largely been overlooked in the debates on financial system and corporate governance reforms. Taking this relationship into account is particularly important in the case of emerging and transition economies, where volatility and financial market development may be closer to that of the U.S. in the early part of the century than of the U.S. today. In addition, our finding that managerial ownership is higher now than in 1935 should help provide guidance in the implementation of "best practices" of corporate governance, such as those promulgated by the National Association of Corporate Directors, which call for boards to "set a substantial target for stock ownership by each director."[6]

---

[6] National Association of Corporate Directors (1995).

CHAPTER 24

Executive compensation as an agency problem

LUCIAN ARYE BEBCHUK AND JESSE M. FRIED

Lucian Arye Bebchuk was born in 1955 in Wroclav, Poland. He earned an LL.M. in 1980 and an S.J.D. in 1984 from Harvard Law School and a Ph.D. in economics in 1993 from Harvard University. When this article was published, he was the William J. and Alicia T. Friedman Professor of Law, Economics, and Finance at Harvard Law School, where he directs the Program on Corporate Governance.

Jesse M. Fried was born in 1963 in Washington, D.C. He received an M.A. in economics in 1989 from Harvard University and a J.D. in 1992 from Harvard Law School. When this article was published, he was Professor of Law at the University of California at Berkeley School of Law, where he serves as co-director of the Berkeley Center for Law, Business, and the Economy.

. . .

Among financial economists, the dominant approach to the study of executive compensation views managers' pay arrangements as a (partial) *remedy* to the agency problem. Under this approach, which we label the "optimal contracting approach," boards are assumed to design compensation schemes to provide managers with efficient incentives to maximize shareholder value. Financial economists have done substantial work within this optimal contracting model in an effort to understand executive compensation practices; recent surveys of this work include Murphy (1999) and Core, Guay and Larcker (2001). To some researchers working within the optimal contracting model, the main flaw with existing practices seems to be that, due to political limitations on how generously executives can be treated, compensation schemes are not sufficiently high-powered (Jensen and Murphy, 1990).

Another approach to studying executive compensation focuses on a different link between the agency problem and executive compensation. Under this approach, which we label the "managerial power approach," executive compensation is viewed not only as a potential instrument for addressing the

Reprinted with abridgments from Lucian A. Bebchuk and Jesse M. Fried, "Executive Compensation as an Agency Problem," *Journal of Economic Perspectives,* 17, 3 (Summer 2003): 71–92. Reprinted with the permission of the American Economic Association.

agency problem but also as *part* of the agency problem itself. As a number of researchers have recognized, some features of pay arrangements seem to reflect managerial rent-seeking rather than the provision of efficient incentives (for example, Blanchard, Lopez-de-Silanes and Shleifer, 1994; Yermack, 1997; and Bertrand and Mullainathan, 2001). We seek to develop a full account of how managerial influence shapes the executive compensation landscape in a forthcoming book (Bebchuk and Fried, 2004) that builds substantially on a long article written jointly with David Walker (Bebchuk, Fried and Walker, 2002).

Drawing on this work, we argue below that managerial power and rent extraction are likely to have an important influence on the design of compensation arrangements. Indeed, the managerial power approach can shed light on many significant features of the executive compensation landscape that have long been seen as puzzling by researchers working within the optimal contracting model. We also explain that managers' influence over their own pay might impose substantial costs on shareholders – beyond the excess pay executives receive – by diluting and distorting managers' incentives and thereby hurting corporate performance.

Although the managerial power approach is conceptually quite different from the optimal contracting approach, we do not propose the former as a complete replacement for the latter. Compensation arrangements are likely to be shaped both by market forces that push toward value-maximizing outcomes, and by managerial influence, which leads to departures from these outcomes in directions favorable to managers. The managerial power approach simply claims that these departures are substantial and that optimal contracting alone cannot adequately explain compensation practices.

The limitations of optimal contracting

The optimal contracting view recognizes that managers suffer from an agency problem and do not automatically seek to maximize shareholder value. Thus, providing managers with adequate incentives is important. Under the optimal contracting view, the board, working in shareholders' interest, attempts to provide cost-effectively such incentives to managers through their compensation packages.

Optimal compensation contracts could result either from effective arm's length bargaining between the board and the executives or from market constraints that induce these parties to adopt such contracts even in the absence of arm's length bargaining. However, neither of these forces can be expected to prevent significant departures from arm's length outcomes.[1]

---

[1] Shareholders could try to challenge undesirable pay arrangements in court. However, corporate law rules effectively prevent courts from reviewing compensation decisions (Bebchuk, Fried and Walker, 2002, pp. 779–781).

Executive compensation as an agency problem

Just as there is no reason to presume that managers automatically seek to maximize shareholder value, there is no reason to expect *a priori* that directors will either. Indeed, directors' behavior is also subject to an agency problem, which in turn undermines their ability to address effectively the agency problems in the relationship between managers and shareholders.

Directors generally wish to be re-appointed to the board. Average director compensation in the 200 largest U.S. corporations was $152,626 in 2001 (Pearl Meyers and Partners, 2002). In the notorious Enron case, the directors were each paid $380,000 annually (Abelson, 2001). Besides an attractive salary, a directorship is also likely to provide prestige and valuable business and social connections. CEOs play an important role in renominating directors to the board. Thus, directors usually have an incentive to favor the CEO.

To be sure, in a world in which shareholders selected individual directors, directors might have an incentive to develop reputations as shareholder-serving. However, board elections are by slate, dissidents putting forward their own director slate confront substantial impediments, and such challenges are therefore exceedingly rare (Bebchuk and Kahan, 1990). Typically, the director slate proposed by management is the only one offered.

The key to a board position is thus being placed on the company's slate. Because the CEO's influence over the board gives her significant influence over the nomination process, directors have an incentive to "go along" with the CEO's pay arrangement, a matter dear to the CEO's heart – at least as long as the compensation package remains within the range of what can plausibly be defended and justified. In addition, because being on the company's slate is the key to being appointed, developing a reputation for haggling with the CEO over compensation would hurt rather than help a director's chances of being invited to join other companies' boards. Yet another reason to favor the CEO is that the CEO can affect directors' compensation and perks.

Directors typically have only nominal equity interests in the firm (Baker, Jensen and Murphy, 1988; Core, Holthausen and Larcker, 1999). Thus, even a director who did not place much value on a board seat would still have little personal motivation to fight the CEO and her friends on the board on compensation matters. Moreover, directors usually lack easy access to independent information and advice on compensation practices necessary to effectively challenge the CEO's pay.

Finally, market forces are not sufficiently strong and fine-tuned to assure optimal contracting outcomes. Markets – including the market for corporate control, the market for capital and the labor market for executives – impose *some* constraints on what directors will agree to and what managers will ask them to approve. An analysis of these markets, however, indicates that the constraints they impose are far from tight and permit substantial deviations from optimal contracting (Bebchuk, Fried and Walker, 2002).

Consider, for example, the market for corporate control – the threat of a takeover. Firms frequently have substantial defenses against takeovers. For example, a majority of companies have a staggered board, which prevents a hostile acquirer from gaining control before two annual elections pass, and often enables incumbent managers to block hostile bids that are attractive to shareholders. To overcome incumbent opposition, a hostile bidder must be prepared to pay a substantial premium; during the second half of the 1990s, the average premium in hostile acquisitions was 40 percent (Bebchuk, Coates and Subramanian, 2002). The disciplinary force of the market for corporate control is further weakened by the prevalence of "golden parachute" provisions, as well as acquisition-related benefits that target managers often receive when an acquisition takes place. The market for corporate control thus leaves managers with considerable slack and ability to extract private benefits.

To be sure, the market for control might impose some costs on managers who are especially aggressive in extracting rents; we later note evidence that CEOs of firms with stronger takeover protection get pay packages that are both larger and less sensitive to performance. The important point is that the market for corporate control fails to impose tight constraints on executive compensation.

Some responses to our earlier work assumed that our analysis of the absence of arm's length bargaining did not apply to cases in which boards negotiate pay with a CEO candidate from outside the firm (for example, Murphy, 2002). However, while such negotiations might be closer to the arm's length model than negotiations with an incumbent CEO, they still fall quite short of this benchmark. Among other things, directors negotiating with an outside CEO candidate know that after the candidate becomes CEO, she will have influence over their renomination to the board and over their compensation and perks. The directors will also wish to have good personal and working relationships with the person who is expected to become the firm's leader and a fellow board member. And while agreeing to a pay package that favors the outside CEO hire imposes little financial cost on the directors, any breakdown in the hiring negotiations, which might embarrass the directors and in any event force them to reopen the CEO selection process, would be personally costly to them. Finally, directors' limited time forces them to rely on information shaped and presented by the company's human resources staff and compensation consultants, all of whom have incentives to please the incoming CEO.

The managerial power approach

The very reasons for questioning the ability of optimal contracting to explain compensation practices adequately also suggest that executives have substantial influence over their own pay. In addition, these reasons suggest that the greater

Executive compensation as an agency problem

is managers' power, the greater is their ability to extract rents. There are limits to what directors will accept and what markets will permit, but these constraints do not prevent managers from obtaining arrangements that are substantially more favorable than those they could obtain by bargaining at arm's length.

One important building block of the managerial power approach is "outrage" costs and constraints. The tightness of the constraints managers and directors confront depends, in part, on how much "outrage" a proposed arrangement is expected to generate among relevant outsiders. Outrage might cause embarrassment or reputational harm to directors and managers, and it might reduce shareholders' willingness to support incumbents in proxy contests or takeover bids. The more outrage a compensation arrangement is expected to generate, the more reluctant directors will be to approve the arrangement and the more hesitant managers will be to propose it in the first instance. Thus, whether a compensation arrangement that is favorable to executives but suboptimal for shareholders is adopted will depend on how it is perceived by outsiders.

There is evidence that the design of compensation arrangements is indeed influenced by how outsiders perceive them. Johnson, Porter and Shackell (1997) find that CEOs of firms receiving negative media coverage of their compensation arrangements during 1992–1994 subsequently received relatively small pay increases and had the pay-performance sensitivity of their compensation arrangements increased. Thomas and Martin (1999) find that, during the 1990s, CEOs of firms that were the target of shareholder resolutions criticizing executive pay had their annual compensation reduced over the following two years by an average of $2.7 million.

The potential significance of outsiders' perception of a CEO's compensation and of outrage costs explains the importance of yet another building block of the managerial power approach – "camouflage." To avoid or minimize the outrage that results from outsiders' recognition of rent extraction, managers have a substantial incentive to obscure and try to legitimize – or, more generally, to camouflage – their extraction of rents. The strong desire to camouflage might lead to the adoption of inefficient compensation structures that hurt managerial incentives and firm performance. This concept of camouflage turns out to be quite useful in explaining many otherwise puzzling features of the executive compensation landscape.

The importance of how compensation arrangements are perceived means that, in the executive compensation area, the transparency of disclosure matters. Financial economists often focus on the role of disclosure in getting information incorporated into market pricing. It is widely believed that information can become reflected in stock prices as long as it is known and fully understood by a limited number of market professionals. In the executive compensation context, however, the ability of plan designers to choose arrangements that favor managers depends on how these arrangements are perceived by a much wider group of outsiders. As a result, the transparency and salience of disclosure can have a significant effect on CEO compensation.

Murphy (2002) and Hall and Murphy (2003) argue that our approach cannot explain increases in managerial pay during the 1990s. In their view, CEO power declined during this period. Given the strengthening of takeover defenses during the 1990s, however, it is unclear whether CEO power diminished during this period. In any event, executive pay increases during the 1990s resulted not from changes in managerial power but rather from other factors, none of which is inconsistent with the managerial power approach.

First, seeking to make pay more sensitive to performance, regulators and shareholders encouraged the use of equity-based compensation. Taking advantage of this enthusiasm, executives used their influence to obtain substantial option pay without giving up corresponding amounts of their cash compensation. Furthermore, the options they received did not link pay tightly to the managers' own performance, but rather enabled managers to reap windfalls from that part of the stock price increase that was due solely to market and sector trends beyond their control. As a result, managers were able to capture much larger gains than more cost-effective and efficient option plans would have provided. Second, because executive compensation has historically been correlated with market capitalization, the rising stock markets of the 1990s, which carried along with them even many poorly performing companies, provided a convenient justification at most firms for substantial pay increases. Third, market booms weaken outrage constraints; exuberant shareholders are less likely to scrutinize and resent generous pay arrangements, in the same way that the recent market declines have made shareholders more prone to do so.

Power and camouflage at work

We illustrate below the potential value of the managerial power approach by discussing four patterns and practices that can be at least partly explained by power and camouflage: the relationship between power and pay; the use of compensation consultants; stealth compensation; and gratuitous goodbye payments to departing executives.

Power-pay relationships

The managerial power approach predicts that pay will be higher and/or less sensitive to performance in firms in which managers have relatively more power. Other things being equal, managers would tend to have more power when i) the board is relatively weak or ineffectual; ii) there is no large outside shareholder; iii) there are fewer institutional shareholders; or iv) managers are protected by antitakeover arrangements. There is evidence indicating that each of these factors affects pay arrangements in the way predicted by the managerial power approach.

Executive compensation is higher *when the board is relatively weak or ineffectual* vis-à-vis the CEO. Core, Holthausen and Larcker (1999) find that CEO compensation is higher under the following conditions: when the board is large, which makes it more difficult for directors to organize in opposition to the CEO; when more of the outside directors have been appointed by the CEO, which could cause them to feel a sense of gratitude or obligation to the CEO; and when outside directors serve on three or more boards, and thus are more likely to be distracted. Also, CEO pay is 20–40 percent higher if the CEO is the chairman of the board (Cyert, Kang and Kumar, 2002; Core, Holthausen and Larcker, 1999). Finally, CEO pay is negatively related to the share ownership of the board's compensation committee; doubling compensation committee ownership reduces nonsalary compensation by 4–5 percent (Cyert, Kang and Kumar, 2002).

The *presence of a large outside shareholder* is likely to result in closer monitoring (Shleifer and Vishny, 1986), and it can be expected to reduce top managers' influence over their compensation. Consistent with this observation, Cyert, Kang and Kumar (2002) find a negative correlation between the equity ownership of the largest shareholder and the amount of CEO compensation: doubling the percentage ownership of the outside shareholder reduces non-salary compensation by 12–14 percent. Bertrand and Mullainathan (2001) find that CEOs in firms that lack a 5 percent (or larger) external shareholder tend to receive more "luck-based" pay – pay associated with profit increases that are entirely generated by external factors (such as changes in oil prices and exchange rates) rather than by managers' efforts. They also find that in firms lacking large external shareholders, the cash compensation of CEOs is reduced less when their option-based compensation is increased. Relatedly, in an examination of Standard & Poor's 500 firms during the period 1992–1997, Benz, Kucher and Stutzer (2001) find that a higher concentration of shareholders results in a significantly smaller amount of options grants to top executives.

A *larger concentration of institutional shareholders* might result in greater monitoring and scrutiny of the CEO and the board. Examining CEO pay in almost 2000 firms during the period 1991–1997, Hartzell and Starks (2002) find that the more concentrated is institutional ownership, the lower is executive compensation. They also find that a larger institutional presence results in more performance-sensitive compensation. Examining CEO compensation in the 200 largest companies during 1990–1994, David, Kochar and Levitas (1998) find that the effect of institutional shareholders on CEO pay depends on the types of relationships they have with the firm. They divide institutional shareholders into 1) those that have no other business relationship with the firm and are thus concerned only with the firm's share value ("pressure-resistant" institutions); and 2) those that have other business relationships with the firm (like managing a pension fund) and are thus vulnerable to management pressure ("pressure-sensitive" institutions). As the managerial power approach predicts, CEO pay is negatively correlated with the presence of pressure-resistant institutional investors and positively correlated with the presence of pressure-sensitive ones.

The adoption of *antitakeover provisions* makes CEOs less vulnerable to a hostile takeover. Borokhovich, Brunarski and Parrino (1997), examining 129 firms that adopted antitakeover provisions (such as a supermajority rule) during the period 1979–1987, find that CEOs of firms adopting such provisions enjoy above-market compensation before adoption of the antitakeover provisions and that adoption of these provisions increases their excess compensation significantly. This pattern is not readily explainable by optimal contracting; indeed, if managers' jobs are more secure, shareholders should be able to pay managers a lower risk premium (Agrawal and Knoeber, 1998). In another study, Cheng, Nagar and Rajan (2001) find that CEOs of Forbes 500 firms that became protected by state antitakeover legislation enacted during the period 1984–1991 reduced their holdings of shares by an average of 15 percent, apparently because the shares were not as necessary for maintaining control. Optimal contracting might predict that a CEO protected by antitakeover legislation would be required to buy more shares to restore the CEO's incentive to increase shareholder value.

Compensation consultants

U.S. public companies typically employ outside consultants to provide input into the executive compensation process (Bizjack, Lemmon, and Naveen, 2000). The use of consultants can be explained within the optimal contracting framework on grounds that they supply useful information and contribute expertise on the design of compensation packages. But although compensation consultants might play a useful role, they also can help in camouflaging rents. The incentives of compensation consultants – and the evidence regarding their use – suggest that these consultants are often used to justify executive pay rather than to optimize it.

Compensation consultants have strong incentives to use their discretion to benefit the CEO. Even if the CEO is not formally involved in the selection of the compensation consultant, the consultant is usually hired by the firm's human resources department, which is subordinate to the CEO. Providing advice that hurts the CEO's pocketbook is hardly a way to enhance the consultant's chances of being hired in the future by this firm or, indeed, by any other firms. Moreover, executive pay specialists often work for consulting firms that have other, larger assignments with the hiring company, which further distorts their incentives (Crystal, 1991).

Pay consultants can favor the CEO by providing the compensation data that are most useful for justifying a high level of pay. For example, when firms do well, consultants argue that pay should reflect performance and should be higher than the average in the industry – and certainly higher than that of CEOs who are doing poorly. In contrast, when firms do poorly, the consultants focus not on performance data but rather on peer group pay to argue that CEO compensation should be higher to reflect prevailing industry levels (Gillan, 2001).

After the compensation consultant has collected and presented the "relevant" comparative data, the board generally sets pay equal to or higher than the median CEO pay in the comparison group. Reviewing the reports of compensation committees in 100 large companies, Bizjack, Lemmon and Naveen (2000) report that 96 used peer groups in determining management compensation and that a large majority of firms that use peer groups set compensation at or above the fiftieth percentile of the peer group. The combination of helpful compensation consultants and sympathetic boards is partly responsible for the widely recognized "ratcheting up" of executive salaries (Murphy, 1999, p. 2525).

After the board approves the compensation package, firms use compensation consultants and their reports to justify executive compensation to shareholders. Examining Standard & Poor's 500 companies during the period 1987–1992, Wade, Porac and Pollock (1997) find that companies that pay their CEOs larger base salaries, and firms with more concentrated and active outside ownership, are more likely to cite the use of surveys and consultants in justifying executive pay in their proxy reports to shareholders. This study also finds that, when accounting returns are high, firms emphasize the accounting returns and downplay market returns.

Stealth compensation

As we document in Bebchuk and Fried (2003a), firms use pay practices that make less transparent the total amount of executive compensation and the extent to which compensation is decoupled from managers' own performance. Among the arrangements used by firms that camouflage the amount and the performance-insensitivity of compensation are pension plans, deferred compensation, post-retirement perks, and consulting contracts.

Most of the pension and deferred compensation benefits given to executives do not enjoy the large tax subsidy that applies to the standard retirement arrangements provided to other employees. In the case of executives, such arrangements largely shift tax liability from the executive to the firm in ways that sometimes even increase the joint tax liability of the two parties. The efficiency grounds for providing compensation through in-kind retirement perks

335

and guaranteed postretirement consulting fees are also far from clear. All of these arrangements, however, make pay less salient.

Among other things, under existing disclosure rules, firms do not have to place a dollar value on – and include in the firm's publicly filed compensation tables – compensation provided to executives after they retire. Although the existence of executives' retirement arrangements must be noted in certain places in the firm's public filings, this disclosure is less salient, because outsiders focus on the dollar amounts reported in the compensation tables. Indeed, the compensation table numbers are used by the ExecuComp database, which is the basis for much of the empirical work on executive compensation.

...

Gratuitous goodbye payments

In many cases, boards give departing CEOs payments and benefits that are gratuitous – not required under the terms of the CEO's compensation contract. Such gratuitous goodbye payments are common even when CEOs perform so poorly that the board feels compelled to replace them.

Compensation contracts usually provide executives with generous severance arrangements even when they depart following very dismal performance. Such "soft landing" provisions provide executives with insurance against being fired due to poor performance. It is far from clear that these arrangements reflect optimal contracting; after all, such provisions reduce the difference in managerial payoffs between good and poor performance that firms spend so much money trying to create. Our focus here, however, is on payments that go beyond the severance arrangements that are contractually specified.

For example, when Mattel CEO Jill Barad resigned under fire, the board forgave a $4.2 million loan, gave her an additional $3.3 million in cash to cover the taxes for forgiveness of another loan and allowed her unvested options to vest automatically. These gratuitous benefits were in addition to the considerable benefits that she received under her employment agreement, which included a termination payment of $26.4 million and a stream of retirement benefits exceeding $700,000 per year.

It is not easy to reconcile such gratuitous payments with the arm's length, optimal contracting model. The board has the authority to fire the CEO and pay the CEO her contractual severance benefits. Thus, there is no need to "bribe" a poorly performing CEO to step down. In addition, the signal sent by the goodbye payment will, if anything, only weaken the incentive of the next CEO to perform.

The making of such gratuitous payments, however, is quite consistent with the existence of managerial influence over the board. Because of their relationship with the CEO, some directors might be unwilling to replace the CEO unless she is treated very generously. Other directors might be willing to replace the CEO in any event, but prefer to accompany the move with a goodbye payment to reduce the discomfort they feel firing the CEO or to make the difficult separation process more pleasant and less contentious. In all of these cases, directors' willingness to make gratuitous payments to the (poorly performing) CEO results from the CEO's relationship with the directors.

It is important to note that, taking managerial power *as given*, providing gratuitous payments to fired CEOs might be beneficial to shareholders in some instances. If many directors are loyal to the CEO, such payments might be necessary to assemble a board majority in favor of replacing him. In such a case, the practice would help shareholders when the CEO's departure is more beneficial to shareholders than the cost to them of the goodbye payment. For our purposes, however, what is important is that these gratuitous payments, whether they are beneficial to shareholders or not, reflect the existence and significance of managerial influence.

Suboptimal pay structures

Pay without performance

Optimal contracting arrangements might call for very large amounts of compensation for executives, if such compensation is needed to provide managers with powerful incentives to enhance shareholder value (Jensen and Murphy, 1990). The problem with current arrangements, however, is that the generous compensation provided executives is linked only weakly to managerial performance. This pay-performance disconnect is puzzling from an optimal contracting view.

The substantial part of compensation that is not equity based has long been criticized as weakly linked to managerial performance. During the 1990s, there was no significant correlation between a CEO's salary and bonus and her firm's industry-adjusted performance (Murphy, 1999). In addition, there is evidence that cash compensation increases when firm profits rise for reasons that clearly have nothing to do with managers' efforts (Blanchard, Lopez-de-Silanes and Shleifer, 1994; Bertrand and Mullainathan, 2001). Furthermore, managers receive substantial non-equity compensation through arrangements that have received little attention from financial economists – such as pensions, deferred pay and loans – and this compensation is also relatively insensitive to managers' own performance.

In light of the historically weak link between managers' performance and their non-equity compensation, shareholders and regulators have increasingly looked to equity-based compensation to provide the desired link between pay and performance. In the early 1990s, institutional investors and federal regulators sought to encourage the use of such compensation, and the last decade has witnessed a dramatic growth in the use of stock options. Unfortunately, however, managers have been able to use their influence to obtain option plans that appear to deviate substantially from optimal contracting in ways that favor managers.

We wish to emphasize our strong support for the concept of equity-based compensation which, if well designed, could provide managers with very desirable incentives. The devil, however, is in the details. Below, we discuss several important features of existing option compensation plans that are difficult to justify from an optimal contracting perspective, but can readily be explained by the managerial power approach: the failure of option plans to filter out windfalls, the almost uniform use of at-the-money options and the broad freedom given to managers to unload options and shares.

It might be asked why risk-averse managers would not use their influence to get higher cash salaries rather than options. Holding the expected value of additional compensation constant, managers would indeed prefer to take the cash. But managers seeking to increase their pay during the 1990s did not have a choice between additional compensation in the form of cash and additional compensation in the form of options with the same expected value. Rather, outsiders' enthusiasm about equity-based compensation enabled managers to obtain additional compensation in the form of options without offsetting reduction in cash compensation. Furthermore, the possible benefits from improved incentives provided defensible reasons for very large amounts of additional compensation. While Apple CEO Steve Jobs was recently able to obtain an option package worth over half a billion dollars, albeit with some outcry, cash compensation of this order of magnitude is (still) quite inconceivable. The fact that better designed options could have provided much more cheaply the same incentives has not been sufficiently salient to make conventional plans patently unjustifiable.

Option plans that fail to filter out "windfalls"

One widespread and persistent feature of stock option plans is that they fail to filter out stock price rises that are due to industry and general market trends and thus completely unrelated to managers' own performance. Under conventional option plans, when the market or sector rises substantially, even executives whose companies perform poorly relative to the market or sector average can make large profits. Paying managers substantial compensation for stock price increases that have nothing to do with their own performance is difficult to explain under optimal contracting. The substantial amount currently spent on

338

rewarding managers for market or sector rises could either be used to enhance incentives (for example, by giving managers a large number of options linked more tightly to managers' own performance) or be saved with little weakening of incentives.

There are many different ways of designing what we call "reduced-windfall" option plans – plans that filter out all or some of the part of the stock price increase that is unrelated to managers' own performance. One approach discussed frequently by academics is linking the exercise price of options to a market-wide index or a sector index (for example, Rappaport, 1999). Another strategy is to condition the "vesting" of options on the firm meeting specified performance targets. These targets can be linked to the stock price, earnings per share or any other measure of firm performance.

When the exercise price of an indexed option is linked to market or sector averages, there is a substantial possibility that the manager will receive no payoff from the option plan. If this possibility were regarded as undesirable, reduced-windfall options could easily be designed to produce a high likelihood of payout. For example, the exercise price could be indexed not to changes in the industry or market average, but rather to changes in a somewhat lower benchmark – say, the stock price of the firm that is at the bottom 20th percentile of the industry or market. Under such an option plan, executives would have, on average, an 80 percent probability of outperforming the benchmark and receiving a payout. But executives would not profit, as they could under conventional plans, when their performance places them at or below the 20th percentile.

Given the wide variety of reduced-windfall options available and their potential benefits, it would probably be optimal in many firms to filter out at least some of the increase in the stock price that has nothing to do with managers' own performance. Yet almost all U.S. firms use conventional stock options under which managers capture the full increase in stock price. In 2001, only about 5 percent of the 250 largest U.S. public firms used some form of reduced-windfall options (Levinsohn, 2001).

Financial economists have made substantial efforts to develop optimal-contracting explanations for why firms do not use reduced-windfall options. We survey the various explanations in our earlier work (Bebchuk, Fried and Walker, 2002, pp. 803–809) and conclude that none of them can adequately explain the widespread failure to screen out windfalls. From the perspective of managerial power, however, the failure to filter out general market or industry effects is not at all puzzling. Under this approach, compensation schemes are designed to benefit executives without being perceived as clearly unreasonable. Given that using conventional options will be legitimate and acceptable (after all, most firms use them) and that moving to indexing or any other form of reduced-windfall options is likely to be costly or inconvenient for managers, the lack of any real movement toward such options is consistent with the managerial power approach.

At-the-money options

Almost all of the stock options used to compensate executives are "at-the-money" – that is, their exercise price is set to the grant-date market price (Murphy, 1999, p. 2509). An optimally designed scheme would seek to provide risk averse managers with cost-effective incentives to exert effort and make value-maximizing decisions. The optimal exercise price under such a scheme would depend on a multitude of factors that are likely to vary from executive to executive, from company to company, from industry to industry and from time to time. Such factors might include the degree of managerial risk aversion (which in turn might be affected by the manager's age and wealth), the project choices available to the company, the volatility of the company's stock, the expected rate of inflation and the length of the manager's contract, among other things. There is no reason to expect that "one size fits all" – that the same exercise price is optimal for all executives at all firms, in all industries and at all times.

It is therefore highly unlikely that out-of-the-money options – options whose exercise price is above the current market price – are *never* optimal. Out-of-the-money options have a lower expected value than at-the-money options because they are less likely to pay off than at-the-money options, and when they do pay off the holder receives less value. Thus, for every dollar of expected value, a firm can give an executive more out-of-the money options than at-the-money options. By giving more out-of-the money options, the firm can increase the reward to the manager for doing particularly well. Out-of-the-money options thus can offer much higher pay-for-performance sensitivity per dollar of expected value than conventional options (Hall, 1999). There is even evidence suggesting that giving managers out-of-the-money options rather than at-the-money-options would, on average, boost firm value (Habib and Ljungqvist, 2000). The almost uniform use of at-the-money options is thus difficult to explain from an optimal contracting perspective. Indeed, economists working within optimal contracting have called this practice a "puzzle" (Hall, 1999, p. 43).

The near uniform use of at-the-money options is not puzzling, however, when examined under the managerial power approach. Everything else equal, executives prefer a lower exercise price. Because at-the-money options might sometimes be optimal and are employed by almost all other firms, their use in any given case will not generate outrage. Therefore, compensation plan designers have little reason to increase the exercise price above the grant-date market price.

Executive compensation as an agency problem

Executives would be even better off, of course, if stock options were issued with an exercise price below the grant-date market price. However, such in-the-money options would create a salient windfall and might generate some outrage costs. Furthermore, in-the-money options would trigger a charge to accounting earnings, which might undermine a main excuse for not using indexed options or other reduced-windfall options – that the use of such options would hurt reported earnings (Bebchuk, Fried and Walker, 2002). Because in-the-money options would thus be difficult or costly for plan designers to use, and at-the-money options are the most favorable to managers within the remaining range of possibilities, a uniform use of at-the-money options is consistent with the managerial power approach.

Managers' freedom to unwind equity incentives

Another problem for the optimal contracting approach is managers' broad freedom to unload their options and shares. When managers unwind their equity incentives, restoring pay-performance sensitivity requires giving them new options or shares. Thus, such unwinding either (1) weakens managers' incentives or (2) forces the firm to give managers new equity incentives to restore incentives to the pre-unwinding level.

Although an executive becomes entitled to options once they have vested, the compensation contract could preclude the executive from "cashing out" the vested options – that is, from exercising the options and then selling the acquired shares – for a specified period after the vesting date. Such a limitation would maintain incentives for that additional period without requiring the firm to grant new options to replace the ones cashed out.

To be sure, restrictions on executives' ability to cash out vested equity instruments impose liquidity and diversification costs that must be balanced against the incentive benefits of restricting unwinding. The efficient arrangement is thus likely to vary from case to case, depending on the executive's and the firm's characteristics. But there is no reason to expect that optimal contracts would generally make the vesting date and the cash-out date identical.

In practice, however, the date on which options vest and the date on which they are exercisable are almost always the same. A minority of firms have created "target ownership plans" that require managers to hold a certain amount of shares (Core and Larcker, 2002). But the targets tend to be rather low, and there often appears to be no penalty imposed for missing them. As a result of weak restrictions on unwinding, managers exercise many of their options well before the options expire and sell almost all of the shares thereby acquired (Carpenter, 1998; Ofek and Yermack, 2000). Shares that are not sold after option exercise are often hedged or partially hedged in transactions that are

341

not reported to the Securities and Exchange Commission (Bettis, Bizjack and Lemmon, 2001).

Managers also typically have freedom to determine the precise time of unwinding, a practice that is also difficult to explain under optimal contracting. Although trading on "material" inside information is illegal, the definition of "materiality" and the difficulties of enforcement are such that managers making selling decisions can use their superior knowledge about the firm with little fear of liability (Fried, 1998). As a result, managers are able to obtain abnormal returns trading in their firm's shares (Seyhun, 1998). It is far from clear, however, that enabling managers to make such profits is an efficient form of compensation.

Even assuming it were desirable to permit managers to unload shares at a certain stage in their contracts, it does not follow that executives should have absolute control over the exact timing of their sales. After all, liquidity or diversification needs are unlikely to arise unexpectedly one morning. Firms could require that sales be carried out gradually over a specified period, perhaps pursuant to a pre-arranged plan. Alternatively, firms could require executives to disclose publicly in advance their intended trades, which would reduce executives' ability to profit from their informational advantage (Fried, 1998). Yet firms generally do not impose any such restrictions.

Because a firm can be held liable if it fails to take reasonable steps to prevent insider trading by its employees, a number of firms have adopted "trading windows" and "blackout periods" to restrict the times during the year when a manager can sell or buy shares (Bettis, Coles and Lemmon, 2000). However, many firms have not put such restrictions in place. And even in firms that have imposed such restrictions, managers who know undisclosed bad news during a trading window may use that trading opportunity to unwind a substantial amount of their holdings. Thus, executives retain the ability to dump shares before bad news becomes public. In one notorious case, Enron insiders sold hundreds of millions of shares before information about Enron's actual financial condition was released and the stock price collapsed.

Although managers' ability to unwind equity incentives early and to control the time of such unwinding cannot easily be explained under optimal contracting, it is quite consistent with the managerial power approach. Broad freedom to unload equity instruments provides managers with substantial benefits that are not particularly conspicuous. The corresponding costs to shareholders from diluted incentives are also not salient. Furthermore, and perhaps most importantly, managers' unwinding of options and shares provides a convenient justification for frequently granting managers new equity-based incentives, thereby boosting their total compensation. Although a system of constant unwinding and replenishing incentives is more costly to shareholders than one that requires managers to hold options and shares for longer periods, it is obviously much better for managers.

The "perceived cost" explanation

Murphy (2002) and Hall and Murphy (2003) put forward a "perceived cost" explanation for the use of conventional, at-the-money options. According to their explanation, executives and directors erroneously perceive conventional options to be "cheap" or even "nearly free to grant" because such options can be granted without any cash outlay and without reducing reported earnings.

We doubt that executives and their advisers cannot grasp the costs of conventional options to shareholders. Assuming that Hall and Murphy are correct in suggesting that managers believe that the stock market is influenced by accounting numbers rather than underlying economic reality, this would at most mean that executives believe that investors underestimate or ignore the costs of options that are not expensed for accounting purposes – not that executives themselves fail to see the significant economic costs that conventional options impose on shareholders (whose ownership interest the options dilute).

One might even be skeptical that directors, many of whom are executives themselves, fail to understand the costs of options to shareholders. Indeed, if directors had so little financial sophistication, then the board-monitoring model of corporate governance is in even worse shape than our analysis suggests. Let us suppose, however, that directors have been oblivious to the true cost of conventional options. If so, such a misperception on the part of directors is best seen not as an alternative to the managerial power explanation, but rather as one of the factors contributing to managers' ability to exert considerable influence over the terms of their pay.

As we discussed earlier, there are several reasons why boards cannot be expected to engage in arm's length negotiations with the CEO over executive compensation; one of them is directors' lack of easy access to accurate, unbiased information. To the extent directors in fact did misperceive the cost of options, such a misperception would simply be part of the informational problem that contributes to directors' willingness to approve suboptimal arrangements. If directors were ignorant about such an important and widely discussed issue as the actual cost of options, they would likely be inadequately informed about other features of compensation arrangements.

In our view, inadequate information is only one of the factors, alongside inadequate incentives and others, that might lead directors to agree to pay arrangements that favor managers. For one thing, directors' confusion over the cost of options cannot explain the systematic relationship between power and pay and managers' efforts to make compensation less salient that we discussed earlier. For many purposes, however, it does not matter whether directors' willingness to accept arrangements that favor executives is the result of conscious favoritism, honest misperceptions, inadequate incentives to exert effort, or some combination of these factors. The important thing is that directors do not adequately represent shareholders' interests in bargaining with managers over their pay and that these pay arrangements consequently depart from the arm's length model in directions favorable to executives.

Costs to shareholders

What are the costs imposed on shareholders by managers' influence over their own pay? To begin with, there is the excess pay managers receive as a result of their power – the difference between what managers' influence enables them to obtain and what they would receive under an arm's length arrangement. Some might think that this problem is only symbolic, and that these rents have little effect on shareholders' bottom line. But a close look at the amounts involved indicates that they add up to much more than small change. In 2000, CEO compensation was on average 7.89 percent of corporate profits in the firms making up the 1500-company ExecuComp dataset (Balsam, 2002, p. 262).

Furthermore, and perhaps more importantly, managers' ability to influence their pay leads to compensation arrangements that generate worse incentives than those that arm's length contracts would provide. Managers have an interest in compensation schemes that camouflage the extent of their rent extraction or that put less pressure on them to reduce slack. As a result, managerial influence might lead to the adoption of compensation arrangements that provide weak or even perverse incentives. In our view, the reduction in shareholder value caused by these inefficiencies, rather than the excess rents captured by managers, could be the largest cost arising from managers' ability to influence their compensation.

To begin, compensation arrangements currently provide weaker incentives to reduce managerial slack and increase shareholder value than likely would be provided by arm's length arrangements. As explained, both the non-equity and equity components of managers' compensation are substantially more decoupled from managers' own performance than appearances might suggest. Shareholders thus might benefit substantially from the improved performance that a move toward optimal contracting arrangements could generate.

Prevailing practices not only fail to provide cost-effective incentives to reduce slack, but also create perverse incentives. For one thing, they provide managers' incentives to change firm parameters in a way that would justify increases in pay. Consider, for example, the familiar problem of empire building. It is commonly believed that the practice of granting options provides managers with incentives not to undertake acquisitions that are value-decreasing for

Executive compensation as an agency problem

shareholders. This is clearly the case, however, only in a static model in which all option grants are made before managers make acquisition decisions. In a dynamic model, managers considering an expansion decision that is somewhat value decreasing for shareholders would have different incentives: While such an expansion would reduce the value of their current options, it may raise their aggregate future compensation by an even greater amount because a larger firm size can be used to justify higher pay.

Furthermore, managers' broad freedom to unload equity incentives can produce substantial inefficiencies. Executives who expect to unload their shares or options have weaker incentives to exert effort when the payoff is not going to be recognized by the market at the time they unwind their equity positions (Bar-Gill and Bebchuk, 2003a). Such executives also have incentives to misreport corporate performance and suppress bad news (Bar-Gill and Bebchuk, 2002). Indeed, such executives also have an incentive to choose projects that are less transparent or to reduce the transparency of existing projects (Bar-Gill and Bebchuk, 2003b). The efficiency costs of such distortions might exceed, possibly by a large margin, whatever liquidity or risk bearing benefits executives obtain from being able to unload their options and shares at will.

Conclusion

There are good theoretical and empirical reasons for concluding that managerial power substantially affects the design of executive compensation in companies with a separation of ownership and control. Executive compensation can thus be fruitfully analyzed not only as an instrument for addressing the agency problem arising from the separation of ownership and control – but also as part of the agency problem itself.

The conclusion that managerial power and rent extraction play an important role in executive compensation has significant implications for corporate governance, which we explore in our forthcoming book (Bebchuk and Fried, 2004). It is important to note, however, that this is an area in which widespread recognition of the problem might contribute to alleviating it. The extent to which managerial influence can move compensation arrangements away from optimal contracting outcomes depends on the extent to which market participants, especially institutional investors, recognize the problems we have discussed. Financial economists can thus make an important contribution to improving compensation arrangements by analyzing how current practices deviate from those suggested by optimal contracting. We hope that future studies of executive compensation will devote to the role of managerial power as much attention as the optimal contracting model has received.

CHAPTER 25

An economist's perspective on the theory of the firm

OLIVER HART

Oliver Hart was born in London, England, in 1948. He received a Ph.D. in economics from Princeton University in 1974. When this article was published, he was Professor of Economics at the Massachusetts Institute of Technology. Since 1993, he has taught at Harvard University, where he is currently the Andrew E. Furer Professor of Economics.

An outsider to the field of economics would probably take it for granted that economists have a highly developed theory of the firm. After all, firms are the engines of growth of modern capitalistic economies, and so economists must surely have fairly sophisticated views of how they behave. In fact, little could be further from the truth. Most formal models of the firm are extremely rudimentary, capable only of portraying hypothetical firms that bear little relation to the complex organizations we see in the world. Furthermore, theories that attempt to incorporate real-world features of corporations, partnerships, and the like often lack precision and rigor and have therefore failed, by and large, to be accepted by the theoretical mainstream.

This article attempts to give lawyers a sense of how economists think about firms. It does not pretend to offer a systematic survey of the area; rather, it highlights several ideas of particular importance, and then explores an alternative theoretical perspective from which to view the firm.[1] Part I introduces various established economic theories of the firm. Part II turns to a newer theory of the firm, based not upon human capital structures, but rather upon property rights. Part III synthesizes this property rights-based theory of the firm with more established theories.

Excerpted from Oliver Hart, "An Economist's Perspective on the Theory of the Firm." This article originally appeared at 89 *Columbia Law Review* 1757 (1989). Reprinted by permission.
[1] Several recent surveys provide other perspectives on this material. See, e.g., Holmstrom and Tirole (1989), Milgrom and Roberts (1988b), Williamson (1988).

An economist's perspective on the theory of the firm

I. Established theories

. . .

C. Transaction cost economics

While the neoclassical paradigm, modified by principal–agent theory, pro-gressed along the above lines, a very different approach to the theory of the firm developed under the heading of transaction cost economics. Introduced in Coase's famous 1937 article, transaction cost economics traces the existence of firms to the thinking, planning, and contracting costs that accompany any transaction, costs usually ignored by the neoclassical paradigm. The idea is that in some situations these costs will be lower if a transaction is carried out within a firm rather than in the market. According to Coase, the main cost of transacting in the market is the cost of learning about and haggling over the terms of trade; this cost can be particularly large if the transaction is a long-term one in which learning and haggling must be performed repeatedly. Transaction costs can be reduced by giving one party authority over the terms of trade, at least within limits. But, according to Coase, this authority is precisely what defines a firm: within a firm, transactions occur as a result of instructions or orders issued by a boss, and the price mechanism is suppressed.

. . .

At the same time that doubts were being expressed about the specifics of Coase's theory, Coase's major idea – that firms arise to economize on transac-tion costs – was increasingly accepted. The exact nature of these transaction costs, however, remained unclear. What lay beyond the learning and haggling costs that, according to Coase, are a major component of market transactions? Professor Oliver Williamson has offered the deepest and most far-reaching ana-lysis of these costs. Williamson recognized that transaction costs may assume particular importance in situations where economic actors make relationship-specific investments – investments to some extent specific to a particular set of individuals or assets. Examples of such investments include locating an elec-tricity generating plant adjacent to a coal mine that is going to supply it, a firm's expanding capacity to satisfy a particular customer's demands, training a worker to operate a particular set of machines or to work with a particular group of individuals, or a worker's relocating to a town where he has a new job.

In situations like these, there may be plenty of competition before the investments are made – there may be many coal mines next to which an electricity-generating plant could locate or many towns to which a worker could move. But once the parties sink their investments, they are to some extent locked into each other. As a result, external markets will not provide a guide to the parties' opportunity costs once the relationship is under way.

. . .

In Williamson's view, bringing a transaction from the market into the firm – the phenomenon of integration – mitigates . . . opportunistic behavior and improves investment incentives. Agent A is less likely to hold up agent B if A is an employee of B than if A is an independent contractor. However, Williamson does not spell out in precise terms the mechanism by which this reduction in opportunism occurs. Moreover, certain costs presumably accompany integration. Otherwise, all transactions would be carried out in firms, and the market would not be used at all. Williamson, however, leaves the precise nature of these costs unclear.

. . .

II. A property rights approach to the firm

One way to resolve the question of how integration changes incentives is spelled out in recent literature that views the firm as a set of property rights. This approach is very much in the spirit of the transaction cost literature of Coase and Williamson but differs by focusing attention on the role of physical, that is, nonhuman, assets in a contractual relationship.

Consider an economic relationship of the type analyzed by Williamson, where relationship-specific investments are important and transaction costs make it impossible to write a comprehensive long-term contract to govern the terms of the relationship. Consider also the nonhuman assets that, in the postinvestment stage, make up this relationship. Given that the initial contract has gaps, missing provisions, or ambiguities, situations will typically occur in which some aspects of the use of these assets are not specified. For example, a contract between GM and Fisher might leave open certain aspects of maintenance policy for Fisher machines or might not specify the speed of the production line or the number of shifts per day.

Take the position that the right to choose these missing aspects of usage resides with the *owner* of the asset. That is, ownership of an asset goes together with the possession of residual rights of control over that asset; the owner has the right to use the asset in any way not inconsistent with a prior contract, custom, or any law. Thus, the owner of Fisher assets would have the right to

348

choose maintenance policy and production line speed to the extent that the initial contract was silent about these.

Finally, identify a firm with all the nonhuman assets that belong to it, assets that the firm's owners possess by virtue of being owners of the firm. Included in this category are machines, inventories, buildings or locations, cash, client lists, patents, copyrights, and the rights and obligations embodied in outstanding contracts to the extent that these are also transferred with ownership. Human assets, however, are not included. Since human assets cannot be bought or sold, management and workers presumably own their own human capital both before and after any merger.

We now have the basic ingredients of a theory of the firm. In a world of transaction costs and incomplete contracts, *ex post* residual rights of control will be important because, through their influence on asset usage, they will affect *ex post* bargaining power and the division of *ex post* surplus in a relationship. This division in turn will affect the incentives of actors to invest in that relationship. Hence, when contracts are incomplete, the boundaries of firms matter in that these boundaries determine who owns and controls which assets.[2] In particular, a merger of two firms does not yield unambiguous benefits: to the extent that the (owner-)manager of the acquired firm loses control rights, his incentive to invest in the relationship will decrease. In addition, the shift in control may lower the investment incentives of workers in the acquired firm. In some cases these reductions in investment will be sufficiently great that nonintegration is preferable to integration.[3]

Note that, according to this theory, when assessing the effects of integration, one must know not only the characteristics of the merging firms but also who will own the merged company. If firms *A* and *B* integrate and *A* becomes the owner of the merged company, then *A* will presumably control the residual

---

[2] This consolidation of ownership and control points to an important lacuna in the property rights approach. The approach makes no distinction between ownership and control, assuming that both rest with the same entity. In most of the formal models that have been developed, such an arrangement turns out to be optimal since agents are assumed to be risk neutral and to have sufficient wealth to buy any asset. If managers were risk averse and had limited wealth, however, this conclusion would no longer be valid. Moreover, from a descriptive point of view, the assumption that owners manage is seriously inadequate; while it may apply to small firms such as partnerships or closed corporations, it certainly does not apply to large, publicly held corporations. For how the ownership/control dichotomy might affect the property rights approach, see infranotes 58–59 [ed.: notes 5 and 6, this version] and accompanying text.

[3] It is important to emphasize that the property rights approach distinguishes between ownership in the sense of possession of residual control rights over assets and ownership in the sense of entitlement to a firm's (verifiable) profit stream. In practice, these rights will often go together, but they do not have to. The property rights approach takes the point of view that the possession of control rights is crucial for the integration decision. That is, if firm *A* wants to acquire part of firm *B*'s (verifiable) profit stream, it can always do this by contract. It is only if firm *A* wants to acquire control over firm *B*'s assets that it needs to integrate.

rights in the new firm. *A* can then use those rights to hold up the managers and workers of firm *B*. Should the situation be reversed, a different set of control relations would result in *B* exercising control over *A*, and *A*'s workers and managers would be liable to holdups by *B*.

. . .

These ideas can be used to construct a theory of the firm's boundaries. First, as we have seen, highly complementary assets should be owned in common, which may provide a minimum size for the firm. Second, as the firm grows beyond a certain point, the manager at the center will become less and less important with regard to operations at the periphery in the sense that increases in marginal product at the periphery are unlikely to be specific either to this manager or to the assets at the center. At this stage, a new firm should be created since giving the central manager control of the periphery will increase holdup problems without any compensating gains. It should also be clear from this line of argument that, in the absence of significant lock-in effects, nonintegration is always better than integration – it is optimal to do things through the market, for integration only increases the number of potential holdups without any compensating gains.[4]

Finally, it is worth noting that the property rights approach can explain how the purchase of physical assets leads to control over human assets. To see this, consider again the GM–Fisher hypothetical. We showed that someone working with Fisher assets is more likely to improve Fisher's output in a way that is specifically of value to GM if GM owns these assets than if Fisher does. This result can be expressed more informally as follows: a worker will put more weight on an actor's objectives if that actor is the worker's boss, that is, if that actor controls the assets the worker works with, than otherwise. The conclusion is quite Coasian in spirit, but the logic underlying it is very different. Coase reaches this conclusion by assuming that a boss can tell a worker what to do; in contrast, the property rights approach reaches it by showing that it is in a worker's self-interest to behave in this way, since it puts him in a stronger bargaining position with his boss later on.

---

[4] In the above we have concentrated on ownership by an individual or by a homogeneous and monolithic group ("management"). However, the analysis can be generalized to include more complicated forms of group ownership, such as partnerships, or worker-, manager-, or consumer-cooperatives. It turns out that these will be efficient when increases in agents' marginal products are specific to a group of individuals of variable composition, rather than to a fixed group. For example, if the increase in an agent's marginal product can be realized only if the agent has access to a majority of the members of a management team, as well as to a particular asset, then it will be optimal to give each of the managers an equal ownership share in the asset and equal voting rights and adopt majority rule. See Hart and Moore (1988), p. 19.

To put it slightly differently, the reason an employee is likely to be more responsive to what his employer wants than a grocer is to what his customer wants is that the employer has much more leverage over his employee than the customer has over his grocer. In particular, the employer can deprive the employee of the assets he works with and hire another employee to work with these assets, while the customer can only deprive the grocer of his custom and as long as the customer is small, it is presumably not very difficult for the grocer to find another customer.

. . .

III. Property rights and the established theories of the firm

. . .

As noted previously, one of the weaknesses of the property rights approach as described here is that it does not take account of the separation of ownership and control present in large, publicly held corporations. In principle, it should be possible to extend the existing analysis to such situations. A public corporation can still be usefully considered a collection of assets, with ownership providing control rights over these assets. Now, however, the picture is more complicated. Although owners (shareholders) typically retain some control rights, such as the right to replace the board of directors, in practice they delegate many others to management, at least on a day-to-day basis.[5] In addition, some of the shareholders' rights sift to creditors during periods of financial distress. Developing a formal model of the firm that contains all these features, and that includes also an explanation of the firm's financial structure, is an important and challenging task for future research. Fortunately, recent work suggests that the task is not an impossible one.[6]

Conclusion

This article began with the observation that the portrayal of the firm in neo-classical economics is a caricature of the modern firm. It then went on to discuss some other approaches that attempt to develop a more realistic picture. The end product to date is still, in many ways, a caricature, but perhaps not such an unreasonable one. One promising sign is that the different approaches

---

[5] See, e.g., Clark (1985), Easterbrook and Fischel (1983), Fama and Jensen (1983b).
[6] See, e.g., Grossman and Hart (1988), Harris and Raviv, (1988), Aghion and Bolton (1988), Kahn and Huberman (1988).

economists have used to address this issue – neoclassical, principal–agent, transaction cost, nexus of contracts, property rights – appear to be converging. It is to be hoped that in the next few years the best aspects of each of these approaches can be drawn on to develop a more comprehensive and realistic theory of the firm. Such a theory would capture the salient features both of modern corporations and of owner-managed firms and would illuminate the issues for economists and lawyers alike.

CHAPTER 26

Ownership and the nature of the firm

LOUIS PUTTERMAN

Louis Putterman was born in 1952 in New York City. He received a Ph.D. in economics at Yale University in 1980. Since 1987, he has been Professor of Economics at Brown University.

. . .

1. Ownership and its components

The production of goods and services commonly requires a large variety of inputs, including financial resources, risk-bearing services, and decision making. Decision making is a necessary input because production takes place in real time, and relevant events, such as mechanical failures, technical innovations, or changes in market conditions, cannot be foreseen when agreements to undertake production are initiated.[1] Financial inputs are required because it is usually worthwhile to employ techniques entailing a lag between the investment of resources and the completion of saleable products. Risk bearing is required when the realizable value of the products cannot be known with certainty at the time that costly effort, materials, and services of capital goods are used up.

In most business firms, decision-making rights are held by persons who are also financial risk bearers and suppliers of funds. The holders of these rights are known as the owners of the firm. Ownership refers to a bundle of rights that an economic agent is entitled to exercise over an asset. Its main components are the right of utilization, the right to the products of the asset, and the right to alienate or dispose of the asset and of these rights of utilization and return (Montias, 1976, p. 116; Ryan, 1987, p. 1029). The firm as an ownable asset is

Adapted and reprinted by permission of the publisher from "Ownership and the Nature of the Firm" by Louis Putterman in *Journal of Comparative Economics*, Volume 17, pages 243–263. Copyright ©1993 by Academic Press, Inc.
[1] The transactions cost school argues that some decisions are left to be taken by specialized agents because renegotiating the duties and rewards of each contributor to the production process would make products uncompetitively expensive. A more complete statement of the problem would also refer to the costs of writing complex contingent contracts; see Williamson (1975) and Hart (1989).

an entity that acts as a legal agent in the marketplace, entering into contractual agreements with other agents in order to produce and sell goods and services. With respect to a firm, the right of utilization means the right to determine what contracts the firm enters into and the right to unilaterally fill in the details of incomplete contracts with some agents, e.g., employees. Revenue rights over the firm mean both a limited or an unlimited obligation for financial liabilities incurred by it and a claim on all earnings accruing to it. The right of alienation means that the bundle of ownership rights may be transferred to another party or parties on mutually agreeable terms.

Holding residual income rights and rights of alienation makes owners of firms risk bearers as well as controllers. Why these functions are bundled together in ownership, why they are usually also linked to the provision of financial resources, and who will own the firm are the questions to which I turn next, while subsequent sections examine the question of ownership concentration, the relationship between equity and nonequity finance, implications of separating ownership from work, and the problem of public ownership. A brief summary concludes the paper.

2. Who owns the firm?

Risk bearing, provision of finance, and decision making are potentially separable functions, but they are usually found together in the firms of market economies. Risk bearing and control over decision making tend to be associated with the same individuals because moral hazard means that the cost of risk bearing is inversely proportional to the degree of control the risk bearer exercises over the risks taken. Risk bearing could be separated from provision of finance if firms could be 100% debt financed. However, as is discussed further in Section 5 [of Putterman, 1993a], risk bearers can attract fixed return financiers at more favorable interest rates if they also place some of their own funds at risk in the firm.

Who will own the firm? Suppliers of machine services, raw materials, and labor could share risk-bearing, financing, and decision-making functions if collective decision-making rules were adopted and if each of the parties were to provide their services without immediate compensation and agreed to accept payment in the form of a share of whatever value is realized. But just as these individuals may not consume equal quantities of finished goods and services because of differences in their income levels and preferences, they may also not find it equally attractive to finance the production process and to bear its risks. Rather, individuals having greater wealth will, as a rule, be more inclined to supply financing and risk-bearing services to the firm. Suppliers of ordinary labor services are usually not in a good position to incur risk or to finance the provision of labor without fairly immediate compensation. In contrast, the suppliers of financial resources that are advanced to pay for wages and materials and to invest in physical capital and in product and marketing research are on average of higher wealth and in a better position to bear risk.[2] If control, risk bearing, and financing go together for the reasons given above, then we can expect to see most agents cede control rights to financiers in return for an insured return to their own participation in the production process.[3]

Pointing to wealth constraints alone constitutes an incomplete explanation of why workers do not finance their own firms to a greater degree than is typically observed. Many workers engage in life-cycle saving, and their pension and insurance funds provide a significant share of the investment funds in capitalist economies. Consideration of how the possibility of portfolio diversification interacts with risk aversion must be added to that of financing capacity.

Having low net wealth, most workers will prefer to invest their savings in a portfolio in which aggregate risk is reduced by judicious diversification. Workers already bear an unavoidable burden of risk linked to the fortunes of the enterprise employing them, since an important difference between labor and financial capital is that the former is relatively undiversifiable. When workers acquire human capital specific to their firms, or when anticipated unemployment or search costs make the prospect of job loss costly, further entanglement with these firms as financiers is particularly undesirable. The diversification motive accordingly works together with workers' relatively low abilities to supply financial resources and bear risk to help explain why most workers do not own their firms (Meade, 1972; Neuberger and James, 1973; Putterman, 1988).

A cost to workers of not providing risk-bearing and financing services to their firms is that they do not control them. This may involve both an agency cost, since owners will have to expend resources on monitoring and otherwise disciplining nonowner employees, and a direct welfare cost, if workers suffer a loss of satisfaction due, for example, to the perception that they are working for the profit of others under conditions they do not control. Whether the low financial capacities and diversification motives for not financing their firms, discussed in the previous paragraphs, in fact lead workers to forego a financial role depends upon their assessments of these costs of not financing as well as on the affirmative costs of financing their firms. High assessments of the risk-bearing costs of financing their firms, or low assessments of the monitoring

[2] For formal models in which the less risk averse or the less liquidity constrained become suppliers of capital and holders of enterprise control rights, see Kihlstrom and Laffont (1979) and Eswaran and Kotwal (1989).

[3] An additional consideration is that control by a subset of agents having similar objectives may make decision making easier than it would be for a set of agents with more heterogeneous goals (Hansmann, 1988). This advantage may or may not be offset by costs with respect to information sharing or lost enthusiasm for implementing the decisions taken.

and direct welfare costs of not doing so, would lead to the commonly observed outcome of nonownership by workers.

. . .

Ownership and work

A basic preoccupation of the literature on the economics of organization has been the problem of the separation of ownership and control in the modern corporation. This paper argues that revenue and alienation rights, on the one hand, and control or utilization rights, on the other, are at most only partially separated in the corporation and that the joining of these rights to the right of control and to the function of supplying risk-bearing capital has been a constant element in the evolution of the modern business firm. Compared with the separation of ownership and control, separation of ownership and work is usually far more complete. While work motivation has now been extensively studied as an agency problem, it is not often noted that the roots of the agency problem of work motivation can be seen as lying precisely in the separation of ownership from work.

A quick scan of the literature on the work motivation problem[4] can bring out the importance and implications of this point. I have suggested that the fact that workers are not ordinarily owners of their firms may be explained by workers' high demand for portfolio diversification given their low wealth, their relatively undiversifiable labor, and the fact that their incomes are already linked to the fortunes of their firms by way of the returns on that labor. Workers paid a fixed wage and able to influence their prospects of continued employment only by avoiding egregious absenteeism, insubordination, and visible acts of sabotage have little economic motivation to work to their full capabilities. Structuring rewards and penalties to motivate worker behavior that is consistent with employer goals thus becomes a central problem facing the firm.

The literature treats this incentive question in various ways depending upon its assumptions about the observability of workers' contributions. In the more relevant and interesting cases, the productive effort of individual workers is not perfectly inferable from output, either because output is a team product or because the quality of individual output, care of machinery, etc., are costly to monitor. Resources are therefore expended on attempts to measure effort and to link payment and employment outcomes to the information thereby obtained. One interesting result is the efficiency wage literature's linking of equilibrium unemployment to the employer's need to make the layoff threat an effective

---

[4] For example, the articles in Nalbantian (1987) and Milgrom and Roberts (1992).

Ownership and the nature of the firm

deterrent to shirking (Shapiro and Stiglitz, 1984). Also of interest are the observations of Bowles (1985), Edwards (1979), and others concerning the influence of the monitoring problem on the employer's choice of production technology, on expenditure on supervision in the workplace, and on the workforce's skills and attitudes via the impact of employer needs on education and socialization systems.

To be sure, a serious challenge to the claim that it is the separation of ownership and labor that creates the characteristic motivation problem of the capitalist enterprise can be posed. It can be suggested that as long as the number of workers in a firm is large, even if workers were to be owners, their profit claims and the dependence of their individual wealth levels on the values of their shares would not suffice to significantly affect their incentives to provide effort, since the level of profits is then not notably affected by the efforts of any one worker. However, as Weitzman and Kruse (1990), note, whether profit sharing significantly influences the behavior of rational, self-interested workers is theoretically indeterminate, because there is a multiplicity of equilibria to the repeated game of effort choice in a profit-sharing team. These equilibria include both a collusion-like response to profit sharing, in which the effect of that payment scheme is as if each worker's share were fully contingent on that one worker's effort, and the Cournot–Nash equilibrium, in which the free-rider problem largely negates the effect of profit sharing.[5] The conclusion reached by purely theoretical reasoning, then, is that the problem of eliciting effort from workers may be fundamentally transformed by profit sharing, or there may be no basic change, and the motivation of the individual worker may be as poorly aligned with that of the organization, as a collectivity of workers, as is that of a typical nonowner worker with respect to a conventional firm.

However, the literature on the growing phenomenon of actual profit sharing suggests that outcomes lying near the collusive end of the spectrum of possibilities are common.[6] A common explanation of these outcomes is that whereas workers in a conventional setting are indifferent to one another's behavior, workers under successful profit-sharing schemes monitor each other's effort

[5] The possibility of the collusive outcome, which follows Friedman (1971), is demonstrated in MacLeod (1988). While such an equilibrium is possible, provided that workers do not have too high a rate of pure time preference, too low an expectation of continued participation in the team, or too much heterogeneity of preferences (see Putterman and Skillman, 1992), the conditions for this possibility are not assurances that the equilibrium will in fact be selected over others. The indeterminateness of the response is an application of the folk theorem (Fudenberg and Tirole, 1991).

[6] See Weitzman and Kruse (1990) and the other papers in Blinder (1990). Evidence of the favorable effects of profit sharing is also recognized by Baker et al. (1988), who contend that economic theory is poorly equipped to explain it.

and use informal sanctions to punish slacking.[7] The increasing popularity of profit sharing validates the suggestion that separation of ownership and work be seen as a cause of the characteristic motivation problem of conventional firms. However, that same popularity raises new questions about the separability of the revenue, alienation, and control elements of ownership. Where profit sharing is implemented with favorable incentive effects in firms that remain otherwise conventional in the sense that control rights and the ownership of equity stakes continue to reside with the nonworker proprietors, partners, or shareholders, it would appear to be the case that problems created by what I have called the separation of ownership and work are at least partially addressed by linking just one element of ownership, revenue rights, to work. Whether the addition of control and alienation, i.e., share ownership, rights to profit sharing leads to further improvements in worker productivity or to gains in workplace satisfaction at given levels of productivity, why participation at the shop-floor level without control over broader business matters appears to be an effective complement to profit sharing, and how the sharing of ownership rights between workers and nonworker owners affects these outcomes are topics which are only beginning to receive serious attention.[8]

. . .

7. Nonprofits and public ownership

While businesses controlled by equity suppliers are the rule in most sectors of the market economy, some goods and services are supplied primarily by organizations to which that description does not apply. . . .

An example of an organizational form that does not make use of the institution of ownership, yet prospers in some niches of market economies, is the nonprofit organization. Candidates for nonprofit provision include partially nonrival or nonexcludable goods that are demanded by too local or specialized a constituency to command public provision. In other cases, referred to as trust goods, asymmetric information between provider and demander generates a preference for the nonprofit form, because the absence of residual claims and control of the nonprofit's board by like-minded demand-side agents provides

---

[7] In addition to mutual monitoring, profit sharing is reported to raise productivity by making workers more willing to share with employers (or co-owners) their observations on ways to increase the efficiency of the production process. For some discussions of mutual monitoring, see Bradley and Gelb (1981) and FitzRoy and Kraft (1986). See also the related discussion of peer pressure by Kandel and Lazear (1992). A formal model of mutual monitoring which roots the incentive to monitor in a trigger strategy-type penalty in a repeated game setup resembling that of MacLeod (1988) is presented in Dong (1991) and Dong and Dow (1993).

[8] See again Blinder (1990) and Bonin et al. (1993).

some assurance against provider opportunism.[9] This last case is interesting in terms of the issues addressed in this paper, because, whereas the existence of a residual claimant and holder of alienation rights is regarded as the best guarantor of efficient resource use where conventional goods are concerned, it is the absence of such an agent that is called for here. Nonprofits will have controlling agents, boards of directors in principle representing those who demand their services, to whom employed managers are answerable, but they will not have owners in the sense of this paper. There is no market for control of nonprofits, and they have no salable equity value.

. . .

State ownership of enterprises or of service-providing agencies again raises interesting questions from the standpoint of this paper. If ownership is to be located in individual decision makers, then the state must be viewed as a medium for exercising the ultimate ownership interests of individuals whose identities and relative degree of control will depend upon the political system in question. A basic problem with the state as a supplier of goods and services is that, while the collective action problem of free-riding with respect to payment for the items supplied can be resolved by using state powers to enforce compulsory taxation, another collective action problem complicates the agency relationship between the citizenry and the state and is not so easily resolved. This problem is highlighted presently in a discussion of proposals for broad public ownership of capital.

In light of the failure of state socialism and the limited emergence of worker control in market economies, some economists have revived the proposal of a socialist market economy in which public funds are allocated to projects according to primarily commercial criteria, with the citizenry receiving equal dividends reflecting the return on social capital.[10] While most economists agree that the production of ordinary goods and services is not the comparative advantage of the state, the literature is unclear on why a maximally decentralized system for allocating socially owned funds in an economy characterized by competitive markets for other inputs and products could not operate as efficiently as a system in which funds are privately owned.[11] One answer that may be offered, however, is that the social ownership economy is unlikely to be as efficient as the economy with privately owned investment funds because the

---

[9] Ben-Ner and Van Hoomissen (1991). See also Fama and Jensen (1983b).
[10] Bardhan and Roemer (1993). In the Langean model of Ortuno-Ortin et al. (1993), noncommercial criteria influence the allocation of public funds through the setting of different interest rates for different sectors to reflect social priorities. See also Yunker (1992).
[11] Regarding the consensus on limiting the role of the state in the production sector, see World Bank (1991, pp. 128–147) and the papers in Putterman and Rueschemeyer (1992).

citizen of the socialist democracy has less incentive to monitor the performance of actual and potential projects due to her inability to arrange a private portfolio whereby to benefit from the information so acquired.[12]

Whereas the individual holding private assets can rearrange her portfolio to include more of the projects found to have better prospects and less of those found to be unpromising, the citizen of the public ownership economy can at most propose a change in the composition of the public portfolio or vote for replacement of the public funds manager whose project choices are suggestive of incompetence. The comparison applies even though few investors in the private ownership world do their own securities analysis work, for in that world investors can discipline the financial intermediaries (banks, brokerage houses, mutual funds) that specialize in such monitoring by entering and exiting relationships with them as their evolving reputations suggest is warranted, whereas only the voice mechanism is open to the citizen in the public ownership democracy. Thus, one way of looking at the problem of social ownership is that it does not take sufficient advantage of one of the main properties distinguishing financial capital from other resources, that it is extraordinarily mobile in character, whereas the best candidates for allocation by the voice rather than the exit mechanism are those resources that are relatively *im*mobile.[13] The upshot seems to be that attempts to achieve greater equality in control over nonlabor resources might better be designed to retain rewards for individuals who are successful in identifying good investment projects.[14]

The aforementioned problem of public ownership may also help to illustrate an advantage of the alienability property of privately owned enterprises. When a market for ownership or control of public property is absent, a force that ideally presses managers to use resources to maximize long-term benefits in the private sector is lacking in its public counterpart. Absence of a tradable enterprise value also deprives decision makers of an indicator of the performance of incumbent managers.[15] Recall, however, that an arrangement under which tradability is absent is seen as desirable in the case of some nonprofit entities. Thus, the circumstances in which a market value indicator is beneficial on balance are not entirely general.

· · ·

[12] The argument summarized here is developed at length in Putterman (1993b, 1993c).

[13] For example, the relative immobility of labor is offered by Freeman (1976), among others, as a reason for having a worker voice in the firm. Note that weak citizen incentives to monitor performance is a problem arising for all public sector functions. It is presumably offset, then, by advantages of public provision in the cases of some categories of goods and services.

[14] A suggestion along these lines is offered, for example, by Roemer (1994).

[15] The cost of capital to the enterprise *may* be a meaningful indicator in the case of public ownership, but only if the public enterprise is sufficiently autonomous that creditors cannot assume repayment by the government itself.

9. Summary

. . .

Ownership arrangements evolve to satisfy the needs of the production sector for financial, risk-bearing, and decision-making services, while reflecting the risk preferences of input suppliers and the need to address the agency problems that arise in the process of balancing these demands and preferences. In particular, firms' demands for the aggregation of funds and financiers' demands for portfolio diversification may not be easy to meet without giving rise to an agency problem of separating owners and decision makers. This conflict is addressed in different ways depending upon the scale and specificity of required capital and the difficulty or ease of monitoring decision making and other activities, but retention of ultimate control rights by the holders of residual claims and alienation rights remains an almost constant element. While concentrated and even substantial inside ownership are also among the solutions that are frequently observed, control by production workers is relatively rare, presumably due to workers' limited wealth and the high cost to them of not diversifying it. The resulting separation of ownership and work is the basic cause of the familiar agency problem between employer and employee.

Where for-profit provision suffers from public good, trust good, or other market failures, government or nonprofit providers may dominate, with interesting implications from the standpoint of ownership relations. However, public ownership of capital in sectors in which such problems are absent or less acute may be inefficient relative to private alternatives because the commonality of a public portfolio exacerbates tendencies to free-ride in the monitoring of funds management.

. . .

References

Abelson, Reid, 2001, "Enron Board Comes under a Storm of Criticism," *The New York Times*, December 16, C4.

Aghion, P., and Bolton, P., 1988, "An 'Incomplete Contract' Approach to Bankruptcy and the Financial Structure of the Firm," Stanford University, Institute for Mathematical Studies in the Social Sciences Technical Report No. 536.

Aghion, P., Bolton, P., and Felli, L., 1997, "Some Issues on Contract Incompleteness," London School of Economics Working Paper.

Agrawal, Anup, and Knoeber, Charles R., 1998, "Managerial Compensation and the Threat of Takeover," *Journal of Financial Economics*, 47(2): 219–239.

Ahmadjian, Christina, and Lincoln, James, 1997, "Changing Firm Boundaries in Japanese Auto Parts Supply Networks," draft, Columbia Business School.

Akerlof, George, 1982, "Labor Contracts as Partial Gift Exchange," *Quarterly Journal of Economics*, 47(4): 543–569.

Akerlof, George A., and Katz, Lawrence F., 1988, "Workers' Trust Funds and the Logic of Wage Profiles," National Bureau of Economic Research Working Paper 2548. (Published in 1989 as "Workers' Trust Funds and the Logic of Wage Profiles," *Quarterly Journal of Economics*, 104(3): 525–536.

Alchian, A. A., 1965, "The Basis of Some Recent Advances in the Theory of Management of the Firm," *Journal of Industrial Economics*, 14: 30–44.

Alchian, A. A., 1968, "Corporate Management and Property Rights," in *Economic Policy and the Regulation of Securities*. Washington, DC: American Enterprise Institute.

Alchian, A. A., and Kessel, R. A., 1962, "Competition, Monopoly, and the Pursuit of Pecuniary Gain," in National Bureau of Economic Research, *Aspects of Labor Economics*. Princeton, NJ: Princeton University Press.

Alchian, Armen, A., and Demsetz, Harold, 1972, "Production, Information Costs, and Economic Organization," *American Economic Review*, 62: 777–795.

Alchian, Armen A., 1969, "Corporate Management and Property Rights," in Henry G. Manne (ed.), *Economic Policy and the Regulation of Corporate Securities*. Washington, DC: American Enterprise Institute for Public Policy Research.

Alchian, Armen, 1984, "Specificity, Specialization, and Coalitions," draft manuscript, February.

Altenberg, Lee, 1990, "An End to Capitalism: Leland Stanford's Forgotten Vision," *Sandstone and Tile*, 14(1): 8–20.

Andersen, Erin, 1985, "The Salesperson as Outside Agent or Employee: A Transaction Cost Analysis," *Marketing Science*, 4: 234–254.

REFERENCES

Andersen, Erin, and Schmittlein, David, 1984, "Integration of the Sales Force: An Empirical Examination," *Rand Journal of Economics*, 15: 385–395.

Aoki, Masahiko, 1984, *The Co-operative Game Theory of the Firm*. London: Clarendon Press.

Arrow, K. J., 1969, "The Organization of Economic Activity," in *The Analysis and Evaluation of Public Expenditure: The PPB System*. 91st Congress, 1st Session, vol. 1, JEC, 47–64.

Arrow, K. J., 1974, *The Limits of Organization*. New York: Norton.

Arrow, Kenneth, 1975, "Vertical Integration and Communication," *Bell Journal of Economics*, 6: 173–182.

Asanuma, Banri, 1989, "Manufacturer–Supplier Relationships in Japan and the Concept of Relation-Specific Skill," *The Journal of the Japanese and International Economies*, 3: 1–30.

Asanuma, Banri, 1992, "Japanese Manufacturer–Supplier Relationships in International Perspective," in Paul Sheard (ed.), *International Adjustment and the Japanese Economy*. St. Leonards, Australia: Allen & Unwin.

Ashenfelter, O., and Johnson, G., 1972, "Unionism, Relative Wages, and Labor Quality in U.S. Manufacturing Industries," *International Economic Review*, 13: 488–508.

Atiyah, P. S., 1979, *The Rise and Fall of Freedom of Contract*. Oxford and New York: Clarendon Press.

Atwood, Jane, and Kobrin, Paul, 1977, "Integration and Joint Ventures in Pipelines," Research Study No. 5, American Petroleum Institute.

Baker, George, 1989, "Price Rate Contracts and Performance Measurement Error," Graduate School of Business, Harvard University.

Baker, George, Gibbons, Robert, and Murphy, Kevin J., 2002, "Relational Contracts and the Theory of the Firm," *Quarterly Journal of Economics*, 117(1): 39–84.

Baker, George P., Jensen, Michael C., and Murphy, Kevin J., 1988. "Compensation and Incentives: Practice vs. Theory," *Journal of Finance*, 63(3): 593–616.

Balsam, Steven, 2002, *An Introduction to Executive Compensation*. New York: Academic Press.

Bardhan, Pranab K., and Roemer, John E. (eds.), 1993, *Market Socialism: The Current Debate*. New York: Oxford University Press.

Bar-Gill, Oren, and Bebchuk, Lucian, 2002, "Misreporting Corporate Performance," Discussion Paper No. 400, Harvard Olin Center for Law, Economics, and Business.

Bar-Gill, Oren, and Bebchuk, Lucian, 2003a, "The Costs of Permitting Managers to Sell Shares," mimeo, Harvard Law School.

Bar-Gill, Oren, and Bebchuk, Lucian, 2003b, "Corporate Transparency and Managerial Incentives," mimeo, Harvard Law School.

Barnard, Chester, 1938, *The Functions of the Executive*. Cambridge, MA: Harvard University Press.

Barnard, C. I., 1962, *The Functions of the Executive*, 2nd edition. Cambridge, MA: Harvard University Press.

Bartlett, F. C., 1932, *Remembering*. Cambridge: Cambridge University Press.

Barzel, Yoram, 1982, "Measurement Costs and the Organization of Markets," *Journal of Law and Economics*, 25: 27–48.

References

Batt, Francis R., 1929, *The Law of Master and Servant*. New York: Pitman Publishing Co.

Baumol, William J., 1959, *Business Behavior, Value and Growth*. New York: Macmillan.

Bebchuk, Lucian, Coates, John IV, and Subramanian, Guhan, 2002, "The Powerful Antitakeover Force of Staggered Boards: Theory, Evidence, and Policy," *Stanford Law Review*, 54: 887–951.

Bebchuk, Lucian Arye, and Fried, Jesse M., 2003a, "Stealth Compensation," mimeo, Harvard Law School and Boalt Hall School of Law.

Bebchuk, Lucian Arye, and Fried, Jesse M., 2003b, "Executive Compensation as an Agency Problem," *Journal of Economic Perspectives*, 17(3): 71–92.

Bebchuk, Lucian Arye, and Fried, Jesse M., 2004, *Pay without Performance*, Cambridge, MA: Harvard University Press.

Bebchuk, Lucian Arye, Fried, Jesse M., and Walker, David I., 2002, "Managerial Power and Rent Extraction in the Design of Executive Compensation." *University of Chicago Law Review*, 69(3): 751–846.

Bebchuk, Lucian Arye, and Kahan, Marcel, 1990, "A Framework for Analyzing Legal Policy Toward Proxy Contests," *California Law Review*, 78: 1071–1136.

Becker, Gary S., and Stigler, George J., 1974, "Law Enforcement, Malfeasance, and Compensation of Enforcers," *Journal of Legal Studies*, 3: 1–18.

Beckmann, Martin, 1983, *Tinbergen Lectures on Economic Organization*. Berlin: Springer-Verlag.

Benassy, Jean-Pascal, 1982, *The Economics of Market Disequilibrium*. Orlando, FL: Academic Press.

Benz, Matthias, Kucher, Marcel, and Stutzer, Alois, 2001, "Stock Options: The Managers' Blessing: Institutional Restrictions and Executive Compensation," Working Paper No. 61, University of Zurich Institute for Empirical Research in Economics.

Ben-Ner, Avner, and Van Hoomissen, Theresa, 1991, "Nonprofit Organizations in the Mixed Economy: A Demand and Supply Analysis," *Annals of Public and Cooperative Economics*, 62: 519–550.

Berhold, M., 1971, "A Theory of Linear Profit Sharing Incentives," *Quarterly Journal of Economics*, 85: 460–482.

Berle, Adolf A., and Means, Gardiner C., 1932, *The Modern Corporation and Private Property*. New York: Commerce Clearing House.

Bertrand, Marianne, and Mullainathan, Sendhil, 2001, "Are CEO's Rewarded for Luck? The Ones without Principals Are," *Quarterly Journal of Economics*, 116(3): 901–932.

Bettis, J. Carr, Bizjak, John M., and Lemmon, Michael L., 2001, "Managerial Ownership, Incentive Contracting, and the Use of Zero-Cost Collars and Equity Swaps by Corporate Insiders," *Journal of Financial and Quantitative Analysis*, 36: 345–370.

Bettis, J. Carr, Coles, Jeffrey L., and Lemmon, Michael L., 2000, "Corporate Policies Restricting Trading by Insiders," *Journal of Financial Economics*, 57(2): 191–220.

Bewley, Truman F., 1999, *Why Wages Don't Fall during a Recession*. Cambridge, MA: Harvard University Press.

REFERENCES

Bizjack, John M., Lemmon, Michael L., and Naveen, Lalitha, 2000, "Has the Use of Peer Groups Contributed to Higher Levels of Executive Compensation?" Working Paper, Portland State University.

Blanchard, Olivier Jean, Lopez-de-Silanes, Florencio, and Shleifer, Andrei, 1994, "What Do Firms Do with Cash Windfalls?" *Journal of Financial Economics*, 36: 337–360.

Blair, Margaret M., 1995, *Ownership and Control*. Washington, DC: The Brookings Institution.

Blair, Margaret M., and Stout, L., 1997, "A Theory of Corporation Law as a Response to Contracting Problems in Team Production," The Brookings Institution Working Paper, available at www.brook.edu.

Blau, P., and Scott, W., 1962, *Formal Organizations*. San Francisco: Chandler.

Blinder, Alan (ed.), 1990, *Paying for Productivity: A Look at the Evidence*. Washington, DC: The Brookings Institution.

Blum, Milton L., 1956, *Industrial Psychology and Its Social Foundations*. New York: Harper and Brothers.

Bolster, Paul, Chance, Don, and Rich, Don, 1996, "Executive Equity Swaps and Corporate Insider Holdings," *Financial Management*, 25: 14–24.

Bonin, John P., Jones, Derek C., and Putterman, Louis, 1993, "Theoretical and Empirical Research on Producers' Cooperatives: Will Ever the Twain Meet?" *Journal of Economic Literature*, 31: 1290–1320.

Bork, Robert, 1954, "Vertical Integration and the Sherman Act: The Legal History of an Economic Misconception," *University of Chicago Labor Review*, 22: 157–201.

Borokhovich, Kenneth A., Brunarski, Kelly R., and Parrino, Robert, 1997, "CEO Contracting and Anti-Takeover Amendments," *Journal of Finance*, 52(4): 1495–1517.

Bowles, Samuel, 1985, "The Production Process in a Competitive Economy: Walrasian, Neo-Hobbesian, and Marxian Models," *American Economic Review*, 75: 16–36.

Bowles, Samuel, 1988, "Social Institutions and Technical Choice," in M. DeMatteo, A. Vercelli, and R. Goodman (eds.), *Technological and Social Factors in Long-Term Economic Fluctuations*. Berlin: Springer-Verlag.

Bowles, Samuel, and Boyer, Robert, 1990, "Labour Market Flexibility and Decentralization as Barriers to High Employment," in Renato Brunetta and Carlo Dell'Aringa (eds.), *Labor Relations and Economic Performance*. London: Macmillan.

Bowles, Samuel, and Gintis, Herbert, 1975, "The Problems with Human Capital Theory," *American Economic Review*, 65: 74–82.

Bowles, Samuel, and Gintis, Herbert, 1976, *Schooling in Capitalist America: Educational Reform and the Contradictions of Economic Life*. New York: Basic Books.

Bowles, Samuel, and Gintis, Herbert, 1982a, "The Crisis of Liberal Democratic Capitalism," *Politics and Society*, 10: 51–93.

Bowles, Samuel, and Gintis, Herbert, 1982b, "The Welfare State and Long-Term Economic Growth: Marxian, Neoclassical, and Keynesian Approaches," *American Economic Review*, 72: 341–345.

Bowles, Samuel, and Gintis, Herbert, 1990a, "Contested Exchange: New Microfoundations of the Political Economy of Capitalism," *Politics and Society*, 18: 165–222.

Bowles, Samuel, and Gintis, Herbert, 1990b, "Bonding and Dismissal in Labor Discipline Models," photocopy, University of Massachusetts.

References

Bowles, Samuel, and Gintis, Herbert, 1993a, "The Democratic Firm: An Agency Theory Evaluation," in Samuel Bowles, Herbert Gintis, and Bo Gustaffson (eds.), *Markets and Democracy: Participation, Accountability, and Efficiency*. Cambridge: Cambridge University Press.

Bowles, Samuel, and Gintis, Herbert, 1993b, "The Revenge of Homo Economics: Contested Exchange and the Revival of Economy," *Journal of Economic Perspectives*, 7: 83–102.

Bowles, Samuel, and Gintis, Herbert, 1995, "Democratic Firms and the Distribution of Wealth," in J. E. Roemer (ed.), *Property Relations, Incentives and Welfare*. London: Macmillan.

Bowles, Samuel, Gordon, David M., and Weisskopf, Thomas E., 1989, "Business Ascendancy and Economic Impasse: A Structural Retrospective on Conservative Economics, 1979–87," *Journal of Economic Perspectives*, 3: 107–134.

Bradley, Keith, and Gelb, Alan, 1981, "Motivation and Control in the Mondragon Experiment," *British Journal of Industrial Relations*, 19: 211–231.

Branch, B., 1973, "Corporate Objectives and Market Performance," *Financial Management*, 2: 24–29.

Brickley, James, and Dark, Frederick, 1987, "The Choice of Organizational Form: The Case of Franchising," *Journal of Financial Economics*, 18: 401–420.

Buchanan, James, Tollison, Robert, and Tolluck, Gordon, 1990, *Toward a Theory of the Rent-Seeking Society*. College Station: Texas A&M University Press.

Buttrick, John, 1952, "The Inside Contracting System,"*Journal of Economic History*, 12: 205–221.

Calvo, Guillermo, and Wellisz, Stanislaw, 1978, "Supervision, Loss of Control, and the Optimum Size of the Firm," *Journal of Political Economy*, 86: 943–952.

Camerer, Colin, and Fehr, Ernst, 2004, "Measuring Social Norms and Preferences Using Experimental Games: A Guide for Social Scientists" (Chapter 3, pp. 55–95), in *Foundations of Human Sociality: Economic Experiments and Ethnographic Evidence from Fifteen Small-Scale Societies* (Joseph Henrich, et al., eds.); Oxford and New York: Oxford University Press.

Canes, M., 1970, "A Model of a Sports League," doctoral dissertation, University of California at Los Angeles.

Carpenter, Jennifer N., 1998, "The Exercise and Valuation of Executive Stock Options," *Journal of Financial Economics*, 48: 127–158.

Chandler, A., 1977, *The Visible Hand*. Cambridge, MA: Harvard University Press.

Chandler, Alfred Dupont, 1962, *Strategy and Structure: Chapters in the History of the Industrial Enterprise*. Cambridge, MA: The MIT Press.

Cheng, Shun, Nagar, Venky, and Rajan, Madhar V., 2001, "Control Versus Risk in Stock-Based Incentives: Evidence from Antitakeover Regulation," Working Paper, University of Michigan Business School.

Cheung, S. N. S., 1969, "Transaction Costs, Risk Aversion, and the Choice of Contractual Arrangements," *Journal of Law and Economics*, 12: 23–42.

Cheung, Steven, 1983, "The Contractual Nature of the Firm," *Journal of Law and Economics*, 26: 1–21.

REFERENCES

Clague, Christopher, 1993, "Rule Obedience, Organizational Loyalty, and Economic Development," *Journal of Institutional and Theoretical Economics*, 149: 393–414.

Clark, J. B., 1900, *Distribution of Wealth*. New York: Macmillan.

Clark, Robert C., 1985, *Principals and Agents: The Structure of Business*. Boston: Harvard Business School Press.

Clarkson, Kenneth W., Miller, Roger LeRoy, and Muris, Timothy J., 1978, "Liquidated Damages Versus Penalties: Sense or Nonsense?" *Wisconsin Law Review*, 1978: 351–390.

Coase, R. H., 1959, "The Federal Communications Commission," *Journal of Law and Economics*, 2: 1–40.

Coase, R. H., 1960, "The Problem of Social Cost," *Journal of Law and Economics*, 15: 143–150.

Coase, R. H., 1964, Discussion, *American Economic Review*, 3: 194–197.

Coase, R. H., 1972, "Durability and Monopoly," *Journal of Law and Economics*, 15: 143–150.

Coase, Ronald, 1991a, "The Nature of the Firm: Origin," 34–47 in Oliver Williamson and Sidney Winter (eds.), *The Nature of the Firm: Origins, Evolution, and Development*. New York: Oxford University Press.

Coase, Ronald, 1991b, "The Nature of the Firm: Meaning," 48–60 in Oliver Williamson and Sidney Winter (eds.), *The Nature of the Firm: Origins, Evolution, and Development*. New York: Oxford University Press.

Coase, Ronald, 1992, "The Institutional Structure of Production: 1991 Alfred Nobel Memorial Prize Lecture in Economic Sciences," *American Economic Review*, 82: 713–719.

Coase, Ronald H., 1937, "The Nature of the Firm," *Economica*, 4: 396–405; reprinted 331–351 in American Economic Association, *Readings in Price Theory*, Chicago: Irwin, 1952; reprinted, 33–55 in Coase, *The Firm, the Market, and the Law*, Chicago: University of Chicago Press, 1990; reprinted, G. J. Stigler and K. E. Boulding (eds.), *Readings in Price Theory*. Homewood, IL: Richard D. Irwin.

Commons, J., 1970, *The Economics of Collective Action*. Madison: University of Wisconsin Press.

Core, John E., Guay, Wayne, and Larcker, David F., 2001, "Executive Equity Compensation and Incentives: A Survey," Working Paper, Wharton School. (Published in 2003 as "Executive Equity Compensation and Incentives: A Survey,"*Economic Policy Review*, 9(1): 27–50.)

Core, John E., Holthausen, Robert W., and Larcker, David E., 1999, "Corporate Governance, Chief Executive Compensation, and Firm Performance," *Journal of Financial Economics*, 51: 371–406.

Core, John E., and Larcker, David, 2002, "Performance Consequences of Mandatory Increases in Executive Stock Ownership," Working Paper, Wharton School. (Published in 2002 as "Performance Consequences of Mandatory Increases in Executive Stock Ownership," *Journal of Financial Economics*, 64(3): 317–340.)

Cox, A., 1958, "The Legal Nature of Collective Bargaining Agreements," *Michigan Law Review*, 57: 1–36.

References

Crocker, K. J., and Masten, S. E., 1991, *"Pretia ex Machina?* Prices and Process in Long-Term Contracts," *Journal of Law and Economics*, 34: 69–99.

Crystal, Graef S., 1991, *In Search of Excess*. New York: Norton.

Cyert, R. M., and Hedrick, C. L., 1972, "Theory of the Firm: Past, Present, and Future: An Interpretation," *Journal of Economic Literature*, 10: 398–412.

Cyert, R. M., and March, J. G., 1963, *A Behavioral Theory of the Firm*. Englewood Cliffs, NJ: Prentice-Hall.

Cyert, Richard, Kang, Sok-Hyon, and Kumar, Praveen, 2002, "Corporate Governance, Takeovers, and Top-Management Compensation: Theory and Evidence," *Management Science*, 48(4): 453–469.

Dahl, Robert A., 1985, *A Preface to Economic Democracy*. Berkeley: University of California Press.

Darby, Michael R., and Karni, Eli, 1973, "Free Competition and the Optimal Amount of Fraud," *Journal of Law and Economics*, 16: 67–88.

David, Parthiban, Kochar, Rahul, and Levitas, Edward, 1998, "The Effect of Institutional Investors on the Level and Mix of CEO Compensation," *Academy of Management Journal*, 41(2): 200–208.

Dawes, Harry, 1934, "Labour Mobility in the Steel Industry," *The Economic Journal*, 44: 84–94.

Demsetz, H., 1967, "Toward a Theory of Property Rights," *American Economic Review*, 57: 347–359.

Demsetz, H., 1969," Information and Efficiency: Another Viewpoint," *Journal of Law and Economics*, 12: 1–22.

Demsetz, Harold, 1983, "The Structure of Ownership and the Theory of the Firm," *Journal of Law and Economics*, 26: 375–390.

Demsetz, Harold, and Lehn, Kenneth, 1985, "The Structure of Corporate Ownership: Causes and Consequences," *Journal of Political Economy*, 93: 1155–1177.

Dickens, William T., Katz, Lawrence F., Lang, Kevin, and Summers, Lawrence H., 1989, "Employee Crime and the Monitoring Puzzle," *Journal of Labor Economics*, 7: 331–347.

Dobb, Maurice, 1925, *Capitalist Enterprise and Social Progress*. London: George Routledge and Sons, Ltd.

Doeringer, P., and Piore, M., 1971, *International Labor Markets and Manpower Analysis*. Lexington, MA: D.C. Heath and Co.

Dong, Xiao-Yuan, 1991, "Production and Monitoring Incentives in China's Collective Farming: Theory and Evidence," Ph.D. dissertation, University of Alberta.

Dong, Xiao-Yuan, and Dow, Gregory, 1993, "Monitoring Costs in Chinese Agricultural Teams," *Journal of Political Economy*, 101: 539–553.

Dow, Greogry, 2003, *Governing the Firm: Workers' Control in Theory and Practice*. New York: Cambridge University Press.

Dow, Gregory, and Putterman, Louis, 2000, "Why Capital Suppliers (Usually) Hire Workers: What We Know, and What We Need to Know," *Journal of Economic Behavior and Organization*, 43: 319–336.

Durbin, E. F. M., 1936, "Economic Calculus in a Planned Economy," *Economic Journal*, 46: 676–690.

REFERENCES

Easterbrook, Frank, and Fischel, Daniel, 1983, "Voting in Corporate Law," *Journal of Law and Economics*, 26: 305.

Eaton, B. Curtis, and White, William, 1982, "Agent Compensation and the Limits of Bonding," *Economic Inquiry*, 20: 330–343.

Eccles, Robert G., 1981, "The Quasi Firm in the Construction Industry," *Journal of Economic Behavior and Organization*, 2: 335–357.

Edwards, Richard, 1979, *Contested Terrain: The Transformation of the Workplace in the Twentieth Century*. New York: Basic Books.

Elster, John, 1979, *Ulysses and the Sirens*. Cambridge: Cambridge University Press.

Eswaran, Mukesh, and Kotwal, Ashok, 1989, "Why Are Capitalists the Bosses?" *Economic Journal*, 99: 162–176.

Fama, E. F., 1970, "Multiperiod Consumption-Investment Decisions," *American Economic Review*, 60: 163–174.

Fama, E. F., 1972, "Ordinal and Measurable Utility," in M. C. Jensen (ed.), *Studies in the Theory of Capital Markets*. New York: Praeger.

Fama, Eugene F., 1976, *Foundations of Finance*. New York: Basic Books.

Fama, Eugene, 1978, "The Effects of a Firm's Investment and Financing Decisions on the Welfare of Its Security Holders," *American Economic Review*, 68: 272–284.

Fama, Eugene, 1980, "Agency Problems and the Theory of the Firm," *Journal of Political Economy*, 88: 288–307.

Fama, Eugene F., and Jensen, Michael C., 1983a, "Agency Problems and Residual Claims," *Journal of Law and Economics*, 26: 327–349.

Fama, Eugene F., and Jensen, Michael C., 1983b, "Separation of Ownership and Control," *Journal of Law and Economics*, 26: 301–326.

Fama, Eugene F., and Jensen, Michael C., 1985, "Organizational Forms and Investment Decision," *Journal of Financial Economics*, 14: 101–119.

Fama, Eugene F., and Miller, Merton H., 1972, *The Theory of Finance*. New York: Holt, Rinehart, and Winston.

Farrell, Joseph, and Shapiro, Carl, 1989, "Optimal Contracts with Lock-in," *American Economic Review*, 79: 51–68.

Fehr, Ernst, and Gächter, Simon, 2000, "Cooperation and Punishment," American *Economic Review*, 90: 980–994.

Fehr, Ernst, and Schmidt, Klaus, 2003, "Theories of Fairness and Reciprocity – Evidence and Economic Applications," in M. Dewatripont, L. Hansen, and S. Turnovsky (eds.), *Advances in Economics and Econometrics – 8th World Congress, Econometric Society Monographs*. Cambridge: Cambridge University Press.

Feldman, J., and Kanter, H., 1965, "Organizational Decision-Making," in J. March (ed.), *Handbook of Organizations*. Chicago: Rand McNally.

Feldman, Martha S., and March, James G., 1981, "Information in Organizations as Signal and Symbol," *Administrative Science Quarterly*, 26: 171–186.

Feller, David E., 1973, "A General Theory of the Collective Bargaining Agreement," *California Labor Review*, 3: 663–856.

Ferguson, Adam, 1767, *An Essay on the History of Civil Society*. Dublin: Boulter Grierson.

References

FitzRoy, Felix R., and Kraft, Kornelius, 1986, "Profitability and Profit-Sharing," *Journal of Industrial Economics*, 35: 113–130.

Freeman, Richard, 1976, "Individual Mobility and Union Voice in the Labor Market," *American Economic Review*, 66: 361–368.

Freeman, Richard B., and Rogers, Joel, 1999, *What Workers Want*, Ithaca, NY: Cornell University Press.

Fried, Jesse M., 1998, "Reducing the Profitability of Corporate Insider Trading through Pre-trading Disclosure," *Southern California Law Review*, 71(2): 303–392.

Friedman, James, 1971, "A Non-Cooperative Equilibrium for Supergames," *Review of Economic Studies*, 38: 1–12.

Friedman, M., 1970, "The Social Responsibility of Business Is to Increase Its Profits," *The New York Times Magazine*, September 13, 32ff.

Fudenberg, Drew, and Tirole, Jean, 1991, *Game Theory*. Cambridge, MA: The MIT Press.

Fudenberg, D., Holmstrom, B., and Milgrom, P., 1990, "Short-Term Contracts and Long-Term Agency Relationships," *Journal of Economic Theory*, 51(1): 1–31.

Furubotn, E. G., and Pejovich, S., 1972, "Property Rights and Economic Theory: A Survey of Recent Literature," *Journal of Economic Literature*, 10: 1137–1162.

Garnier, Germain, 1815, *Abrege elementaire des principes de l'Economie Politique*. Paris: Agasse.

Ghemawat, Pankaj, 1995, "Competitive Advantage and Internal Organization: Nucor Revisited," *Journal of Economics and Management Strategy*, 3: 685–717.

Gillan, Stuart, 2001, "Has Pay for Performance Gone Awry: Views from a Corporate Governance Forum," *Research Dialogue*, TIAA CREF Institute, 68: 1–16.

Gintis, Herbert, 1976, "The Nature of the Labor Exchange and the Theory of Capitalist Production," *Review of Radical Political* Economics, 8(2): 36–54.

Gintis, Herbert, and Ishikawa, Tsuneo, 1987, "Wages, Work Discipline, and Unemployment," *Journal of Japanese and International Economies*, 1: 195–228.

Gleitman, Henry, 1995, *Psychology*. New York: W. W. Norton.

Goetz, Charles J., and Scott, Robert E., 1983, "The Mitigation Principle: Toward a General Theory of Contractual Obligation," *Virginia Law Review*, 69: 967–1025.

Golbe, Devra, and White, Lawrence, 1988, "Mergers and Acquisitions in the United States Economy: An Aggregate and Historical Overview," *Mergers and Acquisitions*, Chicago: University of Chicago Press for the NBER.

Golbe, Devra, and White, Lawrence, 1993, "Catch a Wave: The Time Series Behavior of Mergers," *Review of Economics and Statistics*, 75: 493–499.

Goldberg, Victor P., 1976, "Regulation and Administered Contracts," *Bell Journal of Economics*, 7: 426–448.

Goldberg, Victor, 1980a, "Relational Exchange: Economics and Complex Contracts," *American Behavioral Scientist*, 23(3): 337–352.

Goldberg, Victor, 1980b, "Bridges Over Contested Terrain: Exploring the Radical Account of the Employment Relationship," *Journal of Economic Behavior and Organization*, 1: 249–274.

REFERENCES

Goldberg, Victor, and Erickson, John R., 1987, "Quantity and Price Adjustment in Long-Term Contracts: A Case Study of Petroleum Coke," *Journal of Law and Economics*, 30: 369–398.

Gouldner, A. W., 1961, "The Norm of Reciprocity," *American Sociological Review*, 25: 161–179.

Granovetter, Mark, 1983, "Loyalty Filters," *American Economic Review*, 73(1): 54–63.

Greenberg, Edward S., 1986, *Workplace Democracy: The Political Effects of Participation*. Ithaca, NY: Cornell University Press.

Greenwald, Bruce, and Stiglitz, Joseph, 1986, "Externalities in Economies with Imperfect Information and Incomplete Markets," *Quarterly Journal of Economics*, 101: 229–264.

Grossman, Sanford J., and Hart, Oliver D., 1980, "Takeover Bids, the Free Rider Problem, and the Theory of Corporation," *Bell Journal of Economics*, 11: 42–64.

Grossman, Sanford J., and Hart, Oliver D., 1984, "The Costs and Benefits of Ownership: A Theory of Vertical Integration," unpublished manuscript, March.

Grossman, Sanford J., and Hart, Oliver D., 1986, "The Costs and Benefits of Ownership: A Theory of Vertical and Lateral Integration," *Journal of Political Economy*, 94: 691–719.

Grossman, Sanford J., and Hart, Oliver D., 1988, "One Share–One Vote and the Market for Corporate Control," *Journal of Financial Economics*, 20: 175–202.

Gustafson, W. Eric, 1959, *Periodicals and Books*, in Max Hall (ed.), *Case Studies in Metropolitan Manufacturing*. Cambridge: Harvard University Press.

Habib, Michel A., and Ljungqvist, Alexander P., 2000, "Firm Value and Managerial Incentives," Working Paper, London Business School.

Hadlock, Charles, and Lumer, Gerald, 1997, "Compensation, Turnover, and Top Management Incentives: Historical Evidence," *Journal of Business*, 70: 153–188.

Hall, Brian J., 1999, "A Better Way to Pay CEO's?," in *Executive Compensation and Shareholder Value: Theory and Evidence*, Jennifer Carpenter and David Yermack (eds.), Kluwer Academic, 35–46.

Hall, Brian, and Liebman, Jeffrey, 1998, "Are CEOs Really Paid Like Bureaucrats?" *The Quarterly Journal of Economics*, 113(3): 653–691.

Hall, Brian J., and Murphy, Kevin J., 2003, "The Trouble with Stock Options," *Journal of Economic Perspectives*, 17(3): 49–70.

Hansmann, H., 1996, *The Ownership of the Enterprise*. Cambridge, MA: Belknap Press of Harvard University.

Hansmann, Henry, 1988, "Ownership of the Firm," *Journal of Law, Economics, and Organization*, 4: 267–304.

Harris, Milton, and Raviv, Artur, 1988, "Corporate Governance: Voting Rights and Majority Rules," *Journal of Financial Economics*, 20: 203–235.

Hart, Oliver, 1983, "The Market Mechanism as an Incentive Scheme," *Bell Journal of Economics*, 14: 366–382.

Hart, Oliver, 1989, "An Economist's Perspective on the Theory of the Firm," *Columbia Law Review*, 89: 1757–1774.

References

Hart, Oliver, and Holmstrom, Bengt, 1987, "The Theory of Contracts," in Truman F. Bewley (ed.), *Advances in Economic Theory – Fifth World Congress*. Cambridge: Cambridge University Press.

Hart, Oliver, and Moore, J., 1988, "Property Rights and the Nature of the Firm," Massachusetts Institute of Technology, Department of Economics Working Paper No. 495.

Hart, Oliver D., and Moore, John, 1990, "Property Rights and the Nature of the Firm," *Journal of Political Economy*, 98: 1119–1158.

Hartzell, Jay C., and Starks, Laura T., 2002, "Institutional Investors and Executive Compensation," Working Paper, New York University Stern School of Business (Published in 2003 as "Institutional Investors and Executive Compensation," *Journal of Finance*, 58 (6): 2351–2374.

Hayek, F. A., 1933, "The Trend of Economic Thinking," *Economica*, 13: 121–137.

Hayek, F. A., 1945, "The Use of Knowledge in Society," *The American Economic Review*, 35: 519–530.

Hayek, Friedrich, 1972, *Individualism and Economic Order*. Chicago: Henry Regnery Company.

Healy, Paul M., Palepu, Krishna G., and Ruback, Richard S., 1992, "Does Corporate Performance Improve after Mergers?" *Journal of Financial Economics*, 31: 135–175.

Heckerman, D. G., 1975, "Motivating Managers to Make Investment Decisions," *Journal of Financial Economics*, 2: 273–292.

Helper, Susan, 1991, "Strategy and Irreversibility in Supplier Relations: The Case of the U.S. Automobile Industry," *Business History Review*, 65: 781–824.

Henderson, Hubert D., 1922, *Supply and Demand*. New York: Harcourt, Brace, and Co.

Henry, Robert S., 1942, *This Fascinating Railroad Business*. New York: Bobbs-Merrill.

Himmelberg, Charles, Hubbard, R. Glenn, and Palia, Darius, 1999, "Understanding the determinants of managerial ownership and the link between ownership and performance," *Journal of Financial Economics*, 53(3): 353–384.

Hirschman, A. O., 1970, *Exit, Voice, and Loyalty*. Cambridge, MA: Harvard University Press.

Hodgeskin, Thomas, 1827, *Popular Political Economy*. London: Charles Tait.

Holderness, Clifford, Kroszner, Randall, and Sheehan, Dennis, 1995, "Changes in Corporate Stock Ownership since the Great Depression," Working Paper, University of Chicago, Graduate School of Business.

Holderness, Clifford G., Kroszner, Randall S., and Sheehan, Dennis P., 1999, "Were the Good Old Days that Good? Changes In Managerial Stock Ownership since the Great Depression," *Journal of Finance*, 54: 435–469.

Holderness, Clifford G., Kroszner, Randall S., and Sheehan, Dennis P., 2000, "The Rise in Managerial Stock Ownership," *Journal of Applied Corporate Finance*, 13(3): 105–115.

Holderness, Clifford, and Sheehan, Dennis, 1988, "The Role of Majority Shareholders in Publicly Held Corporations," *Journal of Financial Economics*, 20: 317–346.

REFERENCES

Holmstrom, B., and Milgrom, P., 1991a, "Multi-task Principal–Agent Analyses: Incentive Contracts, Asset Ownership, and Job Design," *Journal of Law, Economics, and Organization*, 7: 24–52.

Holmstrom, Bengt, 1982a, "Moral Hazard in Teams," *Bell Journal of Economics*, 13: 324–340.

Holmstrom, Bengt, 1982b, "Managerial Incentives – A Dynamic Perspective," in *Essays in Economics and Management in Honor of Lars Wahlbeck*. Helsinki: Swedish School of Economics.

Holmstrom, Bengt, 1996, "The Firm as a Subeconomy," draft, Department of Economics, Massachusetts Institute of Technology.

Holmstrom, Bengt, and Milgrom, Paul, 1987, "Aggregation and Linearity in the Provision of Intertemporal Incentives," *Econometrica*, 55: 303–328.

Holmstrom, Bengt, and Milgrom, Paul, 1990, "Regulating Trade Among Agents," *Journal of Institutional and Theoretical Economics*, 146: 85–105.

Holmstrom, Bengt, and Milgrom, Paul, 1991b, "Measurement Cost and Organization Theory," Working Paper, Stanford University.

Holmstrom, Bengt, and Milgrom, Paul, 1994, "The Firm as an Incentive System," *American Economic Review*, 84: 972–991.

Holmstrom, Bengt, and Ricart i Costa, Joan, 1986, "Managerial Incentives and Capital Management," *Quarterly Journal of Economics*, 101: 835–860.

Holmstrom Bengt, and Roberts, John, 1998, "The Boundaries of the Firm Revisited," *Journal of Economic Perspectives*, 12(4): 73–94.

Holmstrom, Bengt, and Tirole, Jean, 1989, "The Theory of the Firm," in R. Schmalensee and R. Willig (eds.), *The Handbook of Industrial Organization*. Amsterdam: North Holland.

Hubbard, Glenn R., and Weiner, Robert J., 1986, "Regulation and Long-Term Contracting in U.S. Natural Gas Markets," *Journal of Industrial Economics*, 35: 71–79.

Hubbard, Glenn R., and Weiner, Robert J., 1991, "Long-Term Contracting and Multiple-Price Systems," NBER Working Paper 3782, National Bureau of Economic Research, Inc. (Published in 1992 as "Long-Term Contracting and Multiple-Price Systems," *Journal of Business*, 65: 177–198.)

Ichniowski, Casey, Levine, David I., Olson, Craig, and Strauss, George, 2000, *The American Workplace: Skills, Compensation, and Employee Involvement*. Cambridge: Cambridge University Press.

Ichniowski, Casey, Shaw, Kathryn L., and Prennushi, Giovanna, 1997, "The Effects of Human Resource Management Practices on Productivity: A Study of Steel Finishing Lines," *American Economic Review*, 87(3): 291–313.

Itoh, Hideshi, 1989, "Coalitions, Incentives, and Risk Sharing," mimeograph, Kyoto University, Japan.

Itoh, Hideshi, 1991, "Incentives to Help in Multi-Agent Situations," *Econometrica*, 59: 611–637.

Jarrell, Gregg A., Brickley, James, and Netter, Jeffrey M., 1988, "The Market for Corporate Control: The Empirical Evidence Since 1980," *Journal of Economic Perspectives*, 2: 49–68.

References

Jensen, M. C., and Meckling, W. H., 1977, "On the Labor-Managed Firm and the Co-determination Movement," unpublished manuscript.

Jensen, M. C., and Meckling, W. H., 1979, "Rights and Production Functions: An Application to Labor-Managed Firms and Co-determination," *Journal of Business*, 52: 469–506.

Jensen, Michael C., 1972, "Capital Markets: Theory and Evidence," *Bell Journal of Economics*, 3: 357–398.

Jensen, Michael, 1983, "Organization Theory and Methodology," *Accounting Review*, 58: 319–339.

Jensen, Michael, 1986, "Agency Costs of Free Cash Flow, Corporate Finance, and Takeovers," *American Economic Review*, 76: 323–329.

Jensen, Michael, 1989, "Eclipse of the public corporation," *Harvard Business Review*, 67: 61–74.

Jensen, Michael, 1993, "The modern industrial revolution, exit and the failure of internal control systems," *Journal of Finance*, 48: 831–880.

Jensen, Michael C., and Meckling, William H., 1976a, "Theory of the Firm: Managerial Behavior, Agency Costs and Ownership Structure," *Journal of Financial Economics*, 3: 305–360.

Jensen, Michael C., and Meckling, William H., 1976b, "Can the Corporation Survive," Center for Research in Government Policy and Business Working Paper No. PPS 76–4. Rochester, New York: University of Rochester. (Published in 1978 as "Can the Corporation Survive," *Financial Analysts Journal*, 31(1): 31–37.)

Jensen, Michael C., and Meckling, William H., 1988, "The Distribution of Power Among Corporate Managers, Shareholders, and Directors," *Journal of Financial Economics*, 20: 3–24.

Jensen, Michael, and Murphy, Kevin, 1990, "Performance Pay and Top Management Incentives," *Journal of Political Economy*, 98: 225–263.

Jensen, Michael C., and Warner, Jerold B., 1988, "The Distribution of Power Among Corporate Managers, Shareholders, and Directors," *Journal of Financial Economics*, 20: 3–24.

Johnson, Harry G., 1963, "The 'Higher Criticism' of the Modern Corporation," *Columbia Law Review*, 63: 399–432.

Johnson, Marilyn F., Porter, Susan, and Shackell, Margaret B., 1997, "Stakeholder Pressure and the Structure of Executive Compensation," Working Paper, Michigan State University, University of Massachusetts at Amherst, Notre Dame.

Jones, Eliot, 1927, *The Trust Problem*. New York: MacMillan.

Joskow, Paul L., 1977, "Commercial Impossibility, the Uranium Market, and the Westinghouse Case," *Journal of Legal Studies*, 6: 119–176.

Joskow, Paul L., 1985, "Vertical Integration and Long-Term Contracts: The Case of Coal-Burning Electric Generating Plants," *Journal of Law, Economics, and Organization*, 1: 33–80.

Joskow, Paul L., 1987, "Contract Duration and Relationship-Specific Investments: Empirical Evidence," *Journal of Law, Economics, and Organization*, 77: 168–185.

REFERENCES

Joskow, Paul L., 1988a, "Asset Specificity and the Structure of Vertical Relationships: Empirical Evidence," *Journal of Law, Economics and Organization*, 4: 95–117.

Joskow, Paul L., 1988b, "Price Adjustment in Long-Term Contracts: The Case of Coal," *Journal of Law and Economics*, 31: 47–83.

Juster, R. Thomas, 1985, "Preferences for Work and Leisure," Chapter 13 in F. Thomas Juster and Frank P. Stafford (eds.), *Time, Goods, and Well-Being*. Ann Arbor: Institute for Social Research, University of Michigan.

Kahn, C., and Huberman, G., 1988, "Default, Foreclosure, and Strategic Renegotiation," presented at the Conference on Economics of Contract Law, Duke University.

Kaldor, Nicholas, 1934a, "A Classificatory Note of the Determinateness of Equilibrium," *The Review of Economic Studies*, 1: 122–136.

Kaldor, Nicholas, 1934b, "The Equilibrium of the Firm," *Economic Journal*, 44: 60–76.

Kandel, Eugene, and Lazear, Edward, 1992, "Peer Pressure and Partnerships," *Journal of Political Economy*, 100: 801–817.

Kaplan, Steven N., 1989, "The Effects of Management Buyouts on Operating Performance and Value," *Journal of Financial Economics*, 24: 581–618.

Kenney, R. W., and Klein, B., 1983, "The Economics of Block Booking," *Journal of Law and Economics*, 26: 497–540.

Kerr, C., 1954, "The Balkanization of Labor Markets," in E. Wight Bakke et al., *Labor Mobility and Economic Opportunity*. Cambridge, MA: Technology Press of MIT.

Kessler, Friedrich, and Stern, Richard H., 1959, "Competition, Contract, and Vertical Integration," *Yale Law Journal*, 69: 1–129.

Keynes, John Maynard, 1933, *Essays in Biography*. London: Macmillan.

Khalil, Elias L., 1994, "Can Transaction-Cost, Competence-Bundle, and Process Theories of the Firms Sustain the Market/Form Dichotomy Thesis?" Working Paper, Ohio State University, Mansfield Campus.

Kihlstrom, Richard, and Laffont, Jean-Jacques, 1979, "A General Equilibrium Entrepreneurial Theory of Firm Formation Based on Risk Aversion," *Journal of Political Economy*, 87: 719–747.

Kihlstrom, Richard E., and Matthews, Steven A., 1990, "Managerial Incentives in an Entrepreneurial Stock Market Model," Discussion Papers 876, Northwestern University, Center for Mathematical Studies in Economics and Management, Science.

Kirzner, I., 1973, *Competition and Entrepreneurship*. Chicago: University of Chicago Press.

Kirzner, Israel M., 1979, *Perception, Opportunity, Profit: Studies in the Theory of Entrepreneurship*. Chicago: University of Chicago Press.

Klein, Benjamin, 1974, "The Competitive Supply of Money," *Journal of Money, Credit, and Banking*, 6: 423–453.

Klein, Benjamin,, 1983, "Contracting Costs and Residual Claims: The Separation of Ownership and Control," *Journal of Law and Economics*, 26: 367–374.

Klein, Benjamin, 1988, "Vertical Integration as Organized Ownership: The Fisher Body-General Motors Relationship Revisited," *Journal of Law, Economics, and Organization*, 4: 199–213.

376

References

Klein, Benjamin, Crawford, Robert G., and Alchian, Armen, 1978, "Vertical Integration, Appropriable Rents and the Competitive Contracting Process," *Journal of Law and Economics*, 21: 297–326.

Klein, Benjamin, and Leffler, Keith, 1979, "The Role of Market Forces in Assuring Contractual Performance," *Journal of Political Economy*, 89: 615–641.

Klein, Benjamin, and McLaughlin, Andrew, 1978, "Resale Price Maintenance, Exclusive Territories, and Franchise Termination: The Coors Case," unpublished manuscript.

Klein, Peter G., and Shelanski, Howard A., 1994, "Empirical Research in Transaction Cost Economics: A Survey and Assessment," Business and Public Policy Working Paper BPP-60, Haas School of Business, University of California, Berkeley. (Published in 1995 as "Empirical Research in Transaction Cost Economics: A Review and Assessment," *Journal of Law, Economics, and Organization*, 11: 335–361.)

Klein, W. A., 1976, "Legal and Economic Perspectives on the Firm," unpublished manuscript, University of California, Los Angeles.

Knight, Frank, 1921, *Risk, Uncertainty and Profit*. London: The London School of Economics and Political Science.

Knight, Frank, 1933, *Risk, Uncertainty and Profit*, preface to the re-issue. London: London School of Economics Series of Reprints, No. 16.

Knight, Frank H., 1965, *Risk, Uncertainty and Profit*. New York: Harper and Row.

Kole, Stacey, and Lehn, Kenneth, 1999, "Deregulation and the Adaptation of Governance Structure: The Case of the U.S. Airline Industry," *Journal of Financial Economics*, 52(1): 79–118.

Kronman, A. T., 1985, "Contract Law and the State of Nature," *Journal of Law, Economies and Organizations*, 1: 4–32.

Kroszner, Randall, and Rajan, Raghuram, 1997, "Organization Structure and Credibility: Evidence from Commercial Bank Securities Activities before the Glass-Steagall Act," National Bureau of Economic Research Working Paper. (Published in 1997 as "Organization Structure and Credibility: Evidence from Commercial Bank Securities Activities before the Glass-Steagall Act," *Journal of Monetary Economics*, 39: 475–516.)

Krueger, Alan, 1991, "Ownership, Agency, and Wages: An Examination of Franchising in the Fast Food Industry," *Quarterly Journal of Economics*, 106: 75–101.

Kruse, Douglas, 1993, *Profit Sharing: Does It Make a Difference?* Kalamazoo, MI: Upjohn Institute for Employment Research.

Laffont, Jean-Jacques, and Tirole, Jean, 1989, "Provision of Quality and Power of Incentive Schemes in Regulated Industries," in W. Barnett, B. Cornet, C. d'Aspremont, J. Gabsewicz, and A. Mas-Colell (eds.), *Equilibrium Theory and Applications*. Cambridge: Cambridge University Press.

LaFontaine, Francine, and Slade, Margaret, 1997, "Retail Contracting: Theory and Practice," *Journal of Industrial Economics*, 45: 1–25.

Langlois, Richard, 2003, "The Vanishing Hand: The Changing Dynamics of Industrial Capitalism," *Industrial and Corporate Change*, 12(2): 351–385.

REFERENCES

La Porta, Rafael, Lopez-de-Silanes, Florencio, and Shleifer, Andrei, 1999, "Corporate Ownership around the World," *Journal of Finance*, 54: 471–517.

Lawler, Edward, 1971, *Pay and Organizational Effectiveness*. New York: McGraw-Hill.

Lazear, Edward, 1989, "Pay Equality and Industrial Politics," *Journal of Political Economy*, 97: 561–580.

Lazear, Edward, and Rosen, Sherwin, 1981, "Rank-Order Tournaments as Optimum Labor Contracts," *Journal of Political Economy*, 89: 841–864.

Leff, Nathaniel H., 1978, "Industrial Organization and Entrepreneurship in the Developing Countries: The Economic Groups," *Economic Development and Cultural Change*, 26: 661–676.

Leffler, Keith B., and Rucker, Randal, 1991, "Transaction Costs and the Efficient Organization of Production: A Study of Timber-Harvesting Contracts," *Journal of Political Economy*, 99: 1060–1087.

Leibenstein, H., 1966, "Allocative Efficiency vs. X-Efficiency," *American Economic Review*, 56: 392–415.

Leibenstein, Harvey, 1979, "A Branch of Economics Is Missing: Micro-Micro Theory," *Journal of Economic Literature*, 17(2): 477–502.

Leibenstein, Harvey, 1982, "The Prisoners' Dilemma in the Invisible Hand: An Analysis of Intrafirm Productivity," *American Economic Review*, 72: 92–97.

Lerner, Abba, 1972, "The Economics and Politics of Consumer Sovereignty," *American Economic Review*, 62: 259.

Levi, Margaret, 1988, *Of Rule and Revenue*. Berkeley: University of California Press.

Levinsohn, Alan, 2001, "A Garden of Stock Options Helps Harvest Talent," *Strategic Finance*, 82: 81–82.

Llewellyn, Karl N., 1931, "What Price Contract? An Essay in Perspective," *Yale Law Journal*, 40: 704–751.

Loasby, Brian J., 1986, "Competition and Imperfect Knowledge: The Contribution of G. B. Richardson," *Scottish Journal of Political Economy*, 33: 145–158.

Lowry, S. Todd, 1976, "Bargain and Contract Theory in Law and Economics," *Journal of Economic Issues*, 10: 1–19.

Lutz, Nancy, 1995, "Ownership Rights and Incentives in Franchising," *Journal of Corporate Finance*, 2: 103–131.

Macaulay, Stewart, 1963, "Non-Contractual Relations in Business: A Preliminary Study," *American Sociological Review*, 28: 55–70.

MacDonald, Glenn, 1984, "New Directions in the Economic Theory of Agency," *Canadian Journal of Economics*, 17: 415–440.

Macgregor, David H., 1906, *Industrial Combination*. London: George Bell and Sons.

Machlup, F., 1967, "Theories of the Firm: Marginalist, Behavioral, Managerial," *American Economic Review*, 57: 1–33.

Machlup, F., and Taber, Martha, 1960, "Bilateral Monopoly, Successive Monopoly, and Vertical Integration," *Economica*, 27: 101–119.

Machlup, Fritz, 1961, *International Trade and the National Income Multiplier*. New York: A. M. Kelley.

MacLeod, Bentley, 1987, "Behavior and the Organization of the Firm," *Journal of Comparative Economics*, 11: 207–220.

378

References

MacLeod, W. Bentley,1988, "Equity, Efficiency, and Incentives in Cooperative Teams," in Derek Jones and Jan Svejar (eds.), *Advances in the Economic Analysis of Participatory and Labor-Managed Firms*, Vol. 3. Greenwich, CT: JAI Press.

Macneil, I. R., 1974, "The Many Futures of Contracts," *Southern California Law Review*, 47: 691–816.

Macneil, I. R., 1978, "Contracts: Adjustment of Long-Term Economic Relations under Classical, Neoclassical, and Relational Contract Law," *Northwestern University Law Review*, 72: 854–906.

Malcomson, James, 1984, "Work Incentives, Hierarchy, and Internal Labor Markets," *Journal of Political Economy*, 92: 486–507.

Malmgren, H., 1961, "Information, Expectations, and the Theory of the Firm," *Quarterly Journal of Economics*, 75: 399–421.

Maness, Robert, 1996, "Incomplete Contracts and the Choice between Vertical Integration and Franchising," *Journal of Economic Behavior and Organization*, 32: 101–115.

Manne, Henry G., 1962, "The 'Higher Criticism' of the Modern Corporation," *Columbia Law Review*, 53: 259–285.

Manne, Henry, 1965, "Mergers and the Market for Corporate Control," *Journal of Political Economy*, 73: 110–120.

Manne, Henry G., 1967, "Our Two Corporate Systems: Laws and Economics," *Virginia Law Review*, 53: 259–285.

March, J. G., and Simon, H. A., 1958, *Organizations*. New York: Wiley.

Marglin, Stephen, 1974, "What Do Bosses Do? The Origins and Functions of Hierarchy in Capitalist Production," *Review of Radical Political Economics*, 6: 60–112.

Marris, R., 1964, *The Economic Theory of Managerial Capitalism*. Glencoe, IL: The Free Press.

Marx, Karl, 1967, *Capital: A Critique of Political Economy, Volume I. The Process of Capitalist Production*. Edited by Frederick Engels, translated from the Third German Edition by Samuel Moore and Edward Aveling. New York: International Publishers.

Masten, Scott, 1988, "A Legal Basis for the Firm," *Journal of Law, Economics, and Organization*, 4: 191–198.

Masten, Scott E., 1984, "The Organization of Production: Evidence from the Aerospace Industry," *Journal of Law & Economics*, 27(2): 403–417.

Masten, Scott E., and Crocker, Keith J., 1988, "Efficient Adaptation in Long-Term Contracts: Take-or-Pay Provisions for Natural Gas," *American Economic Review*, 75: 1083–1093.

McAfee, R. Preston, and McMillan, John, 1991, "Organizational Diseconomies of Scale," mimeo, University of California, San Diego.

McConnell, John J., and Servaes, Henri, 1990, "Additional evidence on equity ownership and corporate value," *Journal of Financial Economics*, 27(2): 595–612.

McManus, J. C., 1975, "The Costs of Alternative Economic Organizations," *Canadian Journal of Economics*, 8: 334–350.

Meade, J., 1971, *The Controlled Economy*, London: G. Allen and Unwin.

REFERENCES

Meade, James, 1972, "The Theory of Labor-Managed Firms and of Profit-Sharing," *Economic Journal*, 82: 401–428.

Meckling, W. H., 1976, "Values and the Choice Model of the Individual in the Social Sciences," *Zeitschrift fur Volkswirtschaft und Statistik*, 112: 545–560.

Merton, Robert, 1995, "Financial Innovation and the Management and Regulation of Financial Institutions," *Journal of Banking and Finance*, 19: 461–481.

Milgrom, P., and Roberts, J., 1986, "Relying on the Information of Interested Parties," *Rand Journal of Economics*, 17: 18–32.

Milgrom, Paul, 1988, "Employment Contracts, Influence Activities and Efficient Organization Design," *Journal of Political Economy*, 96: 42–60.

Milgrom, Paul, and Roberts, John, 1988a, "An Economic Approach to Influence Activities and Organizational Responses," *American Journal of Sociology*, 93: S154–S179.

Milgrom, Paul, and Roberts, John, 1988b, "Economic Theories of the Firm: Past, Present, and Future," *Canadian Journal of Economics*, 21: 444.

Milgrom, Paul A., and Roberts, John, 1990a, "Bargaining Costs, Influence Costs, and the Organization of Economic Activity," in James E. Alt and Kenneth A. Shepsle (eds.), *Perspectives on Positive Political Economy*. Cambridge: Cambridge University Press.

Milgrom, Paul, and Roberts, John, 1990b, "The Economics of Modern Manufacturing: Technology, Strategy, and Organization," *American Economic Review*, 80: 511–528.

Milgrom, Paul, and Roberts, John, 1992, *Economics, Organization, and Management*. Englewood Cliffs, NJ: Prentice-Hall.

Milgrom, Paul, and Roberts, John, 1993, "Johnson Controls, Inc.: Automotive Systems Group: The Georgetown Kentucky Plant," Stanford Graduate School of Business, Case S-BE-9.

Minahan, John, 1988, "Managerial Incentive Schemes and the Divisional Structure of Firms," mimeograph, University of Massachusetts.

Mitchell, Daniel E. B., and Kimbell, Larry J., 1982, "Labor Market Contracts and Inflation," in Martin Neil Baily (ed.), *Workers, Jobs, and Inflation*. Washington, DC: The Brookings, Institution.

Monsen, R. J., and Downs, A., 1965, "A Theory of Large Managerial Firms," *Journal of Political Economy*, 73: 221–236.

Monteverde, Kirk, and Teece, David, 1982, "Supplier Switching Costs and Vertical Integration in the Automobile Industry," *Bell Journal of Economics*, 13: 206–213.

Montias, J. Michael, 1970, "The Price Mechanism in Socialist Countries – Discussion," *American Economic Review*, 60: 321–323.

Montias, John M., 1976, *The Structure of Economic Systems*. New Haven, CT: Yale University Press.

Morck, Randall, Shleifer, Andrei, and Vishny, Robert W., 1988, "Management Ownership and Market Valuation: An Empirical Analysis," *Journal of Financial Economics*, 20: 293–315.

Morris, Charles, 1980, *The Cost of Good Intentions*, New York: W.W. Norton.

380

References

Mulherin, J. Harold, 1986, "Complexity in Long-Term Contracts: An Analysis of Natural Gas Contractual Provisions," *Journal of Law, Economics, and Organization*, 2: 105–117.

Murphy, Kevin J., 1999, "Executive Compensation," in *Handbook of Labor Economics*. Orley Ashenfelter and David Card (eds.), North Holland, 2485–2563.

Murphy, Kevin J., 2002, "Explaining Executive Compensation: Managerial Power vs. the Perceived Cost of Stock Options," *University of Chicago Law Review*, 69: 847–869.

Muth, John F., 1960, "Optimal Properties of Exponentially Weighted Forecasts," *Journal of the American Statistical Association*, 55: 299–306.

Myerson, R., 1979. "Incentive Compatibility and the Bargaining Problem," *Econometrica*, 47: 61–73.

Nalbantian, Haig R. (ed.), 1987, *Incentives, Cooperation, and Risk Sharing: Economic and Psychological Perspectives on Employment Contracts*. Totowa, NJ: Rowman and Littlefield.

National Association of Corporate Directors, 1995, Report of the NACD Blue Ribbon Commission on Director Compensation. NACD, Washington, D.C.

Nelson, Charles R., 1973, *Applied Time Series Forecast for Managerial Forecasting*. San Francisco: Holden-Day.

Nelson, R., 1959, *Merger Movements in American Industry, 1895–1956*. Princeton, NJ: Princeton University Press.

Nelson, Richard R., and Winter, Sidney G., 1982, *An Evolutionary Theory of Economic Change*. Cambridge, MA: Harvard University Press.

Neuberger, Egon, and James, Estelle, 1973, "The Yugoslav Self-Managed Enterprise: A Systemic Approach," 245–284 in Morris Bornstein (ed.), *Plan and Market: Economic Reform in Eastern Europe*. New Haven, CT: Yale University Press.

Newman, Andrew, 1995, "Employment Contracts, Finance, and the Distribution of Wealth," in J. E. Roemer (ed.), *Property Relations, Incentives and Welfare*. London: Macmillan.

Nilsson, Eric, 1989, "International Trade and the Social Relations of Production," Ph.D. dissertation, University of Massachusetts.

North, Douglas, 1981, *Structure and Change in Economic History*. New York: Norton.

Novaes, W., and Zingales, L., 1995, "Capital Structure Choice When Managers Are in Control: Entrenchment versus Efficiency," NBER Working Paper No. 5384, available at gsblgz.uchicago.edu.

Nove, Alec, 1958, "The Problem of Success Indicators in Soviet Industry," *Economica*, 25: 1–13.

Nutter, Warren, 1951, *The Extent of Enterprise Monopoly in the United States 1899–1939*. Chicago: University of Chicago Press.

Ofek, Eli, and Yermack, David, 2000, "Taking Stock: Equity-Based Compensation and the Evolution of Managerial Ownership," *Journal of Finance*, 55(3): 1367–1384.

Ortiz, Fernando, 1963, *Contraputo del Tabaco y el Azucar*. Barcelona: Editorial Ariel.

Ortuno-Ortin, Ignacio, Roemer, John E., and Silvestre, Joaquim, 1993, "Investment Planning and Market Socialism," in S. Bowles, H. Gintis, and B. Gustafsson

REFERENCES

(eds.), *The Microfoundations of Political Economy: Problems of Participation, Democracy, and Efficiency.* Cambridge: Cambridge University Press.

Pagano, Ugo, 1985, *Work and Welfare in Economic Theory.* Oxford: Basil Blackwell.

Pagano, Ugo, 1988, "Determinazione Endogena dei Diritti di Proprieta in un Economia di Mercato," Working Paper, University of Siena.

Palay, Thomas M., 1984. "Comparative Institutional Economics: The Governance of Rail Freight Contracting," *Journal of Legal Studies*, 13: 265–287.

Pearl Meyers & Partners, 2002, *Executive Pay Trends: Looking Forward and Looking Back.*

Pejovich, S., 1969, "The Firm, Monetary Policy and Property Rights in a Planned Economy," *Economic Inquiry*, 7(3): 193–200.

Pencavel, John, 2001, *Worker Participation: Lessons from the Worker Co-Ops of the Pacific Northwest.* New York: Russell Sage Foundation.

Penrose, E., 1958, *The Theory of the Growth of the Firm.* New York: Wiley.

Perrow, Charles, 1983, *Normal Accidents: Living with High-Risk Technologies.* New York: Basic Books.

Plant, Arnold, 1932, "Trends in Business Administration," *Economica*, 12: 45–62.

Powell, Walter, 1996, "Inter-Organizational Collaboration in the Biotechnology Industry," *Journal of Institutional and Theoretical Economics*, 152(1): 197–215.

Preston, L. E., 1975, "Corporation and Society: The Search for a Paradigm," *Journal of Economic Literature*, 13: 434–453.

Publishers' Association v. Newspaper and Mail Delivery Union, 1952, 114 N.Y.S. 2d401.

Putterman, Louis, 1984, "On Some Recent Explanations of Why Capital Hires Labor," *Economic Inquiry*, 22: 171–187.

Putterman, Louis, 1988, "The Firm as Association versus the Firm as Commodity: Efficiency, Rights, and Ownership," *Economics and Philosophy*, 4: 243–266.

Putterman, Louis, 1993a, "Ownership and the Nature of the Firm," *Journal of Comparative Economics*, 17: 243–263.

Putterman, Louis, 1993b, "Exit, Voice, and Portfolio Choice: Agency and Public Ownership," *Economics and Politics*, 5: 205–218.

Putterman, Louis, 1993c, "Incentive Problems Favoring Noncentralized Investment Fund Ownership," pp. 156–168 in P. Bardhan and J. E. Roemer (eds.), *Market Socialism: The Current Debate.* New York: Oxford University Press.

Putterman, Louis, 1995, "Markets, Hierarchies, and Information: On a Paradox in the Economics of Organization," *Journal of Economic Behavior and Organization*, 26: 373–390.

Putterman, Louis, and Rueschemeyer, Dietrich (eds.), 1992, *States and Markets in Development: Synergy or Rivalry?* Boulder, CO: Lynne Rienner.

Putterman, Louis, and Skillman, Gilbert, 1992, "The Role of Exist in the Theory of Cooperative \Teams," *Journal of Comparative Economics*, 16: 596–618.

Radner, R., 1970, "Problems in the Theory of Markets under Uncertainty," *The American Economic Review*, 60: 454–460.

Rajan, Raghuram G., and Zingales, Luigi, 1997, "The Firm as a Dedicated Hierarchy," University of Chicago Working Paper, available at gsblgz.uchicago.edu.

382

References

Rajan, Raghuram G., and Zingales, Luigi, 1998, "Power in a Theory of the Firm," *Quarterly Journal of Economics*, 113(2): 387–432.

Rajan, Raghuram G., and Zingales, Luigi, 2001, "The Firm as a Dedicated Hierarchy: A Theory of the Origins and Growth of Firms," *Quarterly Journal of Economics*, 116(3): 805–851.

Rappaport, Alfred, 1999, "New Thinking on How to Link Executive Pay with Performance," *Harvard Business Review*, 77(2): 91–101.

Richardson, G. B., 1972, "The Organization of Industry," *Economic Journal*, 82: 883–896.

Richardson, G. B., 1990, *Information and Investment: A Study in the Working of the Competitive Economy, with a New Foreword by David Teece*. Oxford: Oxford University Press.

Riordan, Michael, 1990, "Vertical Integration and the Strategic Management of the Enterprise," in M. Aoki, B. Gustafsson, and O. Williamson (eds.), *The Firm as a Nexus of Treaties*. London: Sage Publications.

Robbins, L., 1932, *An Essay on the Nature and Significance of Economic Science*. New York: Macmillan.

Robertson, D. H., 1930, *Control of Industry*. London: Nisbet and Co.

Robinson, E. A. G., 1931, *The Structure of Competitive Industry*. London: Nisbet; and Cambridge: Cambridge University Press.

Robinson, E. A. G., 1934, "The Problem of Management and the Size of the Firm," *The Economic Journal*, 44: 242–257.

Robinson, Joan, 1932, *Economics Is a Serious Subject: The Apologia of an Economist to the Mathematician, the Scientist and the Plain Man*. Cambridge: W. Heffer and Sons.

Roe, Mark, 1994, *Strong Managers, Weak Owners: The Political Roots of American Corporate Finance*, Princeton, NJ: Princeton University Press.

Roemer, John, 1994, *A Future for Socialism*. Cambridge, MA: Harvard University Press.

Ross, S. A., 1973, "The Economic Theory of Agency: The Principal's Problem," *American Economic Review*, 62: 134–139.

Ross, S. A., 1974, "The Economic Theory of Agency and the Principal's Similarity," in Michael Balch, Daniel McFadden, and Shih-yen Wu (eds.), *Essays on Economic Behavior under Uncertainty*. Amsterdam: North-Holland.

Ryan, Alan, 1987, "Property," in John Eatwell, Murray Milgate, and Peter Newman (eds.), *The New Palgrave: Dictionary of Economics*. New York: Stockton Press.

Samuelson, Paul, 1957, "Wages and Interest: A Modern Dissection of Marxian Economics," *American Economic Review*, 47: 884–912.

Schelling, T., 1971, "On the Ecology of Micromotives," *The Public Interest*, 25: 61–98.

Scherer, R., and Ross, David, 1990, *Industrial Market Structure and Economic Performance*, Boston: Houghton Mifflin Company.

Schmidt, Peter, and Strauss, Robert P., 1976, "The Effect of Unions on Earnings and Earnings on Unions: A Mixed Logit Approach," *International Economic Review*, 17: 204–212.

REFERENCES

Schor, Juliet B., and Bowles, Samuel, 1987, "Employment Rents and the Incidence of Strikes," *Review of Economics and Statistics*, 64(4): 584–591.

Scott, Richard, 1981, *Organizations*. Englewood Cliffs, NJ: Prentice-Hall.

Segal, Ilya, and Whinston, Michael, 1997, "On the Transaction Cost Determinants of Vertical Integration," draft, Department of Economics, Northwestern University.

Selznick, Philip, 1948, "Foundations of the Theory of Organization," *American Sociological Review*, 13: 25–35.

Selznick, Philip, 1949, *TVA and the Grass Roots: A Study in the Sociology of Formal Organization*. Berkeley: University of California Press.

Seyhun, H. Nejat, 1998, *Investment Intelligence from Insider Trading*. Cambridge, MA: The MIT Press.

Shapiro, Carl, and Stiglitz, Joseph, 1984, "Equilibrium Unemployment as a Worker Discipline Device," *American Economic Review*, 74: 433–444.

Shepard, Andrea, 1993, "Contractual Form, Retail Price, and Asset Characteristics," *Rand Journal of Economics*, 24: 58–77.

Shove, G. F., 1933, "The Imperfection of the Market: A Further Note," *The Economic Journal*, 43: 113–124.

Shubik, M., 1970, "A Curmudgeon's Guide to Microeconomics," *Journal of Economic Literature*, 8: 405–434.

Shleifer, Andrei, and Vishny, Robert W., 1986, "Large Shareholders and Corporate Control," *Journal of Political Economy*, 94(3): 461–488.

Silver, M., and Auster, R., 1969, "Entrepreneurship, Profit and Limits on Firm Size," *Journal of Business*, 42: 277–281.

Simon, H., 1959, "Theories of Decision Making in Economics and Behavioral Science," *American Economic Review*, 49: 253–283.

Simon, H. A., 1955, "A Behavioral Model of Rational Choice," *Quarterly Journal of Economics*, 69: 99–118.

Simon, H. A., 1957, *Models of Man*. New York: Wiley.

Simon, Herbert, 1951, "A Formal Theory of the Employment Relation," *Econometrica*, 19: 293–305. Reprinted in *Models of Man*, 1957, New York: Wiley.

Simon, Herbert, 1991, "Organizations and Markets," *Journal of Economic Perspectives*, 5: 25–44.

Slade, Margaret, 1996, "Multitask Agency and Contract Choice: An Empirical Assessment," *International Economic Review*, 37: 465–486.

Smith, Adam, 1937, *The Wealth of Nations*, Cannan edition. New York: Modern Library. Originally published in 1776.

Smith, Clifford, and Watts, Ross, 1992, "The investment opportunity set and corporate financing, dividend, and compensation policies," *Journal of Financial Economics*, 32: 263–292.

Sonnenschein, Hugo, 1987, "Oligopoly and Game Theory," John Eatwell, Murray Milgate, and Peter Newman (eds.), in *The New Palgrave: A Dictionary of Economics*. London: Macmillan.

Spence, Michael, and Zeckhauser, Richard, 1971, "Insurance, Information, and Individual Action," *American Economic Review*, 61: 380–387.

References

Steinherr, Alfred, and Thisse, J-F, 1979, "Are Labor-Managers Really Perverse?" *Economics Letters*, 2: 137–142.

Stigler, George, and Friedland, Claire, 1983, "The Literature of Economics: The Case of Berle and Means," *Journal of Law and Economics*, 26: 237–268.

Stiglitz, Joseph, 1975, "Incentives, Risk, and Information: Notes toward a Theory of Hierarchy," *Bell Journal of Economics*, 6: 552–579.

Stiglitz, Joseph E., 1977, "The Theory of Local Public Goods," in *The Economics of Public Services*, Martin S. Feldstein and Robert P. Inman (eds.), London: Macmillan, for International Economic Association.

Stinchcombe, Arthur L., 1983, "Contracts as Hierarchical Documents," unpublished manuscript, Stanford Graduate School of Business.

Stuckey, John, 1983, *Vertical Integration and Joint Ventures in the Aluminum Industry*. Cambridge, MA: Harvard University Press.

Stulz, Rene, 1988, "Managerial Control of Voting Rights: Financing Policies and the Market tor Corporate Control," *Journal of Financial Economics*, 20: 24–54.

Stulz, Rene, 1996, "Rethinking Risk Management," *Journal of Applied Corporate Finance*, 9: 8–24.

Summers, C., 1969, "Collective Agreements and the Law of Contracts," *Yale Law Journal*, 78: 527–575.

Tajfel, Henri, 1970, "Experiments in Intergroup Discrimination," *Scientific American*, 223: 96–102.

Taylor, Curtis, and Wiggins, Steven, 1997, "Competition or Compensation: Supplier Incentives Under the American and Japanese Subcontracting Systems," *American Economic Review*, 87(4): 598–618.

Teece, David J., 1976, *Vertical Integration and Vertical Divestiture in the U.S. Petroleum Industry*. Stanford, CA: Stanford University.

Teece, David J., 1980, "Economics of Scope and the Scope of Enterprise," *Journal of Economic Behavior and Organization*, 1: 223–247.

Teece, David J., 1982, "Towards an Economic Theory of the Multiproduct Firm," *Journal of Economic Behavior and Organization*, 3: 39–63.

Teece, David, Rumelt, Richard, Dosi, Giovanni, and Winter, Sidney, 1994, "Understanding Corporate Coherence, Theory and Evidence," *Journal of Economic Behavior and Organization*, 23: 1–30.

Thomas, Randall S., and Martin, Kenneth J., 1999, "The Effect of Shareholder Proposals on Executive Compensation," *University of Cincinnati Law Review*, 67: 1021–1081.

Thompson, E. A., 1970, "Nonpecuniary Rewards and the Aggregate Production Function," *Review of Economics and Statistics*, 52: 395–404.

Tiebout, Charles M., 1956, "A Pure Theory of Local Expenditures," *Journal of Political Economy*, 64(5): 416–424.

Tirole, Jean, 1986, "Hierarchies and Bureaucracies: On the Role of Collusion in Organizations," *Journal of Law, Economics, and Organization*, 2: 181–214.

Trivers, R. L., 1971, "The Evolution of Reciprocal Altruism," *Quarterly Review of Biology*, 46: 35–57.

REFERENCES

Tufano, Peter, 1996, "Who Manages Risk? An Empirical Examination of Risk Management Practices in the Gold Mining Industry," *Journal of Finance*, 51: 1097–1138.
Turner, John C., 1987, *Rediscovering the Social Group: A Self-Categorization Theory*. Oxford: Basil Blackwell.
Urquhart, David, 1856, *Familiar Words as Affecting England and the English*. London: Trubner & Co.
Usher, Abbott P., 1921, *Introduction to the Industrial History of England*. London: G. C. Harrap and Co., Ltd.
Veblen, Thorstein, 1964, *Absentee Ownership and Business Enterprise in Recent Times: The Case of America*. New York: B. W. Huebsch, reprinted by Augustus M. Kelly.
von Stackelberg, H., 1934, *Marktform and Gleichgewicht*. Vienna: Springer-Verlag.
Wade, James B., Porac, Joseph, and Pollock, Timothy, 1997, "Worth, Words, and the Justification of Executive Pay," *Journal of Organizational Behavior*, 18: 641–664.
Walton, Mary, 1997, *Car: A Drama of the American Workplace*. New York: W.W. Norton.
Watts, Ross L., and Zimmerman, Jerod, 1978, "Auditors and the Determination of Accounting Standards, an Analysis of the Lack of Independence," Working Paper GPB 7806, University of Rochester, Graduate School of Management.
Weisbach, Michael, 1988, "Outside Directors and CEO Turnover," *Journal of Financial Economics*, 20: 431–460.
Weitzman, Martin L., and Kruse, Douglas, 1990, "Profit Sharing and Productivity," in Alan S. Blinder (ed.), *Paying for Productivity: A Look at the Evidence*. Washington, DC: The Brookings Institution.
White, Harrison, 1981. "Where Do Markets Come From?" *American Journal of Sociology*, 87: 517–547.
White, Horace, J., Jr., 1936, "Monopolistic and Perfect Competition," *American Economic Review*, 26: 645.
Williamson, O. E., 1964a, "The Economics of Antitrust: Transaction Cost Considerations," *University of Pennsylvania Law Review*, 122: 1439–1496.
Williamson, O. E., 1964b, *The Economics of Discretionary Behavior: Managerial Objectives in a Theory of the Firm*. Englewood Cliffs, NJ: Prentice-Hall.
Williamson, O. E., 1970, *Corporate Control and Business Behavior*. Englewood Cliffs, NJ: Prentice-Hall.
Williamson, O. E., 1975, *Markets and Hierarchies: Analysis and Anti-Trust Implications*. New York: The Free Press.
Williamson, Oliver E., 1967a, "Hierarchical Control and Optimum Firm Size," *Journal of Political Economy*, 75: 123–138.
Williamson, Oliver E., 1967b, "The Economics of Defense Contracting: Incentives and Performance," in *Issues in Defense Economics*. New York: National Bureau of Economic Research.
Williamson, Oliver E., 1971, "The Vertical Integration of Production: Market Failure and Considerations," *American Economic Review*, 61: 112–123.
Williamson, Oliver, 1979, "Transaction-Cost Economics: The Governance of Contractual Relations," *Journal of Law and Economics*, 22: 233–261.

References

Williamson, Oliver, E., 1985, *The Economic Institutions of Capitalism: Firms, Markets, and Relational Contracting*. New York: The Free Press.

Williamson, Oliver, 1988, "The Logic of Economic Organizations," *Journal of Law, Economics, and Organization*, 4: 65.

Williamson, Oliver, 1994, "Evaluating Coase," *Journal of Economic Perspectives*, 8: 201–204.

Williamson, Oliver, Wachter, Michael, and Harris, Jeffery, 1975, "Understanding the Employment Relation," *Bell Journal of Economics*, 6: 250–278.

Williamson, Oliver E., and Winter, Sidney G. (eds.), 1991, *The Nature of the Firm: Origins, Evolution, and Development*. New York: Oxford University Press.

Wilson, R., 1968, "On the Theory of Syndicates," *Econometrica*, 36: 119–132.

Wilson, R., 1969, *La Decision: Aggregation et Dynamique des Orders de Preference, Extrait*. Paris: Editions du Centre National de la Recherche, Scientifique.

Wolfson, Mark A., 1983, "Empirical Evidence of Incentive Problems and Their Mitigation in Oil and Gas Tax Shelter Programs," unpublished manuscript, Stanford University.

World Bank, 1991, *World Development Report 1991*. New York: Oxford University Press.

Yermack, David, 1996, "Higher Market Valuation of Companies with a Small Board of Directors," *Journal of Financial Economics*, 40: 185–213.

Yermack, David, 1997, "Good Timing: CEO Stock Option Awards and Company News Announcements," *Journal of Finance*, 52: 449–476.

Yunker, James A., 1992, *Socialism Revised and Modernized: The Case for Pragmatic Market Socialism*. New York: Praeger.

Zingales, Luigi, 1998, "Corporate Governance," in *The New Palgrave Dictionary of Economics and the Law*, P. Newman (ed.). New York: Macmillan.

Printed in Great Britain
by Amazon